SOUTHEAST ASIA EMERGES

A CONCISE HISTORY OF SOUTHEAST ASIA FROM ITS ORIGIN TO THE PRESENT

STEVEN WARSHAW

diablo press

Copyright 1964, 1974, 1979, 1987, and 1988 DIABLO PRESS, Inc.
Berkeley and San Francisco
P.O. Box 7042, Berkeley, California 94707

ORDER DESK; (800) 445-6638, 2 Acorn Lane, Colchester, VT. 05446

PRINTING HISTORY
First edition as part of Asia Emerges

First Printing
1964

Second Printing
1966

Third Printing
1967

Revised and expanded as SOUTHEAST ASIA EMERGES
1974

Second printing as SOUTHEAST ASIA EMERGES
1975

Third printing as SOUTHEAST ASIA EMERGES
1979

Fourth printing as SOUTHEAST ASIA EMERGES
1985

Fifth printing as SOUTHEAST ASIA EMERGES
1987

Sixth printing as SOUTHEAST ASIA EMERGES
1988

Library of Congress Cataloging in Publication Data

Warshaw, Steven.

   Southeast Asia emerges.

   (The Asia emerges series, 5)
   First published in 1964 as part of Asia emerges, by
A. J. Tudisco; rev. and expanded.
   Bibliography: p.
   1. Asia, Southeastern-History. I. Bromwell, C.
David, joint author. II. Tudisco, A. J., joint author.
III. Tudisco, A. J. Asia emerges. IV. Title.
DS511.W37   959   73-93982

ISBN 0-87297-021-3 Paper Edition

Printed in the United States of America

CONTENTS

Preface and Acknowledgments, ix

PART I
The Region and Its History

1
SOUTHEAST ASIA IN PERSPECTIVE, 1–21

Religious Forces, 2–10
Buddhism. Islam. Confucianism. Taoism.
Families, Villages, Cities, 10–16
Land, Climate, Resources, 16–19
The Economy of Southeast Asia, 19–20
Tradition and Change, 20–21

2
EARLY INFLUENCES, 22–40

Immigrants, 22–24
India, 24–36
Khmers. Lao. Thais. Burmans. Malays. Filipinos.
China, 36–37
Vietnamese.
Mongols, 37–38
Muslims, 38–40

3
WESTERN COLONIAL RULE, 41–66

The Origins of Colonialism, 41–43
The Colonies as Extensions of the West, 43–50
Spanish. Dutch.
The Colonies as Producers for the West, 50–64
Dutch. British. French. The United States.
The Independent State of Siam, 64–66

4
THE GROWTH OF NATIONALISM, 67–82

Dutch East Indies (Indonesia). British Malaya. Burma.
French Indochina. The Philippines.

5
WORLD WAR II AND ITS AFTERMATH, 83–103

The Japanese Conquest, 83–85
Southeast Asia's Response, 85–87

Contents

5 ... Continued

The Tides of Nationalism, 87–102
Burma. Thailand. Laos. Cambodia.
Tonkin, Annam, and Cochin China (Vietnam).
Malaya. Indonesia. The Philippines.
The War in Retrospect, 102–103
The Rise of Marxism. The Geneva Conference.

PART II
The Independent Nations

1
BURMA, 105–123

Social Conditions and Cultural Life, 105–112
Ethnic groups. Religion. Education, language, and the arts.
Recent Political Developments, 112–116
Post-independence. Further organizing efforts.
Current conditions.
Economic Conditions and Problems. Trends.
Foreign Relations, 120–122
The Future of Burma, 122–123

2
THAILAND, 125–145

Social Conditions and Cultural Life, 125–132
Ethnic groups. Religion. Education, language, and the arts.
Recent Political Developments, 132–138
Post-independence. Further organizing efforts.
Current conditions.
Economic Conditions and Problems, 139–141
Sources of current problems. Trends.
Foreign Relations, 142–144
The Future of Thailand, 144–145

3
LAOS, 147–163

Social Conditions and Cultural Life, 148–152
Ethnic groups. Religion. Education, language, and the arts.
Recent Political Developments, 152–157
Post-independence. Further organizing efforts.
Current conditions.
Economic Conditions and Problems, 157–161

Contents

Sources of current problems. Trends.
Foreign Relations, 161–162
The Future of Laos, 162–163

4
KAMPUCHEA, 165–183

Social Conditions and Cultural Life, 165–170
Ethnic groups. Religion, Education, language, and the arts.
Recent Political Developments, 170–179
Post-independence. Further organizing efforts.
Current conditions.
Economic Conditions and Problems, 179–181
Sources of current problems. Trends.
Foreign Relations, 182
The Future of Kampuchea, 182–183

5
VIETNAM: THE PATH TO UNITY, 185–198

Two Countries, One People
Social Conditions and Cultural Life, 185–193
Ethnic groups. Religion. Education, language, and the arts.
Political Developments, 193–194
The Two Governments, 194–198
Post-independence: the North. Post-independence: the South.

6
THE VIETNAM WAR (1956–75), 199–211

Causes and Effects, 199–201
Economic conditions. Political developments.
The American Role, 201–211

7
THE PEOPLE'S REPUBLIC OF VIETNAM: THE USES OF POWER, 212–223

Recent Political Developments, 212–216
Economic Conditions and Problems, 216–220
Foreign Relations, 220–221
The Future of Vietnam, 221–223

8
INDONESIA, 225–245

Social Conditions and Cultural Life, 225–230

Contents

Ethnic groups. Religion. Education, language, and the arts.
Recent Political Developments, 231–238
Post-independence. Further organizing efforts.
Current conditions.
Economic Conditions, 238–241
Sources of current problems. Trends.
Foreign Relations, 242–244
The Future of Indonesia, 244–245

9

MALAYSIA, 247–265

Social Conditions and Cultural Life, 247–254
Ethnic groups. Religion. Education, language, and the arts.
Recent Political Developments, 254–258
Post-independence. Further organizing efforts.
Current conditions.
Economic Conditions and Problems, 259–262
Sources of current problems. Trends.
Foreign Relations, 262–263
The Future of Malaysia, 263–265

10

SINGAPORE, 267–277

Social Conditions and Cultural Life, 267–271
Ethnic groups. Religion. Education, language, and the arts.
Recent Political Developments, 271–274
Post-independence. Further organizing efforts.
Current conditions.
Economic Conditions and Problems, 274–276
Sources of current problems. Trends.
Foreign Relations, 276
The Future of Singapore, 276–277

11

THE PHILIPPINES, 279–307

Social Conditions and Cultural Life, 279–282
Ethnic groups. Religion. Education, language, and the arts.
Recent Political Developments, 282–299
Post-independence. The Aquino Administration.
Economic Conditions and Problems, 300–303
Sources of current problems. Trends.
Foreign Relations, 303–306
The Future of The Philippines, 306–307

Contents

APPENDIXES

A. ASIAN STATISTICS, 308

B. GLOSSARY, 308–312

C. ROMULO STATEMENT, 337–338

D. VIETNAMESE DECLARATION
OF INDEPENDENCE, 314–316

E. HO CHI MINH LETTER TO L.B. JOHNSON, 316–317

F. VIETNAMESE CONSTITUTION (EXCERPTS), 317–318

G. NFL MANIFESTO, 319–320

H. HO CHI MINH'S LAST WILL, 320

I. LE DUC THO STATEMENT, 321–322

J. PRG VICTORY STATEMENT, 323

K. HO CHI MINH POEM, 324

L. LAOTIAN PEACE AGREEMENT (EXCERPTS), 325

M. PROGRAM FOR CAMBODIA, 326–328

N. SUHARTO STATEMENT, 329–330

O. FERDINAND MARCOS' PHILOSOPHY, 330–336

P. MARTIAL LAW IN THE PHILIPPINES, 337–340

Q. THE BURMESE WAY TO SOCIALISM, 340–344

R. BIBLIOGRAPHY, 345–348

S. INDEX, 349–356

© by Rand McNally & Co., R.L. 64-SF-11

PREFACE AND ACKNOWLEDGMENTS

Southeast Asia Emerges completes a series of four concise histories which provide an introduction to the major regions of Asia: the *Asia Emerges Series.* The series' purpose is to focus the most important of Asia's many parts into a single clear image. Together the four books are designed to generate respect for Asia, with its intriguing past, complex present, and enormous potential.

Southeast Asia Emerges is needed for different reasons than the other books in the series. Relatively few single sources exist about the region that it covers. Though Southeast Asia has become increasingly meaningful to the rest of the world, the data needed to understand it are scattered in hundreds of journals, texts, speeches, and photographs. *Southeast Asia Emerges* assembles the essential data, not as a work of original scholarship, but to bring into clear, readable focus the history of an area in which world peace is at stake every day.

The development of *Southeast Asia Emerges* required strenuous effort over an extended period, and this commitment could not have been fulfilled without the talents of Tom Koberna, the editor. Mr. Koberna drove the writer to his farthest limits and generously shared his own excellent talents to produce a better book. In the process he demonstrated the indivisible commitment to truth that characterizes the noblest members of his profession.

Southeast Asia Emerges, like the other books in the series, is an extension of materials gathered for the popular text, *Asia Emerges.* Through their work on that book the co-authors, C. David Bromwell and A. J. Tudisco, indirectly helped in the preparation of the present volume, which is completely new. The author is also grateful to the many researchers at the University of California, Berkeley, and Stanford University, Palo Alto, whose critiques of the research in the *Asia Emerges Series* helped to increase its usefulness. A special note of gratitude is due to Dr. Raymond N. Tang, whose generous contributions of historical photographs made it possible to illustrate *Southeast Asia Emerges.* Most of the photographs of contemporary scenes were supplied by the Pacific Area Travel Association, San Francisco, whose efforts to explain Pacific countries to the rest of the world have been invaluable to many researchers. Other photographs were supplied by the United Press and the Associated Press. The area maps were supplied by Rand McNally and by the U.S. Government Printing Office, publishers of the fine *Area Handbook Series* written by faculty members of American University. Recent photographs from the Philippines were supplied by the Philippines' Consulate-General, San Francisco.

Rice, Southeast Asia's major crop, requires patient cultivation and joint efforts. It grows best in areas where the rainfall exceeds 72 inches a year.

PART 1

CHAPTER 1
SOUTHEAST ASIA IN PERSPECTIVE

EAST OF INDIA, the mighty Himalayas turn southward and descend in long chains for 2,000 miles to the sea. There they vanish, to reappear again in the form of a volcanic arc of islands extending for 3,400 miles toward China. This whole vast area, consisting of the mainland peninsula and strings of more than 10,000 islands, is Asia's frontier—Southeast Asia.

Deep within this land lie some of Asia's most puzzling contradictions. It has dense jungles in which headhunters search for prey, but they stalk near modern plantations. It produces an outpouring of some of the world's most valued products—gold, oil, tin, rubber, and jewels, but contains starving millions who depend on a single grain, rice, for their barest survival. Some of its parts are the most densely populated sections on earth, but it has land to spare and enormous potential power. The region is hot, humid, and rainswept and so supports a rich plant and animal life.

For centuries the rest of the world has looked upon Southeast Asia as an extension of other places. Even its name did not exist until World War II, when military strategists needed a new way to refer to the colonial lands that the Japanese were overrunning. Westerners used to call Southeast Asia "Further India" or "Far Eastern Tropics." Thus they implied that it was a part of India or China, the giant countries on either side of it. Its states were seen as confederations of people whose roots lay elsewhere. Their languages, religions, customs, skin colors, and values seemed to spring from everywhere in the world. Indians, Chinese, Arabs, Portuguese, French, British, Dutch, and Americans helped to make its history. Its own ancient faith was modified by many other religions from abroad: Buddhism, Islam, Christianity, Confucianism, and Taoism.

This swirling blend of peoples, religions, and customs is at last forming cohesive nations: Burma, Thailand, Laos, Kampuchea (Cambodia), Vietnam, Indonesia, Malaysia, the island city-state of

1

Singapore, and the Philippines. The peoples of Southeast Asia are increasingly shaping their own destinies and now have begun to affect the history of the world in their own right. Yet Southeast Asia itself remains subject to immense social, economic, and international pressures. Strategically placed, it has been battered by rival powers while struggling to overcome historic problems of poverty, rebellion, racial conflict, and over-population. To understand this complex part of the world it is necessary to examine the whole region's past and present ways of life.

RELIGIOUS FORCES

Hunting and agricultural societies depend upon natural forces for their survival. When will the rains come? When will they end? Will they be too heavy or too light? How large will the crop be? These and similar questions tend to reinforce the conviction that individuals are not in control of their own destinies. The forms that religious beliefs take are affected by such questions, and the beliefs can, in turn, link vast numbers of people, influencing culture, attitudes, and outlook.

In Southeast Asia, the early hunting and agricultural societies developed a form of religion that underlies its modern life. This ancient form of religion is called animism, a belief that a governing spirit dwells within every living or non-living thing. The spirits were thought to live in trees, rocks, and fields, in people and animals. Emotions and dreams were regarded as traces of these invisible, indestructible powers. Animists believe that these spirits can be persuaded to act for good or for evil. A hunter may try to appease the spirit that controls his prey through a magical symbol or a gift of food. On the island of Kalimantan (Borneo), the members of some Negrito tribes offer the heads of strangers to the spirits of the dead.

The people of Southeast Asia incorporated animism into other religions. Hinduism and Buddhism were introduced first, and Islam much later. Confucianism helped to shape those societies that are closest to China. In the sixteenth century, Christian missionaries arrived from Europe. Today, almost half the 398 million people in Southeast Asia are Muslims who live in Indonesia, Malaysia, and the Philippines. The Burmese, Thai, Khmer, Lao, and many Vietnamese are primarily Buddhists. Christianity is strongest in the Philippines, where 95 percent of the people profess it. There are also scattered communities of Taoists, followers of another Chinese philosophy.

Significant as they are, all of Southeast Asia's religions are influenced by animism, "and it is hardly an exaggeration to say," wrote one scholar, "that [Southeast Asians] are all of one religion." People of all faiths still go regularly to fortune tellers and sorcerers for

The daughter of Prince and Monique Sihanouk practiced an ancient Hindu dance in modern Cambodia. Indian traditions persist among the Khmer and Balinese people.

personal advice. They consult the stars, planets, and more earth-bound signs. A devout Christian may place a symbol in his field to plead with spirits for a better crop. A pious Muslim may ask an oracle whether to allow his son to marry. A Buddhist monk may treat an illness with prayers before an animist altar. Yet its imported religions reflect historical patterns of thought in Southeast Asia, and it is impossible to understand the region without understanding them.

Buddhism. Buddhism arose from the teachings of Siddhartha Gautama (ca. 503–483 B.C.). He was an Indian prince who refused to accept the claims of Hindu priests (Brahmans) that they were socially and spiritually superior to the masses of people. Rejecting the idea of social caste and of sacrifice to Hindu gods, Gautama taught that anyone could secure salvation. His teachings appealed not only to Indians but also to millions of other Asians as well.

Long before Gautama lived, Hindus developed the principle of transmigration of souls. This belief holds that every living thing has a soul that survives when its body dies. After painful wandering, the soul may become bound to a higher or lower form of life, depending on how its former owner behaved. According to the Hindu Brahmans, the individual could save his soul from a miserable future existence by strictly observing his social and religious obligations.

Gautama accepted the idea of the transmigration of souls, but he claimed that the soul may be spared misery through self-discipline rather than through the fulfillment of duty. A soul's wandering, he taught, is caused by the lust of its owner for possessions, power, or relationships. Gautama said that since all things are constantly changing it is pointless to crave them, for by the time they are gained both they and their owners are different from when they were first perceived.

Gautama said that individuals could liberate themselves from craving, thereby achieving an ultimate peace, by accepting the *Four Noble Truths:* that existence is sorrow, that the origin of sorrow is desire, that sorrow ceases when desire ceases, and that the way to end desire is to follow the "Eightfold Path" to the correct life. This path consists of right belief, the renunciation of sensual pleasure and cruelty to any creature, the practice of moderation in speech, conduct, occupation, and effort, and finally, meditation and contemplation.

Gautama described the world as a tragic place in which birth, age, death, contact with the unpleasant, and separation from the pleasant produce sorrow. "...every wish unfulfilled is sorrow—in short, all the...components of individuality are sorrow," he said. But self-discipline leads to moderation in all things and serves to eradicate sorrow. The total elimination of the craving which causes sorrow is called *Nirvana*, which literally means a "blowing out" of the flame which is the soul. Its natural result is peace, which is an end of the soul's wandering.

Because of the clarity of his thought, Gautama was called Buddha—the "Enlightened One." From the social point of view the most significant aspect of Buddha's message was his plea for universal love. He offered the individual a way to be saved, although the way was hard. On the other hand, the Brahmans of India had created a social system in which darker skinned people were forever condemned to live among the lower castes. Brahmanism had given rise to the cult of the *devaraja*, the idea that the king could be identified with gods. In a society ruled by a god-king the people had little choice but to be obedient followers, but the Buddhist king could be expected to show compassion and sensitivity to the people he ruled.

Buddha's ideas spread quickly through India. Buddhist monks went from village to village in selfless pursuit of the Four Noble Truths. Some Buddhist teachers began to say that Buddha himself was a god. They claimed that it would have been impossible for him to have become a god without having been reborn many times, each time at a higher level. If this were true of Buddha it probably was also true that other individuals were preparing for Buddha-hood through succeeding rebirths, or reincarnations. The teachers called a previous incarnation of a Buddha a *bodhisattva*, meaning someone who achieved Nirvana but who preferred to live on earth to help others.

Nirvana, they said, was not only a state of eternal bliss, but a definite heaven over which the original Buddha presided. These teachers also conceived of hell as a place of perpetual suffering.

In the first century A.D. a group of reformers persuaded the Indian emperor to call a conference of Buddhists. There, they split the religion into two schools. They called their own school the "Mahayana" ("Greater Vehicle") and referred to the older one as the "Hinayana" ("Lesser Vehicle"). The Mahayanists allowed the individual a wider interpretation of Buddha's teachings than the Hinayanists. They gave the individual many bodhisattvas to worship in place of the abstract ideal upon which the older school of Buddhism insisted. The Mahayanists permitted people to feel they had achieved salvation through a sense of commitment to Buddhism. In contrast, the Hinayanists offered salvation only to those people who fulfilled specific demands, such as entering the monastery. The Mahayana school quickly became more popular and drove the followers of Hinayana into southern India and Ceylon. For this reason the two schools have ever since been called the "northern" and "southern" branches of Buddhism.

Ultimately Mahayana Buddhism was spread overland to China, Korea, and Japan. The Chinese in turn brought it to Vietnam, the only Southeast Asian country in which it was adopted. Buddhism in Vietnam became fused with Confucianism and Taoism. Burma,

This almost life-sized head of a Buddhist teacher (Bodhisattva Avalokitesvara) was made in the Khmer Kingdom late in the twelfth century.

Cambodia, Thailand, and Laos all adopted the school of "Hinayana," to which they restored its rightful name, Theravada ("Teachings of the Elders").

In Southeast Asia the Mahayanists and Theravadists closely followed the teachings of their Indian counterparts. The Mahayanists of Vietnam opened schools and actively sought the participation of their community in religion. They did not develop a religious hierarchy, however, and allowed each Buddhist temple to manage its own affairs. By contrast, the Theravadists of other Southeast Asian countries taught largely by example and maintained an impressive hierarchy, culminating in the chief of state. Throughout Southeast Asia, Buddhist monks are thought to be closer to Nirvana than ordinary people. They are respected and followed as models of moderation, self-control, and compassion.

Islam. The people of Indonesia and Malaysia accepted Islam ("Submission to Allah") after the arrival of Muslim merchants in the thirteenth century. They were persuaded to do so chiefly because the Muslims refused to trade with the members of other faiths and in many cases demanded conversion. However, the Muslims of Southeast Asia made Islam an expression of their own complex religious ideas. First, they fit it into their system of animism. For example, the

The jeweled elephant is a symbol of this Muslim leader's power in Indonesia.

Muslims of the Middle East, where Islam originated, believe in angels and devils (*djins*). These naturally seemed to correspond with the spirits of animism. The Southeast Asians simply gave their spirits Muslim names.

Second, the Southeast Asians integrated Islam into their Hindu and Buddhist heritage. They built their Islamic mosques on the sites of Hindu or Buddhist temples. Hinduism, which eventually disappeared in Southeast Asia except on the island of Bali, has been expressed there for centuries through the continual retelling of the Hindu epics, the *Ramayana* and the *Mahabharata*. The names of the main characters in Hindu stories, like the animist spirits, became Muslim names. The sacred image of the great bird of the Hindu god Vishnu was retained but identified as the garuda bird, the "roc" in the *Tale of the Arabian Nights*. This bird today is part of the Indonesian flag.

In the Middle East, religious behavior is governed by a strict code (*sharia*) which grew out of the revelations of Muhammad (570–632 A.D.). After his death his followers compiled the sacred book of Islam, the *Qu'ran* (Koran), and other Arabic texts. These works require Muslims throughout the world to practice a uniform system of rituals, duties, and laws which are addressed to the one God (Allah).

Muslims believe that Allah alone has power over humans, who can only praise him and beg him for mercy. Allah is believed to have created all things with a purpose and to have given humanity the purpose of ruling nature in his name. Life is governed by fate (*kismet*) which can only be reverently accepted. The prophets of Islam, of whom Muhammad was the foremost (after Adam, Noah, Abraham, Moses, and Jesus), are the guides whom humans must respect if they want the love of Allah.

Muslims throughout the world express their piety through the *Five Pillars of the Faith.* The first pillar is the *shahada,* a statement that the believer must make once in his life out of a complete commitment and repeats daily afterward: "I swear that there is no God but Allah, and Muhammad is His Prophet." He must pray five times a day in ritualized postures. He must give charity, especially to the state if Islam is the state religion. He must fast during the ninth month of the Muslim year, Ramadan (called Puasa in Indonesia), eating nothing from dawn until nightfall. Finally, once in his life the devout Muslim must make a pilgrimage (*hadj*) to the holy city of Mecca, in Saudi Arabia.

Islam has no priesthood and depends upon the devotion of its members for its propagation. The Muslims of Southeast Asia interpret their religion in a way that is characteristic of their region. They are devout, but emphasize the ceremonies and pageantry of the faith more than its specific regulations. It is not unusual to find Indonesian

Muslims eating forbidden foods and foregoing some daily prayers. In fact, a noted geographer wrote, "in many of the more backward islands [Islam] represents little more than a thin veneer on a scarcely concealed pagan base." Yet most Malaysians and Indonesians follow Muslim religious principles and expect their governments to be Muslim in outlook.

Muslims everywhere feel an obligation to organize society according to their principles. They may accomplish it through social or commercial means, but violence is not ruled out. Islam holds that the state is an instrument of religion and that Muslims, in the words of the *Qu'ran*, "are the best community produced for mankind." It stresses the equality of all people, whatever their faith, but urges Muslims to work together in support of their religion.

Confucianism. The Chinese philosopher Confucius (ca. 551–479 B.C.) urged his followers to respect the fixed rights of others in all relationships. The members of families are the first to experience this mutual respect, which Confucius called "humanitarianism" (*jen,* pronounced "ren" or "run"). Each of them is expected to know his place in relation to the others. Through this knowledge the individual is able to avoid the conflicts that plague less civilized societies and to help make the family a harmonious social unit.

Confucius taught that the father, as head of the family, deserved the greatest measure of respect. The eldest son was next highest in authority, and the family's women were granted authority in varying degrees. Each individual not only received respect but was required to give it, thus linking the family firmly through bonds of love. The apostles of Confucius taught that in addition to humanitarianism the cardinal virtues are righteousness, propriety, wisdom, and faithfulness.

On the social level Confucianism extended the family system of ethics to friends, members of government, and finally to the emperor. All people were expected to give and receive respect in varying degrees. This system was translated into the structure of government by a class of highly educated men called mandarins. The emperor permitted this group to form his bureaucracy, excluding all others by means of a civil service test for which it took years to prepare. Peasants were able to take the test but were almost never able to prepare for it. Thus the wealthy mandarins controlled the government for centuries, basing their power on their ability to read and write the difficult Chinese language.

A mysterious force called "Heaven" was said to have created the natural conditions on which Confucianism was based. Without its support, the Confucianists thought, the social system would collapse. This idea assumed that emperors had a divine right, or "Mandate of

Wearing garments resembling those in Confucian China, the family of Ngo Dinh Diem, South Vietnam's first chief of state, met with a Catholic prelate.

Heaven," to rule. But if the country suffered reverses, there were always rebels who would claim that the Mandate had been withdrawn. The bureaucracy continued to run the country whether dynasties rose or fell.

Confucianism fit in well with Vietnamese traditions. The principle of patrilineal descent (in which the father is considered the source of family relationships) was part of the culture, and it reinforced the Confucian idea that the father is supreme in the family. The concept of an orderly society appealed to the Vietnamese, who regard themselves as an especially gifted, efficient people. Finally, the Chinese influenced Vietnam more than any other country in Southeast Asia. Their ideas of government and of a separate mandarin class permeated Vietnamese society. The Vietnamese had originated in China and brought with them the idea of ancestor worship which is inherent in Confucianism.

Taoism. Taoism is a minor faith in Southeast Asia today. It is concentrated in South Vietnam. Before the arrival of European colonizers in what is now North and South Vietnam, Taoism was a popular cult, and its ideas have not completely disappeared from Vietnamese society.

Taoism is based on the book *Tao teh ching* ("The Book of the Way of Life"), which is said to have been written by Lao-tze (born ca. 604 B.C.). Lao-tze rejected Confucianism, with its demands for obligations and rigid social order. Instead, it pointed out that humans are part of nature. Real power, Lao-tze said, is obtained when people behave the way water does, accepting change, ever flowing, finding their own level, persistent but yielding. He wrote: "Nature does not have to insist. [It] can blow for only half a morning, rain for only half a day. And what are these winds and these rains but natural? If nature does not have to insist, why should man?"

Taoism suggested that humans apply its philosophy of "quietism" in their governments as well as in their own lives. This philosophy urged rulers to allow their people as much freedom as possible, shielding them from material needs while permitting them to experience life in their own contemplative, dispassionate way. Taoism was often mystical, suggesting spontaneous creativity in harmony with nature.

Taoist ideas comforted the Vietnamese people while their rulers were accepting Confucian principles. They offered an escape from the demands for order that were often imposed by the government. Through its faith in nature and belief in mystical spirits, it often seemed to resemble the animism that predated the arrival of the Chinese conquerors.

Families, Villages, Cities

Families. Life throughout Southeast Asia is centered on the family. The region's agricultural villages foster conditions in which family members are more dependent on one another than they would be if they lived in cities. In the different Southeast Asian countries

The ceremonial cremation of a dead king in a "Dragon Ship" testified to popular belief in spirits in Laos.

families may vary in size, but invariably are linked by bonds of mutual concern, esteem, and economic need.

There are two types of families in Southeast Asia, the nuclear and the extended. The nuclear family consists of parents and their children, all sharing a small house, hut, or apartment. This type pre-dominates in Burma, Thailand, Kampuchea, Laos, and on two of Indonesia's most heavily populated islands, Java and Sumatra. The extended family consists of the wives and children of the family's sons, as well as the parents and children. Extended families are the rule in Vietnam, Malaysia, the Philippines, and on Indonesia's less populated islands.

Southeast Asia's family life also differs from country to country with respect to the treatment of women. In general, Southeast Asian women are treated with greater esteem than they are in India, China, or Arabia. They have more social and economic independence. Even the Muslims of Malaysia and Indonesia ignore the Islamic custom of veiling their women from the eyes of men (*purdah*). Burma, Thailand, and Laos extend greater rights to women than Cambodia, Malaysia, and the Philippines. In both Thailand and Indonesia women often manage family finances and are able to buy and sell properties. By contrast, the father is usually the undisputed manager of the household in North and South Vietnam. In most Southeast Asian countries women have not been able to vote until recent years.

Throughout the region marriages are arranged by the parents of the prospective groom. At their son's request they seek a bride for him among families with their own social, cultural, and financial position. After making their choice they will often ask an astrologer to confirm it by consulting the stars. A man may marry as many as four women in Indonesia, Malaysia, Kampuchea, and among many traditional families in Vietnam. Usually only very wealthy men take more than one wife, however.

Only three Southeast Asian populations share the reverence for ancestors that has lasted for centuries in China and India. They are in North and South Vietnam, where Confucianism prevails, and on the island of Bali, a refuge for Hindus in Muslim Indonesia. Among these same populations people reckon their descent from the father of the family alone, and he is almost invariably the most respected member of their families. In other Southeast Asian places fathers are esteemed but not revered, and people rarely think of distant ancestors or family traditions. In some countries the disregard of lineage is so complete that family names are not used or even borne. These countries include Burma, Kampuchea, Laos, and Malaysia.

Families in a few Southeast Asian countries have special personal characteristics. The Thais seem freer and more independent than their neighbors. The Filipinos seem more interdependent and form large kinship groups that are related to both the father's and mother's side of the family. Filipinos also usually have godfathers (*compadres*) and godmothers (*comadres*) who are chosen for them to provide them with care and security as they grow older. But in all of the countries of Southeast Asia families are similar in one respect: they teach their members moderation, compassion, and charity—values stressed by their great religions. People are expected to show respect for others in all of their relationships and to cause no one to feel shame or inadequacy. But the greatest esteem is reserved for those who have become successful in politics, the professions, or education.

Villages. Of Southeast Asia's 398 million people about 75 percent, or 299 million, live in the rural areas. The overwhelming majority are rice growers. In every country the dominant ethnic group slowly drove out the previous lowland occupants and began intensive agriculture. As a result, each country today has areas which are settled by specific ethnic groups.

The older lowland occupants almost invariably fled to higher ground. In Burma, Thailand, Laos, and most other Southeast Asian countries Negrito and other interior people still search for food in the high mountains. Negritos are a small, dark people. They live in family groups of about fifty members, each claiming food-gathering rights over about 25 square miles. There are only about 25,000 of them now. Below them in the mountains are 15,000,000 other tribesmen who grow dry rice by the slash-and-burn method. They chop and cut vegetation over a large area of forest, burn it, and use the ashes to fertilize the field that they have cleared. After about two years the land becomes eroded. Then the families move their village to another part of the forest to repeat the slash-and-burn process, which destroys forests and results in land that is barren for twenty-five years.

By far the largest percentage of Southeast Asia's population lives in the lowlands. There farmers cultivate over 1,000 varieties of rice, in addition to significant but much less important crops. Rice-growing is in large part a community activity. People work together to level the ground and build dikes. Within the "paddies" formed by the dikes they retain sufficient water for the rice to grow. The dikes also prevent the water from sweeping away the rich soil. Rice-growing involves entire villages. The farmers plant the rice seeds in beds. After about five weeks they transplant the tender seedlings to the flooded fields. To prepare the soil for this task they churn, plough, hoe, and weed it with their bare hands and with the help of bullocks and oxen.

Across the land during planting season, thousands of farmers may be seen stooping for hours from the waist. They root the seedlings beneath the fine mud, often singing or chanting as they go. The plants survive only if their tops are above the water. Therefore

This village of Meo tribesmen in Laos consists of clustered huts in a clearing in a dense forest. The trench is a defense against guerrillas.

members of the village have the job of controlling the water level of the paddies. Depending on the type of rice grown, the plants will mature within 60 to 300 days. Then the harvest, another community venture, takes place.

Rice growing in paddies is called wet rice cultivation. Since it requires intensive labor, communities that practice it are among the most densely populated in Southeast Asia. The average density of the wet-rice area of Java, for example, is well over 1,400 people per square mile. Java, with a population of more than 80 million in an area of over 51,600 square miles, is the most closely packed region in the world. By contrast, Great Britain has 56 million in 94,000 square miles. Some parts of the wet-rice delta in North Vietnam have densities approaching Java's.

Another kind of rice-growing involves dry strains. That is, the plants need much less water and can be grown on mountainsides. They are less productive than the wet-rice strains but are planted widely, especially in the Philippines and Indonesia.

Rice cultivation lends itself to the village life that is the basis of society throughout Southeast Asia. Villages contain from 50 to 3,000 people whose object is to supply all of their own needs. In addition to serving as their own food growers they must be carpenters, weavers, potters, and boatbuilders. In countries where water is the principal means of transportation they are often expert navigators, sailors, and fishermen. Whatever they cannot make they gain by bartering, trading their own surpluses for the goods of other villagers.

The water which helps them to raise their food may also damage Southeast Asians. Funguses, insects, and rodents thrive in the moist climate. Timbers rot, and most construction is deliberately made of temporary materials. In the mountains the slash-and-burn cultivators build their houses with bamboo and palm leaves. In Vietnam and Java, villagers weave bamboo into wall material. They tie it to wooden frames which they build on ground-level foundations. Throughout the rest of Southeast Asia, houses are placed on stilts three to six feet high. The space under the house is protection against floods and animals. It allows cooling air to flow beneath the houses and eliminates some of the moisture that tends to rot the timbers.

Southeast Asian houses are small. They range in size from about 10 by 20 feet to about 25 by 40 feet. In most rural areas they are clustered, but in some places they are lined along waterways. In a few regions such as Kalimantan (Borneo) the strings of houses form connected structures called "longhouses."

Cities. Southeast Asians have been building cities since the arrival of the first Indians about the time of Christ. The seafaring Indians traded in small villages on the coastlines, where communities grew. The Indian concept of a socially superior king, separated from the people by priests, led to the development of courts that became cities. The Indians believed that kingdoms were meant to resemble the universe, with kings in the place of gods. They had a complex image of what the universe must be like and duplicated it in the construction of their court cities. The famous Angkor Wat in Kampuchea (Cambodia), as we will see, is a later development of the Indian desire to reflect mythology in royal architecture.

Some of the older cities still existed when the Europeans began to arrive in the sixteenth century. The objective of the Westerners in Southeast Asia was to take out agricultural products and raw materials and to bring their own manufactured products for sale. Therefore they built up the coastal cities into enormous marketplaces. Unable to persuade the easygoing, agricultural Southeast Asians to enter commerce, industry, and construction, they imported Chinese and Indians for those purposes. Today there are more than twenty million people of Chinese ancestry and more than three million of Indian ancestry in the cities of Southeast Asia. These minorities have preserved their ancestral cultures in their new land. At the same time, their commercial and financial activities have enabled them to prosper at the expense of the Southeast Asians. Both factors have provoked lasting anger among the major ethnic groups.

Ultimately the Western powers dominated every Southeast Asian country except Thailand. Their enterprises attracted other foreigners to the cities. Freebooters and merchants came from every part of the world to claim some of the enormous profits in tin, rubber, gold, oil, or spices. Still, throughout the colonial period the major cities contained surprisingly few Southeast Asians. The local populations refused to surrender their agricultural societies, although many were drawn to the Western-owned mines and plantations.

For millions of Southeast Asians, conditions prevailing since World War II have changed that point of view. Guerrilla warfare in the countryside has caused untold numbers of people to leave their farms and to stream into the metropolitan areas. Countless others were driven from their rural homes by bombing or terrorism. Finally, young people have been drawn from the country to the cities to escape subsistence labor, to find industrial jobs, security, or education. Saigon, Bangkok, Manila, and Kuala Lumpur are among the fastest growing cities in the world. The process of urbanization in Southeast Asia has begun and will not stop. The region now has ten cities with more than a million people, four with more than two million, and one, Djakarta, with more than 6.5 million.

There are sharp contrasts between the rich and poor in the metropolitan areas. Millions of people live in slums. They surround the lavish, well-guarded homes and hotels of successful business and professional people. The cities themselves stand in stark contrast to the

The independent city-state of Singapore has become one of the world's most prosperous financial centers and a headquarters for oil exploration.

quiet, thatched villages in the distant countrysides. In both urban and rural areas malnutrition and disease are rampant.

The growing urbanization of Southeast Asia does not mean that the land is overcrowded as a whole. On the contrary, in the context of Asia there are relatively few people. The population density in Southeast Asia is 205 per square mile, while in India it is 605, in China it is 282, and in Japan, 827. By comparison, density in Europe is 176 and in the United States, 65.3.

Thus in much of Southeast Asia there is land to spare. It is the maldistribution of population and poor land use, not the shortage of land, that has greatly contributed to social tension. We have seen that the cities grew because of Western activities and that the lowlands are crowded because of the intensive labor required there for rice growing. Other factors which are chiefly geographical and cultural also generate conditions that have made the future of Southeast Asia precarious.

LAND, CLIMATE, AND RESOURCES

Extending from the eastern tip of the Himalayas, Southeast Asia's peninsula consists of a series of mountainous spines stretching southward, and of broad valleys lying between them. The land extends 2,000 miles into the ocean toward Australia. A chain of 10,000 equatorial islands comprises the second feature of the region. There is evidence that millions of years ago these islands were joined to the

Southeast Asia's rivers
are a major source of food,
irrigation, and transportation.

continent of Asia. They form the Indonesian and Philippine archipelagoes.

On the great peninsular land mass of Southeast Asia six rivers descend from the heights of eastern Tibet. From west to east they are the Irrawaddy, Sittang, Salween, Chao Phraya, Mekong, and Red rivers. Most of the population of the peninsula lives near the rivers. The Burman, Thai, Khmer, Lao, and Vietnamese people live in the lowlands formed by these rivers. They comprise more than half of the population of the peninsula.

Most of Southeast Asia's population growth has been near the rivers, in the lowlands. The average rate of increase now stands at 2 percent a year, .2 percent more than the average rate for the entire world. It is adding almost eight million people a year. But the growth rate is much higher in some countries than in others. While the increase is only 1.1 percent in Singapore, it is more than twice that in Burma, Kampuchea, Malaysia, the Philippines, and Vietnam. The populations of some Southeast Asian countries will double by the end of the century.

Rivers are the basis of life for most of the region's millions. They provide the irrigation, drinking, and washing water, the recreation and sewage disposal. They are the highways and source of alluvial land without which the region would be incapable of supporting its present population. The rivers expand and contract seasonally, providing a rhythm to life that imposes itself on all human activities. Depending on the state of the rivers, people, plant or prepare to plant. Whether they are trading, weaving, or boatmaking they know that the rivers will determine their lives.

Changes in the rivers depend on the climate. All of Southeast Asia, and much of the rest of the continent, too, undergoes winds called monsoons (the Arabic word for "seasons"). The exact cause of the monsoons is still unknown, but probably they result from changing air masses over land and sea. Between mid-May and mid-October the southwest monsoon sweeps inland from the Bay of Bengal. As it passes from ocean to land it gathers moisture which becomes torrential rain. In winter the flow of the monsoon is reversed. The air mass over the continent chills and descends. It drives air southward, causing a dry period about equal with the rainy one.

The southwest monsoon deposits widely differing amounts of rain in the different areas of Southeast Asia. Most areas receive more than 60 inches of rainfall, but some undergo four times that amount. A minimum of 72 inches a year is needed for the cultivation of wet rice. Southeast Asia's highest rainfall is at Akyab on the coast of Burma, where the annual average is 204 inches. The lowest is at Luang

A volcanic eruption on Bali created tens of thousands of refugees in 1963.
There are hundreds of active volcanoes in Indonesia and the Philippines.

Prabang, where a little over 51 inches falls annually. Singapore is
about midway, with 92.9 inches.

There is no comparable variation in temperature. The average
annual temperature at sea level is about 80 degrees F., except in
North Vietnam, where in winter it may average only 62 degrees F.
Temperatures throughout the year vary little in any one region.
What does change, principally, is the humidity.

Moisture in Southeast Asia produces an amazingly diverse plant
and animal life. Rain forests develop solid canopies of shrubs and
plants. Within them there are hundreds of varieties of reptiles,
mammals, and insects. Some trees soar 180 feet above the forests, and
at their base there are brilliant flowers, shrubs, and bamboos. Some
areas are so densely choked with vines that they are impassable.

Not all of Southeast Asia is so lushly overgrown. Parts of the high,
windswept north are barren. Regions such as the Plain of Jars in Laos
and the Korat Plateau, which comprises about a third of Thailand,
are relatively stark because they are dry. But much of Indonesia,
Malaysia, the Philippines, and the forests of the peninsula contain
some of the world's most magnificent natural scenes. In the island
countries, smoldering volcanos supplement the drama of the environ-

ment. More than a hundred of them are still active on Java alone. On Krakatao, in the Straits of Sunda, an eruption in 1883 destroyed most of the island. The resulting tidal waves drowned 36,000 people. Another disastrous eruption took place on the island of Bali early in 1963. The island countries are also subject to typhoons and earthquakes.

Southeast Asia's land and climate provide some of the world's best conditions for growing rice, sugar, rubber, tea, and spices. Rice is grown everywhere, but the other major crops do best in isolated parts of the region. Burma, Kampuchea, and the Philippines are major sugar producers. The British introduced the first rubber plants from Brazil in the 1870's, and ever since most of the world's natural rubber has been produced on the Malay Peninsula and Indonesia. Burma and Thailand provide some of the best sources teakwood. There are valuable oil deposits in Burma, Malaysia, and Indonesia, and recently more have been discovered off the coasts of Vietnam and Kampuchea. Gold in the Philippines, tin in Burma and Thailand, and coal in Vietnam are among the region's other valuable minerals. Coffee and tea are grown in the Philippines, Indonesia, Malaysia, and Vietnam.

THE ECONOMY OF SOUTHEAST ASIA

Most of Southeast Asia's energies go into the development of a food supply for its own population. Since World War II it has introduced more double-cropping, irrigation, and improved strains of rice seed which have contributed to substantial progress in agriculture. But while food production is rising, so is the population, often at a greater rate. Some of the region's countries are able to use only a small part of their land. Burma, for example, is able to cultivate only 10 percent of its land because of mountainous terrain. For the same reason Laos cultivates only 30 percent of its land.

In a subsistence economy countries have little to export. Southeast Asia's industries are meager. Most of them are situated near the coasts, near markets and transportation established by the West during colonial times. The governments of Southeast Asia have developed vigorous plans to increase industrial production but rarely does industry produce more than a quarter of the gross national product. Progress has been slow because of the shortage of capital, the lack of industrial experience, and the destruction caused by war.

Despite these shortcomings, the economies of Southeast Asia have immense importance and potential. The region's raw materials are indispensible to the world's industrial countries. While Southeast Asia needs to import such manufactured goods as chemical fertilizers and machinery, it is able to export vital supplies of tin, rubber, and oil. It was chiefly to gain these materials that the West colonized Southeast Asia and Japan opened World War II in the Pacific. Today almost every nation in the West, and the new Japan, too, looks to Southeast Asia for continued supplies of raw materials. At the same time, most of the countries of the region must import food and capital to survive and grow.

The per capita income in Southeast Asia is extremely low, ranging from only $180 a year in Burma to a high of $7100 a year in Singapore. In Western terms those are small amounts of money to earn a year, but the same standards cannot be applied in Asia. Most Southeast Asians grow their own food and make their own clothing. They spend nothing for these items, which are normally large parts of any Western budget. They use no cash, but employ the barter system for many of their purchases. Yet they live marginal lives, for food supplies are uncertain.

There is no doubt that although the enormous populations in Southeast Asia are subsisting, they earn too little. The poor have almost no chance of changing their economic position. As populations increase so do social tensions and shortages. Disease, starvation, and early death are constant threats. It is to control the mounting problems in Southeast Asian societies that the region's governments have been changing rapidly.

TRADITION AND CHANGE

For centuries life in Southeast Asia has been based on the family, religion, and the village. Slowly it began to change under the impact of colonial rule. Families were broken up as the Western entrepeneurs drew individuals out of them for work on the plantation and factories. Then World War II began, and one of its effects was to erode the authority and moral systems prescribed by religion. Finally, the nationalist movements following the war resulted in governments which needed to gain the loyalty of their people in order to exist. The efforts of these governments to create nations, combined with the challenge presented to them by rebel groups, have tended to break down the average Southeast Asian's commitment to his village.

This breakdown of village life has been a complex process. In Southeast Asia there is a general consciousness that customs may be limited to small regions. Local laws and standards are enforced by village courts and social pressures. People believe more in horoscopes than in government. But in recent years they have been compelled to become more political. With the advent of guerrilla warfare they have had to favor one side over the other. Their loyalty was the prize for which the two sides fought. Bombing and ground action caused many people to move from their villages. Others were persuaded to move by the economic plans of the new nationalist movements, which worked intensively to launch new projects. Still others have moved because they were unable to survive economically in their villages.

Thus the cities are growing at the expense of the villages and almost certainly will grow more. People in cities have less regard for traditional behavior. The young often live alone and forgo contact with their rural families. Most urban quarters are too small for large families, and money and jobs are scarce. All of these factors tend to break down strong family ties in Southeast Asia. But urbanization is also bringing some benefits. It increases the chances that people will become more skillful in commerce and industry, that women will become more independent, and that the young will gain better educations.

Southeast Asia is emerging from a long period in which change took place slowly, and now the speed of events is quickening. In this new phase of its history it is no longer made up of scattered societies, but consists in an interdependent unit which is becoming increasingly significant in the world. Each of the ten nations of the region is groping for ways to satisfy needs on which the survival of millions depends. They have been struggling to modernize their economies while their people are often divided politically and culturally. At the same time they are unwilling and probably unable to abandon the traditions and values that have made Southeast Asia unique.

Today, Southeast Asia is struggling to achieve its own identity, free of domination by outside powers. Whether it can gain the autonomy that it seeks depends on many factors, many of which lie in its history. To understand what the region may become, therefore, it is essential to know not only its hopes, plans, and capacity, but also its history.

CHAPTER 2

EARLY INFLUENCES

LONG BEFORE RECORDED HISTORY HUMANS hunted in the jungles of
what is now Indonesia. Anthropologists classify them as Australoids,
a long-headed, dark-skinned, wavy-haired people who were a little
more than five feet tall. They were fishing and gathering food, using
single-edged axes. at a time when much of the rest of the world was
covered by ice (Pleistocene Age).

From about 10,000 to 5,000 B.C. the hunters made a transition to
an agricultural society. They were apparently joined by a people who
centuries before originated in Central Asia and so are called Mongoloids. The immigrants came from western China, where they lived in
villages. The Malay people were brown-skinned and slightly taller
than the Australoids. They introduced the arts of making cloth, pots,
and woodcarvings. A later group of Malay immigrants followed them
from China and brought the ability to make and shape bronze and
iron. Their bronze drums, used for religious purposes, are still found
in the islands of Southeast Asia and in Vietnam. Their culture is called
"Dong-Son," after the Vietnamese village in which the drums were
first found.

The Malays were accomplished sailors and traders. They occupied
the best coastal sites and forced the older population back into the
interior. The Australoid population continued to practice slash-and-
burn agriculture and nomadic hunting. Meanwhile the Malays
appear to have introduced wet-rice cultivation into the lowlands,
thus permanently changing the future development of Southeast
Asia. They kept cattle and probably ducks and chickens, raised their
bamboo houses on stilts to escape the hazards of heavy rains, and
practiced ancestor worship. Like many other people who originated
in Central Asia, they held women in high regard.

While the islands were being settled by the Malays, other migrants
were arriving in the peninsula of Southeast Asia. They came over the
high mountain passes of the north and east. The mountains of Southeast Asia are crossed more easily than those of India, though passage is

difficult. The people who immigrated were from Central Asia and China, as well as from the Malayo-Polynesian islands. Within the two thousand years before Christ they came slowly but steadily, until by the birth of Christ they were well established in coastal villages. Their wet-rice paddies began to spread across the river deltas.

Some islanders began to move to the peninsula, but there they soon confronted new immigrants who were arriving overland, the Mons. Like the islanders the Mons were Mongoloids, but they came directly from Central Asia rather than through China. They shared the islanders' basic cultural tendencies, particularly the willingness to grant relative equality to women. The Mon people settled at the southern tip of what is now Burma, where they dominated the region's richest land and its major sea lanes. Other Mongoloids followed them over the mountains, arriving from Tibet. They followed the Mons' pattern of wet-rice cultivation near coastal villages.

The Mons were settled in the delta of the Irrawaddy River when a much smaller group, the Khmers, began to arrive from southeast China about the first century B.C. After 500 years of wandering through the peninsula of Southeast Asia, the Khmers established a kingdom covering most of what was to become Kampuchea (Cambodia) and Laos. As we will see, under the influence of Indian culture the Khmer kingdom became one of the most artistically accomplished societies in Southeast Asia.

The Vietnamese were a third group of immigrants whose influence has persisted to the present day. According to their legends they came from central China precisely in the year 2879 B.C. and settled near the Annamite Mountains, in the center of what are now North and South

Rice cultivation and bullocks were brought to Southeast Asia in prehistoric times by immigrants who came overland from Central Asia and by sea from China.

Vietnam. No records exist to confirm that date. However, Chinese historians reported that the Yüeh people were displaced from their kingdom south of the Yangtze River in 333 B.C. The Yüeh migrated to the south (*nam*) and later were unified as the Nam Yüeh, or Nam Viet. The Nam Viets were conquered by China in 111 B.C.

The Mons, Khmers, and Vietnamese began to arrive at a time when the first great empires were arising in India and China. The reasons for their migrations are not clear, but apparently it was to escape domination by India and China. Later they were followed by the Burmans of Central Asia and the Thais of South China. Each of these immigrant groups displaced earlier, less aggressive settlers who had occupied the river valleys.

Not long after the immigrants settled in Southeast Asia, Indian traders arrived and peacefully spread their culture among them. Indian customs, religion, and literature blended with Southeast Asia's predominately Mongoloid ideas, creating one of the most important aspects of the region's history. The Chinese came, too, but as conquerors. Their unique culture, technology, and government were indelibly imprinted in what was to become North Vietnam. Ultimately they were driven out, but their ideas remained. Finally, Mongols came from Central Asia and Muslims from India and the Middle East.

The people of Southeast Asia struggled to keep their own identity while these overwhelming influences were affecting them. Their own traits were blended with the succeeding foreign cultures. The degree to which Southeast Asians preserved their identity, and the unique cultural blend that resulted, is the subject of this chapter.

India

A wall of mountains blocks overland communication between India and Southeast Asia. It is the sea that makes possible relationships between them. In the days when sailing vessels dominated trade, Asia's monsoon winds were a dependable source of power. They swept Indian ships eastward in the summer and back home in the winter. A large part of India's international trade was focused on its northwest, or Coromandal Coast. There, traders from the state of Gujarat loaded sturdy little ships with oil-filled jugs, fabrics, and jewels to trade in Southeast Asia for spices, metals, forest products, and food.

The Indian traders, or Gujaratis, were disinterested in establishing colonies, but they did maneuver for commercial advantages. A number of Gujaratis began to live in Southeast Asia to negotiate trade agreements which became profitable because of India's demand for spices. Some of the wealthier Gujaratis married into the families of Southeast Asian rulers. Having attained riches and authority, they were admired by Southeast Asians. The members of many local courts copied the Gujaratis' Indian culture. At first Indian culture had no attraction for the general population, but its appeal increased with the introduction of Indian religions.

Beginning about the first century, the "Indianization" of Southeast Asia's coastal villages progressed steadily for a thousand years. The word "Indianization" has long been used by scholars to suggest how deeply Indian culture penetrated the societies of Southeast Asia. On the eastern coast of what is now South Vietnam, for example, a people called the Chams lived about the second century A.D. They worshipped the Hindu deities of India—Siva the god of destruction, change, and reproduction; and Vishnu, the god of preservation and permanence. But Buddha, too, was worshipped as he was in India. The two Indian religions of Hinduism and Buddhism existed side by side in the state of Champa.

Khmers. More enduring evidence of Indianization exists in the lands settled by the Khmers. We have no complete record of this people, but their story has been pieced together from indirect evidence. It tells of a Hindu named Kaudinya who landed with a group of settlers in the delta of the Mekong River. The Hindu settlers blended with the Khmers, and Kaundinya became the Khmer ruler.

Under the leadership of Kaundinya and his successors the Khmers advanced up the Mekong River and down into the Malay Peninsula. The Khmer kingdom eventually included much of present-day Kampuchea, Laos, southern Thailand, and northern Malaysia. For almost five hundred years the Khmers dominated the trade culture of the Southeast Asian peninsula, instilling the Indian arts and language. However, they did not bring the Indian idea of social castes.

Like many other Indians, Kaundinya believed in an ancient Hindu myth concerning society. This myth had been brought to India by Aryan invaders. It described the universe as a mechanism presided over by the gods. In great detail it told how the gods lived in the top of the sacred mountain of Meru which revolved on the central axis of the universe. Below these gods were humans, living on a continent surrounded by six circles of land and seven oceans. A rock wall lay beyond these oceans.

In this thoroughly organized world the ruler lived in an elevated position closer to the gods. Below him were the priests, or Brahmans, and below them, in descending order, were the warriors, merchants, and laborers. A special group of outcastes could belong to none of these groups. Skin color was the basis of this caste system. Since the Aryan conquerors were fair skinned and the Indians whom they conquered were darker, they gave higher positions to lighter skinned people.

Accepting at least part of the caste system, the Khmers revered Kaundinya as "King of the Mountain." (Because of this title the Chinese began to refer to Kaundinya's land as Funan, a word that was derived from the local word *phnom*, or mountain. Funan is the name most often used by people referring to Kaundinya's dynasty.) In India Kaudinya was religious, and no doubt he encouraged the rise of a priesthood in Southeast Asian society. He directed thousands of laborers to build a royal court resembling a mountain and attracted craftsmen and farmers to live near it. In addition, he enlisted an army to defend his authority against tribal chiefs who might oppose him. The Funan Dynasty established by Kaundinya was conquered by another group of Khmers, the Chen, in the sixth century. But this conquest merely spread Indianization farther into Southeast Asia. The Chen people retained Funan's traditions and expanded its empire throughout western Kampuchea and southern Thailand.

The new kingdom was called Chenla. It became so large that it was divided into two sections, Water Chenla and Land Chenla. Water Chenla exerted a powerful influence on the people of the islands, where it carried on extensive trade. From 790–802 it was ruled by a prince on the island of Java. This prince made the mistake of appointing a rebellious Khmer leader to govern his new colony. In 802 this Khmer liberated Water Chenla. Taking the name Jayavarman II, he ruled a new empire from Tonle Sap ("Great Lake") in the center of what is now Kampuchea (Cambodia). Later he built a new capital on a site called Angkor, for which his dynasty is named. From Angkor he contrôlled an area that extended from central Vietnam to the Gulf of Thailand.

The two Chenlas were reunited under the Angkor Dynasty, and the Indianization of this part of Southeast Asia continued. During this so-called Khmer Classical Period the Indian epics, written in the original Sanskrit, were spread throughout the central part of the peninsula. The Chenla people accepted the Indian cult of the god-king (*devaraja*). Jayavarman II was the source of all law and the owner of all land. He controlled a bureaucracy of more than 4,000 officials. Often he added the officials' daughters to his harem in order to insure bureaucratic loyalty.

The god-like supremacy of the king was symbolized in enduring stone by Jayavarman and Suryavarman II (ca. 1112–1150). On the river of Siemreab the Khmers erected a massive group of buildings, covering an area as large as many cities. The buildings were made of sandstone and laterite, but were so large that they have lasted through the centuries. Elaborately planned and decorated, their construction must have required many thousands of laborers.

Jayavarman II (802-850 A.D.) used this capital at Angkor to symbolize
the ancient Indian belief that the king could be identified with a god.

The most famous buildings of the group were built at Angkor for
Jayavarman II. Their construction reflects the Khmer (and Hindu)
acceptance of Aryan mythology, for they recreate in stone the universe that it described. The builders of Angkor built an enormous
moat, behind which there is a wall with four high gates. Four roads
lead from the gates to a central pyramid-temple in which the king
and god were thought to be united. Lining the roads are statues that
represent the forces of good and evil. The most celebrated of the
pyramid-temples, Angkor Wat, shows the magnitude of the under-
taking at Angkor. It became the burial place for Suryavarman II. The
building is square. Each side is 660 feet long, or twice the size of a
football field. The skill with which it was built indicates that the
Khmer had a good working knowledge of both mathematics and
geometry. On the outside of the structure there are 1,760 life-sized
carvings of spirit-dancers. The intricate carvings cover the stone to its
height of 220 feet. Inside, near the mausoleum, are hundreds of
symbols of the god and of the king.

Angkor became a thriving commercial center very much run by its
women merchants. Its prosperity enabled Suryavarman II to extend
the country's ricefields by increasing its irrigation and roads. He also
expanded the empire through wars against the Chams, Vietnamese,
and Burmans. Eventually the kingdom was called Kambuja (later
westernized as "Cambodia"), after a legendary figure who is said to
have led the Khmers before the rule of Jayavarman II. Kambuja held
much of Annam and Champa during the eleventh and much of the
twelfth centuries. However, in 1177 Champa rallied its forces and
struck back. It invaded and destroyed the Khmer capital at Angkor.

The sacred capital was not regained until 1181. Then Jayavarman VII drove out the Chams and added the buildings known as Angkor Thom to the other structures. He also led the Khmers into conquests of large parts of Burma and the Malay Peninsula.

During this period rebellions threatened the unity of the country. The Angkor Dynasty had clearly reached its peak and was beginning to decline. The Khmer people could no longer accept without question the idea that their king was divine. His wars and lavish behavior were too great a price to pay for the cult of the *devaraja* (god-king). The extravagant ways of the god-king were proving too great a burden for the peasants.

Another Indian influence on the Khmers was Theravada Buddhism, which was spreading throughout Southeast Asia. As we have seen, the Theravadists accepted the Hindu teaching that the soul survives the death of the body. However, they added to the Buddha's belief that the individual can take steps to gain everlasting peace. Brought by monks from Ceylon, Theravada Buddhism was increasingly accepted throughout the future countries of Cambodia, Burma, Thailand, and Laos. Its focus on self-mastery tended to undermine the idea that the king was supreme. At last Kambuja's monarchy became too weak to resist invaders. It was attacked from both east and west. In 1353 its capital at Angkor Thom was captured, and in 1431 it was finally destroyed. Angkor was left to the jungle.

Although the Angkor Dynasty fell, Kambuja survived. It resisted the attacks of its neighbors (whose histories we will next examine) and established its capital near Phnom Penh. During the fifty-year reign of Ang Chan (1516–66) the country dedicated itself to Buddhism. Yet the change of religions did not bring peace. Ang Chan involved Kambuja in repeated wars with the Thais and Vietnamese. In its turn it became a prize for which its aggressive neighbors fought. Still, Kambuja was able to maintain its independence until 1864. At that time it did not fall to a Southeast Asian power, but to a European one.

Lao. The neighbors who attacked Angkor Thom in 1353 and 1431 were fascinated by the Indianized culture that they confronted. They had come from China only a century before and had nothing to equal the achievements of the Khmers. At Angkor they seized thousands of works of Khmer art and carried the entire troupe of Khmer royal dancers home with them.

These people were the Lao, a branch of the Thais who had settled in what is now Laos and Thailand. They originated in Yünnan, South China, where they had developed the powerful kingdom of Nan Chao ("South of the Clouds"). In 1253 Kublai Khan's Mongol armies drove this Chinese people southward into the peninsula of

Southeast Asia. The Lao-thais settled in the valley of the upper
Mekong River, in a region inaccessible to the Khmer Empire. However, they became related to the Khmer by marriage and established
a country called Lan Xang ("Million Elephants"), which was later
called Laos.

With the development of Lan Xang, the Indianization of Southeast
Asia reached its northernmost point. The Khmer relatives of the Lan
Xang king sent him relics and images of the Buddha, including a
famous gold statue called the Prabang which had been brought from
Ceylon. Buddhism became Lan Xang's official religion, although
most Laotians did not give up their belief in animism. By 1376 Lan
Xang was a prosperous country of 300,000 with a central government
and Buddhist schools. Its army was strong enough to resist those of
Siam and Burma.

In the sixteenth century the Lao took over the neighboring Thai
state of Chiengmai, where they later developed a large Buddhist
temple complex (*wat*). In this temple they placed an emerald Buddha
and other religious symbols. In the eighteenth century the Thais came
to enslave the Lao and seize their wealth, including the Prabang
Buddha. In the early nineteenth century the fragments of the Lan
Xang Empire were subject to the Thais. By the end of the century
they were an important part of the struggle between the Thais and
the French for control of the central part of the Southeast Asian
peninsula.

Thais. The main branch of the Thai people settled west of the Lao
after leaving China. The Thais encountered the Mons there and were
deeply influenced by them. The Mons lived at the southern tip of the
future country of Burma, and they modeled their culture closely on
the one they saw in nearby India. Because of their Mon contacts, the
Thais quickly became Indianized and began to practice Buddhism.
At the end of the thirteenth century they established a kingdom called
Chiengmai in the upper basin of the Mekong River. The Burmans
repeatedly attacked them there, and they began to edge southward
toward the Mons. After seizing the Mon capital, the Thai king sought
out the artisans of neighboring Burma to build Buddhist shrines for
him. For this reason many of the historic buildings of Siam—what
was to become Thailand—resemble those of Burma. Thus Thai culture reflects Indian concepts, but its language and architecture also
retain many of their original Chinese elements.

Another Thai kingdom, called Sukothai, was founded to the north
of Chiengmai. It became Indianized through the Khmers, on whose
land it was developed. Its third king, Rama the Great, introduced the
Theravada school of Buddhism to his country after discovering it in a
Malay kingdom that he conquered. Rama borrowed the script used

The ruins of this fifteenth-century Thai temple contain a monumental image of Gautama Buddha which is characteristic of Mahayana Buddhism in Southeast Asia.

by the Mons and Khmers, both of whom he defeated, to create the first Thai alphabet. He was proud of these accomplishments and of his ability to government. Rama maintained peace with China and developed a prosperous land. "The lord of the country," he boasted of his rule, "levies no tolls on his subjects.... Whoever desires to trade elephants, does so; whoever desires to trade horses, does so; whoever desires to trade silver and gold, does so."

Under Rama, the Thai empire became an absolutist monarchy that was more powerful than the neighboring kingdom of the Khmers. It developed a strongly centralized government, with provincial, district, and village administrations. Its officials had both territorial responsibilities and functional ones. For example, a peasant who was a carpenter would have to deal with a local official who was in charge of construction. The country had a social ranking system, but one which still allowed for promotion and demotion. Rama ruled for forty years. Soon after his death in 1317, however, the kingdom was absorbed by one begun near the future city of Bangkok.

This new kingdom was called Ayuthia (Siam). Founded in 1350, it was to last for four hundred years. It was centered on an island in the Chao Phraya River, where its capital could easily be defended. There, too, it could enjoy the benefits of trade between the Malays to the south and Khmers to the east. Culturally, Ayuthia borrowed heavily from the neighboring Khmers, whose land it often attacked. It adopted Khmer arts and forms of government, particularly the concept that the king was divine. Thus like all of its neighboring states it became thoroughly Indianized.

Trade with China increased during the fourteenth century, when the Chinese developed a commercial fleet. Ayuthia became the principal agent for this trade and so won China's recognition and support. It attacked the Muslim ruler of Malacca when he tried to trade directly with China in the early fifteenth century. The invasions of Malacca marked the beginning of a conflict between the Buddhist Thais and the Muslim Malays that has never ceased.

Throughout the fifteenth century Ayuthia expanded rapidly at the expense of its neighbors. It invaded the kingdoms of Sukothai, Chiengmai, and Khmer. Thus most of the ports in the Gulf of Thailand were in its control when the Chinese ships arrived. Ayuthia's increased commerce enabled its kings to gain new powers. Its bureaucracy was expanded under King Trailok (1448–88), who insured greater continuity for the kingdom by naming his own successor. This policy allowed the country to avoid the bloody conflicts that often followed the death of kings in neighboring Burma. King Trailok also solidified his hold over remote areas by granting land to people who aided his administration. He would give a governor as much as 4,000 acres and a farmer about 10.

The people of Ayuthia were energetic and extremely proud of their culture, maintaining an independence that was to endure throughout their history. They were conquered by the Burmans in 1556 but later rebelled and defeated both the Burmans and the Khmers, extending their borders almost to the present frontiers of Siam (Thailand). By the end of the sixteenth century their lands included many of the former Mon states at the southern tip of the peninsula. After an invasion of Burma the Thai armies were driven back, but were joined by thousands of Mon refugees who feared the Burmans. Thus the future country of Thailand absorbed more elements of the Indianized culture that so profoundly affected it.

Burmans. The Mon people spread Buddhism and other Indian ideas to the Burmans as well as the Thais. The Burmans were a Tibetan tribe that descended the northern mountains about the middle of the eighth century. They first overcame the Pyus, earlier Tibetan immigrants who had an Indianized culture just north of the Mons. By the middle of the eleventh century they expanded their kingdom southward until they reached the kingdom of the Mons.

The Burman king, Anawratha, became a Buddhist in 1056, about 12 years after he came into contact with the Mons. His conversion illustrates the power of the Indianized cultures. Anawratha was eager to gain possession of Buddhist scriptures held by the Mons and asked politely that they be sent to his capital at Pagan, on the Irrawaddy River. The Mon king refused, calling the Burmans barbarians. Thereupon, Anawratha became enraged and pursued his campaign southward until his conquest of the Mons was complete.

Through these wars Anawratha created the Burman kingdom out of the states on the western coast of Southeast Asia's peninsula. He dedicated his kingdom to Buddhism. Enslaving 30,000 Mons, he ordered them to turn Pagan into one of the architectural marvels of the world. They filled the city with temples and shrines, and its soaring spires have ever since proclaimed to distant travelers the devotion of the Burman rulers.

We have seen how the Mons previously Indianized the Thais, who like the Burmans are related to the Chinese. Through their similar effect on the Burmans they caused Indian, Chinese, and Southeast Asian cultures to blend on the peninsula. The Burmans had only recently come from Tibet and brought no written language or mathematical skills. By the eleventh century they began to use the written language of the Mons and in time gained many of the other skills that the Mons had learned from the Indians.

In 1084 a warrior named Kyansittha ("Soldier Lord") came to power and ruled over a united Burma for twenty-eight years. A devout Buddhist, he constructed Pagan's Ananda pagoda and encouraged missionaries to spread the use of the new written language. Burma by this time was wealthy enough to trade exten-

Monuments built in the eleventh century in Pagan, Burma, encouraged Buddhism throughout Southeast Asia and today remain shrines for the faithful.

sively with China and India. It also sent a ship bearing help for Buddhists who wanted to rebuild their holiest shrine at Benares, India. Within fifty years after Kyansittha's death, almost everyone in Burma was a Buddhist.

The great wealth in Burma was a result of irrigation projects financed by the central government. The country was never short of food. As early as the eleventh century it had an extensive meat and dairy industry and raised fish in artificial ponds. It was one of the largest rice growers in Southeast Asia. It also produced gold, silver, and gems which it traded for Indian luxuries.

Despite its prosperity, Burma had basic weaknesses in its social system. Burman kings appointed provincial rulers, who were not allowed to will their authority to their sons. As a result, after the death of either the provincial ruler or the king there were bloody struggles for power. The officials kept slaves who were either con- quered people or those who fell into debt. A third serious weakness was a growing Buddhist monkhood to which citizens gave large gifts of nontaxable land. The monks spent fortunes on their own pleasure, violating their pledges to lead simple lives.

Burma's geographical position made it vulnerable to invasion from China. For centuries the Chinese have seen Burma as the best route to the Bay of Bengal. We will see how, in the thirteenth century, a Mongolian dynasty in China invaded Burma and stripped its treasuries and holy shrines. This assault shattered the Burman empire by allowing another people from China, a group of Thais who called themselves Shans, to take some of its eastern lands. To the south, the Mons also rebelled and restored their old state, and to the northwest the Arakanese declared independence. Thus the Mongol invasion resulted in Burma's division into many small states. In spite of Burma's collapse as an empire, it remained a center of Buddhist art and poetry, as well as trade. Burma never ceased to produce surplus goods that made it the envy of its neighbors.

Part of the Burmese empire was restored in the mid-sixteenth century in a form that lasted two hundred years. However the Burmans, Mons, Thais, Arakanese, and Shans fought each other continually during this period. For the first time Europeans appeared in Burma to take advantage of the divisions there. They were Portuguese mercenaries who controlled all of Lower Burma for several years. After finally defeating the Portuguese in battle, the Burmans moved their capital out of Lower Burma, where the hostility of the Mons had made the country vulnerable to the Portuguese. In 1634 the new capital was established at Ava in Upper Burma. This move isolated the government from European visitors for almost 2½ centuries. Nevertheless, its inland position did not save it from a final assault by the Mons. They seized the capital city of Ava in 1752, ending the second Burmese empire.

The third and last Burmese empire was established by a soldier named Alaungpaya in 1752. He attacked the Mons who had seized Ava and gained a victory so complete that they could no longer act as ;' political force in Burma. Some Mons fled to Thailand, and the rest became integrated into Burmese society. Alaungpaya thought that British and French traders on the coast were partly responsible for the Mon attack on the Burmans. He executed these traders, ending Western influence in his country until the nineteenth century. Alaungpaya memorialized the end of the war with the Mons by founding the city of Rangoon, which in Burman means "peace." Later, Rangoon became an active port.

Throughout the eighteenth century the Burmans continued their expansion in wars against the Thais. Concerned about this new power, the Chinese sent armies into Upper Burma on four separate occasions, but each time they were defeated. Burma continued to grow and by the end of the eighteenth century it ended its military campaigning and concentrated on internal developments. Economically self-sufficient, it had few contacts with the outside world. On the west it confronted the British in India, and on the east the Thais and Chinese.

Malays. As late as the eighth century the Malays were an Indianized people. From the time of Christ they had a significant ocean-going trade with India and borrowed freely from Indian ideas about architecture, literature, and religion. One center of this trade was the port of Kedah, north of the Strait of Malacca. Another trading center was on the island of Sumatra.

From the sixth to the thirteenth centuries the trade focusing on Sumatra was controlled by a kingdom called Sri Vijaya, which began to spread to Java and other nearby islands early in its history. On Java it overthrew a kingdom called Sailendra ("King of the Mountain"), another Indianized society.

Sri Vijaya became the greatest maritime power in its region. The precious metals, woods, and spices of Southeast Asia brought fleets of merchant ships from India, the Middle East, and Africa to the busy ports of Java and Sumatra. Sellers of Chinese porcelains, silks, and jades met the Europeans on the islands and at Kedah on the Southeast Asian peninsula. By the end of the thirteenth century commerce was profitable enough for a prince of Sumatra to build a new port on the island of Singapore. Extending its power over the main islands and the Malay Peninsula, Sri Vijaya prospered, both by shipping its own products and by taking a percentage of the income from the trade of others.

Borobudur ("Monastery on the Hill") was built in central Java, *ca.* 850 A.D., as a memorial to Buddha. The intricately carved stones cover almost 10 acres.

Competitors for Sri Vijaya's business arose to the north and south of the thriving empire during the thirteenth century. The port of Kadiri on the island of Java bid for control of the spice trade and gained spectacular successes because it was close to the Moluccas, or "Spice Islands." These islands were the world's chief source of cloves and pepper. Moreover, Kadiri was close to the Banda Islands, the only source of nutmeg. Thus it prospered until the mid-thirteenth century. Then Mongol invaders struck, destroyed Javanese governments, and quickly withdrew.

A new empire, called Majapahit, arose from the ashes of Kadiri after the Mongol invasion. Beginning in 1293, it expanded into areas where Sri Vijaya and lesser kingdoms had controlled the spice trade. In a series of wars with the shrunken and disunited empire of Sri Vijaya, which by then was confined to the islands of Sumatra, the kingdom demolished its last major rival in the area. These conflicts were called the Majapahit Wars. During the latter part of the fourteenth century Majapahit conquered western Borneo, southern Celebes Island (now Sulawesi), and the Moluccas. Its power extended to the Malay Peninsula. States everywhere in Southeast Asia sent tribute to it.

During this period, the great wealth stored in solitary sailing ships at sea appealed irresistibly to pirates in Southeast Asia. These pirates played an immense role in the region's history. Hiding in the coves of Sumatra, they sailed out to prey on vessels bound for Singapore, Malacca, Achin, Madura, and Penang. To avoid them Majapahit built new harbors on Sumatra's northeast coast, but none of these new ports were as secure from pirates as Malacca. This Malay port was situated at the narrowest point of a strait separating Sumatra from the peninsula. Forty miles from the opposite shore, it was a safe harbor overlooking the straits. At the height of Majapahit's power, this factor helped to produce a major shift in trade from Java and Sumatra to Malacca.

Filipinos. Another Malay people affected by the Indians were the Filipinos (who did not gain this name until much later). The first large migration of Filipinos reached the islands about 700 B.C. They came from the mainland of Southeast Asia in canoes called *barangays.* About 300 B.C. many more Malays arrived, spreading up the Borneo coast. They moved to the Sulu Archipelago, then to the northernmost islands of what were to become the Philippines. They brought with them a knowledge of rice cultivation and iron tools. The Filipinos had no central government, but divided themselves into large kinship groups that developed legal systems. Culturally, they considered themselves to be part of Sri Vijaya, where other Malays were building an Indianized society. They were rice growers and fishermen rather than traders, and so their contacts with India were remote. They established enduring contacts with China, however.

CHINA

Vietnamese. The Yüeh people who migrated from China during the fourth century B.C. settled near the Gulf of Tonkin, and it was there that Chinese culture took root. During the more than eight centuries that they ruled Tonkin, the Chinese introduced water buffaloes, metal plows, and other bronze tools. They also brought Confucianism, their written language, and their forms of government. They divided the country into groups of five to fifty cooperating families, or communes, each with its own administrative council. The councils collected taxes and supplied soldiers to the central government while supplying other necessary services to its people. Thus the Chinese helped the Vietnamese to become a vigorously self-governing people instead of the less well organized slash-and-burn cultivators who previously occupied the area.

The Vietnamese demonstrated a unique pride in their culture from the outset of their history. They built monuments to two sisters who organized a rebellion against the Chinese in 39 A.D. The sisters fought for four years and finally drowned themselves rather than be captured. The Vietnamese rebellions continued, reaching their peak in the sixth century. By then the Vietnamese were spread over the Red River Delta, where Chinese-inspired reclamation projects made rice cultivation possible. The Chinese haughtily referred to their subject land as "Annam"—Pacified South, a term that angered the Vietnamese. Nevertheless, the Vietnamese acknowledged Chinese power over them by paying tribute, all the while clinging to their own traditions and speech.

The Vietnamese were able to drive the Chinese out of the Red River Delta in 939. Then after almost 30 years of instability they formed the first of four Vietnamese dynasties that ruled the country almost continuously until 1788. The Vietnamese developed a strong central government based on China's Confucian system. Their gentry class was similar to the one in China, where all bureaucrats were required to pass a civil service test that only the gentry could understand. Yet even while following the Chinese model in government the Vietnamese were adopting Buddhism in their personal lives. The Vietnamese apparently gained Buddhist ideas from the Chams, a people who lived south of them and were among the first Southeast Asians to trade with India.

Vietnam grew and prospered. As its population increased its government built vast public works, such as dikes and roads. It became strong enough to resist a Chinese invasion in 1076. It also fought off a Khmer attack from the west and soon afterward began a series of assaults against the Chams and Khmers. These attacks were continual for the next 800 years, causing its neighbors to regard Vietnam as one of the most aggressive states in Southeast Asia. The frequent cry, "March to the South," characterized one of its most enduring policies. Vietnam steadily fought the Chams, reducing them to a small part of the lower peninsula. The Viet king who finally accomplished this is considered one of the country's greatest rulers. He was Le Thanh Tong, who died in 1497.

MONGOLS

After overrunning China early in the twelfth century, the Mongols looked for new lands to conquer. They first subdued Korea and attempted an invasion of Japan. After failing to conquer Japan, they turned to Southeast Asia. In 1257–58 the unbeatable Mongol horsemen overwhelmed Annam and Champa. Throughout the remainder of the thirteenth century they received tribute from the northern states of Southeast Asia. When they were refused tribute in Burma they devastated and looted the great city of Pagan.

The Mongols encountered a strong will to resist in Vietnam. There the kingdom of five million, mostly farmers, defeated the Mongols twice during the thirteenth century. After the second battle a Mongol force of 500,000 appeared. The Vietnamese, led by Tran Hung Dao, induced the invading horsemen to attack at Haiphong during a monsoon. He shattered the enemy force and has been a legendary hero among the Vietnamese ever since.

Although they were defeated in Vietnam, elsewhere in Southeast Asia the Mongols lingered and withdrew only when they wished. The collapse of the Mongol empire took place after the death of Kublai Khan at the end of the thirteenth century. By 1368 the Chinese were able to rebel and to drive the Mongols back into Central Asia. That event signalled the end of Mongol influence over Southeast Asia.

The Mongols left many new kingdoms and situations throughout Southeast Asia. As we have seen, they helped to establish the Majapahit empire on Java. In South China, their raids caused waves of Thais to descend into the Southeast Asian peninsula. On the western side of the peninsula they left a shattered Burman kingdom which was not able to reassert Burman rule until the mid-sixteenth century. Finally, in Vietnam the Mongols left a weakened people who were forced to accept a Chinese government for 22 years (1406–28) before they could regain control over their own country.

MUSLIMS

Muhammad, (570–632 A.D.), founder of the Islamic faith, was originally a member of the merchant class and encouraged his followers to engage in trade. By the eighth century the Muslims had great fleets of trading ships that sailed with Asia's monsoons. In Southeast Asia the first Muslim ships began to arrive from India during the middle of the thirteenth century. Soon afterward, an immense trade with India's Muslims sprang up. The Turkish Muslims then ruled northern India from their capital at Delhi. They conducted most trade from the port of Cambay, north of Bombay on the western coast of the subcontinent. Merchants journeyed between the ports and Delhi through the state of Gujarat on India's northwest coast. Thus they were known as Gujaratis.

The Gujaratis were famous for their command of the spice trade. Their goal in Southeast Asia was to load up with the spices of Java, Sumatra, and the Malay Peninsula and to carry them back to the Middle East. There, Europeans eagerly bought their cargo, which included the metals, gems, and fabrics of Southeast Asia as well as its spices.

As trade flourished, both the Muslim Gujaratis and the rulers of Java, Sumatra, and the Malay Peninsula grew wealthy. The Muslims took advantage of this economic bond to convert the previously Hindu or Buddhist Southeast Asians to Islam. Many Muslim traders took up residence in the local communities. Then they refused to do business with non-Muslims. Thus the local ruler who refused conversion turned down great commercial advantages. If the local ruler accepted Islam, he often received secure trading privileges— and sometimes a Muslim princess for his bride.

Despite these inducements, some rulers of Southeast Asia bitterly rejected Islam. This was the case with the Hindu kingdom of Majapahit, in Java. However, Majapahit was unable to control the pirates who swarmed on its northwestern coast. The Muslims could control them. Therefore early in the fourteenth century the Muslims began to take power on the island of Sumatra, a possession of Majapahit. During the course of the century they infiltrated more and more of Majapahit's lands. By the end of the century the Muslim merchants dealt Majapahit a crushing blow by shifting the center of Southeast Asian trade to the Malay Peninsula.

The new focus of trade was in the Strait of Malacca. This change was to have far-reaching implications for the history of the world. Malacca was well placed for ocean trade between Asian countries. All ocean-going vessels between India and China had to sail beneath the guns of the city. Whoever held the straits was able to regulate all East-West ocean traffic. The Muslims assured themselves the control of Malacca by placing it in charge of a pirate who was an exiled prince of Majapahit. They told him that he could turn the post into the region's official Muslim trading station (entrepôt, or "warehouse city"), but only on condition that he accepted their faith. This he did, taking the name Iskander Shah.

By similar tactics, the Muslims advanced their faith throughout the region. The bulk of Malays generally accepted the beliefs of their rulers, once the rulers had been converted to Islam. Muslim bases extended as far north as the island of Luzon, in the Philippines. Among the Philippine Islands Muslim influence was largely confined to the Sulu Archipelago, however.

Malacca became the hub of Muslim commercial activities in Southeast Asia. By levying a tax of up to six percent on all trade, the city created a vast bazaar for merchants from Asia, with quarters for Malays, Chinese, Arabs, Filipinos, Persians, and Sumatrans. Although Malacca was a Muslim City, Hindu ideas and practices never completely disappeared. For example, beginning in 1446, the city was ruled by a sultan, but the symbols of his power remained the royal umbrella and sacred dagger that accompanies every Indian prince.

During the fifteenth century China became increasingly interested in ocean trade and helped Malacca by clearing the seas of pirates. Greatly strengthened by this, Malacca grew and became the main port on the route between East and West. To the Muslims it represented Islam's response to Buddhism, which prevailed elsewhere in Southeast Asia. The Muslims deplored Indian political and religious ideas, which seemed to them weak and imprecise. The Indianized cultures believed that life has many sides, symbolized by many gods. But the Muslims saw it as an opportunity to serve Allah, by combat if necessary. In earlier times, Hindu ideas brought about a wealth of visual arts and dance in the islands of Southeast Asia. These arts were suppressed by Muslim rules forbidding artists to represent living things in their work and denying women the right to dance. Under Muslim influence Southeast Asians ceased building the enormous temples dedicated to the cult of the god-king. Instead they began to build mosques, shaped in their own unique, square style. The vast array of real and mythological characters in Hinduism and Buddhism gave way to Muslim decorative arts.

At the time of their greatest power in Malacca, the Muslims were not far from total defeat at the hands of newcomers to Asia, the Portuguese. Muslim influence collapsed 44 years after the death of their most powerful ruler, Sultan Mansur Shah (1459–77), whose tombstone rightly said, "The world is but transitory; the world has no permanence; the world is like a house made by a spider."

CHAPTER 3

WESTERN COLONIAL RULE

OVER A PERIOD OF FOUR HUNDRED YEARS Europeans caught glimpses of Southeast Asia from their Crusades (1100-1300), their contacts with the Mongols, and the writings of Marco Polo (1254-1323). During the late fifteenth century these glimpses were focused into the image of a land that could instantly improve their lives. Europe had become an enormous consumer of meat. Each year as winter approached European farmers had to slaughter their animals in autumn, for they lacked the means to keep them longer. The Europeans needed spices to pickle, preserve, and season their meats. Their demand for spices grew with each passing winter of bland diets and wasted foods. Through their trade with Muslims the merchants of Europe learned of the great wealth in the Moluccas— the legendary "Spice Islands"—and dreamed of going there themselves. The first Western sailors to make these voyages were the Portuguese, whose eastward thrusts began 450 years of Western intervention in Southeast Asia.

THE ORIGINS OF COLONIALISM

It was the Portuguese who first rounded the Cape of Good Hope, in 1488. Ten years later they reached India by sea. This momentous voyage to India, led by Vasco da Gama in 1498, was a direct threat to Muslim traders who controlled both land and sea routes to Southeast Asia. In 1508 the competition between the Portuguese and Muslims resulted in a great sea battle near Diu, in the Indian Ocean. The Portuguese won, gaining the freedom to continue their efforts to reach the Spice Islands.

The founder of Portugal's Asian empire was a visionary admiral named Alfonso de Albuquerque (1453-1515), who considered it his country's destiny to supplant the Muslim commercial monopoly. Despite harassment and on one occasion imprisonment by his fellow officers, Albuquerque established a chain of bases extending from the Persian Gulf to the islands of Southeast Asia. Within two years after Portugal made him Viceroy in 1509, Albuquerque sailed into

Malacca harbor with eighteen ships and bombarded the town until the sultan surrendered. But the pivotal base in the Portuguese chain was Goa, on the west coast of India. The sultans of Southeast Asia wanted Indian fabrics, not European products, in exchange for their spices. Therefore Albuquerque bought Indian textiles at Goa before sailing to the Moluccas. Other Portuguese bases were established at Ceylon, Bantam, Timor, and Amboyna, and trading posts on the coasts of Siam, Burma, and Cambodia.

The Portuguese maintained their authority by threatening military action against the sultans who ruled near their bases. Armed with European-made guns, they took part in local disputes and demanded tributes from weaker sultanates. Malacca supplied a different kind of revenue. No Muslim sea captain passed through the straits without paying a heavy toll to the Portuguese.

Portugal's stations in Southeast Asia are often called a "garrison empire." The small country of Portugal had few men to spare for its operations in Southeast Asia. None of its Asian bases ever contained more than a few hundred Portuguese soldiers. When necessary these men were supplemented by local mercenaries. In time, the Portuguese soldiers in Southeast Asia also were willing to fight for whoever paid them. They felt abandoned far from home, having the sole function of making larger profits for the spice merchants. Some of them deserted and became pirates who preyed on ships in the Straits of Malacca. A few Portuguese Catholic missionaries came, but they failed to make many converts to Christianity. Portugal's

The Portuguese explorer Vasco de Gama (1469–1524) showed Europeans how to reach Asia by sailing around Africa.

From their main Asian base here on India's Malabar Coast, the Portuguese set out under Viceroy Alfonso de Albuquerque to control the spice trade.

venture into Southeast Asia thus became too weak to continue. By 1640 the Portuguese were unable to defend Malacca, and this important base fell to the Dutch. Afterward Portugal retained its bases in India, but its empire in the rest of Southeast Asia gave way to succeeding waves of Europeans.

THE COLONIES AS EXTENSIONS OF THE WEST

Spanish. Observing the profits that their neighbors the Portuguese were reaping in the spice trade, the Spanish decided to find their own routes to Southeast Asia. Their first expedition to the area was headed by a hired Portuguese, Ferdinand Magellan, who navigated five ships around the southern tip of South America and across the Pacific Ocean. Magellan was killed by a Filipino chief during that voyage in 1521, but his crew continued to the Moluccas. There they loaded their ships with spices and returned to Spain.

Just twenty-five years before Magellan's great voyage, Spain and Portugal had agreed to divide the world's newly discovered lands between them. The Moluccas were granted to Portugal under this agreement, and Spain was forced to seek other territories in Southeast Asia. This the Spanish did in the St. Lazarus Islands, which in 1542 they renamed Las Felipinas to honor their prince, the future King Philip II.

Spain's role in the Philippines was profoundly affected by its discovery that it could reach the islands by way of its colony in Mexico. From the Mexican port of Acapulco Spanish galleons were swept by trade winds and currents into the Pacific and back again. The Spanish sent a small force to the Philippines in 1564. They began conquests by forming alliances with local tribes that wanted help against rivals. By 1584 Spain claimed control over all of the islands except Sulu and Mindanao, which were fortified by hostile Muslims.

When taking the Philippines the Spanish did not face the problems encountered by other European colonists in Southeast Asia. There was no interference from China, which wanted only to trade with the islands. There were no close neighbors of nearby European powers to fear. The Spanish built a capital at Manila, on the island of Luzon, in 1571. To this port the Spanish galleons brought Mexican silver, and the Chinese delivered silks and porcelains. Despite Chinese pirates, Spain prospered. Soon their Mexican coins were the standard currency throughout Southeast Asia's trading centers.

But the Spanish came for more than trade. They wanted to turn the Philippines into a country resembling Spain. To accomplish this they needed to pacify the inland tribes, and they did so through missionaries. The tribes were barely exposed to Indian and Muslim cultures and were still animists. Most of them accepted baptism and pledged themselves to be loyal Christians.

After making conversions the Spanish introduced their system of government. In pre-Spanish times the islanders had a form of government called the barangay, named for the log-boat that carried settlers from the mainland centuries before. The usual barangay included about a hundred related families headed by a *datu*, or chieftain, who was aided by hereditary nobles. In place of this system the Spanish created townships, or *barrios*, which were headed by Spanish magistrates, nobles, priests, and a few island chiefs.

Spain's program for the Philippines was characterized by the increasingly complex government that it developed there. It began its administration with a Governor-General, but in 1589 placed the islands under the control of a Viceroy, who ruled from Mexico City. The Viceroy appointed a court and treasurer who represented the king. This government then set about changing the communal land system that had existed in the islands for centuries. The Spanish established the *encomienda* system, through which thousands of acres of the best farmland were placed under the control of the Spanish nobles. The encomienda (Spanish for "to entrust") was a franchise from the king enabling a favored few to arrange for production on "his" land. Variations of this labor system were developed in other Spanish colonies, including the American southwest and California.

The new landowners were expected to collect taxes, to convert their workers to Christianity, and to protect the population from bandits, disease, or starvation. As payment for these services the government allowed the nobles or priests to keep part of the taxes they collected and to occupy the land. In some cases the system brought security and employment to people. In time, however, the farmers fell into economic bondage. Many of them rebelled, but the Spanish fought them vigorously and rejected all appeals to reform the system.

Catholic priests were among the largest landowners in the Philippines. They were given massive land grants for converting most of the population in the northern two-thirds of the islands. Filipinos resented the priests for exploiting labor, but respected them for their other work. The priests organized the first schools and hospitals in the islands. They also set up seminaries which performed educational functions and arranged for the construction of the College of Santa Tomás in Manila in 1611.

The priests were largely responsible for introducing other aspects of Spanish culture to the Philippines. They designed churches and other buildings in the styles that were popular in Spain, creating plazas that became the focus of island life. They encouraged the Filipinos to adopt the Spanish language, clothing, and foods and introduced them to new crops from the Americas, including tobacco, corn, sweet potatoes, avocados, and peanuts.

As the priests gained control of increasing amounts of land the peasants began to identify them with the ruling class. The priests were often the chief visible agents of the *cacique* class. They administered the educational, health, charity, tax, and public works systems. They certified whether or not obligations to the government had been discharged, supervised elections and budgets, censored the arts, and helped to control the allocation of crops.

The noblemen meanwhile were turning Manila into one of Southeast Asia's busiest ports. They gathered velvets, jewels, silks, ivory, and forest products for shipment to Mexico. The booming trade brought hundreds of ships to the harbor. To manage their commerce the Spanish began to hire Chinese merchants during the early seventeenth century. The Chinese population increased rapidly, and soon the Spanish became concerned that they would be overwhelmed by the new minority. In 1603 an incident took place which caused the Spanish to murder 23,000 Chinese. The massacre crippled trade severely by frightening Chinese sailors away. Later the Spanish had to plead with China to send more ships and merchandise to Manila.

During the seventeenth century the Philippines became an increasing problem for Spain. Dutch and Muslim pirates preyed on the island trade. The king and Church officials began to use the Philippines as a place to send unwanted persons. The colonial administration itself became incompetent and corrupt. The landowning priests inspired fear more than respect, and both they and the nobles taxed the peasants mercilessly.

Throughout Spanish rule and as recently as World War II many villages in the Philippines were almost untouched by the economic progress in other nations.

The Philippines entered a long period of decline after Spain began to lose its colonies in North America. After 1825 the number of Spaniards in the islands dwindled to fewer than 5,000. Spain's monopoly over the Philippines trade began to crumble when the port of Manila was opened to the ships of other countries. Then Philippine coffee, hemp, and sugar were eagerly sought in European and American markets and were carried there under many different flags.

The arrival of new merchants and traders exposed Filipinos to political ideas inspired by the American and French revolutions. Young Filipinos began to go abroad to study, and when they came back most of them demanded independence for their country. The Spanish governments refused to let this group organize, but their repression merely served to unite the Filipinos. They executed forty-one Filipino soldiers for participating in a mutiny in Cavite in 1872, but quickly learned that by doing so they had inspired a revolutionary movement. The murdered soldiers have been considered martyrs in the Philippines ever since.

The nationalists were led by José Rizal, who helped to organize what was called the "Propaganda Movement." A poet, novelist, sculptor, and physician, Rizal's political writings were widely distributed in the radical newspaper *La Solidaridad*, founded in 1889. His novels, including *The Lost Eden* (1886) and *El Filibusterismo* (1891) aroused Filipinos to the problems of corruption and social abuse in their country. The Spanish exiled Rizal but he returned and they finally executed him in 1896.

While Rizal advocated pacifism and reforms, others, including Andreas Bonifacio and Emilio Aguinaldo, advocated violent revolt. Bonifacio was murdered during a dispute within his revolutionary movement, but Aguinaldo continued to lead a rebellion in central Luzon. After fighting the Spanish bravely for a year Aguinaldo conceded that his cause was hopeless. The Spanish paid him 600,000 pesos to abandon the struggle and leave for Hong Kong. His surrender and acceptance of the money crushed the hopes of the revolutionary movement in the Philippines.

But the movement was not dead. Spanish repression had united the landlords (*caciques*), the educated class (*ilustrados*), and the peasants (*taos*) in the hope that the Philippines could gain independence. In earlier times each of these groups had benefited in varying degrees from the activity of the Spaniards. Their European colonizers had given them a sense of nationhood, a government, a marketing system, and a number of cities. For better or for worse, the Spanish had introduced a new language, culture, and religion to the Philippines. Having absorbed these changes, the Filipinos were ready to seek the control of their destinies as a fully self-governing people.

Dutch. Throughout the sixteenth century Dutch ships called at Lisbon to load up with the spices that the Portuguese were bringing from Southeast Asia. They delivered the cargo throughout Europe and so benefited from Portugal's successes in Asia. In 1595, however, the Portuguese decided that neither the Dutch nor the English would share in the wealth that their empire was generating. They closed the port of Lisbon to the ships of both countries and as a result doomed their empire to a fatal competition.

A number of Dutch sailors knew the routes to Asia as well as the Portuguese, with whom they often traveled. With the help of their government they financed voyages direct to Southeast Asia, where they loaded their ships with nutmeg, mace, and cloves. The Dutch developed a merchant fleet which in 1601 alone made 65 voyages between the Netherlands and the Spice Islands. They began attacking Portuguese ships and bases, particularly Malacca, and in 1602 defeated a Portuguese fleet off Java. Within the next fifteen years the Dutch seized almost every major base in Portugal's withering Southeast Asian empire. Malacca held out until 1640, but surrendered after a siege of six months. The Portuguese empire in Southeast Asia was reduced to a few minor outposts, notably on half of the island of Timor, northwest of Australia.

The Dutch goal was to gain a monopoly over the profitable spice trade. To this end they harassed the ships of their only important rival in the region, England. In 1623 their Governor-General, Jan Pieterszoon Coen, drove the English out. He executed ten of them, as well as nine Japanese and one Portuguese whom he said had conspired with them to take over Amboyna, an island near Sumatra. After this incident, known as the "Massacre of Amboyna," the English steered clear of the islands.

Coen then proceeded to develop the small port of Djakarta, which became known as Batavia. Through the Dutch East India Company, a private corporation chartered by the Netherlands to rule Dutch possessions from the Cape of Good Hope to the Straits of Magellan, he proposed vastly expanded trade. Coen recognized that the Company would have to do much more than trade in spices, because the increasing supply of spices was driving prices down on the European market. He wanted the Company to serve as the main commercial agent for the worldwide markets demanding Asia's silks, porcelains, copper, gemstones, and rice.

At first, colonial expansion was far from Coen's mind. His intention was to dominate Asia's sea lanes from Batavia. He was drawn into expansion, however, because smugglers and pirates were threatening the Dutch economic monopoly. To fortify Batavia the Dutch took over adjacent islands and enlarged the town. Dutch expansion on Java was at the expense of the Javanese, who were so disinterested in shipping that they freely allowed the Dutch to use their ports. By the end of the seventeenth century the Dutch controlled the western third of the island. They took tribute from local rulers but refused to interfere in political or social affairs. Their purpose for being on Java was to generate business, not to affect local life, they said. But increasingly they were forced to govern the society that they ruled.

The city of Batavia (Djakarta) was built solely to accommodate Dutch needs. However, it exercised a direct influence over the political, social, and cultural life of the island. The city was the center to which people went to pay tribute, sell goods, or deal with international agents. All roads led to Batavia. These links with the interior of Java caused the Dutch to take a new view of the direct participation in farming, rather than merely serving as agents for it. They created sugar and coffee plantations on which Chinese immigrants labored for low wages. By the beginning of the eighteenth century sugar and coffee had replaced spices as the leading Dutch export. These new products were developed just in time for the Dutch, it turned out, for the spice market was dying.

Like the Portuguese before them, the Dutch had relatively few men to spare for their colony. Even fewer women came to Java, a fact which caused Dutch men to marry Javanese women. The Dutch were able to manage Java, despite their shortage of managers, by gaining the services of local authorities in Javanese villages. They allowed these authorities to share in the great profits from their "Tribute System." Under this system the Dutch took fixed amounts of all of the crops raised on the island. Their local agents collected the tribute—usually rice—and carried it to Dutch warehouses after keeping some of it for themselves. Thus the Dutch were able to run Java's economy with no more than a few hundred men.

The Dutch later recognized that the tribute given them would have greater value if they could control the rest of the market for it. They therefore developed a marketing system called "contingents

Seizing the island of Java from the Kingdom of Mataram, the Dutch set up a base at Batavia (the present city of Djakarta) and began to colonize.

and forced deliveries." Through this system the Dutch took their tribute (contingents), but required that the rest of the crop be sold at prices which they set (forced deliveries). By this means and by limiting the size of the harvest they exercised total control of the market.

The social problems caused by Dutch colonial methods began to accumulate in Java about the middle of the eighteenth century. Javanese farmers became increasingly rebellious as they were forced to work on plantations. Dutch agents were hated and looked upon as traitors. Jobless Chinese roamed the island and in 1740 seemed so threatening that the Dutch encouraged the Javanese to murder 10,000 of them. Then the Javanese turned against the Dutch, who promptly suppressed the rebels with their superior organization and arms.

After 1750, the Dutch East India Company was plagued by incompetence and bribery. The Dutch government, after a long conflict with officials of the Dutch East India Company, finally dismissed them and took over the direct rule of Java in 1800. When Napoleon Bonaparte of France conquered the Netherlands he sent his own governor to Java. French rule was harsh, and the Javanese welcomed the British who came to take over Dutch colonies from Napoleon in 1811.

The British placed Java under the administration of Thomas Stamford Raffles, who attempted to collect taxes in the form of cash rather than commodities. The effect was to place increasing numbers of farmers into debt, forcing many more to move to Batavia. Raffles also introduced an efficient civil service, with a central government and a network of local administrators.

The Colonies as Producers for the West

The Napoleonic Wars (1803–1815) marked a turning point both for Europe and Southeast Asia. The European powers had to pay for the enormous debts of the wars, but they also needed capital and resources to press forward with the Industrial Revolution. The invention of the steamship and development of the Suez Canal in 1859–69 caused them to see Southeast Asia in a new light. Instead of merely trading with their Southeast Asian colonies, they looked to them as suppliers of raw materials and as markets for their manufactured products. The Netherlands, Great Britain, and France were part of this process. Later, after it completed its transcontinental railroad in 1869, the United States joined them.

Dutch. After the defeat of Napoleon at Waterloo, the British returned Java to the Dutch. In search of greater agricultural production on the island, the Dutch introduced the "Culture System," a term which refers to the closely controlled agricultural economy that they developed.

Under the Culture System the Dutch required a fixed amount of labor each year—represented by either 20 percent of the crop or by 66 working days—from the head of every family. In effect this was a much greater tax than the Dutch had levied under the old Tribute System, under which revenues were a percentage of whatever the Javanese chose to produce. The Culture System permitted the Dutch to adjust their exports from Java to the demands of markets in Europe. Through their total control over the supply of exports the Dutch were also able to control the price.

The Culture System was an official monopoly of the Dutch government, and it brought enormous profits to the Netherlands.

To the Javanese, it was an unbelievable burden. The system gave the island's farmers the responsibility of paying their taxes before they paid themselves. Many farmers had to work 200 days a year for the Dutch. Javanese agriculture expanded rapidly, but it was owned by foreigners rather than by local producers.

In 1825 Dutch policies led to a rebellion that lasted five years. The Javanese were furious because the Dutch appeared less willing than the British to respect their local laws. Led by Prince Diponegoro, they declared a Muslim holy war against the Dutch, many of whom they ambushed and slaughtered. The Dutch defeated and exiled Diponegoro in 1830, but ever since he has been honored as the first champion of Indonesian nationalism. Following their suppression of the rebellion, the Dutch took over all of the islands which are today part of the country of Indonesia.

The disorders on Java brought Dutch colonial methods to the attention of reformers in the Netherlands. After 1848 these reformers campaigned continuously. Eventually they forced their country to write a new constitution that prohibited non-Javanese from owning land in the islands. However, the farmers were so deeply in debt that they often gave the Dutch control of their lands. The Culture System, moreover, was continued until a Dutch colonial officer named Eduard Dekker, writing as "Multatuli" in a book called *Max Havelaar*, dramatized how brutal the system had become.

During the twenty years after the publication of *Max Havelaar* in 1860, the Dutch government slowly withdrew from its monopolies over Javanese agriculture. In 1870 it introduced its so-called "Liberal System"—which proved to be less than liberal for the Javanese. The new system was characterized by an Agrarian Law that allowed private businessmen to lease plantations for up to 75 years, both on Java and on the outer islands. This resulted in the enormous expansion of plantations on Java and Sumatra. It also resulted in great profits for Dutch businessmen and continuing misery for local farmers. On the new private plantations workers were far from their families and villages, laboring under foremen who had no concern for them. The plantation owners collected workers from remote parts of the islands and even from China. As the number of Chinese increased during this period, many of them drifted to the cities, where they had long dominated trade. Finally, the growth of plantations cut off the local farmers from new lands that they might have developed for themselves as their own soil was depleted. Thus the plantation workers earned no more than they had in the villages, but worked for low wages while witnessing the erosion of their society and culture.

The Liberal System further oppressed Indonesian farmers as prices for three of its major products, sugar, coffee, and tobacco, rose in Europe. The Dutch government did not end its monopoly over sugar until 1890 and kept the one over coffee until 1910. Dutch officials forced both the farmers and the plantations to supply their mills with sugar at fixed prices, which they manipulated to control the supply. They drew tens of thousands of Javanese and Sumatrans from villages to raise more sugar.

All of these agricultural programs required substantial administration, and corps of young Dutch businessmen came to the islands with their families to operate them. The Dutch expanded Indonesia's cities and dominated them completely, setting up their own schools, churches, and government institutions. They kept Indonesians out of the administration, preferring to bind them to farm labor. Impoverished Indonesians swarmed to the cities, but found that the only way of life open to them there was to work at odd jobs. Meanwhile they had to live in shacks near the comfortable homes of the Dutch.

The Dutch tried to soften the effects of colonialism through their Ethical Policy. Under this plan the Dutch offered to repair the damage they had done to village culture. They began teaching programs and encouraged handicrafts and food production on small farms. But it was too late for the Dutch to remedy the damage they had done to Indonesian cultural life. Java's population increased from twenty million to forty million from 1880 to 1930. Throughout the Great Depression of the 1930s, millions of Indonesians were starving and homeless. Far from pacifying the Indonesians, the educational programs begun under the Ethical Policy did little more than awaken them to a need to be rid of the Dutch.

The Dutch had created an enormous expansion of agriculture in Indonesia. They introduced specialized agriculture and cash crops that later became the basis of the country's modern economy. They also were the developers of Indonesia's cities and original civil service. But against these mixed benefits, as the Dutch entered the last phase of their occupation of the islands, Indonesians were forced to measure the disruption that colonialism brought to their society. Under the Dutch a land of small farmers had become one of enormous farm businesses, but at great cost.

British. By the end of the eighteenth century Great Britain was able to break the Dutch monopoly in Southeast Asia by opening trade routes directly to China from bases in India. One of India's principal exports was tea, which it sold ɛo Europe, but the Chinese wanted silver, not European goods in exchange for their tea. The British tried to gain silver in North Borneo but were unable to defend their bases there. A private British citizen, Francis Light, managed to gain his country's first permanent base in Southeast Asia by offering military help and an annual salary to the Sultan of Kedah. The sultan granted him the island of Penang in the Straits of Malacca, never realizing that Light was unauthorized to negotiate for his country. Light quickly turned Penang into a thriving base which later gained additional territory, called Prince Wellesley, on the mainland. This success of Light gave Great Britain its foothold in Southeast Asia.

By 1818 Britain's policies in Southeast Asia were guided by Thomas Stamford Raffles, who used Penang to establish a second base on the island of Singapore. Following Francis Light's methods, he offered the local sultan military support and funds for what was largely a swamp containing a few houseboats. Raffles then became secretary of the British East India Company and bought Singapore from its sultan. He turned its fine natural harbor into a free port where foreign sailors could bring cargoes without paying the duties imposed at Dutch ports. This greatly increased Singapore's trade, and it soon rivaled the Dutch base at Batavia, in Java.

Britain's growing power on the Malay Peninsula gave it a strong position in negotiations with the Dutch. The British proposed to separate their interests from Dutch interests in the region. Concerned chiefly with Java, the Dutch agreed to a treaty enabling each of the countries to develop its own region. The British received Malacca and recognition of their activities in Singapore and Malaya. The Malayan islands and peninsula had been linked socially, culturally, and economically for centuries. This one stroke divided the Malay people and led inevitably to friction in later years.

Britain's first extension of authority in the region took place on

The Raffles Hotel on Singapore, named for the British founder of the port, was visited by many of the world's commercial leaders as the city prospered.

the island of Borneo. There, the Sultan of Brunei gave land to a young Briton named James Brooke, who helped him to suppress a rebellion. In 1841 Brooke established himself on the Sarawak River, where he gained the title, "White Raja of Borneo." He and his son Charles expanded their holdings until their territory surrounded Brunei. In 1888 the Brooke family turned its lands over to Great Britain. At the same time a group of businessmen who had formed the North Borneo Company in Sabah gave their territories to Britain. Both lands became crown colonies.

On the Malay Peninsula it was more difficult for the British to maintain control. The governments there were fragmented. The British administration—called the Straits Settlements of Singapore, Malacca, and Penang—rarely dealt with the small sultanates in the interior. In 1874 the British decided that they could no longer ignore the tin mining and potential for rubber production in the interior. They began to speak of the moral problems and unjust taxation among the sultanates. Soon they were extending their authority over the entire peninsula by offering weaker sultans alliances against stronger ones.

By 1896, Britain was able to join its Borneo and Malay Peninsula lands into an association called the Federated Malay States. Since the Straits Settlements offered British citizenship to their residents they were not made part of the Federation. A new, centralized government was established at Kuala Lumpur, where British civil servants helped to spur unprecedented investments and economic growth. Public projects, including roads, dams, communication, and transportation were extended throughout the peninsula as the markets for Malay tin and rubber grew.

These developments on the Malay Peninsula coincided with striking British gains elsewhere in Southeast Asia. The British began an active commercial relationship with the Burmese. Their East India Company began to hire Burmese shipbuilders in Rangoon and to buy Burma's products, especially teakwood, for resale in Britain. To develop this trade they needed political stability in Burma, however. In the Arakan Mountains of Western Burma rebels were attacking the Burmese government and taking refuge in India by escaping over the unguarded border. To protect its commercial interests Britain decided to intervene in this protracted war.

Britain's first effort to control Burma's internal disputes took place in 1824. Its solution to the problem of Burmese unrest was to make parts of Burma a protectorate. Demanding rights over Arakan and Assam to the northwest and Tenasserim to the south, the British sent an army into Burma and after two years of warfare forced the Burmese king to submit. A British resident was set up in Ava, the

Burmese capital, to insure continuing trade with the East India Company.

The Burmese had been relatively self-sufficient and secure behind their mountains for centuries. They systematically developed their food supply through irrigation and by improving their fishing and dairy industries. They participated in international trade, too, by selling minerals and acting as brokers between India and China. Burmese society was an enlightened one that held only a few slaves, and those only for indebtedness. Unlike China, India, Japan, and much of Europe, Burma allowed women to attain high positions in commerce and the arts.

But Burma lacked the unity to defend itself against the British. Border warfare was only part of its problem, for the death of every Burmese king led to civil wars. When the king died in 1846 his son, Pagan, began to murder his rivals and their families. Britons who witnessed this annihilation were shocked, and in Britain their reports gave rise to talk of "civilizing" the Burmese. Within six years British hostility toward the Burmese was fanned by a report by British sea captains who said they had been imprisoned in Burma. Soon a British army left Madras, India, and within a year (1852) it seized every port in Lower Burma.

In Upper Burma, the king tried to resist further British expansion by forming alliances with other Western countries. Burma relinquished its traditional isolation and began to send students to European schools. It also developed new roads and industries and in 1857 held the first Great Synod of Buddhism in almost 2,000 years. But these tactics failed to hold off the oncoming British, who annexed all of Burma in 1885 on grounds that the Karens, an eastern mountain people, were in rebellion. A combined British, Indian, and Karen army subdued the Burmese and placed the country under the direct control of the British Viceroy of India.

The Viceroy replaced all local government in Burma, except in the lands occupied by minority people. At the outset of his rule he brought the country considerable material progress. He lowered taxes, began an efficient civil service, and extended railroads and communications systems. The British began to reclaim swamps for ricelands in Lower Burma, and soon paddlewheel boats were moving regularly between settlements and the lumber, mineral, and food production sites. As trade increased Rangoon became a great seaport. From its wharves the British shipped teak, rice, and later oil, tin, silver, and wolfram.

Despite this increasing prosperity, the effects of British rule on Burmese society were generally oppressive. By governing the country as part of India, the British ignored Burma's own history and culture. They replaced the authority of the traditional village leader, the headman, with British trained civil servants. The British considered the Burmese less able to govern than the Indians, many of whom were installed in the Burmese government. They also encouraged the Chinese to join the civil service. In addition, Indians and Chinese also ran most of Burma's shops and businesses.

Nor were Burmese farmers safe from the dislocations caused by British rule. They rarely understood the legal code that the British compelled them to obey. Before the British arrived all land belonged to the king. Farmers understood that the royal land was theirs to cultivate and always managed to compromise with creditors before losing their rights. The British changed this with their concept of private land ownership, which allowed moneylenders to foreclose on impoverished farmers. An Indian merchant group called the Chettyars were the major moneylenders. As the British increasingly put Burma on a cash basis the Chettyars began to make loans at high interest rates and soon had possession of most of Lower Burma.

Finally, British rule tended to erode Burma's ancient culture, particularly Buddhism. The British did not want their government to support any single religious group and so cut off public subsidies to the monks. The British also began to build a public education system that tended to deprive the monks of their historic teaching function. The Buddhists became discouraged and by 1900 surrendered all claims to moral leadership in Burma. For the first time in their history Buddhist monks began to play a socially subversive role, attacking the British and giving refuge to nationalists who sabotaged British facilities.

The British poet Rudyard Kipling had written of the "white man's burden," implying that Westerners were superior to Asians and Africans and had an obligation to share their abilities with the less privileged people. In Burma, the British clearly demonstrated their sense of moral superiority, yet they applied it only where it was profitable. They imposed their government only over the Burmans, who were capable of supplying them with surplus rice, minerals, and timber. They allowed Burma's mountain people, who were unable to pay for British government, to remain autonomous.

By the last stage of their rule the British had brought substantial benefits to the Burmans. The country's population had increased from four million in 1834 to 8.5 million in 1891 and 10.5 million in 1901, yet it had plenty of food. The increasing population was due in large part to British public health methods that tended to control the death rate. Highway, river, and railroad transportation facilities were much improved. However, against these gains the Burmese were forced to weigh the negative effects of British rule.

Some of these negative effects were: hostilities among ethnic groups caused by the British use of minorities in government, the army, commerce, and industry; the destruction of Burmese self-government and culture, including the monarchy, educational system, and religious organizations; and the removal of Burmese from the control of their own economy.

During the last half of the nineteenth century the British assumed more direct control of other Southeast Asian territories beyond Burma. On North Borneo they took over Sarawak (1841), Sabah (British North Borneo) (1846), and the Sultanate of Brunei (1877). They also captured large parts of the Malay Peninsula. In 1896, after a period of warfare among the Malay states, Britain persuaded the four central states (Perak, Selangor, Negri Sembilan, and Pahang) to federate. The Federated Malay States were among Britain's most important suppliers of tin and rubber and after World War I were said to have generated more income than any other part of the British Empire. The British allowed them to control domestic policy, but closely supervised their foreign policy and economy.

French. Like the British, the French regarded themselves as superior to Asians, but there was a difference in the colonial views of the two countries. The British saw themselves as *morally* superior, bound by an obligation to teach a code of behavior. The French, on the other hand, thought themselves *culturally* superior and regarded their colonial subjects as part of "Outer France." In this view the Southeast Asians no longer existed to serve themselves, but the homeland until they could become "civilized"—that is, more thoroughly French.

It was with this objective that French missionaries and traders visited Southeast Asia during the seventeenth century. They tried to gain access to Vietnam and Siam by selling arms to warring sides,

The French pressed these Vietnamese men into military service and extended their empire over Tonkin, Annam, Cochin China, Laos, and Cambodia.

but were forced out. Finally a French bishop named Pigneau de Behaine managed to open the door to the empire by developing a small private army in Vietnam. He used this force to bring a member of the Nguyen family to the throne. In 1802 this ruler took the name Gia Long to signify that he had united the territories of Saigon, then called Gia Dinh, and Hanoi, then called Thanh Long. It was Gia Long who first used the name "Vietnam" for the combined lands under his rule.

Gia Long moved the capital to the city of Hué, where his dynasty was to rule until 1945. French priests lived at the court, although Gia Long never became a Catholic. The emperor knew it would be profitable to study Western ideas. He made friends of the priests, some of whom became mandarins. But Vietnamese Confucians were never pleased by the close relationship between Gia Long and the French. They saw French and Catholic influence spreading among villagers who were always ready to model themselves on the members of the court.

The three emperors who succeeded Gia Long were far less receptive to the French. During their rule many priests were murdered in Vietnam, which was suffering from the effects of war with Siam and the inflation that resulted from it. Catholics in villages were persecuted, too, causing anger and threats of reprisal in France. In defense of their priests and converts the French sent an army to Vietnam in 1858. This army seized Da Nang and three years later invaded Saigon. Vietnam was forced to cede to France that part of the southern delta which the French later called Cochin China. By 1883 the French had extended their "protection" throughout the northern part of the country, bringing Vietnam's independence to an end. By this time they had also persuaded Cambodia to break away from Siam and put itself under French protection.

Immediately after seizing Vietnam, the French were challenged by China. The Chinese sent an army into Tonkin, Vietnam's northernmost province, but were quickly defeated. In addition, the French were resisted by groups of Vietnamese rebels who fought scattered battles throughout the country for almost sixteen years. The rebels did not succeed in driving out the French, but they had shown they could fight an extended guerrilla war. This same kind of fighting was later used against the French and Americans with greater success.

To the anger and humiliation of the Vietnamese, the French restored the name that Chinese imperialists had given the country long before—Annam (the "Pacified South"). They allowed the emperor and his Confucian officials to maintain a government at Hué but closely supervised it and were the ultimate governors them-

selves. In 1887 the French organized Cochin China and the protec-
torates of Annam, Tonkin, and Cambodia into the Union of Indochina. Six years later they extended their protectorate to four small
kingdoms west of Vietnam, where the Siamese were threatening.
They called this new territory Laos. Placing it under the rule of one
of the kingdoms, Luang Prabang, they made it part of the Union of
Indochina.

We have seen that the French regarded colonies as distant
branches of the homeland and governed them to serve the homeland's needs. In Vietnam they developed an economy meant to serve
France rather than the Vietnamese people. Frenchmen held every
major position in the civil service. To meet demand in France they
tried to introduce or expand the production of silk, cotton, and
tobacco in Vietnam, but failed to raise large quantities of these
crops. Then they turned to rice production and at the same time
tried to build a market for rice at home. Through irrigation and
drainage projects they opened vast new ricelands in the Mekong
Delta, increasing the number of acres almost 500 percent between
1880 and 1939. Rice production was increased from 284,000 metric
tons in 1880 to 1.4 million metric tons in 1939. French plantations
began to produce large quantities of coffee and rubber, although
neither of these crops approached rice in importance.

In the north the French built factories to help them process local
minerals. The most important mineral product was coal; zinc, tin,
and cement were among the others. Thus while the south became
increasingly agricultural, the north also became industrial, a fact
that was to have great future importance.

The growth of Vietnam's economy did not necessarily mean
greater benefits for the Vietnamese people. France and its colonies
bought half of the country's products and supplied at least half of its
imports. A small class of Vietnamese, who received French educations and were Roman Catholics, shared in the economic advances
with the French. But mostly it was the colonists who profited. In
effect they transferred part of France to Vietnam. They built
hospitals in Saigon and Hanoi, staffing them with European specialists. They also developed a public school system. However, these
new institutions were meant to serve the French and their agents,
not the general population.

The French ruled with similar effects in Laos and Cambodia.
Administrating Laos with relatively few officials—only 70 in
1904—they ended slavery, introduced French schools and legal
codes, and defended the region against attacks from neighboring
kingdoms. Their Cambodian protectorate was begun at the request
of the Cambodian king, who was under attack by the Thais in 1859.

Their "protectorate treaty" enabled them to live in Cambodia under their own laws, to use Cambodian land in any way that they pleased, and to trade without tariffs on their commerce, in exchange for supporting Cambodia's King Norodom.

The French government of Vietnam, Laos, and Cambodia was not altogether damaging to the colonial people, as has been charged. The French greatly expanded areas under cultivation by improving the dikes of North Vietnam and the irrigation, drainage, and canal systems of both the North and the South. They increased the number and amount of crops grown in the country and brought industry to the North. By their public health methods they helped to reduce malaria and yellow fever. The works of great French thinkers reached the Vietnamese people, who reëvaluated their own obsolete Confucian system as a result.

But all of these advances were primarily for the comfort and profit of the colonists and were often made at the expense of Vietnamese society. The public health and educational systems were used by the families of colonial administrators and their supporters, not the Vietnamese people. The French imposed their own laws, economic concepts, and government on a society based on village life and the family.

To benefit from the economies of its Indochinese possessions, the French introduced the use of cash. The effect was to reduce self-sufficiency in the villages. Many farmers had to specialize in the production of "cash crops." The use of cash also became part of one of the most destructive aspects of French rule, the system of private land ownership. Before the French arrived, the lands of Vietnam, Laos, and Cambodia were owned by kings who granted cultivators rights in them. The French began to sell rights in land. Gradually a class of absentee landlords, speculators, and moneylenders arose. These private landowners dispossessed thousands of farmers who were forced to borrow at high interest rates. The landowners worked closely with French administrators and businessmen, whose culture they imitated. Together the French and their Vietnamese followers created plantations on which landless farmers worked for low wages. Families were divided as laborers sought jobs on the plantations and in cities.

To develop the plantations the French often reclaimed land and added to it acreage formerly owned by the villages in common. The cost of the reclamation, transportation, and communications projects was piled on the farmers in the form of taxes. This burden was combined with costs of producing for French consumption and of importing French consumer goods, both of which were required by the French administration. As population in Vietnam grew from 5.1 million in 1830 to 23 million in 1936, there was less and less land for the Vietnamese to divide among themselves. Countless thousands of farmers were impoverished.

The population increases produced surplus workers who tried to find jobs in the northern factories and the southern plantations. There was insufficient work for them, yet the French failed to devise an effective employment or welfare program. Their objective was to take profits out of the country, and they expected the Vietnamese, Laotians, and Cambodians to work for them while being "civilized." By the time World War II began the French owned almost all of Vietnam's industries and most of its plantations. The rest were owned by an elite class of French-speaking Vietnamese.

In Vietnam, the French introduced Chinese to serve as commercial brokers between the farmers and themselves. The Chinese developed almost all of the country's shops to sell goods that the French made of Vietnamese products. Thus the Vietnamese were the last to benefit from the French-controlled products. Their anger grew, particularly as they watched their young people being drawn to French culture. Throughout Indochina people were increasingly isolated from their own traditions, government, and culture at a time when nationalism was reaching explosive dimensions everywhere in Asia.

The United States. We have seen how the Philippine patriots despaired in their struggle against Spain. Two years after the defeat and exile of General Emilio Aguinaldo the United States came to their aid. A mysterious explosion sank the U.S. battleship *Maine* in the harbor of Havana, Cuba, early in 1898. Immediately afterward the United States became embroiled in the Spanish-American War,

These Philippine patriots, led by Emilio Aguinaldo (2nd row, center), demanded attacks against Spain and later against the United States.

and it quickly carried the conflict to the Philippines. The spirit of nationalism in the islands suddenly was revived.

In preparing for the war the United States counted heavily on discontent among the populations of Cuba and the Philippines. Insurgents in both colonies were contacted and offered arms and money if they would attack the crumbling Spanish authority. To form their alliance with the Philippine rebels, the Americans sought out Emilio Aguinaldo and offered to help him fight the Spanish. Aguinaldo accepted the offer, and an American ship secretly returned him to the Philippines.

While Aguinaldo formed an army behind Spanish lines the Americans began their advance by sea. On May 1, 1898, Admiral George Dewey surprised and sank the Spanish fleet in Manila Bay. He had apparently been studying charts of Philippine waters long before the war began and was well prepared to make the surprise attack. Within three months after his victory American troops marched into Manila.

The triumphant Filipinos expected that the war would result in their independence and began to organize a government, but they were to remain a subject people. After ending the war with Spain, the Americans began an agonizing debate over the Philippines. Some Americans, chiefly in the Republican Party, wanted to annex the islands. They were led by Theodore Roosevelt, former Assistant Secretary of the Navy, who argued that the U.S. needed the Philippines to continue its westward expansion into the Pacific. A much smaller group of Americans thought that the annexation of the Philippines would be a dangerous first step toward an American empire. In a speech to a group of Protestant ministers, President McKinley revealed that he had been torn by the issue until a voice in the night persuaded him that "there was nothing left for us but to take them all, and to educate the Filipinos, and uplift and civilize and Christianize them. . . . And then I went to bed . . . and slept soundly."

When the Philippine nationalists realized that the Americans were not going to leave they began to attack U.S. troops. This so-called "Tagalog Rebellion," named so because it was concentrated among Tagalog-speaking people on Luzon, was a brutal jungle war in which more than 100,000 Filipinos died of famine and disease. The U.S. ordered 70,000 soldiers and 50,000 sailors into the battle, inflicting 16,000 casualties on the Filipinos and suffering 4,200 dead and 2,800 wounded itself. All of Asia watched the guerrilla war drag on for two years (1899–1901). Nationalists in China and Japan offered to help the Filipinos, but the rebel leader, General Aguinaldo, was finally forced to accept U.S. rule.

The Spanish transplanted their culture to the Philippines, bringing their customs, religion, form of government, and the architecture shown above.

On July 4, 1901, the United States placed the administration of the Philippines under a commission headed by William Howard Taft. The commission was ordered to respect traditions in the islands but at the same time to compel the islanders to follow "certain practical rules of government which we (Americans) have found essential. . . ."

Filipinos were stunned when Taft confirmed the land grants that had been made by the Spanish king. They had hoped Taft would fulfill promises of reform. He dissipated some of their fears by buying most of the 400,000 prime acres of land owned by priests and reselling it to Filipinos at lower prices. He also limited the amount of land held by private individuals and corporations and tried to end confusion about land ownership by guaranteeing titles. Unfortunately only the landlords (*caciques*) and the educated class (*ilustrados*) were able to benefit from Taft's land reforms. They alone had the money to buy the land sold by the government or the ability to understand the new land laws.

The Philippines became an important producer for the United States. Four-fifths of its exports went to the U.S., and three-fifths of all that it bought abroad came from the U.S. Americans refused to call it a colony, yet it was clearly a ward of the American economy.

In many ways Filipinos benefited from their relationship with the United States. American soldiers helped to eliminate the sanitation problems that were a major cause of typhoid and cholera epidemics. Other serious diseases, including smallpox and tuberculosis, were brought under control through the construction of hospitals and the development of educational campaigns. The Americans built modern water supply systems in the cities and new roads to the main population centers in rural areas. American businessmen made sub-

stantial investments in Filipino sugar plantations, lumber companies, mining, real estate, and light industry.

But many Filipinos contended that there were disadvantages to
their American government. Under the Americans their land was
controlled by the same class that owned it under the Spanish—the
large owners and the Church. Less than one-fifth of 1 percent of the
population owned 21 percent of the arable land. Farm wages in
1939–40 were about 15 cents a day. There was malnutrition and
even starvation in many areas. The economy was increasingly
geared to the needs of the United States, without whose patronage
the entire economic system would have collapsed. American businessmen with large amounts of capital were able to dominate
international trade in the islands because they enjoyed legal "parity"
with Filipinos—a point that the Americans insisted upon in their
agreements with the Philippines. Finally, the Filipinos were inex-
perienced in business and government and tended to help friends
and relatives whenever they gained power. Thus they often became
lost in the maze of American administrative systems, and the help
that they gave to others was called bribery and corruption.

THE INDEPENDENT STATE OF SIAM

Siam, alone among Southeast Asian kingdoms, maintained its
independence of the West with a combination of skillful diplomacy
and the benefits of geographical position. During the seventeenth
century France tried to dominate Siam through a Greek adventurer
named Constantine Phaulkon, who was in their pay. Phaulkon
became a friend of the Siamese king and would have given the
French the access they wanted to one of the richest courts in Asia,
but Thai nobles executed him. Then they closed Siam to the West,
beginning a policy that lasted 135 years.

While isolated from the West, Siam began to trade more with
China and fought a series of wars with the Burmese and other adjacent kingdoms. (It was after one of these wars in 1781 that the
country took the dynastic name of a new king, Siam, and dropped
its old name, Ayuthia.) The Siamese were brilliant fighters and by
the late eighteenth century captured so much of northern Burma
and western Cambodia that the Sultan of Kedah called in the
British to help oppose them. After the British were settled into the
Malay Peninsula the Siamese offered to work with them by granting
them trading privileges. They carefully avoided domination by the
British, however, by granting the same rights to the United States.
This policy of playing one Western power against another was a
principal source of Siam's diplomatic strength.

Siam's financial stability was another reason that it was able to maintain independence. Its king financed his activities by levying taxes on foreign trade. Provinces neither took nor gave money to the royal treasury, for they were able to complete all of their projects through a system by which their people built public works for them. During four to six months every year all males over eighteen helped in police or military work, or built roads and irrigation projects. They served without pay, and slavery was their only alternative to their obligation. About a third of all Siam's males were slaves during the nineteenth century.

Slavery and court polygamy in Siam were made known to the West by the writing of Anna Leonowens, a widow hired by King Mongkut to teach English to his children from 1862-67. (Her book was turned into the musical play *The King and I* in 1944.) The book and play failed to show it, but Monkut was a sophisticated man who knew history and many languages. He greatly expanded Siam's trade and contacts with Westerners, but he continued to deny them the opportunity to divide and conquer his country.

Mongkut's son, Chulalongkorn, became king when he was only 15. He rapidly modernized Siam by abolishing forced labor, slavery, and prostration in the presence of the king—a practice that humiliated foreign visitors. Through a new system of taxation and free labor he financed schools, roads, and communications. King Chulalongkorn maintained that "All children from my own to the poorest should have an equal chance of education." Through his reforms and willingness to borrow the best ideas that he saw abroad Chulalongkorn helped to maintain Siam's independence and freedom. Many of his friends and advisers were educated in the West, and they ended Siam's traditional isolation.

Siam's independent role proved useful to the British and the French, who flanked the centrally placed Southeast Asian state in Burma and Indochina. Siam's position prevented friction between them. The Siamese periodically made concessions to balance their two powerful neighbors against one another. Despite British and French gains, Siam managed to hold on to large parts of the Korat Plateau and the former Cambodian provinces of Batdambang and Siemreab.

To the south, a different situation developed. There the British, allied with the Malays, forced Siam to surrender Kedah, Perlis, Kelantan, and Trengganu in 1909. But Siam turned this concession into a diplomatic victory. In exchange for ceding the land it per-suaded the British to limit their extraterritorial rights in Siam. Thus once again Siam proved that it could fend off the West.

Siam's contacts with other countries were further increased under Chulalongkorn's successor, King Vajiravudh (1910-1925). Educated at Oxford, Vajiravudh was impressed with British and American administrators and invited them to help run Siam's foreign trade. He astutely sent a token force to join the Allies during World War I, assuring Siam of secure borders and a place at the peace table after the war.

Siam's absolute monarchy was challenged in 1932, when the country's stability was threatened by the effects of the Great Depression. A group of aristocrats confronted the king and demanded that he sign a constitution. The king authorized a document written by Pridi Banomyong, a professor of law who was closely associated with two army colonels, Phya Phahol and Phibul Songgram. These three men, all Western educated, were to dominate Siamese politics for the next quarter century.

Political parties quickly developed under the new constitution. One was led by Pridi, who wanted to nationalize raw materials, industries, and land. The other party was supported by a military group that distrusted Pridi and soon drove him out of the country. Pridi had immense popular support, however, and regained his position in government. Siam held its first election in 1934. When it was over Phya, Pridi, and Phibul were still in control of the government.

In 1935 the king resigned and retired to England. He was replaced by his ten-year-old nephew, Ananda Mahidol, who was studying in Switzerland and remained there until 1945 while a regent governed for him. Phibul slowly installed more military men in office. When Phya retired as prime minister in 1938, Phibul replaced him. Pridi, however, succeeded in gaining the post of minister of finance.

Despite their antagonism, Phibul and Pridi were surprisingly effective together in government. Their common objective was to replace the foreigners in the government with Thais. In 1939 they revised the revenue code to place heavier taxes on the Chinese and Europeans who owned most of Siam's businesses. They also closed some Chinese schools and newspapers and rounded up and deported some Chinese opium addicts.

To build Thai enterprises the government gave subsidies, founded technical schools, and sent many students abroad for training. A wave of nationalism swept the country. Although Western manners and clothing were officially encouraged, the Thais reminded each other of their ancient traditions and culture. They reflected this national pride in 1939 by giving Siam a new name, *Muang Thai*, meaning "Land of the Free," or Thailand.

CHAPTER 4

THE GROWTH OF NATIONALISM

*What is the Principle of Nationalism? (It) is equivalent to
the "doctrine of the state." The ... people have shown the
greatest loyalty to family and clan, with the result that...
there have been family-ism and clan-ism but not real
nationalism. Foreign observers say that (we) are like a
sheet of loose sand. Why? Simply because our people have
shown loyalty to the family and clan but not to the nation
—there has been no nationalism. The family and the clan
have been powerful unifying forces; again and again (the
people) have sacrificed themselves, their families, their
lives in defense of their clan... But for the nation there has
never been an instance of the supreme spirit of sacrifice.*

This statement was made by Dr. Sun Yat-sen, leader of the
Chinese Nationalist Party, about his people in 1924. It applied
equally to Southeast Asians. Before Westerners arrived Southeast
Asians thought of themselves as members of religious, ethnic, and
cultural groups rather than of nations. Government was limited to
families, local leaders, and councils. The monarchies unified large
populations but were identified with single ethnic groups. Southeast
Asian kings ruled largely self-sufficient people who considered
themselves part of local communities rather than as citizens of a
nation.

At the beginning of the twentieth century Japan, China, and
India were leading Asians toward a new idea of society—a society in
which Asians were no longer subject people. The Japanese kept their
independence of the West and in 1905 won a war against a major
Western power, Russia. Under Sun Yat-sen's leadership in 1912 the
Chinese overthrew the Manchu Dynasty and began a long struggle
to overcome the effects of Western economic domination. In India
Mohandas K. Gandhi became the undisputed leader of nationalistic
forces. He organized nonviolent campaigns against India's British
rulers, saying, "We believe that it is the inalienable right of the

Indian people, as of any other people, to have freedom and to enjoy the fruits of their toil and have the necessities of life."

In the remarks of Sun Yat-sen and Gandhi lay the basis of the nationalist movements that were sweeping across Asia. The Asians were demanding the right to control their own destinies. Above all, they wanted governments that represented their own interests and embodied their own customs and institutions. Most Asians were un-aware that self-rule was possible until the Japanese began to challenge Western power. As exceptional stresses began to develop in Western society, more and more Asians were awakened to the possibility of national freedom, independence, and self-government.

Ironically, it was Western colonialists who introduced the idea of nationhood into Southeast Asia. The Westerners joined remote areas with railroads, communications systems, and markets, turning isolated villages into cohesive societies. They introduced the use of cash, which promoted economic interdependence and the develop-ment of cities. But probably nothing promoted nationalism as much as Western culture itself. The Westerners encouraged local civil ser-vants to learn European languages and gave commercial favors to the few Southeast Asians who could afford to become westernized. The introduction of Western language and culture enabled many Southeast Asians to communicate with one another for the first time, for in none of the colonies was a single language known everywhere. The sons of westernized Southeast Asian families went to Europe and the United States to study and returned home with revolution-ary ideas about freedom and independence—ideas learned from the works of Voltaire, Rousseau, Locke, Jefferson, and Marx. They expected to apply what they had learned in their own countries.

But the Westerners infuriated this group of educated Southeast Asians by their attitude of superiority. While teaching the principles of democracy and equality in their own countries, the Westerners practiced autocratic rule in their colonies. The colonial administra-tors refused to mingle socially with Southeast Asians. They kept separate living quarters, schools, and clubs. Southeast Asians were denied the right even to come near most Western sections, except as servants. The most highly trained Southeast Asians were expected to give way to Westerners in public places, and they were made to use special terms of respect when dealing with Westerners.

The West's refusal to allow local self-government was a further cause of anger in Southeast Asia. Local people never rose to promi-nence in their own civil service, except in the Philippines and Malaya. In every European colony the Western administrators imported foreigners to operate commerce, industry, or government, rather than training local personnel for those jobs. This policy usually developed because the local people were unwilling or unable to leave their traditional jobs in agriculture. Nevertheless, Southeast Asians blamed the Westerners for introducing large foreign groups into important positions in their communities.

The nationalists in Southeast Asia argued that self-government was the remedy for most of the region's problems. Though nationalists often disagreed over questions of political and economic policy, they were able to unite in opposition to the West. Southeast Asian nationalists first tried to promote popular unity by calling attention to cultural achievements in Southeast Asia, hoping to instill pride among people who were struggling to achieve a sense of personal worth. Between the two world wars the nationalists concentrated on reform rather than revolution. Few of them dared to hope for complete independence from what seemed to be the invincible colonial powers. In Indochina and Indonesia, Ho Chi Minh and Achmed Sukarno spoke of sovereignty, independence, and industrialization for their countries. Most other nationalist leaders would have been willing to settle for more liberal colonial governments.

The calls for reform turned to cries for revolution during the 1930s. This change was caused by the Great Depression, which

Southeast Asians saw the colonialists draw vast wealth from their land and take most of the profits abroad. The British developed these tin mines in Malaya.

sharply cut the demand for Southeast Asia's products. In place of self-sufficient villages, colonial governments had created many specialized economies that were dependent on the sale of rubber, tin, oil, and rice. The sudden drop in the prices of these products brought ruin to many farmers and workers. At the same time, impoverished millions saw that their agricultural efforts were still benefiting the West and the Chinese, Indians, and upper classes that best served Western interests.

The economic distress during the Depression was particularly severe because Southeast Asia's population had dramatically increased under colonial rule. In 1830, the population of the entire region was only 25.8 million. By 1930, it had soared to 150 million. This astonishing increase of almost 570 percent compared with increases of only 300 percent in India and Japan and 200 percent in China during the same period. Starvation, unemployment, poor housing, and inadequate clothing produced demands for change in Southeast Asia. But the colonial governments were powerless to bring about change while the world economy was depressed. Both the people and their governments turned to violence during the Great Depression. There were strikes, boycotts, and finally armed attacks by both sides.

The most dedicated nationalists to emerge from these conflicts came to believe that the West would never relent in its colonial practices. These nationalists became revolutionaries who looked to the Soviet Union for guidance. The Soviet Union provided a powerful example of an undeveloped country that had used revolution to change its society and develop an alternative to the economic systems of the West. It was because the Soviet Union stood in opposition to the West that many Southeast Asian nationalists were drawn to its program for revolutionary change. This program was based on the ideas of Karl Marx (1818–1883), whose philosophy underlies every modern communist and socialist government.

According to Marx, economic activity underlies and shapes all historical changes. His theory of history states that every society is a result of a class struggle. The dominant class wins political and economic power because it is able to increase production. But in time this dominant class loses control of the economy and is replaced. During the nineteenth century, Marx said, the industrialized working class would succeed the capitalists, who themselves were the successors of feudal nobles. Marx expected these industrial workers (proletariats) to "centralize all instruments of production in the hands of the state" and to promote an abundance so universal that neither classes nor government would be necessary.

During the Russian Revolution of 1917, the leading interpreter of

At the height of nationalist activity in their Southeast Asian colonies the British were forced to patrol the streets continuously. This is Singapore.

Marxism, V. I. Lenin (1870–1924), applied Marx's theory of class struggle to the conditions in Southeast Asia. He said that the people of Western colonies represented a working class which was struggling against Western capitalists, and he maintained that the West would collapse without its colonies. The Soviet Union later tested this theory by offering revolutionary training and weapons to nationalist leaders throughout Asia. As a result, many Southeast Asian leaders either became communists or socialists or were strongly influenced by Marxist-Leninist ideas.

Yet neither communism nor socialism had all of the answers needed by Southeast Asia. Like the religions and philosophies imported centuries before from China, India, and the Middle East, Marxism was blended with existing political ideas in the region. The final stages of colonialism and the rise of nationalist movements in Southeast Asia are described in the remainder of this chapter.

Dutch East Indies (Indonesia). The Dutch "Liberal System" of colonial government began in 1870 and lasted through the 1920s. Under this system Dutch investors were not able to own land but could lease land on a long-term basis. Consequently more plantations were established, and more farm workers were drawn from villages to work in remote areas. The Dutch imported Chinese laborers to supplement the Indonesians.

The Liberal System enabled the Dutch to take most of the best land in the islands, thus denying local farmers land for expansion. There was no escape for the farmers, therefore, when their taxes were too high or their masters were too cruel. Countless thousands of farmers were forced to give up their land. The Indonesians gained no more income from the Liberal System, though it was intended to relieve their hardships. But the Dutch, it turned out, gained substantial benefits from the Liberal System. Drawn to the islands by cheap labor and raw materials, many more Dutch arrived, especially after the opening of the Suez Canal in 1869. The Dutch hired Indonesian and Chinese workers to build cities for them while they extended their investments in sugar, rubber, tin, tobacco, and finally oil. In time the Dutch allowed other Westerners to invest in the Dutch East Indies.

Early in the twentieth century the Dutch tried to soften the harmful effects of their economic policies through a program called the Ethical Policy. This plan recognized that the Dutch bore some responsibility for the deteriorating conditions in the islands. The Ethical Policy enabled the Dutch government to help some small farmers expand their rubber and rice production, and it subsidized a few schools for Indonesians.

But Indonesian nationalists regarded the Ethical Policy as an inadequate solution to the growing problems caused by the colonial rule. They pointed out that the Dutch did nothing to limit the numbers and power of the Chinese minority. Chinese immigrants were moneylenders, tax collectors, and labor contractors for the Dutch. In 1908 one group of Javanese intellectuals formed their own economic, social, and cultural organization, *Budi Utomo* ("Noble Endeavor."). The aim of this organization was to help Indonesians assert their own culture and overcome poverty. The movement also sponsored its own schools to encourage interest in Indonesian arts.

Another nationalist group was the *Sarekat Islam*, founded by Muslim merchants on Java in 1911. Its original goal was to protect the Muslim trade in batik cloth from Chinese competition. But the Sarekat Islam soon devoted its energies to the cause of Indonesian nationalism. During the 1920s the organization was seriously weakened by the split between radical and moderate members and the rise of political parties.

The upsurge of Indonesian nationalism caught the Dutch government off guard. Under pressure from liberal reformers in the Netherlands, the colonial administration in 1916 created an advisory council chosen by local leaders—the Voksraad. However, this body had no law-making power. The chairman and half of the members of the Voksraad were appointed by the Dutch, who had the power to veto the council's recommendations. In reality, the legislative branch of government remained firmly in Dutch control.

As part of their response to Dutch capitalism, the Indonesian nationalists began to join socialist or communist movements. In 1926–27 the country's labor unions were almost all controlled by communists and called a general strike. The Dutch took harsh measures against them, arresting more than 13,000 strikers. With the suppression of the unions the leadership of Indonesian nationalism passed to a few young students, many of whom had been educated in Holland.

The leading student nationalists were Achmed Sukarno and Muhammad Hatta, who organized the National Indonesian Party in 1927. Sukarno and Hatta advocated a policy of non-cooperation with the Dutch and called for the use of violence when necessary. Once again the Dutch colonial government resorted to drastic measures. In 1929 the colonial administration officially dissolved the party, arrested its leaders, and exiled Sukarno, Hatta, and other nationalist leaders. Even the name "Indonesia" was outlawed. Yet the nationalists continued their campaigns of sabotage and terrorism.

By the mid-1930s the growth of Japanese military power threatened the safety of the Dutch East Indies. In an effort to gain popular support the colonial authorities adopted a more conciliatory attitude toward the Indonesian nationalists. In one major concession they decentralized the colonial administration. The Dutch East Indies were divided into a number of provinces. Each province was headed by an appointed governor who was advised by a council in which Indonesians were in the majority. Moderate Indonesians were encouraged by this move and offered to cooperate with the Dutch in exchange for a promise of more self-rule. The Dutch refused. As World War II began in Europe, the Dutch were still clinging to their colonial power, but they had begun to realize that the forces of Indonesian nationalism were irrepressible.

British Malaya. The people of Malaya were slow to conceive of themselves as the members of a nation. Most Malays were governed by sultans who had been organized into a loose confederation by the British. This government represented its people well in all of their ethnic and religious concerns. Each of the four states in the Malay Federation had its own heritage, and the population as a whole had no strong sense of national purpose.

Nationalist zeal in Malaya was also reduced by British policies. Although they took substantial profits out of the country, the British helped the Malays to improve their economic position. They allowed the Malays considerable self-rule, and many Malays never considered the British oppressive. Malays were allowed to join the civil service and maintain their standards of culture and system of land ownership.

The Malays preferred agriculture to commercial and financial occupations. To establish businesses and tin mines, therefore, the British imported Chinese.

But British commercial activity inevitably increased ethnic tensions on the peninsula because the Malays were unwilling to change their way of life. To develop large rubber plantations and tin mines the British imported thousands of Indians and Chinese. Both the Indians and Chinese quickly took over Malaya's commercial and financial enterprises. Friction between the Malays and Chinese were especially severe because the British began to appoint Chinese to collect their taxes. The need for these appointments was based on the British policy of taxing luxuries brought to Penang, Malacca, and Singapore—the "Straits Settlements." The British used Chinese tax agents because many of their revenues came from opium-smoking and gambling, both prevalent "luxuries" in the Chinese community. When these same agents tried to collect taxes from Malay farmers there was often violence.

There were no more than 300,000 Malays on the peninsula when the Straits Settlements were being developed during the 1850s. By 1911 there were more than 1.5 million and at least 900,000 Chinese and 267,000 Indians. By 1940 the Chinese outnumbered the Malay population in Singapore. Much of the new population was added in 1909 through Britain's acquisition of the states of Perlis, Kelantan, Trengganu, and Kedah from Thailand. These states accepted British advisers but declined to join Malaya and so were called the Unfederated States.

Thus Malaya was made up of districts whose people were largely self-governing and who therefore did not consider the British oppressive. Nor did the education of Malays promote unrest, as it had in other Western colonies. The Malays were largely concerned with agriculture and their Muslim way of life. They accepted the limited education offered to them by the British. Throughout Malaya, only the wealthy Chinese and Muslim families developed private schools.

The seeds of nationalism were planted, but they grew slowly, chiefly in the cities. Young Muslims became conscious of progress in the West and wanted to reform both their religion and their economy. The Young Malay Union became active in the 1930s. Inspired by Indonesian nationalists, this group of intellectuals agitated against the British. Its arguments were blunted, however, because the Malays were among the more prosperous people in Southeast Asia and were not prepared to rebel. The independence movement in Malaya therefore lay dormant until World War II, when it suddenly arose as vigorously as in Southeast Asia's other colonies.

Burma. As the twentieth century began, Burmese nationalists were nursing a burning hatred of British rulers, Indian moneylenders, and Chinese laborers. Burma was a prosperous and relatively peaceful country before foreigners arrived in the nineteenth century. The Burmese yearned for a time when they could take over their own land again.

Burmese nationalism gained its first great impetus in the aftermath of World War I, when President Woodrow Wilson championed the right of self-determination for all people. The growing success of Indian nationalists also stimulated Burma to begin organizing against the British. Each step that India took toward self-government increased the activity of the nationalist movement in neighboring Burma. In 1906 a number of ordinarily nonpolitical religious groups began to demand self-government through the Young Men's Buddhist Association.

The British gave Burma a new constitution in 1921, establishing a two-level government resembling one that they had organized in India. Under this government the British allowed the Burmese to elect an assembly which the colonial administration often consulted. On the surface, this administrative change appeared to be a step toward self-government in Burma. Beneath the surface, Burmese nationalists, however, saw ominous signs that the new government was more dependent on Britain than ever, for the whole regime was placed under the authority of the British government of India.

The British provoked Burmese nationalists in many other ways. They refused to allow either Burmans or the ethnic minorities into the highest posts of government and the imperial police. The Burmans were not even permitted in the civil service, which was run by Indians, Chinese, and Karens. The colonial administration did little to resolve such important social problems as the growing number of Burmans who were being evicted from their farms by moneylenders. This issue became crucial after World War I, when Indian financiers owned almost 40 percent of the land in Lower Burma. As prices for rice, tin, rubber and oil fell during the Great Depression, the desperate Burmese rioted against both their landlords and the British, forcing the colonial government to take action.

In 1935, the British Parliament decided to increase home rule for Burma by separating the governments of India and Burma. Through the Burma Act it established a Burmese senate and also placed cabinet ministers in the colony under the authority of the Burmese assembly. In spite of these changes, the Burmese nationalists continued to protest the lack of true self-rule. The nationalists pointed out that the British governor retained absolute veto power over the government and had sole authority over foreign affairs and defense.

During the 1930s, the two leading Burmese nationalists were Dr. Ba Maw and U Saw. Dr. Maw's followers dominated the Burmese assembly until 1939, when U Saw was swept into office as prime minister. After the defeat of his party, Maw began to collaborate with Japanese undercover agents, who were beginning their plan to take over the country. U Saw was also in touch with the Japanese. He established his own newspaper, the *Sun*, which was vigorously anti-British. During a visit to England the British arrested U Saw on suspicion that he was plotting with Japanese agents in Portugal. They held him in Africa until after the war.

The most important pro-Japanese group in prewar Burma was made up of students at Rangoon University. This group called itself the "Thakins" ("Masters") to defy the British who reserved that term for themselves. Thirty members of this group (the "Thirty Comrades") went to Japan for military training just before World War II broke out. Later they went to Thailand, where they organized the Burma Independence Army. This army quietly prepared to help the Japanese drive the British out of Burma. But the Thirty Comrades were not pro-Japanese as much as they were nationalists and, they claimed, socialists or communists. Demonstrating the unity of Burmese nationalists, the Thirty Comrades were given valuable aid by young Buddhist monks who resented British policies. Some of the monks became guerrillas. Others organized anti-British strikes and boycotts. In one campaign the monks forced the British to remove their shoes before entering pagodas—an act which the British considered beneath their dignity.

The Burmese often fought each other as well as the British during

Many Burmese nationalists, including Prime Minister U Saw, called on the Japanese to help them against the British.

the 1930s. There were riots among Muslim, Indian, Chinese, labor, and student groups. In spite of these differences the nationalist drive for independence remained uppermost among the political issues in Burma. As the students and monks led the way, the ranks of the independence movement attracted more and more members of the professional and skilled classes.

After Japan's invasion of Manchuria in 1937, Burma became an important link in a supply system established by the West to help the defenders of China. Thousands of tons of ammunition and food were hauled over the Burma Road, which extended to Chungking in South China. A group of Americans and Chinese called the "Flying Tigers" helped to carry provisions to China by air over Burma. Their dangerous flight over the windswept Himalayas became known throughout the world as the "Hump." The British also funneled most of their aid to China through Burma.

French Indochina. The desire for independence persisted in northern Vietnam since the Chinese were expelled in 939 A.D. During colonial times the keen sense of national identity in the Tonkin region, caused the Vietnamese to fight the French at every turn. The French expected the Vietnamese to be loyal to France. This attitude merely angered the Vietnamese, who reserved patriotism for their own people. Nationalism among the Vietnamese was powerfully stimulated when the French forcibly recruited 100,000 Vietnamese soldiers and workers for service in Europe during World War I. Thousands of these men returned from the war filled with resentment against the French, yearning for national self-determination.

Nationalism in Indochina contributed to the rise of political parties after World War I. Most of these parties advocated moderate reforms such as higher wages and better opportunities in education and government. When the French ignored these demands the moderation gave way to revolutionary ideas. Operating secretly, leading Confucian scholars in Vietnam made contact with anti-French groups in China and Japan. The Confucian scholars regarded rebellion as their most honorable recourse against oppressive government.

The French resistance to reform movements in Vietnam caused the nationalists to respond by promoting widespread terrorism during the 1920s. The Vietnamese Nationalist Party was founded in Canton, China, in 1925, and immediately afterward sent underground agents to Hanoi. These agents proved ineffective against French opposition. Colonial troops were sent to crush local revolts, and in 1930 a French army shattered nationalist forces at Yen Bay, northwest of Hanoi. After their defeat at Yen Bay the leaders of the nationalist army moved to Yünnan, China, where many of them joined the communist movement.

A young Confucian named Nguyen Tat Thanh was the most active nationalist leader. Later this man took the name Ho Chi Minh ("He Who Enlightens"). Ho Chi Minh was born in the mountainous province of Annam in 1890. When he was 19 he went to France for military service and developed a burning hatred of French capitalism. Later he became editor of a newspaper called *Le Paria* ("The Pariah") and wrote hundreds of articles attacking the French colonial system. Ho Chi Minh helped to found the French Communist Party during the 1920s and then spent two years in the

Ho Chi Minh led the communist attack against the French in Vietnam.

Soviet Union, where he studied and translated the works of Marx and Lenin into Vietnamese. Later he became a communist agent in Shanghai, China, and made secret visits to Vietnam to found the Communist Party there.

Ho conceived of the struggle for self-determination in two parts. First he proposed to unite all of Vietnam's nationalist groups to fight for political independence from France. Once this victory was secured, he believed, Vietnam could begin modernizing its society and developing a communist economy.

At the outset of his campaigns Ho believed that the French could be defeated through political means. He worked for national elections. The French tried to destroy his organization, the League for the Independence of Vietnam (Viet Minh), but it continued to gain strength. The Viet Minh's popularity was due in part to the widespread opposition of the French, who were detested by intellectuals and peasants alike. The nationalists stood for independence and land reform, both of which the French bitterly opposed. In time Ho Chi Minh concluded that the French would never accept a political defeat and began to work for revolution.

The more moderate Vietnamese hoped that the stern policies of the occupation force would be tempered because of the efforts of the emperor of Annam, Bao Dai. This young ruler was a student in France when he took the throne in 1925, and his supporters in Vietnam thought that his experience there might some day make him an able mediator between the French and the nationalists. Bao Dai returned to Vietnam in 1932, when he was 19, and announced that he would work for the reform of Vietnam's economy and the unification of its three parts. The French refused to cooperate with him, however, and the emperor's youthful dreams of leading a new national government were ended. The French allowed Bao Dai to remain in the imperial palace at Hué, but they continued to govern Vietnam as three parts of Indochina: Tonkin, Annam, and Cochin China.

The Philippines. The Nacionalista Party became dominant in the Philippine assembly (established in 1907) soon after the establishment of American rule. Its platform called for full independence for the islands. Philippine nationalists were encouraged by the election of President Woodrow Wilson in 1912. Wilson began to mismantle the bureaucracy that his Republican predecessors has built for the islands and he declared that it was his intention to grant independence to the Philippines.

The leader of the nationalists, Manuel Quezon, had fought against the Americans as well as the Spaniards. His schoolteacher parents had given him a Catholic education and helped him to study for the priesthood. Quezon proved unsuitable as a novice but

Filipino nationalists blamed the United States for the slums of Manila, among the worst in the world, and increased their demands for independence.

was given a chance to run one of the plantations owned by the Catholic Church. This experience interested Quezon in administration. He studied law, entered politics, and from 1906–16 served as the Philippines' Resident Commissioner in the U.S. Congress, where he carried the cause of independence into the political arena of Washington. Quezon pleaded eloquently with congressmen and diplomats, urging them to support sovereignty for the Philippines.

By 1916, President Wilson had recalled all but 582 of the 2,600 American administrators in the islands. In that same year Quezon persuaded the Congress to pass the Jones Act, which permitted the islanders to elect their own senate and control their own budget, subject to a veto by the American governor-general. This political victory made Quezon a hero in the Philippines. Most Filipinos expected that ultimately he would be able to gain the full independence that Wilson had promised for the islands. But the movement toward independence was halted by America's entry into World War I.

During the 1920s, the Republican administrations of Warren G. Harding and Calvin Coolidge reversed Wilson's policy toward the Philippines. They denied that the islands were ready for independence and sent General Leonard Wood to Manila to tighten American controls there. After the Great Depression began in 1929, however, American public opinion began to shift in favor of independence for the Philippines. Many Americans realized that by granting independence they could block the flow of cheap goods and low-paid workers from the Philippines to the United States. The Americans expected to impose tariffs and immigration quotas on the Philippines after independence was granted.

In 1931 the U.S. Congress passed the Hare-Hawes-Cutting Bill, which promised independence to the islands after a ten-year transition period. But the bill contained no provision to protect Philippine industries from American competition while the country was getting on its feet. Quezon opposed the bill and in 1934 persuaded the Congress to pass the Tydings-McDuffie Bill. This measure provided for independence after ten years too, but during the interim assured the Filipinos that they could ship their sugar, coconuts, oil, and cordage to the United States duty-free. The United States kept its veto power over the Filipino economy, judiciary, and foreign policy, and it also retained the right to station troops in the islands until independence.

The passage of the Tydings-McDuffie Bill began what many Americans called the "Commonwealth Stage" of the Philippines. The U.S. government hoped that during the decade preceding independence, the Philippines would gain enough political and economic experience to resist foreign control. The Americans continued to see the islands as a line of defense against any future expansion by Japan, and they contended that their own type of democracy would help keep the Philippines strong. But Filipinos accepted only part of the political structure that the United States wanted them to adopt. Quezon was elected president of the Philippines in 1935 and soon boasted that he had "more power than President Roosevelt ever dreamed of." He believed in a one-party system and closely controlled all political appointments in the islands, right down to village schoolteachers. By raising fears of Japanese sabotage, Quezon persuaded the Philippine National Assembly to pass an Emergency Powers Bill in 1940. Under this legislation he was able to force civilians to work for the government, outlaw strikes, commandeer all transportation, change the entire educational system, and control food production.

Quezon's position was unlike that of the leaders of any fully democratic countries. The American political writer John Gunther said that

> ... his (Quezon's) knack of getting along well with both rich and poor, with the miserably fed peasants of the countryside as well as the Spanish millionaires in Manila, is probably his single most valuable characteristic. The masses adore him because he gives them something. The rich eat out of his hand—when he isn't eating out of theirs—because he guarantees their survival. By using both he has built up an irresistible machine.

Thus Southeast Asia progressed from a "loose sheet of sand" to-

ward a community of nations. The European concepts of nationalism and Marxism and the American concept of democracy became
part of the region. But just as Hinduism, Buddhism, and Confucianism earlier were blended with Southeast Asian ideas, so nationalism,
Marxism, and democracy became Southeast Asian in special ways.
Lacking ethnic cohesiveness, uniform languages, and highly
developed economies, the emerging nations of Southeast Asia could
not build political structures resembling those in the West. Tonkin,
with its powerful cultural unity, was the sole exception. Tonkin's
emerging version of Marxism closely resembled the Chinese interpretation of communism.

The powerful ideas which gripped Southeast Asians just before
World War II were being turned into realities by individuals who
represented deep traditions in the region. The word *charismatic*
applies to each of them, for each symbolized the essence of the
people he led. Aung San in Burma, Sukarno in Indonesia, Ho Chi
Minh in Indochina, and Manuel Quezon in the Philippines each had
the strength and ability to apply the new ideas to their own cultures.
Yet the Marxism they created in Burma, Indonesia, or Vietnam was
not identical to Marxism in the Soviet Union. Nor was Quezon's
practice of democracy identical to democracy in the United States.
The world drew closer to global war. As it did, Southeast Asia's
political character began to take form.

CHAPTER 5

WORLD WAR II AND ITS AFTERMATH

THE JAPANESE CONQUEST

THE OUTBREAK OF WORLD WAR II in Europe presented Japanese imperialists with the irresistible lure of enormous gain. Not far from Japan lay Europe's Southeast Asian colonies, rich in the raw materials which Japanese industrialists were seeking. These colonies were indefensible while their European masters were recoiling from the sudden German assault. The Japanese were eager to incorporate the countries of Southeast Asia into an independent "Asian Co-Prosperity Sphere" which they could dominate. When the colonial governments rejected their plan, the Japanese decided to initiate it by force. They built their strength for the time when the European governments would be too weak to resist.

In 1940, Germany's conquest of the Netherlands and France alerted the Japanese to begin the attack on Southeast Asia. The invasion plan which they executed changed the history of the region for all time, for it caused Southeast Asians to struggle for independence more desperately than ever before. For three centuries the colonial people had been led to think of Westerners as invincible. Now with a few swift blows the Japanese boldly shattered that illusion, seizing lands which the Westerners promised they would never surrender. The Japanese assault in Southeast Asia put an end to Western colonial rule. World War II proved to Southeast Asians that they could and should get rid of their colonial masters.

The first phase of the Japanese attack began with demands on France after the French surrendered to Germany in June, 1940. Crushed by waves of tanks and planes, the French sadly watched German troops march into Paris. The French government collapsed. French officials who believed it was futile to resist the Germans established a new government in the city of Vichy. A group of "Free French" under General Charles de Gaulle fought on in league with the British, but essentially France was unable to maintain its former government or empire. Accordingly, the Japanese informed the French that they were moving into French

83

Indochina. Within two months after France's defeat, the Vichy government acknowledged that Japan was "preëminent" in Asia.

The Japanese did not evict the French colonial administrators from Indochina, nor did they claim to have replaced the French imperialists. Instead, they compelled the Vichy government to allow them the exclusive use of the colony and its raw materials. This arrangement meant that the Japanese did not have to establish costly new governments to administer the French districts of Tonkin, Annam, Cochin China, Laos, and Cambodia. And while their troops were stationed in Indochina's military bases, harbors, depots, and airports, they avoided accusations that they were setting up a new empire. Meanwhile Indochina's vital rice, tin, antimony, manganese, and tungsten all began flowing toward Japan.

The second phase of the Japanese conquest of Southeast Asia began in mid-1941 when Japan formed an alliance with Thailand. The Thais had long sought to capture lands owned by Laos and Cambodia on the Mekong River and were encouraged by the Japanese to seize them. Ships of the Free French defeated the Thais off Indochina, but the Japanese forced them to withdraw. The Thais took the important Cambodian provinces of Batdambang and Siemreab. When Laos called for help against the Thais the French offered that country their "protection." In this way France's Vichy government helped Japan to cement its important relationship with Thailand.

The third and final phase of Japan's conquest of Southeast Asia began the day after the attack on Pearl Harbor. On December 8, 1941, Japanese planes roared out of the airport in Saigon, the chief city in Cochin China, and laid waste to what the whole world believed was the impregnable fortress of Singapore. The British had only two capital ships in Singapore's harbor. Both vessels were sunk. Meanwhile a Japanese army moved swiftly out of Thailand and into Malaya, where on February 15, 1942, the British surrendered. Some 30,000 Japanese soldiers herded 100,000 Britons into prisons and labor camps.

This victory stunned the British, humiliating them in the eyes of their colonial subjects. But it was only the first in a series of attacks that the Japanese executed with precision throughout the region. Early in 1942 a Japanese army invaded the Dutch East Indies and conquered it within three months. At the same time another Japanese force struck westward toward Burma. There, the Japanese met heavy resistance from British and American forces. The Americans were stationed in the country to defend the vital Burma Road, which extended 1,000 miles between Mandalay and Yünnan,

These Japanese planes were among the hundreds that attacked Western positions from Burma to the Philippines as the war began in the Pacific.

South China. The Japanese wanted to close the Burma Road in order to reduce the support that Britain and the United States sent over it to China, where Japan had been fighting since 1937. By the Spring of 1942, the Japanese controlled all of Burma. Meanwhile, Thailand was persuaded to declare war on the Allies, and Japanese troops were besieging the remnants of American forces in the Philippines. Thus within five months after the attack on Pearl Harbor, the Japanese occupied most of Southeast Asia.

SOUTHEAST ASIA'S RESPONSE

Relatively few Southeast Asians supported the Japanese during the conquest. Some militant nationalists in Burma and Indonesia welcomed the invading armies as liberators. Others passively accepted the changes. But most of the region's population was confused and angered by the invasion. Why, Southeast Asian leaders demanded, had the Western powers refused to train local self-defense forces which could resist attack? These leaders concluded that Western governments were not only incapable of protecting them, but also were unwilling to let them protect themselves.

During the early stages of the occupation the Japanese slogan "Asia for the Asiatics" enjoyed considerable appeal. The Japanese gained popular support by releasing nationalist leaders from Dutch, British, and French prisons and by forbidding the use of European languages. But within a short time, Southeast Asians realized that their new Asian masters were no better than their old European masters had been. Japanese administrators insisted that the conquered peoples show them respect and used force to insure obedience. Throughout the war, Southeast Asians were compelled to sacrifice food and raw materials to the needs of Japan's military machine. The Japanese often demanded that the local populations work harder for the war effort. Their police, the Kempitai, instilled terror into the population. The Kempitai murdered thousands of Chinese in Singapore and rounded up Malayans for forced labor. The needs of the Japanese army and wartime conditions sharply reduced available rice supplies, causing widespread starvation.

After the Americans recaptured the Philippines in 1944, the Japanese sensed that they might soon need more support from Southeast Asians and changed their policies in order to win it. They reduced the demands for food and forced labor, although they still compelled British and American prisoners to build roads, bridges, and railways in remote jungles. In the provinces of Indochina the Japanese finally ordered the French out. They urged Laos, Cambodia, and Vietnam (the provinces of Tonkin, Annam, and Cochin China) to declare independence. The "independence" that they granted, however, was within the framework of the Japanese-dominated Co-Prosperity Sphere. It meant little more than the transfer of the colonies to the Japanese Empire.

Aroused by Japanese policies, many Southeast Asian nationalists organized guerrilla bands to fight the Japanese. Even nationalists who initially cooperated with the invaders began to take up arms against them. One of these was Aung San, a fiery Burman who helped the Japanese until 1944. After that date he began to attack the Japanese with the help of the British. In Tonkin, Ho Chi Minh became the rallying point of nationalist resistance. His small guer-

Armed with American rifles, mortars, and bazookas, these Burmese guerrillas fought the Japanese behind the lines of combat during World War II.

rilla army harassed the Japanese in the jungles of the Indochinese peninsula. With American aid, Ho was able to liberate several provinces. In the Philippines, a number of guerrilla organizations offered courageous resistance, notably on the island of Luzon.

The battle for Southeast Asia caused severe destruction to much of the region. The economy was damaged first by the Western colonialists who blew up mines, factories, oil wells, harbors, railways, and mills when they learned that the Japanese were preparing to invade. In Burma, the Philippines and other parts of Southeast Asia, the struggle between the defending armies and the Japanese resulted in the devastation of vast areas. Third, the Allies bombarded most areas intensively by sea and air, both in order to dislodge the Japanese and deprive them of vital products. Finally, Southeast Asia was further damaged when guerrilla forces rose up against the Japanese, who destroyed facilities as they left.

Among the millions of Southeast Asians who suffered during the war, this destruction produced a strong desire to be rid of all foreigners. The intensity of their feeling varied in different parts of the region, depending on what the population had experienced during the war.

THE TIDES OF NATIONALISM

Burma. In the last chapter we saw that a group of Burmese student leaders defiantly called themselves Thakins ("Masters"), assuming the title that the British reserved for each other. Some Thakins, led by Aung San, studied guerrilla warfare in Japan and shortly before World War II went to Thailand to raise an army of Burmese nationalists. These student leaders were personally selected by Aung San and became known as the "Thirty Comrades." Their Burma Independence Army helped the Japanese drive the British and Americans out of Burma in the Spring of 1942.

The war caused severe economic and social damage in Burma. The departing British forces destroyed anything that might have proved useful to the Japanese. They flooded or dynamited mines, oil wells, and train stations. The country's vital harbors were dynamited. Before the war, Burma's commerce and the lower levels of its civil service were operated by about a million Indians. More than half of this Indian population so feared the invading Japanese that they left for India before the invaders arrived. Thus Burma suffered a shortage of management skills.

The opening of the war also intensified Burma's ethnic conflicts. When the British left Burma, the nationalists attacked the ethnic minorities who made up most of the British colonial army in Burma. The Burma Independence Army demanded that the Kachins,

Within nine months after the attack on Pearl Harbor Japanese troops celebrated their conquest of Burma in front of British headquarters in Rangoon.

Chins, Karens, and Eurasians lay down their arms. Fearing attack, the minorities resisted the nationalists, and thousands of people died in the resulting battles.

The Japanese established a puppet government under a former Burmese prime minister named Ba Maw. They made Aung San the minister of defense, never realizing that his ultimate goal was to liberate Burma from Japan as well as from Britain. Aung San secretly headed the Anti-Fascist Organization and in 1944 called on the British for help against the Japanese. As the Japanese prepared to evacuate Burma, Aung San's guerrillas joined the British in the battle for the capital city of Rangoon.

After the war, Aung San's organization became known as the Anti-Fascist People's Freedom League (AFPFL). The AFPFL demanded complete independence for Burma. This coalition of socialists, communists, and nationalists was basically Marxist in its political and economic viewpoint. Therefore it was determined to resist British colonialists, who announced they were determined to restore the prewar government to Burma. In 1945–46 the AFPFL formed an army of 100,000 to fight the British if necessary. A conflict was averted only by the election of the socialist Labor Party in Great Britain. The new British government was far more sympathetic to its colonial subjects than Britain's Conservative Party had been.

In 1946 Britain's new prime minister, Clement Attlee, invited Aung San to a conference in London. Afterward he issued a momentous proclamation, offering Burma complete independence and membership in the Commonwealth if it chose.

Aung San returned to Burma to face the urgent problems confronting the people of Burma. These problems included severe food shortages, high prices, and bandits in the countryside. Guerrillas representing opposing communist groups were beginning to fight each other in the villages. The Karens, Shans, and many of the Indians and Chinese were unwilling to accept the rule of the Burman people.

It was in this chaotic situation that a general election was held in Burma in April, 1947. An overwhelming majority of Burmese supported Aung San and his policy of seeking complete independence. After his election victory, Aung San made great efforts to persuade the minorities to accept the new Burmese constitution. Only the Karen tribesmen refused, demanding an independent state of their own. But Aung San never had a chance to negotiate a peaceful settlement with the Karens. On July 19, 1947, two gunmen burst into a cabinet meeting and assassinated him and seven others. Aung San's chief political rival, U Saw, was tried and hanged for this crime. U Nu, a Thakin and close friend of Aung San, became Burma's prime minister.

Negotiations between the Burmese and the British continued. Finally on October 17, 1947, British and Burmese representatives signed a treaty in London, whereby Burma became a free nation. The new state chose not to join the British Commonwealth. On July 4, 1948, the Union of Burma was proclaimed.

Thailand. The United States refused to accept Thailand's declaration of war against the Allies. The Americans said that the struggle of the Thai underground against the Japanese was proof that Thailand really fought for the Allies. Great Britain, France, and the Soviet Union had demands to make on the Thais for having declared war, however. The British called on Thailand to ship 1.5 million metric tons of rice to starving Malayans as a gesture of good will. The French forced the Thais to return the lands they had taken from Laos and Cambodia. Finally, the Soviet Union demanded that Thailand repeal legislation which outlawed the Communist Party. France and the Soviet Union both threatened to keep Thailand out of the United Nations if their demands were not met.

After granting these war claims, Thailand organized a new government under Pridi Banomyong, the law professor who had become the leader of the nationalist movement. Pridi helped to write a new constitution. The new basic law, announced in 1946, created a parliament of two houses. The lower house was made up of elected officials who then chose the members of the upper house. Thailand's two major political parties, the Constitutional Front and the Cooperative Party, gained a victory for Pridi and put his backers into the upper house. For the first time a Thai prime minister thus won the support of a democratically chosen parliament. But success proved short-lived for Pridi.

During the war years the hereditary king of Thailand, Ananda Mahidol, had been in Switzerland. He and his brother, Bhumibol Aduljadej, were students there. King Ananda returned to Thailand in 1945 and informed Pridi that he was resuming his royal duties in government. Then, just two weeks after Pridi's triumph at the polls, the king was found murdered in his bed. As the dead king's brother took the throne, Pridi was accused of masterminding the assassination. Pridi's government collapsed, plunging Thailand into political chaos. Pridi himself was forced to flee the country. With his departure, Thailand lost its only strong national leader.

Laos. We have seen how during World War II the Japanese formed an alliance with the Thais and encouraged them to seize the land in the northeast, in French Indochina. But these lands belonged to four Lao-Thai kingdoms which demanded protection against further raids by Thailand. At the suggestion of the Japanese, the French reorganized these kingdoms, called Luang Prabang, Vientiane, Xieng Khouang, and Champassak. The combined population of these kingdoms was about 2½ million. The French called this new protectorate "Laos."

The king of Luang Prabang, Sisavang Vong, ruled Laos through a government headed by his eldest son, Prince Phetsarath. The prince led a group of nationalists who insisted upon declaring independence of France as the Japanese withdrew. But soon French paratroops landed in Laos. They forced the king to remove Prince Phetsarath from government and announced that Laos would be restored to status as a colonial "protectorate."

The Laotian nationalists by this time had formed an organization called the Lao Issara ("Free Lao") and were in contact with anti-French guerrillas led by Ho Chi Minh in Vietnam. A combined force of Laotian and Vietnamese guerrillas tried to dislodge the French, but it was defeated. Laotian nationalist forces were scattered. Many of them went to Thailand, where they formed a government in exile under Prince Phetsarath.

The French offered Laos limited autonomy but rejected the idea of complete independence. French officials helped to draw up a new constitution in which powers were divided among a king, prime minister, legislature, and independent judiciary. The king agreed to work with the French, and in 1947 Laotians voted to select the members of a new constitutional assembly. The assembly, once elected, was to organize a government for Laos.

This development in Laos caused a division among the leaders of the Lao Issara (Free Lao) who were in Thailand. Prince Phetsarath

At the end of World War II the French moved swiftly to recover their lost colonies in Indochina, but they faced nationalists who demanded independence.

insisted that the nationalists continue to press for complete independence. His two half-brothers, Prince Souvanna Phouma and Prince Souphanouvong, also wanted independence but disagreed over how to get it. Souvana Phouma was willing to accept French promises of limited self-government. Souphanouvong, on the other hand, refused to trust the French. He flew to Hanoi, where he formed an alliance with Ho Chi Minh. Prince Phetsarath and his followers remained in Thailand until the Thai government changed and they were forced to leave.

In 1949, the French seemed to be carrying out their promise of limited autonomy for Laos. In that year the colonial administration formed the French Union. Under this arrangement, Laos and other parts of French Indochina were allowed to manage their own domestic affairs. Laos was even permitted to join the United Nations, and when it did so it was promptly recognized by France, Great Britain, the United States, and Thailand. Laotian foreign affairs, international trade, and important parts of its economy were still managed by France, however.

By the early 1950s, more and more of France's energies in Indochina were being poured into the war against guerrillas in Vietnam. The French had no troops to spare for duty in Laos. Therefore, they decided to organize an army of Laotians which they hoped could resist the growing number of guerrilla attacks in their country. By this gesture, the French demonstrated their inability to remain in the country much longer. In 1954, Laos became a fully independent nation.

The proclamation of independence did not halt the efforts of Prince Souphanouvong. He not only opposed the French, but also the ruling class in Laos. With Ho Chi Minh's help he continued to organize a movement later called the Lao Patriotic Front (Neo Lao Hak Sat, or NLHS). Souphanouvong declared that the NLHS would join with Vietnamese nationalists to fight both the French and Americans and then reform the Laotian economy. In 1953 Souphanouvong led a guerrilla force into the mountains of northern Laos, establishing a new headquarters from which he said the battle would be directed.

Cambodia. Following their policy of shattering Western empires as they withdrew from Southeast Asia, the Japanese encouraged Cambodia to declare independence from France in 1945. Cambodia's ruler, King Sihanouk, pledged himself to keep this independence but was overwhelmed when the French forces returned after the war. While the king dealt with the French, the head of the independent government, Son Ngoc Thanh, led a force of nationalist guerrillas into the north. In a remote jungle headquarters the guerrillas organized Cambodian nationalists into an army called the Khmer Issarak or Khmer Serei ("Free Khmer.")

The French offered Cambodia limited autonomy, and in 1946 the country's electorate—its adult males—selected the members of a Consultative Assembly. The Assembly was charged with the task of drafting Cambodia's first constitution and did so with the help of the French. But the draft constitution was rejected by Cambodian nationalists. They wanted it to provide for a more democratic government. In 1947, the nationalists won control of the National Assembly.

Under an arrangement to which King Sihanouk agreed in 1949, Cambodia joined the French Union. This gave the country the right to control most of its domestic affairs but acknowledged France's right to direct its foreign affairs. Cambodian nationalists refused to accept this agreement. Instead, the militant Khmer Issarak joined the National Front for Indochina in 1951, pledging itself to drive the French from Cambodia. Thus nationalists throughout the Union— including those for Vietnam and Laos as well as Cambodia— organized to fight the French.

King Sihanouk ruled with increasing authority in order to control the mounting resistance against the French. The king assumed the post of prime minister. Recognizing that the independence movement was irresistible, he flew to the major capitals of the West, begging support for the complete independence of his country. But Sihanouk got little support. Thus the stage was set for a political and military struggle that would have far-reaching consequences.

Under the continuing pressure of the independence movement, Sihanouk at last decided that the only way to preserve Cambodia's peace was to break off with the French. The king announced that he would no longer cooperate with France. He joined a small army of Cambodian soldiers who were preparing to fight the French in Siemreab. France was under heavy attack throughout its Indochinese colonies. The French could not defend themselves against any coalition of insurgents led by the Cambodian king. On November 9, 1953, France finally yielded and granted full independence to Cambodia. The Cambodian people credited Sihanouk with this victory. In triumph, Sihanouk returned to his capital, cheered by people along the way as their liberator.

Tonkin, Annam, and Cochin China (*Vietnam*). When they were near defeat in World War II the Japanese replaced the French administration with an "independent" government in Vietnam. This new administration was headed by Bao Dai, former emperor of Annam. Japan expected Bao Dai to organize a Vietnamese force capable of resisting the returning Allies. The Emperor tried, but failed to inspire his people. The Vietnamese were battered by the effects of starvation, warfare, and misrule. They wanted neither the French nor the Japanese in their country. In the north, many Vietnamese rallied around the nationalist leader, Ho Chi Minh. Ho had developed an armed force within the framework of the Vietnam Independence League, or Viet Minh. The Americans helped him to build it, hoping for his support against the Japanese.

Although he was a devoted communist, Ho carefully allowed a wide range of political beliefs to exist within the Viet Minh. He did so for two reasons. First, he knew that he could not impose the will of the communists, who numbered only 5,000, on the population of more than twenty million. Second, he had organized resistance to the Japanese with funds from the ruling Nationalist Party in China. The Chinese arrested Ho for communist activities inside of China in 1942. They released him the following year and gave him funds to organize an anti-Japanese underground in Vietnam. He was 52. Ho's real name was Nguyen Tat Thanh, but he also was called Nguyen Ai Quoc ("Nguyen the Patriot"). After he left China he was called Ho Chi Minh ("He Who Enlightens"). Soon, his new name was known throughout the world.

Ho Chi Minh refused to cooperate with the new government established by Bao Dai. That government squandered Western aid to make its officials comfortable. The intelligent but frivolous Bao Dai was often called the "night club emperor." Ho set up his own

Ho Chi Minh's "National Liberation Army" replaced the retreating Japanese during World War II, and then fought the French in the Indochina War.

government in Tonkin. There, the Japanese were weakest, for they were unable to reach Ho's forces in their jungle headquarters west of Hanoi. Ho emerged from the jungle when the Japanese surrendered. As Ho's officials took over public offices, Bao Dai was forced to acknowledge that Ho was the only Vietnamese capable of establishing a stable government. Bao Dai abdicated, gave the imperial seal to Ho, and offered to become an adviser in the new administration.

On September 2, 1945, Ho declared that the three subdivisions created by the French would be unified as the Democratic Republic of Vietnam. Soon afterward, the Viet Minh formed a "National Liberation Army" (NLA) to defend the country in case the French tried to return. That the French would return became certain after a conference of Allied leaders in Potsdam, Germany, in 1945. The Potsdam Conference agreed that the British would accept the surrender of the Japanese south of the sixteenth parallel and that the Chinese would accept the surrender north of the parallel. Ten days after the British landed, the French arrived, too. French troops quelled rebellious Vietnamese, who believed they had been betrayed by the Allies. After hearing Allied proclamations that all subject people would be given the right to self-determination, the Vietnamese were confident that they would be allowed to form a unified, independent country when the Japanese were defeated. But this confidence was shattered when the British ordered the Japanese to help them subdue the Vietnamese.

North of the sixteenth parallel, the Chinese were inclined to sympathize with the Vietnamese nationalists. The Chinese began to cooperate with Ho Chi Minh after he dissolved the Communist

Party and seemed willing to help Chinese officials run the country. In effect, Ho eliminated his rivals by bribing and flattering the Chinese. However, the Nationalist government of China was secretly negotiating with the French. In exchange for diplomatic benefits the Chinese gave the French the right to land troops in the north.

The French would have landed troops immediately, but they confronted the army of Ho Chi Minh. To overcome Ho's objections to their landing, the French promised Ho they would recognize his Democratic Republic of Vietnam as a "free state" within a new French federation of Vietnamese states. The French also promised to stop the war against the nationalists in the south and to permit a national election in which all Vietnamese would decide whether the country should be reunited.

Ho accepted the assurances of the French. He allowed French troops to land at Haiphong Harbor. Soon afterward this agreement broke down. The French continued the war in the south, excusing their apparent violation of the agreement on grounds that guerrillas had attacked their troops. Then the French claimed that the national elections they had promised could not be held during a period of unrest. Finally, the French announced that Ho's Democratic Republic could not be a completely "free state" but would be subject to ultimate French authority.

Ho Chi Minh flew to Paris and tried to persuade the French to abide by what he believed was a firm agreement. Meetings between the two sides produced no basic change in the French position. The conference in Paris ended in 1946 when the French announced they were setting up a separate Republic of Cochin China. With hopes for a unified country shattered, Ho Chi Minh returned to Vietnam.

The failure of the Paris conference caused the two sides to prepare for war. The French poured troops, tanks, artillery, and automatic weapons into their bases near the cities of Tonkin. Meanwhile, the Viet Minh sought to gain popular support by issuing a constitution that guaranteed personal freedom, including the right to own private property. At the same time the Viet Minh passed laws limiting rents to 25 percent of the annual crop, thus gaining the friendship of more peasants. During this period the communists needed the support of all Vietnamese nationalists and did not insist upon a communist economy.

The war between the French and the Viet Minh—the "Indochina War"—began on November 20, 1946. French customs agents arrested the captain of a Chinese junk and demanded that he pay a harbor tax. Moments later, a Viet Minh vessel intercepted the French ship and arrested its crew. Soon there was shooting throughout the harbor. With a massive display of strength, French ships began to shell Haiphong. Planes later bombed the city, and infantrymen forced the Viet Minh to retreat into the jungle. The French reported 6,000 casualties, mostly Vietnamese civilians, in this first battle of the war. Ho Chi Minh later estimated that the number of dead Vietnamese reached 20,000.

The Viet Minh general, Vo Nguyen Giap, proved to be a master of guerrilla war. The French confidently took over Vietnam's roads and cities but found themselves with no enemy to confront. Their vehicles were useless and subject to ambush in the narrow mountain passes. Their weapons, though technically superior to the Viet Minh's, were useless against vanishing targets. Giap's troops moved through the jungles mostly at night. Lacking trucks, guerrilla troops were supplied by peasants who were individually assigned quotas of supplies to carry over prescheduled distances. Using secret jungle paths, tunnels, and trenches, they carried and hid their food and ammunition. Fighters and supply teams resumed their roles as farmers during the day, blending indistinguishably with the rest of the population.

Under these conditions the French found it impossible to carry out the program they called "pacification"—by which they hoped to control villages and so deny food and manpower to the Viet Minh. The French had been warned by Bao Dai that "even if you were to...reestablish a French administration here, it would no longer be obeyed; each village would be a nest of resistance, every former friend an enemy, and your officials and colonists themselves would ask to depart from this unbreathable atmosphere."

Bao Dai's prediction increasingly came true. In 1949, hoping to draw the support of at least some of the peasants away from Ho Chi Minh, the French recalled Bao Dai from Hong Kong, where he had taken refuge. He became chief of state in Vietnam. Then the French combined the three Vietnamese districts with Laos and Cambodia. The French promised these new Associated States of Indochina meant a new stage of freedom for all three countries. But the French did not relinquish their control. Demoralized, officials under Bao Dai steadily diverted public funds to themselves. The French, meanwhile, were paying a heavy price for the war. None of their defenses, including a costly series of forts, was able to stop the guerrillas from slipping through their lines. French troops slowly were driven southward. Although by 1953 the United States was paying for half of the cost of the war, the other half alone was crippling the French economy.

In 1953 Giap sent troops to help guerrillas in Laos, where he had a supply of food and munitions. The French pursued this force and

The French built a series of forts to block nationalist guerrillas in Vietnam, but they were driven back, besieged, and finally beaten at Dienbienphu.

then took a position in the village of Dienbienphu, about ten miles from the Laotian border on a road junction. In the center of a basin surrounded by hills the French built a fort into which they airlifted troops, tanks, and artillery. Giap ordered a siege of this small French army, which consisted of about 20,000.

Although Giap had twice as many soldiers as the French, he had no more than ten engineers and 24 artillery pieces. In high caves hidden from strafing French pilots, the guerrillas fired down at the entrenched men. Meanwhile the French trusted to their superior equipment and flew in more men and ammunition, hoping that the enemy would run out of men and supplies. But the guerrillas persisted. By March, 1954, it was the French rather than the guerrillas who were unable to carry on. When the fatigued French army became desperate, a brutal ground assault began, and by March 13, 1954, the guerrillas were overrunning the fort. As the remaining French soldiers were forced to begin a long march to Viet Minh prison camps, the world knew that the Battle of Dienbienphu had marked the end of the French Empire in Indochina.

Malaya. The Malayans calmly accepted the Japanese occupation. They were permitted to run their own government, and friction arose only when Japan gave the country's four northern provinces to Thailand in 1943. The Malayans also suffered heavily from Allied bombardments and from Japanese demands for their labor.

During the occupation, Malaya's Chinese minority did not fare as well as the Malayans. Japan had been fighting in China since 1937 and regarded Chinese everywhere as its enemy. Japanese soldiers murdered the Chinese and seized their property. In frantic escapes from their persecutors, the Chinese fled from the cities and took refuge in the high jungles. Many of them became guerrillas. Ultimately this force grew to 6,000 active fighters. These guerrillas were armed and trained by British agents who considered them the only army capable of attacking the Japanese inside of Malaya.

But the British did not find it necessary to invade their former colony because the Japanese surrendered before an invasion could take place. On resuming power, the British sought to restore order but soon found that the Chinese were not willing to give up all of their arms. The military successes of communists inside of China had inspired the Chinese in Malaya to rebel there, too. The British prepared to deal harshly with this rebellion and meanwhile tried to reorganize the government in order to do so.

In a previous chapter we saw that the interior Malay states were governed by Muslim rulers called sultans. The sultans protected their power and generally refused to accept any British intervention in their affairs. After the war, the British persuaded the sultans that a central government was needed for mutual security and development. The British proposed to unite the sultanates with the Straits Settlements (Malacca, Penang, and Singapore). This so-called Malayan Union was briefly declared but never joined by the sultans, who were afraid that the Union would force them to give more political power to the Chinese minority. The sultans formed the United Malays National Organization (UMNO) and pressed the British for a less centralized government.

In 1948 the British relented and returned to a loose agency called

The Japanese assault on Malaya and Singapore brought exceptional hardship there among Chinese, many of whom formed a guerrilla army with communist leaders.

the Federation of Malaya. The Federation governed the country through a British high commissioner who managed the country's international affairs. Meanwhile the sultanates, Penang, and Malacca, created a Federal Legislative Council to administer the rest of the government. Singapore was excluded because of its large Chinese population. The Chinese were not granted citizenship rights in the new Federation. Nor did the sultans lose any authority over the populations they governed.

When the plan for the Federation was announced, Malayan communists declared that it represented a return to colonialism. They began to attack public buildings and communications. Public officials were assassinated, and guerrilla warfare began. Throughout the 1950s, agitators in Singapore tried to drive out the British by organizing strikes and riots. Only full independence would satisfy them, the communists said. The British responded that in the absence of colonial authority the country's Chinese, Indian, and Malay populations would massacre one another. As evidence, the British pointed out that most voters cast ballots along ethnic lines in the 1951 election.

By 1952, there was some progress toward ethnic harmony. In the capital city of Kuala Lumpur, a group of Malays and Chinese joined forces and won an important election. This coalition called itself the "Alliance Party." Four years later, the Alliance Party won the support of a major part of the Indian community and gained 51 of the 52 seats in the Federal Legislative Council.

The British continued their efforts to reduce ethnic tensions by enlisting the various ethnic communities in joint public works. The Alliance Party, however, insisted that it needed no further help to hold the country together. In 1957, therefore, the British granted full independence to the Federation of Malaya, which included the former Straits Settlements of Penang and Malacca and the Malay states of the peninsula. Singapore remained a crown colony, and opposite it on the island of North Borneo Sabah, Sarawak, and the sultanate of Brunei also remained British possessions.

Indonesia. The Japanese overran Indonesia during the first three months of 1942. Divided over which side to support in the war, the Indonesians did not resist. There was little fighting, yet the Indonesians paid a price for their position as a Western colony in Asia. While trying to escape from the oncoming Japanese, the Dutch destroyed many industries and oil refineries. The unguarded Dutch plantations fell into the hands of squatters who had to plant crops on them in order to survive. The Indonesians suffered severe food shortages and were on the verge of starvation throughout the war.

Having long accepted the idea that the Dutch were invincible, the Indonesian nationalists were stunned by the ease with which the Japanese took the islands. At first the Indonesians offered to cooperate with the Japanese, whom they regarded as liberators. The Japanese freed nationalist leaders from Dutch prisons and put Dutch administrators in their place. The Japanese substituted a Malay dialect called Bahasa Indonesia for the Dutch language and allowed the Indonesians to take high positions in the civil service for the first time. The Japanese also created a single nationalist organization called Putera under two Indonesian leaders, Achmed Sukarno and Muhammad Hatta. Putera developed a 120,000-man army called Peta, whose leaders warned the Dutch not to return. Encouraging nationalist hopes, the Japanese promised that Indonesia would soon become independent.

But the Indonesian nationalists soon decided that the Japanese were unlikely to help them. Japanese soldiers did not respect local religious practices or cultures. They drained the economy of food and raw materials and put Indonesians to work on their projects. Indonesians began to form underground movements to resist the Japanese. The most active of these underground movements were dominated by socialists. Indonesian communists formed a separate group. While pretending to be working with the Japanese, Sukarno headed a third underground organization.

By 1945, it was evident that the Japanese were in full retreat. Knowing that the Dutch would try to return in force, the nationalists debated how to deal with them. Some believed that it would be wise to show support for the Allies by attacking the departing Japanese. Sukarno and Hatta wanted to persuade the Japanese to grant them independence before the Dutch returned. To force this issue, a group of students kidnapped Sukarno and Hatta. The students demanded that Sukarno and Hatta make an anti-Japanese gesture and declare independence. But it was too late to take action. On the night of the kidnapping, Indonesia learned that the Japanese had surrendered without granting independence.

Then Sukarno wrote a brief declaration of independence. On August 17, 1945, he read it to a group of Indonesians in front of his house in Djakarta. Japanese soldiers were nearby but did not stop him. In September, 1945, a British army arrived to receive the Japanese surrender. But the British learned that Indonesian nationalists had formed an army to defend their new nation. The Dutch came immediately after the British, and the war for Indonesian independence began. This war was to last five years and ultimately took the lives of thousands of Indonesians, Dutch, and British. In the end, however, independence prevailed.

The Philippines. The United States placed the defense of the Philippines under the command of General Douglas MacArthur in 1935. General MacArthur repeatedly assured the people of the islands that they were secure under the protection of the United States. They were stunned, therefore, when Japanese soldiers came swarming onto their beaches in December, 1941. MacArthur's army contained 90,000 troops, 80 percent of them Filipinos. This army quickly retreated. Although the capital city of Manila was declared an open city, the Japanese bombed and occupied it on January 2, 1942. The defending forces retreated to the nearby peninsula of Bataan, where they were besieged for months. Many Filipinos and Americans died of starvation and disease as well as of bombing.

President Roosevelt ordered MacArthur to leave Bataan for Australia in 1942. Soon afterward the president and vice president of the Philippines, Manuel Quezon and Sergio Osmena, also left and set up government in exile. The departing officials all echoed Mac Arthur's famous promise to the Filipinos : "I shall return!" But behind them an exhausted U.S.-Filipino army of 36,000 surrendered on Bataan during April of 1942. On May 6 another U.S. army, consisting of 11,500 men, surrendered on the island fortress of Corregidor.

The Japanese established a puppet regime in the Philippines under José P. Laurel, a former justice of the Philippine supreme court. Laurel and many other Filipinos had little choice but to cooperate with the Japanese. In the interior, however, guerrillas fought on. While supplying the jungle fighters from the air, the U.S. Air Force continually bombed Japanese positions. Finally, on October 20, 1944, American troops landed at Leyte. There, the U.S.

Attacked first by the Japanese and then by the American fleet, air force, and invasion army, much of the Philippines was devastated during the war.

Navy had decisively routed the Japanese fleet. After retaking the island of Luzon, MacArthur announced on July 5, 1945 that all of the Philippines had been liberated. Tens of thousands of people died during the long years of war. By 1945 the Filipinos were weary, bankrupt, starving, and seemed to lack even the means to survive. They could foresee only bleaker days ahead. Yet under these conditions, the people of the Philippines prepared for independence.

The War in Retrospect

Before World War II a relatively small group of Southeast Asian leaders was urging nationalism upon populations which were more concerned with subsistence than with politics. The war demonstrated the interrelationship between political and economic concerns. Because of the early military successes of the Japanese, Southeast Asians reëvaluated their belief that Western governments could not be overthrown. Large populations became determined to show that they were capable of self-government and could create nations as prosperous as those in the West. By the time the war ended, Southeast Asians were prepared to follow their nationalist leaders into the uncertainties of independence.

Nationalism in Southeast Asia doomed the efforts of colonial countries to return after the war. The former colonies vigorously rejected such compromises as the French Union and the Malay Federation. Militant nationalist leaders were able to accomplish their goals through guerrilla warfare, a technique they had developed while fighting against the Japanese. In Southeast Asia's rugged terrain, a few guerrillas became more than a match for dozens or even hundreds of better equipped soldiers. But many guerrillas, it turned out, were not fighting for nations alone. They wanted to create wholly new societies with wholly new economic systems.

The rise of Marxism. The most effective nationalist leaders studied in Western schools and there sought explanations for colonialism. For the most part, their investigations took place between the two world wars, when all national economies were in the depths of the Great Depression. After the Bolshevik Revolution in 1917, the Soviet Union tried to export communist revolutionary ideas. To the Southeast Asians, the ideas of Karl Marx (1818–83), a German writer who had inspired the Soviet Revolution, offered an attractive alternative to Western capitalism. In one degree or another Achmed Sukarno, Pridi Banomyong, Ho Chi Minh, and others became Marxists. Throughout the struggle for independence all of them pledged to establish "Marxist" governments—dedicated to socialism or communism—after their nations were created.

The plans advanced by these Marxist leaders proposed national economies which were owned and operated by the government. Since all Southeast Asian countries were predominately agricultural, land was to be nationalized. The leaders differed in the amount of individual freedom they were willing to allow people in the nations they were planning. Socialist leaders such as Pridi wanted people to participate directly in government decisions through elections. Communist leaders such as Ho Chi Minh considered political parties divisive and wasteful. Ho expected people to sacrifice individual freedoms in order to rally behind one party and leader who would organize them and respond to their needs.

We will see in later chapters that the application of Marxist ideas alone could not solve the complex technical and social problems in Southeast Asia. Nevertheless, within twenty-five years after the end of World War II there were strong Marxist movements in all Southeast Asian countries. They originally were small but became popular through alliances with growing nationalist forces. These movements ranged from relatively small groups in Thailand and the Philippines to the total communist government in North Vietnam.

Within ten years after World War II, every Western colony in Southeast Asia was able to call itself independent. We have seen that in Burma, Malaya, and the Philippines, independence was granted without a struggle. France granted independence to Laos, Cambodia, and North and South Vietnam only under the pressures of war. During the post-World War II period, other countries were led to participate in the trend toward independence.

The Geneva Conference. Soon after the French defeat in Indochina, Great Britain and the Soviet Union called a conference of nations in Geneva, Switzerland. All of the major powers attended, and so did the governments of most Southeast Asian countries. The purpose of the conference was to stabilize Southeast Asia, where political changes were threatening to cause World War II.

The governments at the conference pledged not to interfere in the internal affairs of Laos, Cambodia, or Vietnam. They said that the people of those countries had the right to vote for the type of government that they wished and set dates on which elections would be held. Until the decision of its electorate was given, Vietnam was split into North and South Vietnam, with a border roughly at the seventeenth parallel.

Thus colonialism ended in Southeast Asia. But the emergence of independent nations did not end the social problems that had been accumulating for centuries. The nature of these problems, the conditions which gave to them, and the way that the new governments sought to manage them is the subject of the second part of *Southeast Asia Emerges.*

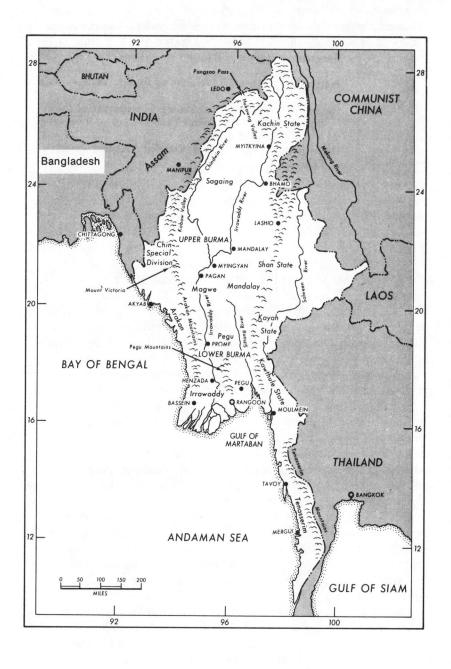

PART II

The Independent Nations

CHAPTER 1

BURMA

A group of Burmese nationalists called the Thakins helped the Japanese to conquer Burma when World War II began in the Pacific. They expected to liberate their country by driving out the British, but soon found they had enabled Japan to dominate Burma. The Thakin leader, Aung San, seemed to be cooperating with the Japanese by becoming defense minister in the occupation government. By the end of the war, however, he was secretly in touch with the British and Americans and was directing an underground movement against the Japanese.

When they had driven out the Japanese, the British tried to rebuild Burma's shattered economy. Meanwhile they promised independence to Burma and authorized an election in which the Burmese could choose to form a sovereign state. Aung San's party, the Anti-Fascist People's Freedom League (AFPFL), won the election and began final negotiations for independence. But while Aung San was developing his program to establish and unite the country, he was assassinated. He died in 1947, less than six months before independence was declared. As bandits, ethnic groups, and rival communists fought one another, the new nation thus began its history in a period of weakness and anarchy.

SOCIAL CONDITIONS AND CULTURAL LIFE

Ethnic groups. The government of Burma recognizes at least 120 ethnic groups, each with its own history and language. The major group, the Burmans, comprise about 72 percent of the 37.6 million people. They originated in Tibet and established themselves in the delta of the Irrawaddy River before 900 A.D.

Like other Southeast Asians who came from Tibet, the Burmans are about 5½ feet or less in height. They have round heads, high

Around the shores of Lake Inle in Burma's Shan State, houses are built on bamboo stilts above the water. Boats provide the main transportation.

cheekbones, brown skin and eyes, and smooth black hair. Their social institutions reflect a cultural heritage in which women are considered inferior to men. Yet Burman women are granted more rights than their counterparts in India or China. They keep their own names in marriage and may return to their parents' home if they are divorced. They are allowed equal inheritance rights with men and usually manage the finances in their families. Kinship in Burma is reckoned through both men and women, a practice which grants Burman women relatively high esteem.

Eighty percent of all Burmans live in villages. Their rural communities are almost always surrounded by bamboo fences to protect them against bandits and wild animals. Beyond these fences lie the fields in the which farmers grow wet rice and other crops by day. By night, the villagers retire behind the fences to houses made of bamboo and wood. The houses are usually raised on stilts to save families from the floods. Normally, a house will contain only a few pieces of furniture and some grass mats for sleeping.

Most villages contain about 500 people and 100 houses. The houses are usually occupied by nuclear families, though some of the larger ones may contain three or four generations of people. As in most Asian families, the father is the focus of authority, but the mother operates the household. The children are called upon to respect their elders but not to revere them. Burman children are allowed almost complete freedom in their early years. They are made to discipline themselves when they are six or seven, after they become students. Remembering the days when they experienced little or no discipline, many Burmans tend to reject efforts to control them as they grow older.

When dealing with each other, Burmans tend to respect accomplishments rather than inherited position. An important sign of this is the lack of family names. Instead of surnames, the Burmans take titles that reveal age, sex, or status when added to their given names. The title "U" is one showing the highest respect for men; "Daw" is its feminine counterpart. Informally, Burmans refer to themselves with the male title "Maung" and the female "Ma."

The Karens are the next largest ethnic group in Burma. With 3.4 million people, they represent about 9 percent of the total population. They are a hill people who during the last century turned to wet-rice farming in the plains of Tenasserim, on the southern coast. The Karens moved from the eastern highlands because of the hostility of the Burmans for them. Early in the nineteenth century, the Karens helped the British conquer the Burmans and later served to police Burma for the colonial government. Now the Karens who live in the plains speak Burmese and experience less friction with Burman culture. A large group of Karens live in Kawthule State, which was created in 1951 to allow them local self-government and separation from the Burmans.

The Shans are the second largest minority in Burma. There are about 2.2 million Shans, or 6 percent of the total population. The Shans are related to the Thais, who came from South China in the thirteenth century. They speak a Thai language but use a Burmese form of writing. Although they live in the highlands, the Shans have highly developed forms of irrigation which enable them to grow wet rice. The Shans lived in 36 princely states before the British arrived. They helped the British during the colonial occupation and so were allowed to keep their small monarchies throughout the colonial period. The Shans preserved their hereditary governments until 1959, when the central Burmese government forced them to break up their large landholdings.

The Arakans are Burma's third largest minority. They include 1.6 million people, or 4 percent of the total population. The Arakan people have lived in the northwestern mountains of Burma at least since the fourth century A.D. They have strong ties with India and Bangladesh, although they have a language and culture resembling the Burman ones. The Burmans have long resented the unwillingness of the Arakans to cooperate with them. During the nineteenth century, the Burmans continually attacked the Arakans. Through fifty years of warfare they reduced the Arakan population from

500,000 to 100,000. It was this massacre which first caused the British to take control of parts of Burma. Since Burma gained independence in 1948, the Arakans have tried to establish an autonomous state but have been rejected by the central government.

Smaller ethnic groups are also influential inside of Burma. There are about 350,000 Mons scattered among the Burmese population. The Mons arrived in Lower Burma centuries ago, probably from India. They were primarily responsible for bringing Buddhism and other aspects of Indian culture to Southeast Asia. Today, most Mons live on the coast of Tenasserim. The smaller ethnic groups in Burma also include the hill tribes. Scattered in many villages which practice slash-and-burn agriculture, the hill tribes grow dry rice in the high mountain areas. They include about 500,000 Chins and 350,000 Kachins.

Finally, Burma includes substantial numbers of Indians and Chinese. Before World War II the Indian population reached one million. About a half million Indians fled when the war broke out. Of those who remained, 400,000 were driven out during the 1960s because the government seized their land or businesses. Before this government action the Chettyars, an Indian sub-caste with a tradition of moneylending, owned about 40 percent of Lower Burma's agricultural land and most of its businesses. Burma has also reacted severely against its Chinese population in recent years. Today its Chinese minority is about 400,000 larger than ever. The Burmans refer to most outsiders with the derisive term, *"kala"* (foreigners), and historically have tended to close their country to outside influences.

Religion. About 80 percent of all Burmese are Theravada Buddhists, although not all practice their religion faithfully. Most Burman homes have shrines for Buddha, and yellow-robed monks can be seen everywhere in the country. Most people practice "duty days," which resemble the Christian Sabbath and are observed four times a month. The spires of pagodas rise above the landscapes in villages and cities. Burma's most famous temple, the golden-spired Shwe Dagon Pagoda, was the monument around which the capital at Rangoon was constructed in 1753.

Theravada Buddhism in Burma has no central monastery, authority, taxing system, or uniform legal code. The people support their religion through charity to the more than 800,000 monks who carry begging bowls through the villages every morning. Many make direct gifts to the pagodas. Most social activities focus on Buddhism, and in the villages they center in the local *wat*, or Buddhist compound which is near every community.

Buddhism was the official state religion until the British arrived. The British disassociated the religion from government and so

Monks pass through
Burmese villages every morning
in search of food.

forced the Buddhist brotherhood, or *sangha,* to seek private contributions. Induced by this action to enter politics, the monks became leaders of the nationalist movement. Immediately after the war they won the full support of the government. The new prime minister, U Nu, wanted to demonstrate to the world that Burma was the center of international Buddhism and in 1954–56 he organized the Sixth Great Buddhist Council in Rangoon. In 1961 U Nu restored Buddhism as the state religion. But as we will see, this move contributed to U Nu's downfall by arousing the anger of the religious minorities. After one year, Buddhism was disassociated from the Burmese government again.

Almost every young Burman man lives for about three months as a novice in a Buddhist monastery. He exchanges his traditional clothing for the saffron-yellow robes worn by the monks, shaves his head, and in a ceremony called the *shinbyu* pledges his commitment to the faith. Buddhist girls have a similar ceremony, called the *natwin,* which involves ear-piercing and often a commitment to a nunnery.

Christianity has a small following in Burma, chiefly among the Karens, about 15 percent of whom were converted by American Baptist missionaries at the end of the nineteenth century. Christianity is still strongly influenced by the ancient practice of animism. Buddhism officially opposes the worship of animist spirits, but some of its literature contains references to them. Similarly, there are overtones of animism in the practices of the Burmese Muslims who live in the Arakan Mountains.

Education, language, and the arts. About 72 percent of Burmese men and 22 percent of Burmese women are literate. The country owes this relatively high rate of literacy to its monasteries. Buddhist monks provided schooling for most of the population until 1963, when the government nationalized education and eliminated both religious and private ethnic schools.

Schools were nationalized for several reasons, the most important of which was the need to build a consciousness of the new Burmese nation. The new public schools also enabled the government to increase its popular support. Following regulations, teachers urged students to repeat political slogans and to dedicate themselves to the success of government policies. Through its new schools, Burma tried to replace the skilled Indians and Chinese whom it had driven out of the country. It designed a uniform national curriculum for the first time, hoping by that means to produce much-needed technical and administrative talent.

The nationalization of schools also enabled the government to use one language, Burman, for the first time. Burman is a tonal language resembling Chinese, with single syllables whose meanings are changed by the tones. In the schools, Burman replaced both English and the many dialects and languages which are spoken and taught by the Buddhist monks. Burman is understood by about 75 percent of the population, while 25 percent speak their own languages. The ethnic minorities resent the spread of Burman speech, but the emphasis on one language has promoted more effective communication in the country than ever before.

In 1966 the government passed the Fundamental Education Act. This measure divided the new school system into primary, middle, and high schools and made education compulsory through the eighth grade. By 1974 the system was enrolling 3.6 million students in its secondary schools and 86,000 in its colleges and universities. No doubt the government has made great strides in the area of education. Still, its progress is difficult for outsiders to measure. Only 2.2 percent of the country's gross national product is budgeted for education. The quality of Burmese teachers declined sharply when foreigners, who did most of the teaching, left the country during the 1960s. There is a shortage of equipment and texts, and new books are often tinged with political ideas. Yet the establishment of the country's first public school system is a monumental achievement.

The government hopes that by controlling the educational system, the press and radio, and thousands of committees, it can make people more politically aware. Everywhere the government stresses the importance of Burma's own traditions, in contrast to those left by the British. Burmese writers and artists have been enlisted in this effort.

Few of the effects of colonialism angered Burmese intellectuals as much as the decline of the arts. Before the British arrived, the court at Mandalay was a vital center for painting, music, dancing, and sculpture. Taking its themes from India, Burma developed its religious architecture into its own unique forms. The heights of Burmese architecture were reached in pagodas which rose everywhere in the country. These structures were made of solid masonry and were richly decorated with Buddhist sculpture. Most of them still exist, but other ancient buildings, made of wood, have decayed. The British banned the use of wood and introduced Roman architecture through their government buildings. When the British ended the monarchy in 1885, they indirectly put an end to Burma's subsidy of the arts.

A cultural revival is taking place today. The Burmese have been particularly skillful in music and the dance, partly because they borrowed highly developed Thai forms of those arts. The Burmese also have their own instruments. One is a set of gongs arranged in a musical scale inside of a circular frame. Another is a series of drums arranged in the same way. Burma's best known form of musical drama is the *anyeint pwe*, in which two male clowns share a stage with one or two female dancers. They often perform for hours before rapt audiences. A similar form is the *zatpwe*, in which stories of the Buddha are dramatized in free outdoor performances. The Burmese also enjoy puppet shows based on the *Ramayana*, the Indian epic that tells the story of Prince Rama, his wife, and their enemies and followers.

In precolonial days, Burma was famous for its brilliant silks, produced both in homes and in industrial centers. Britain's shipment of its own textiles to Burma halted that industry. Today, new centers are being developed for weavers, lacquerware makers, and woodworkers. Once, Burma's wood sculptors filled the country's public buildings with their carvings of birds, flowers, and scrolls. These artists were restricted during the colonial period because of the reduced use of wood. Instead, they turned to the production of carved furniture and other household items. They also worked with copper, gold, and silver, producing sculpture and jewelry that became the admiration of the world.

Throughout the period of the monarchy, Buddhist monks produced almost all of Burma's literature. The Burmese began to write modern novels at the end of the nineteenth century. In 1920 the University of Rangoon was founded, and its faculty helped to encourage translations and the creation of new works. Then writers began to simplify the elaborate works of the religious writers. English literature was regarded as a model. Burmese literature became intensely political before World War II, borrowing most of its radical themes from Western writers. Today, many of its most popular writers are novelists who consider themselves Marxists or communists.

RECENT POLITICAL DEVELOPMENTS

Post-independence. Civil war broke out in Burma within six months after the new nation became independent in January, 1948. Bandits and rival communist groups roamed the countryside, seizing villages. Detachments of fugitive troops from China, defeated by the communists there, moved into the eastern territories occupied by the Shan people. The most serious threat came from the Karen tribesmen in the Irrawaddy Delta. We have seen that under the British the Karens and other minorities were used to police the Burmans. They and other minorities fought for the British against the combined Japanese-nationalist force during the war. Against this background of hostility, it seemed impossible to unite the Burmans and the ethnic minorities in one country. The Karens fought well. By the Spring of 1948 they held most of Burma's rural areas. With their communist allies they set up a headquarters in Mandalay and by 1949 controlled more than half of the rice-belt area.

In 1949, the remnants of the Burmese army were placed under the command of Lieutenant-General Ne Win, one of the "Thirty Comrades" who led the fight for Burma's independence. Through well planned assaults, Ne Win beat back the Karens and communists. In 1951 Ne Win reduced some of the ethnic tensions by offering the Karens a separate state within the Union of Burma. This state, called the Kawthule Special Region, was formed in the Salween District. (It differed from the Karenni State, a part of the Shan Plateau occupied by the Red Karens, who renamed their region the Kayah State to distinguish it from the Karen lands.)

Ne Win's compromise ended most but not all of the fighting. Some of the Karens refused to accept the agreement and fought on. Other minorities also continued guerrilla warfare. One of the largest factions was made up of Muslims who wanted to join the newly organized Muslim state of Pakistan. They occupied an inaccessible part of the Arakan Mountains, in the northwest. Supplied by their fellow Muslims in East Pakistan (now Bangladesh), they fought the Union of Burma until 1961, when they finally surrendered.

General Ne Win urged
socialist policies
in Burma.

Further organizing efforts. Having gained some relief from the civil war, Burma scheduled its first general elections in 1951. The Anti-Fascist People's Freedom League (AFPFL), the nationalist organization that led the country to independence, won a majority of the votes. This strengthened U Nu's tenure as prime minister. But the increasing tensions in Burmese society caused a split to occur within the AFPFL. Burmese socialists were opposed to capitalist trends in the economy and to the country's unwillingness to support North Korea during the Korean War. The socialists withdrew from the AFPFL and formed their own party. Unable to prevent the party's disintregration, U Nu resigned in 1958. U Nu said, however, that his withdrawal was only temporary and that he would run for office again in two years. He suggested that meanwhile a "caretaker" government be formed.

The new government was placed under Ne Win, who mistrusted the parliamentary form under which the country had been operating. Ne Win considered parliamentary government to be an expression of British, rather than Burmese ideals. Sweeping aside the constitution of 1947, he arrested several hundred political opponents and put the army in direct control of the administration. Ne Win quickly produced some impressive results. He reduced crime and improved public services. Ne Win thus remained one of the country's most respected leaders when he returned the government to civilians in 1960, as promised.

A national election was held, and U Nu was chosen again to head the government. U Nu had campaigned on the promise that he would make Buddhism the state religion. This pledge was difficult to keep, though U Nu struggled for a year to carry it out. As he did so, Muslims and Christians increasingly protested his use of public funds for Buddhism. At the same time, violence flared again among the ethnic minorities. As the political and economic situation deteriorated, Ne Win came forward once again, announcing in 1962 that with the support of the army he was returning to power.

Ne Win imprisoned U Nu, but later released him. Then he ended the threat of rebellion by offering separate territories to each of the large ethnic groups which were in rebellion. States were formed in which the Burmans, Shans, Kachins, Karenni (Kayah), Karens, and Chins each could keep their own cultures and religions. The minority regions were linked to the Union of Burma through a house of Parliament, the Chamber of Nationalities. But the real rulers of Burma were seventeen army officers who formed a "Revolutionary Council" under Ne Win. Denouncing colonial methods and capitalism, these officers guided the country toward what they said were "Marxist" goals.

Current conditions. The military was comparatively new in Burma, having been organized just before World War II. Under Ne Win, it became the principal force binding the country together. The military government of Ne Win quickly passed legislation designed to increase the regulation of public health, welfare, education, transportation, and the judicial system. Within two years the government increased the number of hospitals from 500 to 2,000. Progress was made in many areas through the Burma Socialist Program Party (BSPP), organized in 1962. Millions of Burmese became involved in government through the party's lectures, debates, and control of the news media.

Ne Win sought broad public support through the development of a nationwide network of "People's Councils." The Councils were designed to communicate an understanding of his policies to the whole population. The government trained thousands of political agents to make contact with the councils and thus with the public at large. At first these agents attacked Buddhism in the belief that it was diverting the Burmese people from urgent political concerns. They soon found that the Burmese would not readily drop Buddhism, and so they recommended that the government adapt itself to the principles of the country's major religion.

After 1965, Ne Win and other members of the Revolutionary Council introduced many Buddhist ideas into their Marxist program. This blend of ideas was expressed in one of their most important declarations, a pamphlet called "The System of Correlation of Man and His Environment," published in 1963. This pamphlet promised that the Burmese government would enforce economic equality through moderate, fundamentally Buddhist means. In the year that it was issued the government drove 250,000 people out of the country by nationalizing foreign-owned property, however. The Chinese, Indians, and Pakistanis who fled Burma took with them technical and administrative skills badly needed in Burma. They included doctors, teachers, and businessmen who were not easily replaced.

By 1969 the People's Councils involved hundreds of thousands of Burmese. The Councils agreed to increase the emphasis on Burma's own version of Marxism, calling for a "unitary" state rather than a federal one. By this they meant that Burma should work for a new, more thoroughly organized government under a new constitution. The councils' program for achieving the unitary state involved five points: ". . . training and education, solidarity of rural bodies, organized management of the rural economy, a peasant-worker alliance, and the setting up of more regional bodies (councils)."

Ne Win followed these suggestions by summoning the Burma Socialist Program Party into its first congress in 1971. The meeting marked the party's development into a "mass-line" organization. Ne Win suggested that it lead the way to a new Burmese constitution that would "prohibit exploitation of man by man or one national group by another and the guarantee of the birthrights of every citizen."

After holding nationwide meetings, the Burmese people ratified their new constitution and elected their first "People's Congress" in 1972. Two years later, just twelve years after he took power, Ne Win's control over Burma was complete. The People's Councils included more than six million members and were functioning in more than two-thirds of the country's fifteen thousand villages. Ne Win and his associates on the Revolutionary Council, dramatizing the change from military to civilian control, resigned from the army. Basically, however, there was no change at all in the extent of their political power and authority.

When Burma held its first elections in fourteen years, only Ne Win and the members of his Burma Socialist Program Party were permitted to run for office. He was elected President, and his overwhelming victory made it appear that the country was united behind him. Opposition which could not express itself at the polls quickly developed, however, in the streets and in the northern mountains. Through massive demonstrations, workers, students, and Buddhists protested the lack of jobs, rising prices, and repression. Meanwhile in the countryside communists were collecting an army of more than ten thousand guerrillas who harrassed the Burmese army. Finally, in inaccessible areas along the borders with China and India, members of the Shan, Kachin, Naga, and Karen tribes were turning to armed struggle to achieve their goal of self-government.

These problems led to instability in Burma for two decades. There were assassination plots and attempted coups against Ne Win. Within a single two-year period Burma was forced to close its universities four times in order to quiet rebellious students. Widespread groups protested the failure of the economy and corruption among high officials. They forced Ne Win to leave the presidency in 1981. But, as head of the Burma Socialist Program Party, he still controlled the country.

In 1988 further riots caused Ne Win, who at the age of 77 was in poor health, to leave politics entirely. Ending 26 disastrous years in power, he at last acknowledged his failures by suggesting that the country hold a referendum leading to a more democratic political system.

The army, however, refused to accept Ne Win's suggestion. Instead it chose a former general, U Sein Lwin, to be president. Burma's new leader named a cabinet made up almost entirely of army officers, crushing hopes for greater democracy and almost certainly condemning Burma to further social unrest. Students, demanding parliamentary elections, rioted immediately. Many were arrested, but their leaders said they would continue protesting.

ECONOMIC CONDITIONS AND PROBLEMS

Sources of current problems. "Three-quarters of its towns and villages were razed to the ground, and the national income was reduced to half the prewar level," A Burmese leader wrote of his country after World War II. Today, for complex reasons, Burma has still not fully recovered from these effects of the war. Recovery was slow, to a large degree, because Burma's leaders had added political problems to the severe economic ones. Hoping to create a socialist society, they had committed the country to the complete redistribution of wealth while planning for economic expansion. Their proclamation of socialism, issued in 1952 under the name "Pyidawaha" (Happy Land), insisted that Burma, while lacking both skills and capital, could develop an ideal state without any foreign help at all. They called for a Burma "in which our people are better clothed, better housed, in better health, with greater security and leisure— and thus (are) better able to enjoy and pursue the spiritual values that are and will remain our dearest possession." This goal prompted the government to give financial aid to communities that improved themselves. Land nationalization, to be described fully later, also began at this point. Burma announced an Eight-Year Plan for Economic and Social development. But it was able to meet onl a few of its goals, chiefly because it was in the midst of a civil war.

Despite the failure of its first socialist plan, Burma began the intensive nationalization of its economy in 1963. Under Ne Win the government took over banking, foreign and domestic trade, and all of the major industries. By 1968 almost every major business in Burma was under government control. Ne Win seized businesses owned by thousands of Chinese and Indians.

Much of the Burmese resentment against foreigners grew out of the fact that Chinese and Indians had dominated their economy since colonial times. The anger of the Burmese reached a high point in 1967-68 when young Chinese in Burma attacked some of them while showing support for China's Cultural Revolution. Retaliating, many Burmese began stoning and burning Chinese homes and businesses. Only a government declaration of martial law could stop the riots. This incident caused the further exodus of skilled foreigners from Burma.

Trends. Ne Win wanted to inspire a national commitment to socialism and so to overcome capitalist tendencies in Burma. He involved most Burmese in government-sponsored cooperatives for consumption, production, and banking. But the incentives that he offered, including decorations stamped "Model Worker" or "Socialist Worker Hero," were inadequate to increase production. While Ne Win was credited with greatly improving public health, welfare, and education, he was unable to strengthen the economy. By 1974 Burma needed foreign loans to finance his projects.

In the past, Burma's agricultural production helped to carry it through bleak economic times, but now this, too, began to slump. Food supplies barely kept up with the annual rise in population. Ne Win blamed drought and decreasing world prices for rice shortages, but his own policies undoubtedly played a part in creating the country's economic problems.

The failure of agricultural production to meet hopes was ominous for Burma. More than 65 percent of the 12 million people in the labor force were involved in agriculture. A few agricultural products including rice, oilcakes, and teakwood made up more than 80 percent of the total exports. Since industry produced less than 11 percent of the gross national product, any decline in agriculture was significant.

From 1967-69, Burma's rice exports fell to a third of the annual average between 1957-66. Its chief trading partners, Indonesia,

Japan, India, and Sri Lanka, all of which were importing foods, became alarmed. They hoped that Burma would expand its efforts to increase its rice crop. Burma was excellent soil and could plant up to 24 percent of its land, but until recently has used only half that much. Another four million acres could be put into production if there were more capital for irrigation and fertilizer.

Until recently, Ne Win has concentrated on reforming existing land ownership rather than expanding into new areas. His administration continued a government policy of breaking up large parcels of land, limiting them to 25-50 acres per family. In 1963 he encouraged committees of villagers to select the tenants for farms which were owned by absentee landlords. After depriving the landlords of the power to select their own tenants, he seized all of their lands.

In addition to breaking up large land holdings, the government began lending money to the peasants. The peasants were charged 7 percent interest, in contrast to the 48 to 60 percent charged by private moneylenders. But the government soon ran out of money and was forced to turn over at least 75 percent of the loans to the private sources. Many farmers defaulted in their repayment to the government and further crippled this program.

The division of large farms into smaller ones contributed to the food shortage. Eighty-six percent of Burmese peasants live on farms of ten acres or less. The remaining 14 percent owned up to the 50-acre maximum, including 43.5 percent of all the cultivable land. On their small parcels the peasants were unable to grow more food than they need for their own families. Thus although the government relieved peasants of their debts, the insecurity involving tenancy, and of the hazards of a fluctuating market system, the farms produced less.

Through most of the 1970's, Burma's rice production fell. People began to hoard rice, and there was none to export. The worst floods in a century raged across a thousand miles of the Irrawaddy River, sweeping away whole villages. Floodwaters, followed in 1975 by a major earthquake, left hundreds of thousands of Burmans homeless. They spread hunger and disease, forcing the proud, isolated Burmese people to turn to foreign aid as their chief source of support. Inflation became a major problem as the demand for food quickly outstripped the supply.

These disasters came at a time when the Burmese government was beginning to question some of its rigorous socialist policies. Even the most committed Burmese socialists had to admit that only 10 percent of the country's transactions took place in the legal marketplace. The rest were part of the black market. More than 65 percent of goods traded with foreigners was smuggled, depriving

This street scene in Mandalay characterizes much that is Burmese. The boys are Buddhist novices, the old man seeks rice, the girl has flowers.

Burma of an important source of revenue.

In 1975, the Burmese government officially agreed that financial incentives were needed to coax more grain from farmers. By drastically increasing the amount that it paid for rice, it suddenly drew far more grain into the marketplace. At the same time it relaxed controls over the economy. Though natural disasters continued to plague Burma, by 1978 there was not only more rice available, but lower prices as well.

This change in Burma's economic program, accompanied by the gradual withdrawal of Ne Win from government, led to the spread of even more incentives to producers. Production, or at least the delivery of goods which had been produced, increased again. The fourth five-year plan, announced in 1983, indicated that the gross national product would rise by almost 6 percent. The economy was no longer wholly dependent upon foreign loans and aid, but reduced them to a third of the budget. Inflation, meanwhile, was driven down to just 5 percent.

In part, the improvement in Burma's economy is also due to the country's increasing production of raw materials. Rubber and teakwood provide Burma with a large part of its foreign exchange. Forests cover almost half of the country and often include the trees which supply these valuable resources. Though expensive to reach and to harvest, they are providing the country with more and more income. Current production is still no greater than it was before World War II, but it is rising.

Burma also has vast mineral deposits, the export of which has been of key importance to the national economy. Until World War

II minerals accounted for 40 percent of Burma's income from abroad. The country's huge tungsten, tin, and lead deposits had been developed with British capital. The silver, lead, and zinc mines in Burma were among the biggest in the world. Burma also produced large amounts of jade, rubies, and sapphires. But the British were forced to destroy many of the mines as they evacuated Burma during World War II. Some are still not rebuilt, nor is transportation adequate to move ores the long distances from the mines to the mills. Today, Burma's income from the sale of minerals is still below the prewar level.

Similarly, the Burmese are struggling to return oil production to prewar levels. During the 1930s Burma produced from 6 to 6.5 million barrels of oil a year. Many of the wells were destroyed during the war, and production did not reach 6.5 million barrels again until 1970. Lately, Burma's petroleum industry has been making steady progress. Without surrendering its rights, the country, when still under Ne Win, began to allow foreign companies to help explore for oil. Production has been increasing, though slowly.

This progress has a cumulative effect. During the six years ending 1981, per capita income has risen from about $80 a year, the lowest in Southeast Asia, to about $174. During the mid-1970s rice production was exactly half the amount averaged during the years 1934-38, but just a decade later there was surplus rice to sell abroad. An economy which only recently seemed ready to collapse, therefore, now seems capable of surviving and perhaps of advancing.

FOREIGN RELATIONS

Burma's historic tendency to isolate itself has dominated its foreign policy since it gained independence. It has remained neutral in the postwar struggles of the Soviet Union, the United States, and the People's Republic of China. Yet no modern country can be completely aloof from world affairs. In recent years Burma has begun to make increasing outside contacts, especially with Communist China.

After Great Britain withdrew from Burma, the country found itself forming new relationships with Asian states. Soon Communist China, instead of Great Britain, was the most influential foreign power in Burma's region. Burma's border with China is 1,300 miles long and impossible to protect. China has claimed some border regions, stating that Britain added them to Burma illegally in 1886. Was it possible, the Burmese wondered, that China might be planning to annex the dissident minorities inside of Burma in an effort to gain a foothold there?

The Burmese became especially frightened after the People's Republic annexed Tibet in 1950. Soon afterward, it became obvious that China was supplying Burmese communists and the rebellious Naga tribesmen, who demanded autonomy within of the Union of Burma.

The issue of these border lands has made Burma's relationship with its giant neighbor especially complex. On the one hand, China and Burma share a political philosophy and a distrust of more highly developed countries. On the other, both China and Burma must serve the ends of nationalism, defending their territories and seeking to improve their economies.

For twenty years after the Chinese revolution it appeared that the goals of nationhood would triumph over those of cooperation. In one case, war between China and Burma became possible when ten thousand defeated enemies of the Chinese communists took refuge in Burma's northern mountains. The new government of China threatened to pursue this small army until at last it was safely transferred to Taiwan. In another case, China's Cultural Revolution spread to the Chinese minority inside of Burma where, in 1967, young Chinese began violent demonstrations. Burmese police were forced to suppress them, arousing Chinese anger. Hostility between the two countries lasted two years.

After these incidents the Burmese, when still led by Ne Win, sought to appease China. Ne Win made three trips to China during his long rule. He gained increased trade and technical help at a time when the Chinese were still sending support to communist and tribal insurgents in northern Burma. These contradictions in the relationship between the two countries continued into the 1980s.

Burma's relations with its other neighbors have generally been friendly but have been jeopardized at times by its internal policies. When Burma nationalized its businesses in 1963 it forced many Indians to leave. Relations with India were strained. The two countries reduced contacts with one another until the 1970s, when they signed agreements designed to correct the injustices of the nationalization. They have since increased their trade.

There have been other signs that Burma is gradually moving away from its historic policy of isolation. Its improved economy is due in large part to gifts and loans that it sought from other countries. Its international contacts have been increased by trade. Though it pursues a policy of strict neutrality between the major powers it has made some contacts with them. Its relationship with the United States improved substantially in 1982 when, for the first time in sixteen years the U.S. granted Burma economic aid. Burma has accepted loans and technical aid from both the U.S. and the Soviet Union. It seems to have no close ties with either country, though certainly it is more in the Soviet camp than in the American one.

One of Burma's most active relationships in the postwar period has been with Japan. The Japanese paid Burma $340 million, plus loans, as war reparations. Japanese technicians have been sent to help the Burmese build major projects, including a hydroelectric plant and dam. Burma has entered into joint ventures with Japan in order to build fertilizer and auto assembly plants and to explore for oil. More than a third of its imports are purchased in Japan.

THE FUTURE OF BURMA

Burma could become one of Southeast Asia's most productive countries. Its natural resources include large deposits of zinc, lead, silver, and oil, all of which are or will be in worldwide demand. It has many undeveloped hydroelectric sites and with effective irrigation could double the amount of land that it has under cultivation. To date, few of these potential benefits have been realized, however, and Burma has been one of the poorest countries in its region.

The government is often blamed for the country's lagging economy. It has poured its energies into the reorganization of Burma's political and economic life. While doing so it has affected methods of production and distribution which in the past made Burma the leading rice exporter in the world. Burma today has decreasing amounts of rice to export, yet there are many reasons besides government policies for its economic decline. These other reasons include worsening climatic conditions, increasing population, and a shortage of capital and skills.

The acquisition of capital probably is the key to the solution of many other problems in Burma. Only 1 percent of the Irrawaddy Delta is double cropped, for example, because the country lacks irrigation and flood control projects which would enable second crops to be grown. Given the capital, Burma could increase its agricultural output substantially in this one area alone. The lack of capital has severely handicapped the development of Burma's petroleum industry. With more funds the country would do much to overcome the problems caused by intermittant droughts and floods. Even population growth, now at 2.02 percent, in contrast to the world average of 1.7 percent, might grow less rapidly if additional capital made Burma more prosperous. That, at least, has been one of the major effects of prosperity in other countries.

In the past, Burma has been willing to deal with foreign investors only in a limited way. It accepted small loans from Great Britain, the United States, and West Germany and has allowed the Soviet Union and other communist countries to help it build dams and other public works. However, it refused to join the Asian Development Bank, which the United Nations organized in 1966 to help its member states acquire capital. Since gaining independence, Burma has continued its traditional isolation and has used the time to place its government in firm control of the economy.

As they move towards ending the country's isolation, Burma's leaders are showing a new openness in diplomacy. They have promised, for example, that they would attend more international meetings in their region. Although thus far they have refused to join most important regional associations, they are beginning to seek the advice of other national leaders in the solution of their problems. One cause of this new policy on Burma's part is the less belligerent posture that Communist China has taken in world affairs in recent years. Burma is likely to be strongly influenced by China's foreign policy because it lies in the shadow of its powerful neighbor.

Domestically, the Burmese have suffered from an excess of government. Ne Win's policies were intended to distribute goods, labor, and capital more equitably, but they proved to be unrealistic. More than a decade after Ne Win took power the Burmese were being forced to evade his socialist program by illegal means. Shortages of food and clothing, combined with inflation, rendered the "People's Shops" useless. Most Burmese knew that the goods distributed in government facilities were limited. Although the government sold the goods at low prices, the lack of things to sell encouraged smuggling, thievery, and resales at much higher prices. There were many reasons for the shortages: rising population, overregulation of the economy, lack of skilled administrators in business and government, and lack of capital were among them. These problems are certain to continue and to accumulate until Burma develops a government more understanding of its limits.

Like all other peoples in Southeast Asia, the Burmese have been groping for their own solutions to the problems of the post-colonial age. They are plainly committed to some form of socialism and to a government with much greater authority than the parliamentary systems in the West. Their new system can only survive, however, if they recognize that they cannot meet Burma's needs without the help of many other nations.

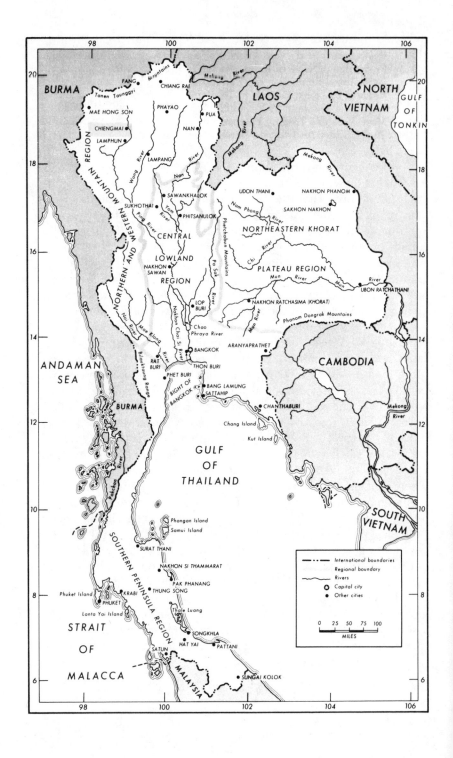

CHAPTER 2

The Independent Nations

THAILAND

Through skillful diplomacy the Thais, alone among Southeast Asian people, preserved their independence of the West. They had a thriving economy and had been trading vigorously with the rest of the world since the middle of the nineteenth century. The Thais cherished their independence but put up little resistance when the Japanese marched into their country at the outset of World War II. Instead, under Japanese pressure they declared war on the Allies and made their valuable supplies of rice, tin, and rubber available to the Japanese. Because they did little fighting they suffered only minor damage during the war.

The United States refused to recognize Thailand's declaration of war because a powerful underground movement was helping the Allies inside of the country. The hero of the underground movement was Pridi Banomyong, a law professor who was the leader of a guerrilla army against the Japanese. Pridi favored a new kind of government for Thailand, one in which the state would own basic industries. Therefore, businessmen and army officers watched apprehensively as he translated his popularity into political victories after the war. As they began their independence, the normally optimistic Thais were sobered by an awareness of the critical problems before them: an unstable political situation, an unusually high birth rate, and an undefined relationship to the other nations of Southeast Asia.

SOCIAL CONDITIONS AND CULTURAL LIFE

Ethnic groups. More than 85 percent of Thailand's 51 million people are ethnic Thais. The Thai people migrated to Southeast Asia from Yünnan, South China, when they came under attacks from the Mongols during the thirteenth century. They absorbed the earlier occupants of their new land. Next, they incorporated Indian ideas

125

into their culture because of their contacts with the Mons, the indianized people who lived in the delta of the Irrawaddy River.

The ethnic Thais are not confined to Thailand. The people of Laos, the country to the north of Thailand, are one of their branches. Another are the Shan people who live in the eastern mountains of Burma. Other Thais are scattered between India and Vietnam. In Thailand, however, they comprise a unified ethnic group who share a common history and culture. They are concentrated in the delta of the Chao Phraya River, where they operate some of Southeast Asia's most productive farms.

Strong central rule is one of Thailand's traditions. For centuries it has been concentrated in a line of kings. The Thai people have an intense love of freedom and individuality, yet respond well to their leaders. These traits enabled them to adapt easily to conditions imposed upon them by the rest of the world. Because of their political and cultural unity the Thais have been able to shape and follow their own independent policies.

The Thais are known everywhere for their optimism and cheerfulness. The country is often called "the land of smiles," although recent social tensions may often cause the smiles to disappear. Most Thais seem to expect things to go well and are inclined to say, *"mai pen rai"* (never mind), if they go wrong.

About 14 percent of Thailand's 51 million people are of Chinese ancestry. The Chinese began large migrations to Thailand during the mid-nineteenth century because of natural disasters and social upheavals in their homeland. They settled in the delta of the Chao Phraya River, where they quickly established monopolies over Thailand's commerce and mining activities. Although their population is relatively small, the Chinese have immense importance in Thailand's economy. The great majority of the Chinese live in cities, particularly Bangkok. Their shops line the streets, and their small mercantile boats are on every river. Most of the tin mining, rubber growing, and teakwood harvesting is in the hands of Thailand's Chinese. They also control the large food processing and distribution industries.

Thailand also has smaller minorities that bring important influences to bear on its society. Near the border with Burma there are about 50,000 Karens, a hill people who speak a Thai dialect. The Karens are mostly farmers who grow dry rice, but they also became famous as soldiers who fought for the British in Burma, where the largest part of their community is based. Thailand also includes about 50,000 Vietnamese, who live along the Mekong River on the eastern border. Many of them came as refugees from wars in Vietnam. In the northern mountains there are some 300,000 members of hill tribes. The most often noted of them is the Meo, a group that the Communist Chinese have been encouraging to seek autonomy. Finally, Thailand has a large minority of Muslim Malays in the south and a much smaller one of Christians. There are almost 1.5 million Malays. They identify themselves with the culture of Malaysia, while the Christians tend to follow European and American traditions.

Religion. About 94 percent of all Thais practice Theravada (Hinayana) Buddhism. Sukothai, the country's first great kingdom, accepted the faith in the thirteenth century. From that time onward, the Thais have had an unbroken commitment to Buddhism. Thailand has about 60,000 monks and more than twice that many temporary monks and novices. Together they comprise the *sangha,* or monkhood.

The sangha maintains itself through charitable contributions and the government support given to the monasteries. Except during a three-month holy season the monks can be seen traveling from village to village, always staying in the local wat, or Buddhist compound. Their yellow robes are seen everywhere. One center of Buddhist life is the city of Chiengmai, about 500 miles north of Bangkok, but every Thai community has its Buddhist pagoda.

Thailand has more than 24,000 monasteries which are the centers of local social activities. The government owns all wat lands in the

Most Thais believe that they accumulate spiritual credit through contributions to monks who pass through communities seeking food each morning.

name of the sangha and subsidizes the monkhood. Thailand's Buddhist hierarchy receives countless private contributions every year, but probably it could not exist without government support. The Thai Ministry of Education maintains a Department of Religious Affairs through which Buddhist properties are administrated and religious materials are created and distributed.

Buddhism's preëminence in Thailand does not eliminate all other religions. About 7 percent of the population practice forms of Indian Brahmanism, Christianity, Confucianism, or animism. Of these religions animism, which predates all others in Southeast Asia, is most often found blended with Buddhism. Thai Buddhists believe that the human being is comprised of a body, a spirit, and a soul. The "spirit" in Thai Buddhism resembles the animist *phi* (spirits) which are thought to reside in all living and inanimate things. According to their concept, the spirit may leave the body when a person is frightened, sick, or overly emotional. It can be persuaded to stay inside the body by gifts or by a person who has magical abilities. Some supernaturally endowed people are regarded as capable of causing foreign spirits to invade bodies and so to cause illness or death. The soul, in contrast to the spirit, is regarded as part of the individual's mind or consciousness.

Other evidence of animism exists in the widespread belief in astrology and in the tributes paid to spirits in most aspects of life. Many homes have miniature dwellings in which people sacrifice food and beg the *chao*, or guardian spirits, for protection, good

There are offerings in the doorways of this miniature house, designed for spirits and placed in a Thai garden.

health, or prosperity. Farmers worship the spirits of the ricefields or the spirits of the weather. There is a mother earth goddess to whom sacrifices are made when the rice seedlings are transplanted. The most respected astrologers in Thailand are the heads of the 4,000 families that are directly descended from India's priestly Brahman (or Brahmin) caste. Each year before the plowing begins Brahmans conduct a mystical ceremony in front of the Thai monarchs and aristocrats.

Thailand's king officially associates himself with Buddhism by setting a model for piety and by appointing the chief of the religious community. This appointee, the Supreme Patriarch, presides over a Supreme Council of Buddhists, which rules a hierarchy similar to the king's civil service.

Education, language, and the arts. Thailand's modern educational system began during the reigns of King Mongkut (1851-68) and his son Chulalongkorn (1868-1910). In 1892 Mongkut opened schools resembling those in England and invited English teachers to work in Thailand. One of these teachers was Anna Leonowens, who instructed the children of the royal family and later wrote the book which became the basis for the popular musical *The King and I.*

The new public school system supplemented an older one offered to the Thai people by their monasteries. Until it was begun the Buddhist monks offered most of the country's formal education, teaching religion, language, and sacred literature, chiefly to the sons of families that could afford education. Almost all Thai boys and many of the girls serve Buddhism for at least a short period in their lives. Thus they were exposed to some education. People who were able to become more deeply educated were among the most respected in the country.

From the days when they monopolized teaching to the present, the Buddhist schools have been financed through both public funds and private contributions. The Ministry of Education supplies them with textbooks and helps to operate the schools at all levels, from the primary ones to two Buddhist colleges in Bangkok. The modern Buddhist schools emphasize language, philosophy, and religion, but they also teach science and mathematics.

Despite the enormous energies poured into both the religious and public school systems, Thailand was slow to spread education among its people. As late as 1950, few Thais had more than three or four years of primary schooling. In 1960 the Thai government required all children under 15 to complete seven years of school. But this law was difficult to enforce. Most children must work and have little time for study. About one-fourth of the students drop out at every grade, and facilities are poor. Relatively few students finish high school.

Today, almost 40 percent of Thailand's 51.7 million people are under 14, and more than 80 percent of this large group attend schools. Chiefly for economic reasons only a fraction go on to high schools or one of the nine universities, however. In 1971 Thailand enrolled 60,000 students in its new Ramkhamhaeng University without examinations, thus tripling the number of its college students. With the help of its Buddhist and public schools Thailand has managed to achieve 84 percent literacy, one of the highest rates in Southeast Asia.

The Chinese minority has its own schools, but the government limits them to four years of education. This restriction was declared after the communist government came to power in China in 1949 and a wave of anti-Chinese feeling swept Thailand. The Chinese are more acceptable in Thailand than in most other Southeast Asian countries, yet for several years during the 1950s the reaction against them was so strong that they were forbidden to teach the Chinese language in upper grades. The government still closely supervises all Chinese institutions.

Schools teach in the Thai language, which government and the press also use. Thai is understood by more than 90 percent of the population. There are regional dialects, but the best known one is used in and around the city of Bangkok. Thai is Southeast Asia's most widespread language, known to millions of people between India and Yünnan, China. Related to Chinese, it chiefly consists in one syllable words whose meanings may be changed completely by one of five tones.

English is the most popular second language and is offered in most schools. The Chinese, as we have seen, must learn Thai if their education goes beyond the fourth grade, but usually they also learn Chinese and perhaps English, too.

Thai art is a blend of ideas from China, India, and Southeast Asia. Its richest period began during the fourteenth century, within a hundred years after the Thai people arrived from China. For 400 years the country produced an outpouring of painting, sculpture, and architecture. Initially, its northern artists recalled and reproduced Chinese pottery and metalwork. Later, the Thais incorporated and expressed concepts of Buddhism learned from the Mons in the south. By the fourteenth century the Thais were producing unique and widely admired forms of art in their kingdom of Ayuthia, but their achievements were largely destroyed by the Burmans in 1767. From that year until the early twentieth century Thai arts suffered a decline.

Chinese and Indian roots are still visible in Thailand's arts. Literature before the nineteenth century was mostly oral and was based on Hindu classics and popular history. In 1802 a famed Chinese novel, *Dream of the Red Chamber*, became the first major prose work printed in Thai. During the twentieth century Western writing increasingly influenced Thai literature.

The Thais adapted Chinese and Indian architecture to their own needs. In Thailand the Indian stupa—a mound commemorating Buddha's death—was developed in its rounded form. Most other buildings were rectangular and often employed the step-like roofs and curving eaves seen in China. Buddhist architects were given full freedom to enrich temple buildings with gold leaf, stained glass, stone mosaics, porcelain, and potteries. They created structures widely noted for their richness of textures and designs. Painting and sculpture reflected Buddhist influences from the thirteenth century onward. They presented images of the Buddha, often in drawings on temple walls and in stucco figures. In recent times Thai architecture has become westernized. Bangkok has attractive parks and luxurious hotels resembling those in the most modern Western cities.

Thai music is based on a seven-note scale that covers the same range as the Western eight-note scale. Therefore it does not resemble Chinese five-tone music, though similar instruments make the two seem related. Until the twentieth century the Thais used counterpoint but no harmony, and they had no written notation.

The Thais have developed one of the world's most intricate arts of the dance. They gained it from the Khmers, who brought it from India.

They repeated about 1,200 anonymously composed pieces, singing them and playing them on flutes, gongs, and an assortment of wind, string, and percussion instruments. The Thais enjoy music. They use it in a popular dance drama called the *khon*, which is based on the Hindu epic, the *Ramayana*, and in shadow plays, folk dance, and festivals. Traveling musicians put on shows from village to village. Many of them specialize in the *like*, a kind of satirical burlesque with music. One of the most colorful musical pageants in Thailand takes place at the end of the Buddhist lent. Royal barges float down the Chao Phraya River while musicians, dancers, and actors perform for the Thai monarchs and throughout the country.

In recent times Thailand has been adopting Western arts into its own styles. Western books, plays, and music are popular among the Thais. At the same time, the country has been trying to preserve its own arts through the University of Fine Arts, the Royal Institute of Thailand, and the Siam Society.

RECENT POLITICAL DEVELOPMENTS

Post-independence. Thailand resumed its independent state when the Japanese withdrew in 1945. There were few debts to pay and no colonial power to resist. Because the Thai underground helped fight the Japanese, the Americans made no demands on the Thais after the war. Great Britain and France took a different view and called on the Thais to make payment for having entered the war. The British demanded that 1.5 million metric tons of rice be shipped from Thai warehouses to Malaya, where people were starving. The French forced the Thais to surrender lands taken from Cambodia during the war. The Soviet Union insisted that Thailand repeal all of its anti-communist laws.

After settling all war claims, the new government was organized by Pridi Banomyong. He directed that a new constitution be written so that the Thais could form their first democratic government. The new basic law, announced in 1946, created a parliament of two houses; the members of the lower house were to be elected by the voters and were to select the members of the upper one. Pridi's supporters won control of both houses in the election that followed. Yet the success of Pridi and his democratically inclined supporters was destined to be short lived.

Within two weeks after he was overwhelmingly elected to parliament and made prime minister, Pridi was in exile. His sudden fall from power took place because the king, Ananda Mahidol, was found murdered in his bed. The entire country assumed that Pridi was responsible for the crime, and he fled under severe attack. The government collapsed, and Thailand was plunged into a period of chaos.

Further organizing efforts. While most Thais were still shocked by the king's assassination and Pridi's departure, a former collaborator of the Japanese took power. His name was Phibul Songgram. He was one of the army officers who had helped Pridi limit the power of the monarchy in 1932. It was Phibul who had declared war on the United States at the request of the Japanese. After the war he was tried as a war criminal, but he was released. Phibul was a field marshal, and most of his political support came from Thailand's army and business community. They regarded Phibul as an effective leader against communism. In addition, he opposed Pridi's plan to increase governmental control over industry.

Phibul seized the government in 1947, declaring that the country was in grave danger of a communist rebellion. After introducing a temporary constitution, he ordered a general election in which he was authorized to stay in office. He was forced immediately to take steps against Pridi's supporters. The army suppressed demonstrators, and may of Phibul's critics were imprisoned.

After stabilizing the country, Phibul gave businesses the right to expand as rapidly as possible, with little government interference. He brought Thailand under a military control that has been almost continuous ever since. In large part his power was based on Thai fears of Communist China. Those fears were aroused when sympathizers of Mao Tse-tung encouraged Muslims and border tribes to rebel in the early 1950s. Many Thais looked upon the large Chinese minority as a potential threat to national security, though Thailand's Communist Party had fewer than 2,000 members. Heeding those fears, in 1952 Phibul banned both the Communist Party and the Central Labor Union, whose 50,000 members were almost all Chinese.

Phibul made these moves after placing Thailand under martial law. He and two fellow army officers controlled the government. They jailed many Chinese and arrested or deported hundreds of their opponents on charges of communist activities. In the northern part of the country they dealt firmly with a guerrilla movement that was growing with the help of the North Vietnamese. The army restricted the activity of the guerrillas, though it failed to eliminate them completely.

Many of Pridi's supporters complained that Phibul was a militarist who cared nothing for the interests of the people. The new king, Bhumibol Aduljadej, appeared to share this view when he ordered the restoration of the civilian-oriented constitution of 1952. Phibul, however, undercut some of the claims made against him by improving schools and public health facilities. He also aligned the country firmly with the West by sending troops to fight alongside the Americans in the Korean War. Under his administration Thailand became a member of the Southeast Asia Treaty Organization (SEATO), which the United States designed to counter the military influence of Communist China.

During his first three years in office Phibul traveled to the United States and England, where he apparently was persuaded to relent in his attacks on his critics. He stopped harassing Chinese and invited more public discussion. He hoped these measures would bring him wider support in the election of 1957. Phibul won that election by the narrowest of margins, however, and according to his opponents would have lost it if he had not resorted to bribery and the intimidation of voters. Weakened by protests after the election, Phibul declared a state of emergency but was unable to keep power. One of the generals with whom he had once shared authority, Sarit Thanarat, replaced him. Phibul fled the country and ultimately settled in the United States.

At length General Sarit was able to lead a new coalition, the National Socialist Party, into power. He installed his deputy, General Thanom Kittikachorn, as prime minister. But the coalition dissolved over the issue of whether or not Thailand should side with the United States in foreign affairs. The U.S. had begun to give Thailand substantial military aid and in 1955 was using Thai bases as part of SEATO.

General Sarit fully supported the alliance with the United States. To enforce his position he became prime minister himself, with Thanom's approval. He arrested political dissenters and made plans to write Thailand's eighth constitution. Sarit continued to suppress government critics, freely detaining suspected communists. His police investigated the Chinese community thoroughly. He soon declared the country well controlled and renewed Thailand's call for foreign investors. But Sarit died in 1963, leaving the country firmly in the hands of the military.

Current conditions. In 1959 the military leaders who controlled Thailand promised the people that a new, democratic constitution would soon be drawn. This document was not delivered until the election campaign of 1969—a full decade late. The very existence of a draft constitution seemed to imply a freer government, but General Thanom, who inherited the government from Sarit, refused to lift the martial law decree by which he held power. His party was reelected in 1969, and he promptly argued that the pressure of communism did not permit his to allow a fully functioning democracy. He gave military officers most of the key jobs in his administration and they, in turn, were backed by or identified with a few wealthy people who controlled the economy. As evidence of a continuing military threat to Thailand he pointed to the incessant attacks by guerrillas in the far north. Thanom ordered the army to redouble its efforts against the guerrillas. At the same time he tried to win general support by providing more government services.

As the 1970s began, it became evident that the United States might soon withdraw its troops and reduce its financial influence in Southeast Asia. While their leaders were considering how to adjust the country to this prospect, the Thais were also forced to regard problems caused by internal dissent, inflation, and falling production. Many Thais began to hoard rice when it was announced in 1972 that the crop had declined by 12 percent from the previous year. The government responded by setting price controls on rice, but this move did not stem the depletion of rice supplies. There were riots at rural mills and among workers in Bangkok.

These events rapidly brought students into the political arena. Previously, students had been aloof from politics, but questions involving the economy and food shortages aroused their concern. They were particularly angered by the fact that Japan was able to buy Thai rice while many Thais were suffering from malnutrition.

Student protests gained new momentum when the issue of government corruption was injected into Thailand's increasingly angry political discussions. Because of the accidental crash of a helicopter in which they were flying, a number of the country's highest officials were found to have been using Thailand's equipment and its best game reserves for their own purposes. This incident led to a student protest at Ramkambaeng University. There, nine students ridiculed the government, charging that it tried to deceive the people with excuses that the helicopter was on a mission of national security.

The helicopter incident flared into one of Thailand's most important issues when the university expelled the students who were critical of the government. Immediately afterward, the students were beaten by thugs who were said to be government agents. Instantly demonstrations broke out in every university in Thailand, forcing the reinstatement of the expelled students. King Bhumibol encouraged all of Thailand's students to keep up the protests, promising that the public would support them if they did.

Soon afterward, the students began their assault on the government again. The chief issue was whether Prime Minister Thanom and his colleagues would permit Thailand to have its long awaited new constitution. At one demonstration more than 400,000 people, students and non-students, marched to the Chitrlada Palace, site of government, to demand one. When the army agreed to produce a constitution within a year most of the demonstrators went home. About 80,000 remained, unwilling to tolerate any further delay. That evening, the encamped demonstrators were attacked by troops using machine guns, tanks, and helicopter gunships. More than a thousand demonstrators were killed or wounded. When King Bhumibol received this news he dismissed Prime Minister Thanom. The army resisted, occupying all radio stations and threatening to renew attacks on the demonstrators. The troops were unable to prevent news of Thanom's ouster from spreading through the press, however. Soon the government fell. Thanom escaped to the United States and Thailand gained its first civilian administration since the end of World War II.

This victory by the students has been called Thailand's "1973 Revolution." It proved how deeply the country's student movement was committed to a struggle against the army officers who had controlled Thailand almost continuously since 1932. The students were pressing for a more neutral policy with respect to the revolutionary movements in neighboring countries. To obtain this objective they demanded that Thailand rely less on financial support from the United States.

The king replaced Thanom with Sanya Thammasak, rector of Thammasat University. Through this appointment of a civilian educator he hoped to appease the students, but military influence was not so easily eliminated from the government. Many high officials were army officers who had been educated in the West. Their power rested on the aid given to the army by the United States, since Thailand could not support its large military establishment alone.

Thus the stage was set for a future collision between students and the military in Thailand. The students were without a leader and were divided over their ultimate political objectives. They feared that Thailand was being steadily isolated in Southeast Asia, but many older Thais began to accuse them of jeopardizing the country's welfare by their demands. While the king remained neutral in order to symbolize national unity, eight political parties arose and competed with one another. During the mid-1970s, this left the army as the most cohesive political force in the country.

Prime Minister Sanya faced some of the most difficult problems in Thailand's history. The rate of inflation in 1974 reached 20 percent—four times greater than the year before. The country's various political factions were unable to agree on the extent to which the electorate should control the government and so could not prepare the new constitution. Meanwhile in the villages, communist insurgents began to step up their attacks and controlled several outlying districts.

Sanya was a former president of the Thai Supreme Court and took the view that Thanom's political prisoners were being deprived of their legal rights. Releasing them, he earned the support of the students and many others who opposed Thanom. Sanya also reorganized the parliament, and while investigating the previous regime learned that Thanom and his colleagues had made personal fortunes while serving in government. These disclosures, combined with programs to stop the bribery of officials and the drug trade, gained a large following for Sanya. On the other hand, he was severely criticized for failing to halt inflation and to draft a new constitution. He resigned in 1974 but was persuaded to return immediately to office by the king and many civilian leaders, including students. The basic problems of his government, however, were as difficult to solve as ever.

Sanya was able to initiate some reforms in land tenure and civil service. However, he urged the country to choose another leader, saying that enduring reforms would be possible only under a government with a popular mandate. In 1975 Thailand took this advice and held what many Thais said was the freest election in the country's history. As evidence of the vigorous dissent in Thailand, 42 political parties sponsored 2,193 candidates for the 269 seats in the National Assembly. No party won a majority, but an Oxford-educated lawyer named Seni Pramoj formed a coalition of minority parties and became prime minister. Seni favored a continuation of Thailand's alliance with the United States but faced a substantial minority in the Assembly, which opposed the Alliance. After only three weeks in office

Thai farmers are among the most productive in Southeast Asia. To sell surplus foods to people in houseboats they created this "floating market."

Seni was forced to resign. He was replaced by his brother. This new leader, Kukit Pramoj, announced that Thailand would follow a neutral policy between the United States, North Vietnam, and Communist China. His new government seemed less stable than many Thais hoped it would be, but most people counted the election as a milestone in Thai history. They knew this was the first time in forty-two years that they could vote for civilians.

Their view proved to be overly optimistic. With almost ten candidates for every seat in the Parliament, Thailand fell into a period of political confusion. The resulting chaos encouraged the military, the best organized group in the country, to crush the young democracy. Army officers charged that communists were seeking to take over the government and used that as a reason to do so themselves.

The military government restored the martial law with which Thailand was long familiar. Police seized thousands of people whom they accused of radical activities. They imposed a curfew, forbade the publication of newspapers, and suspended all rights which had been guaranteed by the constitution. For more than two years leading army officers competed for high positions. They paralyzed the government. Meanwhile communist and Muslim terrorists nagged at the nation's peace, raiding villages and planting bombs in cities in separate efforts to change the direction of the state.

By the 1980s, it appeared that Thailand was under external as well as internal jeopardy. More than half a million Kampucheans (Cambodians) were flooding over the Thai border. They were driven by fear of Vietnamese who demanded the surrender of their former leaders, headed by Pol Pot. While war with Vietnam threatened, Thais were rioting to protest poverty, rising prices, and crime. Many of these problems were brought about by the worst drought in a quarter century, for it had crippled Thailand's ability to produce rice.

In the midst of this turmoil, the government of Thailand came under siege in its own country. The prime minister, General Prem Tinsulanond, had come to power in 1980 during one of the fourteen coups since the establishment of constitutional government in 1932. Terrorists plunged out of crowds repeatedly to hurl bombs or fire pistols at him. Rival officers organized plots to seize his power Yet Prem survived. In 1988, after the longest tenure in office ever achieved by a prime minister, Prem voluntarily resigned. A coalition of five parties replaced him with another military man, a former major general named Chatichai Choonhavan.

ECONOMIC CONDITIONS AND PROBLEMS

Sources of current problems. Thailand's kings controlled the country's trade until the nineteenth century. Reacting to an effort by France to seize their country in 1688, they dealt with China but not with the West. Early in the twentieth century the Thais saw that France was again becoming a threat through its influence in Indochina. To counter this threat the Thais signed a commercial treaty with Great Britain, opening the way to full-scale Western activities in Thailand. A second agreement with Great Britain gave the West the same rights in trade and travel that the Chinese had enjoyed in Thailand for several hundred years. This agreement, the Bowring Treaty of 1855, also granted the British the right of extra-territoriality, under which they could apply their own laws to Britons in Thailand. The Bowring Treaty was to remain in effect for seventy years.

The vast new trade stimulated by Thailand's foreign agreements caused the Thais to begin the intensive development of their economy. Their population was less than six million when the Bowing Treaty was signed, and the only surplus they sold abroad consisted of a little sugar and cotton. The arrival of Western manufactured goods motivated them to expand their ricefields so that they would have products to sell to the West. They developed a rubber industry, and their Chinese community began to mine tin. Rice, rubber, and tin became their main products for export; their tin export business alone grew into the third largest in the world. Teak, and to a lesser extent tobacco and corn also became important crops.

The challenge of the French in Indochina caused the Thais to extend their government into northern lands which they thought the French might try to seize. During the early 1900s they built railways to their farthest borders and put steamships on the many branches of the Chao Phraya River. Thus Thailand ceased its

The water buffalo, originally brought from China, enables the Thais to cultivate their flooded ricefields. This scene is in Thailand's central lowlands.

dependence on small boats and local river transport. It became the only country in Southeast Asia to develop on its own, in response to, rather than under the domination of the West.

The expansion of Thailand's economy made the country one of the world's major rice exporters. Beginning with totals of about 200,000 metric tons in 1870, it was exporting more than 10 million metric tons within a century and up to 13 million metric tons a year by the mid-1970s, ranking second only to the United States.

The country's rice farms are almost all in the hands of the Thais, who prefer agriculture to commerce, industry, and mining. Only 10 percent of the Thai population lives in cities. For this reason Thailand's Chinese-speaking minority has taken control of its businesses and industries. This relatively small community of about 7 million owns and operates Thailand's entire marketing system, from milling to exporting. The 38 million ethnic Thais, meanwhile, not only farm but also supply the products for the substantial handicraft and fishing industries. These markets, too, are dominated by Chinese.

Thailand's major handicrafts include silk and cotton, weaving, pottery-making, and silver-craft. The number of people in these trades is small compared with those growing rice, however. More than 75 percent of the labor force is involved in agriculture, and more than 70 percent of agriculture is dedicated to the production of rice.

Most farming in Thailand is accomplished by hand labor, supplemented by water buffaloes and elephants. A chief reason for the lack of machinery is that almost all of the farms are relatively small. This condition developed because of historical patterns of land ownership. Before the nineteenth century the king owned all of the country's land, allotting it in grants of 10 to 4,400 acres to whoever could make it produce. The size of the king's grants depended on the recipient's occupation and social status. During the nineteenth century social pressures ended slavery and bonded indebtedness, and economic ones forced the largest landowners to give up their holdings. This left the country with small, self-reliant farmers and only a few large ones. Small farms were further subdivided because Thai families tend to will their land equally to all of their children, male and female, when they die.

Thailand packs 51 million people into an area of 198,500 square miles. Thus it has twenty times the population of Oregon with only twice Oregon's land. There are 230 Thais per square mile. To its present enormous density it is adding even more, as much as 2.3 percent a year. At that rate the number of Thais may double within thirty-one years.

This rising population has especially affected farmers. Some 96 percent of them are deeply in debt. Most own a little land but also have to work as tenants on other people's land in order to bring enough food back to their families. As tenant farmers they are charged up to half of whatever they can grow, and to this staggering burden they must add the costs of buying tools, seeds, and animals for their labors. Most of them have to borrow at high rates of interest in order to pay expenses.

Trends. The government has tried to shape a more balanced economy through five-year plans. Under these plans it has made substantial progress by extending grants and loans to investors. Often its capital for these loans has taken the form of credits from the U.S., the U.N., a few of its wealthier neighbors, or public and private investors. By using the money to create a more skillful population Thailand has managed to diversify its economy more than ever. The auto assembly, textile, and drug industries are stronger now. When Thailand was an ally of the U.S. during the Vietnam War it greatly increased its cash reserves. All of these factors have served to make Thailand an economic leader in its region.

Yet this progress cannot obscure the essential fact that rice remains the major source of its income. There are major problems associated with Thailand's rice production. Only about 24 percent of its 127 million acres can be cultivated. Much of this land is in the delta of the Chao Phraya River, which has a fine alluvial soil but less than forty-one inches of rain a year. That's only two-thirds the amount needed for the successful growing of wet rice.

The Thais have been able to achieve astonishing production in their delta because of their management of the waters of the often raging Chao Phraya River. Almost 60 percent of the rice and 75 percent of the exports are produced in the delta because of dikes and dams which at least partly confine the floods. Vast irrigation and reclamation projects are under way. Not even they have been enough, however. The annual flooding still limits lowland farmers to one crop of rice a year.

Outside of the delta more than half of the land is forested or can only be used for grazing. In 1970 the government announced that to keep pace with population growth it would have to increase the total amount of land under cultivation by 12 million acres by 1990. It reached half of this goal within five years of its estimate and almost all of the rest soon after. The new acreage is being used to produce rubber and corn as well as rice.

Much more land is needed. The further expansion of agriculture is essential if Thailand is to gain the economic stability it needs.

FOREIGN RELATIONS

During the colonial period Thailand was the only independent country in Southeast Asia. It was able to resist colonization by refusing to allow any single Western power to control its economy. After a long period of isolation during the seventeenth century it treated all Western countries equally, giving no one of them any commercial advantages. Independent and cohesive, it kept a strong military force which enabled it to serve as a buffer between colonies of Great Britain and France.

Since World War II, Thailand has increasingly been forced to take sides between the East and the West. China became threatening to the Thais when it revealed in 1953 that it was setting up a Thai Autonomous People's Republic in Yunnan, just over the border. It suggested that Thailand be replaced by a "People's Republic of Ayuthia" which would include the former region of Siam, Burma's Shan State, Laos, and Yunnan.

Thailand responded to China's proposal with characteristic independence, by aligning itself more completely with the United States. Its friendship with the U.S. began in 1950, when the Americans were trying to confine Communist China. In 1954 Thailand joined the Southeast Asia Treaty Organization (SEATO), which the U.S. had organized. It took a vigorous role in SEATO and sent troops to fight in to fight beside Americans in Korea, South Vietnam, and Cambodia.

Much of Thailand's foreign policy has been shaped by its relationship with the United States. From bases in Thailand, the Americans sent bombers across Southeast Asia during the Vietnam War. The U.S. Central Intelligence Agency used Thailand as headquarters for its activities in Southeast Asia.

The trend of this relationship changed abruptly when the U.S. withdrew its troops from South Vietnam in 1973. Under pressure from students who opposed military expenditures, the Thai government retreated from its alliance with the United States. In 1975 it renounced the alliance, and American troops left the country soon afterward. Only a policy of this kind, the Thais thought, could placate their powerful communist neighbors.

But neutralism proved impossible because Southeast Asia's immense strategic value brought new forces into play. China and the Soviet Union began to complete for influence in the region. The Vietnamese, supported by Soviet arms and advisers, invaded Kampuchea (Cambodia) in a move which aroused the anger of Communist China. The Vietnamese were determined to install a puppet government in Kampuchea. To that end they drove troops supporting the former government across the border into Thailand. More than a half million refugees, pursued by the Vietnamese army, fled into the mountains of eastern Thailand and begged for help. The Thais tried to feed and protect them but found their resources and patience strained when the Vietnamese continued their attacks.

This situation presented a military as well as an economic problem. The proud Thais quickly rose to drive out the invading Vietnamese. The struggle was limited to areas near the border, but it threatened to widen. For centuries Thailand and Vietnam competed to control Kampuchea (Cambodia). At last, in recent years, Kampuchea took a neutral stance and served as a buffer between the two hostile states, but that neutrality ended during the Vietnam War. Now, according to the Thais, Vietnam wants not only to control Kampuchea but to annex it. If that proves true, war between Thailand and Vietnam may be only a matter of time.

The activity of Vietnam and the Soviet Union in Kampuchea has increased the desire of the U.S. to support Thailand. For the same reason Chinese seem willing to offer help. Thailand, a member of the Association of Southeast Asian Nations (ASEAN), has also gained at least moral support from other members of that group, which also includes Malaysia, the Philippines, Indonesia, Brunei, and Singapore, as well as Thailand.

THE FUTURE OF THAILAND

Thailand is committed to private enterprise in a part of the world that has been powerfully affected by communism. The Thais, cohesive and independent, have refused to yield to the wave of instability around them. This is mostly due to the fact that theirs was never a Western colony and was not seriously damaged during World War II. When the war ended they had no reason to react emotionally to the West and so gained maximum benefits from a relatively strong economy.

Thailand needs great strength to keep its independence among countries so strongly opposed to its views. To some extent this strength has been blunted by its own military governments. The Thai people have never had a chance to work out their own problems, but have had solutions imposed on them by governments organized to defend the state. Under such conditions people tend to be less loyal than they would be to a country that allows them freedom. But Thailand has never been democratic. Lacking a tradition of peaceful dissent, it has long been government by its military. Probably the army will remain the most potent political force as long as enemies are at the borders.

Every year the government imports substantial amounts of farm machinery and fertilizer to raise production. The amount of food produced is increasing, but commerce and industry are growing faster. In the 1960s, agriculture made up 40 percent of the gross national income, but it has been slipping steadily and now may be no more than 25 percent.

By contrast to the 75 percent of Thailand's labor force which is in agriculture, commerce and industry employ only 18 percent. This much smaller number, however, contributes up to half of the gross national product. This suggests that enormous wealth is being concentrated in the hands of a few. Luxurious new buildings are rising in Thailand's cities. Expensive cars fill the streets, and a tide of consumer goods is available in urban markets.

The explosion of prosperity may be dangerous because as little as 5 to 10 percent of the population now controls up to half of the country's capital. The gross national product has been increasing by as much as 6 percent a year, but farmers are less well off than ever before while merchants and financiers are prospering. Total economic gains seem not well enough distributed to meet the needs of the growing population. The trade deficit has been reached record highs, presenting a grave threat to the whole economy.

Bangkok's main downtown avenue is broad, well lit, and lined with modern apartment buildings and shops. Not far away, however, there are slums.

These problems are magnified by population increases. The number of Thais tripled between 1855 and 1941 and redoubled within the thirty-five years after that. During the last ten years along it increased by another 25 percent. The 1.8 percent by which Thailand is now growing is well above the world average of 1.7 percent and may prove dangerous.

Internal conflicts have not prevented the Thai government from working effectively to help the economy keep pace with population growth. It has been developing new land and industry. Periodically it has planned for more daring projects, such as the construction of a canal to encourage trade across the narrow Kra Peninsula in the south. Its main port, Bangkok, is seventeen miles from the ocean. Bangkok must be further developed to accommodate the increased trade which the country must have to remain independent.

All of Thailand's activity must be accomplished with the knowledge that the nation lies in a dangerous part of the world. Restless enemies are at its gates. In every Southeast Asian country ethnic minorities are seeking to break away from existing governments. Along with communist guerrillas, they have used terrorism to gain their ends.

The Thais have kept their independence and the integrity of their country by refusing to accept fashionable political trends. Their government has changed only slightly while all of governments around them have been overthrown. Whether or not they can keep resisting trends will depend not only on their own courage and unity, but on the economic and political support of other countries.

PEOPLE'S REPUBLIC OF CHINA

102

106

22

Mekong River

Phong Saly

PHONG SALY

NORTH VIETNAM

BURMA

Muong Luong
Nam Tha

HOUA KHONG

LUANG PRABANG

Samneva

HOUA PHAN
(Sam Neua)

Mekong River

SAYABOURY

Luang
Prabang

XIENG KHOUANG

Sayaboury

Xieng Khouang

GULF
OF
TONKIN

VIENTIANE

BORIKHANE

Paksane

18

Vientiane

KHAMMOUANE

Mekong River

THAILAND

Khammouane
(Thakhek)

Demarcation line

PEOPLE'S REPUBLIC OF CHINA

BURMA

N. VIETNAM

LAOS

HANOI

THAILAND

S. VIETNAM

KHMER REP.

SAVANNAKHET

Savannakhet

VAPIKHAMTHONG

SARAVANE

Saravane

SOUTH
VIETNAM

Khong Sedone

Pakse

SEDONE

ATTOPEU

Attopeu

Chompassak

0   25   50   75 100
          MILES

CHAMPASSAK

SITHANDONE

KHMER REPUBLIC
(Cambodia)

Khong

14

102

106

CHAPTER 3

The Independent Nations

LAOS

When World War II began Laos consisted of the four landlocked kingdoms of Luang Prabang, Vientiane, Xieng Khouang, and Champassak. These kingdoms were governed as an administrative subdivision of French Indochina. After the defeat of France by Germany, the Japanese moved into key parts of French Indochina, but they allowed French administrators to remain there. Later they persuaded the French to merge the four kingdoms into one colony called Laos. As the Japanese were retreating in 1945, they encouraged Laos to declare independence of the French.

The French returned to Laos as World War II was ending and demanded the right to restore their colonial rule. A few wealthier Laotians welcomed them, but a nationalist named Prince Phetsarath wanted to liberate Laos. Phetsarath had two half brothers who shared his leadership of the Laotian nationalist army. One, Prince Souvanna Phouma, gave up resistance. Souvanna Phouma accepted leadership of "neutralist" Laotians when the French offered Laos limited independence in 1951. Phetsarath's second half-brother, Prince Souphanouvong, pledged to gain the complete independence and reform of his country. His attacks, opened with the help of North Vietnamese guerrillas, weakened the French. In 1953 the French lost a decisive battle to the Vietnamese nationalists. After this battle they agreed at the Geneva Convention of 1954 to grant complete independence to Laos, as well as to Vietnam and Cambodia. But although it became independent, Laos did not gain the reform that Souphanouvong and his Vietnamese allies wanted. For this reason, the guerrillas fought on.

SOCIAL CONDITIONS AND CULTURAL LIFE

Ethnic groups. The name "Laotian" is given to 60 ethnic groups who share the nation of Laos. The Laotians all belong to the family of Thai-speaking people who were driven out of South China by the Mongols during the thirteenth century. The ethnic Lao live along the Mekong River and its tributaries and so are called the Lao Lum, or Valley Lao. The Lao Thai occupy the foothills. The Lao Theung, or Mountainside Lao, live in higher altitudes and speak a Mon-Khmer dialect. They are sometimes called by the derisive name "*kha*," meaning slave.

There are many tribes in the highest regions. They are called the Lao Sung, or Mountaintop Lao. Their largest group is called the Meo. Other mountain-dwelling groups speak Tibeto-Burman languages. Moreover, in the cities there are many French, Thai, Vietnamese, and Chinese. They represent less than five percent of the population but exert a much greater influence than that number suggests because they dominate commerce and industry.

Religion. The Laotian people have been Theravada Buddhists since the fourteenth century, when their king was given a sacred sculpture called the Prabang Buddha by his father-in-law, ruler of the Khmer. The sculpture came from Ceylon (now Sri Lanka), traditional storehouse of Theravada Buddhist relics. Buddhism spread slowly in Laos. By the sixteenth century it was the most powerful religious movement in Vientiane, the kingdom to the south of Luang Prabang, as well as in Luang Prabang itself.

Today, Buddhism plays an important role in the lives of all Southeast Asians. It especially affects Laotians because they are the least urbanized people in their region. Theravada Buddhism is Laos' official religion and is practiced by almost all the ethnic Lao, who

Laotian village life centers on Buddhism.

comprise about half of the population. Under a 1947 constitution the government closely supervises Buddhism, and the king himself is the religion's "Supreme Protector." He appoints the head of the faith, subject to formal regulations and the approval of its leaders. Since 1959 the government's Ministry of Religious Affairs has controlled most of its important activities, including its building projects and finances.

Buddhism occasionally has become political when repressed, as it did in South Vietnam and Burma. In Laos the monkhood, or *sangha*, has been given no cause to involve itself in political affairs. The monks, or bonzes, are pledged to lives of detachment. By their own decision they deny themselves worldly pleasures and may not even offer spiritual advice unless they are asked to give it. They have no formal church or taxing mechanism. Their survival depends entirely upon the charity of their followers and the support of the state. Rising at 5 a.m. every day, almost all of the members of the sangha circulate through the cities and villages with begging bowls. Before noon they return to the local *wat*, or Buddhist compound, to eat, pray, study, meditate, teach, or perform a few simple chores. A survey in 1970 indicated that Laos had 1,833 wats and 4,316 bonzes, with perhaps 10,000 novices. Males over 20 may join the sangha or leave it at will, and all Laotian Buddhists are expected to do so for at least a short time. Laotian women may become Buddhist nuns.

Animism in Laos, which predates Buddhism there, holds that spirits, or phi, exist with special force in the "primary elements" of earth, air, fire, and water. Even Buddhism accepts this belief in Laos and includes references to phi in its scriptures. Former monks and village elders are said to know how to quiet angry spirits. Almost every home, Buddhist or not, has an altar in which sacrifices

The Luang is the principal Buddhist complex (*wat*) in Vientiane.

may be placed for the spirits. Buddhist wats have spirit altars in the form of miniature houses on stilts. Each miniature house is said to contain the spirit of the founder of the wat, and its keeper visits it regularly to inform this phi of important changes in the community of Buddhists.

The human spirit is thought to be another aspect of phi worship. Many Laotians think that it is made up of 32 parts, twenty of which are inherited from the father and twelve from the mother. The loss of one part may cause sickness and the loss of all of them are thought to cause death. When the body dies the parts, or *kwan*, reassemble with other free-floating kwan in another body. Thus Laotians express their version of the ancient Hindu concept of transmigration.

Among the 45 percent of Laotians who live above the foothills, phi worship is universal. Some of the Lao Theung, who live just above the Valley Lao, are Buddhist, but their faith is mingled with spirit worship. Laotian communists discourage the practice of Buddhism and animism in the provinces under their control. They have not been able to destroy either faith, however, and even the communists have been forced to suggest that their political doctrine is in harmony with the religions.

Education, language, and the arts. The rugged, often impenetrable terrain in Laos isolates many ethnic groups and prevents the

Laotians used this cave as a medical school in wartime.

development of a uniform national culture. There is a national school system, but guerrilla warfare and the lack of funds has hampered its development. Schools were part of the monasteries until 1947 and were slow to develop under government control. Today there are only 204,000 primary and secondary and 542 college students among a population of 3.6 million.

Lao Tai is the official language in Laos, but many administrators and members of the elite prefer French. Lao Tai is used in government documents, schools, and the press but is barely known by the non-Lao speaking people who make up 45 percent of the population. Moreover, different groups of ethnic Lao change the number of tones that give the language's words their meaning. There are at least sixty dialects in addition to separate languages of the Mon-Khmer, Tibeto-Burman, and Miao-Yao families. Besides, foreign-born tradesmen still often speak their ancestral Chinese, Vietnamese, or French, and students who learn Lao Tai in schools may often live among families where another language is spoken.

The arts and architecture in Laos express a unique culture, yet have their origins in India. The songs, poetry, and dance that are so important in Laotian life usually describe scenes from the Hindu epics, the *Ramayana, Mahabharata,* and *Panchatantra* ("Beast Fables"), rather than local tales. Laotian literature has been preserved mostly by word of mouth. Printing equipment has been limited, and books have been produced chiefly by monks who used religious themes.

Buddhist works in Laos drew inspiration from the *Tripitaka* ("Three Baskets"), the repository of Theravada Buddhist scriptures in Ceylon (Sri Lanka). Many of them are renderings of Hindu tales, and all Laotians know the *Jatakam,* a collection of 550 stories describing the lives of Siddhartha Gautama before he became the Buddha, or Enlightened One.

Many of the finest works of Laotian architecture have been lost because they were constructed of temporary materials. Its plaster and wooden temples have often decayed or been destroyed by plants, molds, and insects that thrive in the tropical climate. Laotians have been especially effective in wood sculpture, but much of their carving has been on funeral pyres which are burned. Laotian sculptors also make fine jewelry or silver and gold.

French archaeologists contributed to the preservation of Laotian culture and often traced and restored the country's ancient wats. The efforts of French scholars revealed how deeply Laotian arts are indebted to the Khmer culture, which in turn borrowed from India. Roofs of the wats in ancient Laos were turned upward in the style of Chiengmai, a Siamese kingdom that was once held by Lao Thai people. Archaeologists found magnificently carved wood in Laotian

temple doors and interiors. The doors showed humans against backgrounds of elaborately carved jungle scenes. Until the Thais invaded
the Lao Thai kingdoms and destroyed their arts in 1826, Laotian
artists were creating Buddhas in wood, brick, bronze, and stone.
The images resemble those found in early Khmer monuments. A
unique feature is that many show standing figures, in contrast to the
sitting Buddhas rendered in most other Asian countries.

Music is an important part of Laotian life, yet the country has no
written musical notation. Musicians perform from memory, or they
improvise. The favorite instrument is the *khene*, a series of four to
sixteen flutes that produce a blend of sounds. Laotians also have
adaptions of the viola, xylophone, and cymbal. They play in sym-
phonies or for a type of folk dance called the *lamvong*. Musical
groups travel from village to village, performing operas drawn from
the *Ramayana*, *Mahabharata*, or Laotian folk tales. In the communist controlled areas musical performances are used to communicate political ideas.

Recent Political Developments

Post-independence. The nations which were parties to the
Geneva Conference of 1954 agreed to allow Laos, North and South
Vietnam, and Cambodia work out their own destinies. The war in
Laos, they decided, could best be resolved if a coalition government
were formed to represent both sides in the dispute. A coalition
government was formed and placed under the leadership of Prince
Souvanna Phouma, the neutralist whose political position was half-
way between those of the French and his half-brother, Prince Souphanouvong. The new government included Souphanouvong, leader
of the guerrilla army in the north, and members of the Royal Lao
Government (RLG). As we will see, Prince Souphanouvong wanted
a communist society in Laos and was closely allied with the communists in North Vietnam.

In proposing the coalition government, the nations at Geneva
hoped that neither the RLG nor the Laotian communists would
gain sufficient political power to overwhelm the other side. Peace
could be maintained only if there were a balance of power. But one
of the two sides was politically overwhelmed in 1958. In the
national election that had been scheduled by the Geneva
Conference, Laotian voters gave 13 of the 21 contested seats to the
communist faction. The United States promptly withdrew its
financial aid to the new communist-dominated government. Therefore, the coalition government of Prince Souvanna Phouma fell.

Laos had carefully fulfilled the goals set out for it by the members
of the Geneva Conference. It had developed a coalition government

and held a national election, yet again faced the threat of war. The contest in Laos took a new form and no longer involved a foreign power fighting local interests. Rather, it involved a struggle between the rulers of Laos and an army of guerrillas led by Souphanouvong, the "Red Prince."

Under the French, political power in Laos was held almost entirely by twenty families whose members held most major public offices. These families held estates in four of the sixteen provinces—Luang Prabang, Champassak, Xieng Khouang, and Vientiane. Many of them owed their wealth to their ability to do business under the French. The ruling families tended to favor cooperation with the West. Immediately after World War II, they led the effort to restore the French Empire in Laos. After the French left Indochina in 1954, the same families won the support of the United States in the fight against the anti-government guerrillas.

To oppose the Royal Laotian Government, Prince Souphanouvong established a government-in-exile in North Vietnam. Later he transferred his headquarters to the jungles of northern Laos. Souphanouvong's government, called the Pathet Lao ("State of Laos"), represented itself as a reform movement in this early statement of its program:

> *Internal policy: (1) Widen the circle of unity throughout the country to include those of all races and religions, of both sexes and all ages, to defeat the French imperialists and their puppet governments and make the country independent, free, and strong. (2) Open the opportunity for people of all tribal groups to the right of liberty and democracy for all. (3) Eliminate illiteracy which makes men deaf and blind. (4) Develop handicrafts and commerce. (5) Sweep out the backward colonial rule. (6) Get rid of gambling and drunkenness. (7) Develop guerrilla forces into regional forces, and further develop into a national army.*

Further organizing efforts. When the government of Souvanna Phouma collapsed, the ruling families of Laos installed an army officer named Phoumi Nosavan at the head of the country. Phoumi had strong U.S. support. Some Laotians said that the U.S. Central Intelligence Agency (CIA) had engineered his rise to power. Far from neutral, he imprisoned Prince Souphanouvong and other rebel leaders for almost a year. Then Souphanouvong and his associates escaped with the help of their guards. They rejoined their army in the northeast and in 1959 resumed their guerrilla attacks on the RLG.

Neither side made much headway at first. Then the balance was abruptly tipped by a young paratrooper named Kong Le. Demanding peace and neutrality, in 1960 Kong Le and his followers seized the administrative capital of Vientiane and urged the government to restore Souvanna Phouma to power. But Phoumi ordered the army to attack these neutralists. Enraged, Kong Le led his troops over to the side of Prince Souphanouvong. Together, the neutralists and insurgent armies were able to win control of almost half of the country. They confronted a growing Royal Lao Army which was led by Phoumi and supplied by the United States.

A massive new war seemed inevitable. To avert it, Great Britain and the Soviet Union summoned a second Geneva Conference to consider the problem of Laos alone. Fourteen countries attended the conference, which was held in 1961-62. At length the leaders of the Royal Government, the insurgent and the neutralist forces agreed to restore the balance gained after the first Geneva Conference. Souvanna Phouma became prime minister, and Phoumi and Souphanouvong became his deputies. But this system of "tripartism" also failed because most of Kong Le's neutralist troops refused to accept it and joined the Pathet Lao troops. The government collapsed and the war was resumed.

By 1964 it was apparent that the Pathet Lao troops were becoming increasingly successful. They took over the strategic Plain of Jars in the northeast and dislodged the remnants of Kong Le's troops there. Frightened by its losses, the Royal Government called on the United States to give it more help. Soon American planes were flying over Pathet Lao territory. The United States announced that its Strategic Air Command was conducting reconaissance flights over Laos. Later Congress learned that the American flights were for the purpose of bombing.

The American flights involved more than 50,000 airmen stationed in South Vietnam, Thailand, Guam, and on aircraft carriers. President Nixon's administration found it politically difficult to commit ground troops to Laos because of domestic resistance to the spread of the Vietnam War. Instead of sending ground troops, he ordered the massive bombing of insurgent positions in 50,000 square miles of land. Jets roared day and night over Laos. They dropped heavy explosives, napalm, anti-personnel explosives, and delayed action bombs. U.S. planes flew at least 300 flights a day over northern Laos and almost 1,200 a day over Pathet Lao territory in the southeast.

The American bombs often fell near villages. Some apparently were intended to destroy the rebels' ability to obtain food. The air war created an estimated 500,000 refugees—about one-sixth of the total population of Laos. At one point more than 375,000 refugees crowded into a single province. Homeless and without food, they

Communist guerrillas held regular "study sessions" in the jungles to achieve unanimity before going into combat. They used Mao Tse-tung's writing.

swarmed into refugee camps. The Americans tried to finance these camps, but the U.S. budget for Laotian refugees totalled only $17 million in 1971. This sum was wholly inadequate for the need. If a similar disaster struck the United States, more than 38 million Americans would be wandering through the country. Seeking food and shelter. And if a proportionate amount of money were spent on them, only a few could be fed.

The U.S. Central Intelligence Agency conducted a separate part of the American war effort. It established two private companies, Air America and Continental Air Services. These airlines supplied food and munitions to the Royal Laotian Army while not seeming to involve the United States openly in the war. Under a second part of its plan, the CIA organized an anti-guerrilla army of the Meo tribesmen who had been displaced by Pathet Lao troops. The undercover agents called this force the *Armée Clandestine* (Secret Army). The manpower of this secret army was supplemented by Cambodians, Vietnamese, Chinese, and Laotians whom the CIA hired for daily food and about $30 a month. By advising the Royal Government to begin a military draft and underwriting all costs, the Americans also helped to increase the Royal Laotian Army from 15,000 to 50,000 by 1964.

, The rebels, meanwhile, were increasing their army, too. In 1965 they took the name *Neo Lao Hak Sat* (NLHS, or Lao Patriotic Front). The NLHS frightened off or assassinated local officials in remote villages. These methods enabled it to increase its territory and to form a new government—the Provisional Revolutionary Government (PRG). The regions which the PRG dominated lay along the borders with North and South Vietnam and so were accessible to the Vietnamese allies of the NLHS.

The NLHS gained the support of the people in the area that it controlled by developing social services and a sense of community. There is no way to check its claims, but the NLHS announced enormous increases in educational, public health, and agricultural benefits. It claimed to be educating 60,000 children in a region where the French educated only 11,000. According to the NLHS, there were 20 doctors and 1,700 hospital beds in its territory in 1970, in contrast to only one Laotian doctor and 200 hospital beds for the whole of the country in 1945. Visitors to the NLHS zone confirmed that food production was rising rapidly because farmers were being shown more effective methods of planting.

The NLHS tried to build further support by persuading peasants to carry out its policies. Villages were organized into "study groups" that administered their own social and economic programs within the framework of the NLHS government. NLHS cadres (spokesmen) were sent into the villages to insure that activities were carried out according to communist doctrine. The cadres gave agricultural, military, economic, and social as well as political advice. They showed peasants how to use fertilizers more effectively, helped to build bombshelters, or aided in the distribution of food. Their foremost goal, however, was to persuade the peasants to accept the political views of the NLHS.

The NLHS had considerable outside help during these early stages of its development. The number of North Vietnamese in PRG territory ranged from a high of more than 100,000 in 1971 to about 30,000 today. Many of these North Vietnamese were relaying materials over the hundreds of miles of the Ho Chi Minh Trail, the complex system of jungle roads and trails that crosses Laos and Cambodia between North and South Vietnam. Soviet and Chinese supplies and munitions also have reached the NLHS in large quantities.

Current conditions. In 1970 the NLHS announced that it would accept a new coalition government if the United States stopped its bombing and withdrew its special forces. It called for a special election in which the whole country would choose its rulers. As negotiations over this proposal began, the war continued. By the end of 1973, the NLHS controlled three-quarters of Laos and was continuing its relentless advance on the Royal Government's administrative capital in Vientiane. Finally an agreement was signed in the Fall of 1973. It provided for a provisional coalition government, to be headed by Souvanna Phouma. The government was to make its decisions unanimously, with each faction directing its own ministries.

Under the coalition government people who had been fighting each other for more than ten years suddenly were made to unite. Members of rival armies began to enforce the peace together in the two capitals, Vientiane and Luang Prabang. The U.S. withdrew its special forces and most of its advisers, though it continued its military and financial aid of the Royal Government. Thailand, which also had troops fighting the guerrillas, recalled them, too.

In less than a year it became evident that this arrangement could only survive if the two members of the coalition remained equals. But the strength of the former Royal Government in the coalition depended upon the support of the United States. Laotian royalists were weakened when American troops abruptly left Vietnam in 1975, for the move suggested that Americans would soon leave all of Southeast Asia. Just as a power vacuum had been created in South Vietnam, drawing the Viet Cong into it, so did one develop in Laotian cities.

Soon after the Viet Cong entered what was then called Saigon (the present Ho Chi Minh City), the Pathet Lao swept into Vientiane, driving the royalists from power. So ended a monarchy that had endured more than six hundred years. A new communist government was established.

The communists of Laos were more merciful to their enemies than those in Vietnam or Cambodia. They allowed many of the royalists to leave the country. Prince Souphanouvong, the first president of the Democratic People's Republic of Laos, guaranteed his defeated half brother, Prince Souvanna Phouma, a secure old age at home. Even the deposed king, Savang Vatthana, was permitted to live, though he was forced to learn communist ways. It was in their reorganization of society that the Laotians showed themselves little different from their determined communist neighbors.

ECONOMIC CONDITIONS

Sources of current problems. Laos is one of the poorest countries in Southeast Asia. Its farmers must consume almost everything that they produce. But even their low income, only $85 a year per person, is not a measure of their poverty. Laos has two economies, one which uses money and one which barters. People who have no money trade food and services for their needs. The income of those who barter is about half that of those who earn money.

Laos' economy is based almost entirely on the production of rice. There are two types of rice. One is grown in the areas that are naturally flooded by the winter monsoon, and one is grown in the highlands. The lowland, or wet rice, begins as seed in one field, then is transplanted into another which is beneath water retained by low dikes. To accomplish the transplanting of seedlings, whole families wade into the flooded fields. They work together, as they will again when the harvest time comes.

The highland, or dry rice, is cultivated in areas dominated by the ethnic minorities. Some hill tribes terrace their land and live on it continuously, but others move every two or three years. These latter tribes practice "slash-and-burn" agriculture, cutting and burning thickets to fertilize the land, then moving while villages to repeat the process when their farms become less productive.

About 45 percent of all Laotians live in the highlands. The land that they occupy consists in steep mountains, rising to about 9,000 feet. The only large flat area is the Plain of Jars, east of the bend of the Mekong River in the center of northern Laos. A plateau about 4,000 feet above sea level, the plain is not fertile and so is not heavily populated. Its name is derived from prehistoric stone jars found in its soil. The prepondrance of mountainous land in Laos has resulted in largely isolated agricultural communities. Laos has about 9,400 villages, each with from 50 to 200 people.

Because of its terrain, Laos is the least urbanized country in all of Southeast Asia. Its five largest cities have a total population of less than 300,000. More than half of this total lives in Vientiane, the administrative capital. The former royal capital, Luang Prabang, has a population of only 25,000.

The population density in Laos is less than forty-one persons per square mile—the lowest in Southeast Asia. But the figure is deceiving. So much of the country is unusable that land is scarce. There are only 1.1 arable acres per person, and the average farm is less than five acres. The rate of population growth has declined from

The central part of Vientiane, administrative capital of Laos, resembles many European villages. The cars and architecture shown here are French.

2.4 to less than 1 percent in recent years, reducing pressures for more land.

In the lowlands, the surging Mekong River sweeps alluvium down from the mountains into the more heavily populated areas. The lowlands include not only the best, but also the most thoroughly cultivated soil in Laos. Only 7,500 of Laos' 91,000 square miles can be used for farming, and most of them are in the lowlands.

To get the most out of their land, many Laotians plant two crops a year. They raise corn, wheat, cotton, coffee, tobacco, or vegetables on acreage where they will grow rice later in the year. Laotian farmers began to double-crop their ricefields in 1967 and within five years increased their 4,000 acres of arable land to 8,000.

Some Asian farmers have had great success planting new higher yielding seed strains. Their great increase in agricultural production has been called the "Green Revolution." The soil and climate in Laos are not well suited for the new seed strains. Nevertheless, some new seeds have been adaptable. The new strains supplemented double-cropping and the addition of new workers to the labor force. They enabled Laos to increase its rice production from 487,000 to 550,000 tons between 1967-69. But the demand for rice has increased, too. The army needed more. So did the growing number of refugees. Thus the benefits of greater production were largely cancelled by the effects of the war.

Intensive American bombing seriously damaged Laotian agriculture. It forced tens of thousands of peasants to leave their farms, shattered dikes and wrecked the country's meager transportation facilities. Capital assets that took villagers years to develop, such as barns, tools, roads, and draft animals, were suddenly destroyed by waves of jets. The rebel control of farmlands denied Laotians food that they desperately needed. By the early 1970s Laos was importing substantial amounts of rice, chiefly from Thailand.

Trends. Laos' need to buy food abroad began to increase rapidly before the war The cost of the rice that it bought began to rise, more than doubling in the two years ending 1968. The years of war that followed reduced the production of timber, the principal crop, by 80 percent. Droughts in the late 1970s often left the country with no more than 5 percent of its normal rice crop. The production of tin and green coffee, the other major sources of income, declined, too.

These problems were compounded by the demands of the new Communist government. Laos introduced programs which resembled those of its allies in Vietnam and Cambodia. More than a third of the shopkeepers in Laos were compelled to abandon their busi-

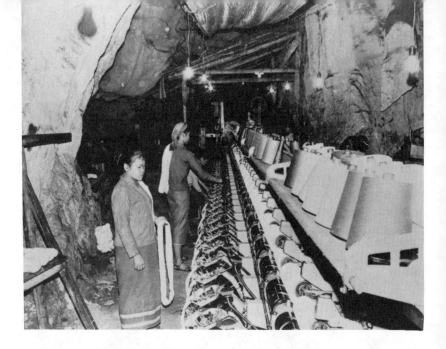

Laos suffers from a severe shortage of capital. When wartime conditions made factory construction impossible, this textile mill was placed in a cave.

nesses and to move to collective farms. As it did in Vietnam and Cambodia, this policy chiefly affected the ethnic Chinese who had long dominated commerce. Such policies drove some of the most talented people in Laos, including many of its most skilled professionals, out of the country. The professional class in Laos had never been larger than one percent of the total labor force. About half of its members were teachers, and most of the others worked for the government. These key jobs, and others, usually were taken over by incompetents.

By the 1980s, Laos was forced to import more than eleven times more than the $14 million that it earned from sales abroad. Laos met this crisis only through the help of other countries. Grain and loans poured into the country, both from allies and former enemies. Meanwhile, Laos yielded in its efforts to establish a rigid form of communism. It began to mix its socialist economy with a capitalist one, offering incentives and other rewards for efficiency. Merchants opened new businesses which rapidly discovered ways to bring more products to the market.

This new policy, combined with better weather, tended to revive the Laotian economy. The country had almost enough rice to feed its people. The government worked to deal with such problems as the lack of skilled people and corruption among public officials. It began building new schools, improving old ones, and greatly increasing the rate of literacy. There was substantially more international trade, and hopes were rising in Laos. But the crisis was far from over. Incomes were still among the lowest in the world.

FOREIGN POLICY

A foreign policy was thrust upon Laos, rather than shaped by it. At first, the French developed the country's international relationships. The French controlled Laotian foreign diplomacy and trade for their own benefit. But World War II accelerated nationalist movements that were spreading throughout Asia. When the war ended the French, with powerful backing from the United States and Great Britain, tried unsuccessfully to continue colonial rule. They failed to win the cooperation of the Laotian people, although the class that profited under their rule tried to help them return.

By the 1950s, other Western powers understood the dangers of leaving France to its own resources in Southeast Asia. China had a Communist government that the United States regarded as menacing. In Vietnam, a guerrilla movement was driving out the best army that the French could array against it. A group of Laotians was developing a similiar guerrilla force with the goal of installing a communist government in their country.

With the outbreak of the Korean War, the United States rapidly developed a foreign policy in which "mutual security" treaties were signed with many Southeast Asian countries. President Eisenhower and his Secretary of State, John Foster Dulles, encouraged Laos to become an independent kingdom when it appeared that the French were unable to hold Indochina. By extending its own military protection to Laos, the United States in effect replaced France as the nation's guardian. Its formal vehicle for the offer was the Southeast Asian Treaty Organization (SEATO). In addition to the United States, SEATO included Great Britain, France, Australia, New Zealand, the Philippines, and Thailand.

Communist China did not directly confront the United States in Southeast Asia. Instead, it preached that revolutions are best made by the people in the countries in which they are taking place. The Chinese gave substantial supplies and advice to the North Vietnamese and Laotians in their war against the French. But they did not send "volunteers" to either country as they did to North Korea in 1950.

Since the borders between Vietnam and Laos are not well defined, it was easy for Vietnamese guerrillas to enter the country and to train Laotian rebels. Thus while the United States became the chief military and economic supporter of the Royal Government, the North Vietnamese and Chinese Communists were the main supporters of the revolutionary movement of 1973. The struggle between these two sides was halted twice, by the Geneva Agreements of 1954 and 1962. But these fragile agreements broke down.

An unexpected shift in alliances followed the departure of the United States from the region in 1975. Instead of China, it was the Soviet Union which gained influence there. Almost immediately after the Americans had gone, seven hundred Soviet technicians appeared in Laos. Others, meanwhile, moved into Vietnam and Kampuchea (Cambodia). They helped to develop Laos' first five-year plan and to build the economy.

With Soviet advice, Laos entered into an economic and military alliance with Vietnam. Its officials flew regularly to Hanoi for guidance. The dependency became so complete that Laotians were arrested for opposing Vietnamese in their own country. This arrangement compelled Laos to resist Chinese influence in its region, for China was a declared enemy of both the Soviet Union and Vietnam.

Nor did the Chinese quietly accept the spread of Soviet power so close to another border. During the 1970s they assigned more than forty thousand laborers the task of building a road from the south of China to a point as far west as the Mekong River. They began transporting supplies to a powerful ethnic minority, the H'mong, which wanted to break away from the Laotian government. The Soviets and Vietnamese responded to this threat, among many others, by entrenching their position. Using local laborers, their technicians supervised the construction of Southeast Asia's largest airport in central Laos. Thus as always in its long history, Laos has become a pawn between great powers, with a foreign policy arranged by others.

THE FUTURE OF LAOS

The government of Laos has changed, but the country's problems have not. Just as it did in recent decades, Laos today must concentrate on raising the total national income, which does not pay for its needs. It must also increase the social services necessary to win the loyalty of its people.

Laos cannot easily develop a professional class. Nor can it readily spread the use of a monetary system among people used to self-sufficiency and barter. Lacking raw materials, there is little chance that it can industrialize. But it can improve the effectiveness of its main occupation, agriculture. In a world increasingly in need of food, this could become a vital and profitable role.

Forests are another aspect of Laotian agriculture. They cover more than two-thirds of the country. During the 1930s, the French found tin in the highlands and began to hire Laotians at low wages to develop the mines. Tin became scarce during and after World War II. Laos' exports of this vital metal began to increase rapidly, tripling during the years 1966-69 alone. Similarly, the country's exports of timber increased for the same reasons. They rose tenfold over the identical period. But the extraction of tin and timber barely dented the supply. Laotian teak reserves remain substantial, and there are insatiatable world markets for this beautiful hardwood.

Under the Royal Government, Laos worked to develop its important hydroelectric resources. Unless it did so it would have to keep importing the expensive fuel oil needed to run thermal plants. During the 1960 the government worked with what were then the countries of Cambodia and South Vietnam, as well as with Thailand, to increase the water resources of the Mekong River. The goal of the so-called Mekong Committee, sponsored by the United Nations, was to develop flood control, irrigation, and electric power for all of the countries bordering on the river.

Laos' communist government today has the same goal, but in a different relationship with its neighbors. Vietnam closely supervises many of the policies of Laos with the help of the Soviet Union. Thailand remains a strong trading partner but is fearful of the communist threat.

Thus the future of Laos lies largely in the hands of outsiders. This strategic land has long served as a buffer between the much stronger nations of Vietnam and Thailand. Now, as it becomes subject to Vietnam and, indirectly, the Soviet Union, its peace and its prosperity are, as always, beyond its control.

Yet Laos has recently begun to show at least faint signs of independence. Late in 1987 Princess Anne of Great Britain became the first member of the British royal family ever to visit Laos, where she went as president of the Save the Children Fund. Its willingness to accept her suggested greater openness on the part of the Laotians. A further sign of reform came in 1988 when the government announced that it would hold its first local elections in thirteen years. But whatever its political direction, Laos must eventually reshape its economy. Its foreign debt has soared over $1 billion at a time when a single bicycle, considered essential by many families, may cost six month's pay.

N.B.: In this chapter the country is referred to as Cambodia or the Khmer Republic until 1977, when its name was officially changed.

KAMPUCHEA

(Cambodia)

The Japanese took control of Cambodia after France was defeated by Germany in 1940. However, they allowed its French administrators to remain in power until 1945, when they encouraged the Cambodians to declare independence of France. The following year, the French returned and demanded that Cambodia accept colonial status again. But although Cambodia was not deeply involved in World War II, it had developed powerful nationalist forces and was determined to fight the French.

By 1946 the French were ready to yield to nationalist pressures throughout Indochina. They offered Cambodia and their other Indochinese colonies a limited form of independence within the framework of a French Union. But the nationalists resisted the formation of the French Union and also demanded constitutional limits on the country's monarchy. By 1949 Cambodia's monarch, King Sihanouk, agreed to bring the country into the French Union. His purpose was to avoid conflict with the French. In response to his move, the nationalists began to organize for war, however. Still hoping to avoid war, Sihanouk joined the guerrillas and called for complete independence from France. The French were hard pressed by the war in Vietnam. They finally gave full independence to Cambodia in 1953. Thus Sihanouk became the hero of his country's independence movement. Then he began a long struggle to keep Cambodia neutral in the gathering conflict between Western countries and their former colonies.

SOCIAL CONDITIONS AND CULTURAL LIFE

Ethnic groups. The ethnic Khmer comprise 85 percent of the 6.3 million people in modern Kampuchea, but the country has significant minorities. The most influential of these, until recently, were 450,000 Chinese who were involved in businesses in the capital city of Phnom Penh and in the Mekong Delta. Most have been driven into farm labor; many have been murdered. Presently the largest minority is Vietnamese, up to 700,000 of whom have recently come to join about 300,000 previously in the country. The Khmer Islam make up a third large ethnic minority. This group consists of about 100,000 practicing Muslims. Finally, there are about 75,000 Khmer Loeu, a mountain people who grow dry rice.

The Khmers do not allow the Chinese to own land or become citizens in their country. Yet they have little fear of the Chinese because they have never been invaded and occupied by China. The Khmers have often intermarried with the Chinese, particularly in the upper classes. As a result, many members of the country's ruling families have Chinese ancestors. Most Chinese, however, maintain their own language and culture.

While they are cordial toward the Chinese, the Khmers have deep fears of the Vietnamese. Tension between these two groups has been severe since 1600, when the Vietnamese began a series of invasions of Cambodia. Hostility between them became more profound during the colonial period, when the French imported Vietnamese to operate the civil service in Cambodia. Throughout the nineteenth century, the Vietnamese gained important positions in government and the professions. Many of them were Roman Catholics and so were regarded as outsiders by the Buddhist Khmers. Seeing the Vietnamese grow wealthier in their country, the Khmers often attacked Vietnamese individuals. Their anger rose to a fever pitch in 1970 because many of them blamed the Vietnamese for the civil war in their country. The Khmers drove at least 100,000 Vietnamese out of Phnom Penh, seizing their businesses and homes.

Despite their intermittant conflicts with the Vietnamese, the Khmers generally enjoy ethnic harmony in their country. Even the smallest ethnic minorities rarely complain of persecution. There are about 20,000 Thais, 5,000 Lao, and lesser numbers of Indian and Pakistanis in the Khmer nation, but they live in relative peace among the Khmers. Because of the preponderance of Khmers, the country has fewer of the ethnic tensions that exist in Indonesia and Malaysia, where ethnic minorities represent much larger sections of the populations.

Religion. Theravada Buddhism has been the dominant religion in Cambodia since the thirteenth century. It replaced a form of Hinduism which was practiced in the court and then spread among the general population which was largely practicing animism. Today, Theravada Buddhism is the state religion in the Khmer nation. Since 1969, the head of the government has appointed many of the leaders of the monkhood, or *sangha.* In making his appointments he follows the recommendations of members of the

This young Khmer
is studying for
the monkhood.

sangha and of his cabinet, which includes a Minister for Religious Affairs. This cabinet officer also governs the monks who head the dioceses (*kun*) into which every province is divided. Thus the state and its religion are closely interlocked.

Both the former Khmer government and the guerrillas who recently defeated it sought the support of the sangha. But the monks are not political and could not even vote until 1972. The Khmer nation has about 100,000 monks, and their main function is to serve as models for Buddhists throughout the country.

The philosophy of Buddhism penetrates every part of the life of the Khmer people. There is a Buddhist compound, or *wat*, in each community. Monks can live or take refuge in the wat. Peasants think of their local wat as a spiritual home and gather there for ceremonies and celebrations. The Khmers have a deep respect for Buddhist monks, who they believe are closer to achieving Nirvana than others. Most people put food in the alms bowls extended by the monks in the mornings. No festival or important occasion is complete without monks to guide it. In homes the monks are not only spiritual counselors, but often physicians. They use ancient treatments, such as herbs and charms, to treat the sick.

Education, language, and the arts. Under the French, the Khmers resisted the development of public schools. They were willing to send their children only to Buddhist monasteries, where education was largely religious. When the country gained full independence in 1953, the Buddhist schools and a few private ones were the only educational institutions in the country.

Cambodia then began to divert large amounts of money into public schools. It recognized that national stability depended on cultural pride in each new generation. Rapidly organizing an efficient educational system, the country began with only 80,000 students in 1963 and by 1970 was teaching more than 1.1 million students in public schools. That represented more than 70 percent of the potential enrollment between the ages of 6–12. To accomplish this, Cambodia spent almost a quarter of its budget on the school system.

Along with its efforts to increase formal education, the government began a campaign to overcome illiteracy. It achieved astonishing results. As recently as 1962, more than 40 percent of the adult population in Cambodia was unable to read and write. Then adult schools were opened everywhere, staffed by volunteers and government employees. Within ten years after the program was begun, Cambodia announced that more than 70 percent of the population was literate.

The Khmer people are also strongly committed to higher education. They have built nine colleges and universities with a total enrollment of about 9,000. While this success in the field of education has been remarkable, it has contributed to social unrest. Once educated, young people tend to live in Phnom Penh so they can use their skills. But the city, crowded and tense, rarely offers work to satisfy educated young people. The rate of unemployment is increasing, and many of the unemployed are skilled people who are dissatisfied with the conditions of their society.

The literacy program has focused on instruction in the Khmer language, which is used by 90 percent of the population. Unlike the Chinese-related languages of Vietnam, Laos, and Thailand, Khmer is not a tonal language. It is closer to Indian speech, and many of its words are borrowed from Sanskrit. But although Khmer is spoken everywhere in the Khmer nation, the members of the upper class still often use French. Diplomats, educators, and financial leaders almost all get their current information from French publications.

The Khmers often deplored the French colonial government, but they appreciated the interest France showed in their culture. The French sent teams of archaeologists to Cambodia to help the Khmers explore their past. Throughout the colonial period the archaeologists repeatedly went into the jungle to find and restore ancient Khmer buildings. They established an institute in Phnom Penh to translate and preserve ancient texts and arts. During this process many Khmer educators learned to speak, read, and write French.

The ruins of Angkor Wat, in the province of Siemreab, are the most famous discovery of French and Khmer archaeologists. Angkor

The god-king presides over Angkor Wat. In a room at the monument's highest point, statues suggest the unity of the rulers of heaven and earth.

Wat is the largest religious structure built anywhere in the world in the last 750 years. The various capitals at Angkor covered an area of 40 square miles. Centuries of jungle growth, moisture, and attacks by insects have eroded the buildings, but massive parts of the construction is still standing, often decorated by magnificent sculptures.

Angkor Wat was apparently planned to represent the faith of the *devaraja* in architecture. This ancient Indian belief maintained that the king could be identified with a god. Indian mythology said that the gods lived at the top of a sacred mountain called Meru. This mountain revolved around the central axis of the universe. People lived at the base of the mountain, in a region surrounded by six circles of land and seven oceans. A rock wall confined this world of gods, people, lands, and oceans.

The parts of Angkor Wat each were intended to symbolize one or more of the elements in the ancient Indian myth. Within a rock wall there were concourses to represent the different lands, moats to represent the oceans, and a central building to represent Meru. Inside of the central building there were images of a Khmer king and of a god. The spirits of the king and the god were expected to meet in the temple. More than one king built his monument at Angkor, and the buildings and their sculpture are still being studied intensively for clues to the people who constructed them.

The Khmers began to use less stone in their buildings after they completed Angkor Wat. They made their temples and palaces of wood which is now decayed. Those constructed in the last two centuries remain, however. They are low, with upturned eaves and richly carved, often painted pediments. Until very recently, modern government buildings were constructed of concrete, with less concern for appealing details.

The French encouraged the Khmers to revive their art of the dance. This art flourished before Thai invasions in the thirteenth and fourteenth century, when the Thais kidnapped the entire Royal Ballet for performances in their own country. Under the French Thai dancers, who by that time had fully absorbed Khmer techniques in their art, were asked to return to Cambodia to help rekindle interest in the art. They succeeded, although when dancing was revived in Cambodia during the 1950s it included Thai costumes and props that did not exist when the art was invented. By the 1970s, Cambodia had an active Khmer Classical Ballet that was widely admired by audiences around the world. The Khmers also developed other arts, especially playwriting and filmmaking. When he was chief of state, Prince Sihanouk and his wife, Monique, were writers and producers of plays and films.

RECENT POLITICAL DEVELOPMENTS

Post-independence. In a previous chapter we saw that the Khmer people credited King Sihanouk with leading them to independence from the French. Sihanouk used this popularity to gain a mandate from the electorate. Until this point he was not able to command large numbers of votes, nor did his supporters control the Cambodian legislature. In 1955, however, Sihanouk seized an opportunity that was given to him because of the defeat of the French in Vietnam.

After the French defeat, the major world powers and most Southeast Asian countries agreed that elections would be held in Vietnam, Laos, and Cambodia. This agreement, called the Geneva Accord of 1954, acknowledged that the people of all three countries had the right to choose their own governments. Cambodia held the scheduled election and in it Sihanouk led his party, the People's Socialist Community, or Sangkum, to a victory that gained it every seat in the National Assembly. Sihanouk himself won more than a million votes, and only 1,800 votes were cast against him.

Cambodia also voted for a constitutional government, but Sihanouk knew that under it he would not be free to carry out his plans for the country's development. He wanted more power for the chief executive—himself. Accordingly, he proposed constitutional amendments that would have concentrated more authority in the king and discouraged free speech. When there were massive protests against his program, Sihanouk took another course. He abdicated, leaving the throne to his father, Norodom Suramarit. Using his new title, Prince, Sihanouk was able to put more of his energies into the leadership of the Sangkum, which promised to modernize and reform Cambodia.

Prince Sihanouk proved to be a master campaigner. While his opponents remained leaderless and divided, he learned to speak directly to the Cambodian people. In his last three years as king he had also served as prime minister under a declaration of martial law. Now as head of the majority party and as the country's most popular political figure he was able to keep this position under the constitution. Later, he was to become president of Cambodia, too.

Under Sihanouk the government borrowed foreign money to

Norodom Sihanouk developed an immense popular following in Cambodia by meeting regularly with the members of his political party, the Sangkum.

develop its transportation, communication, mineral deposits, and managerial skills. Sihanouk also pressed for more international trade and tourism in Cambodia. He adopted these policies over the objections of a group that wanted Cambodia to sever all foreign contacts in order to achieve self-sufficiency. Still another group was willing to accept foreign aid but not the social reforms that Sihanouk thought were necessary to build the economy.

Although Sihanouk accepted loans from the United States and other Western countries, he worried about the effect they would have on his country. His fears increased when President Diem of South Vietnam was overthrown and murdered in 1963. Sihanouk suspected that Diem's fall from power was due to his dependence on the United States. Sihanouk discovered a plot against his own life by the Khmer Serei ("Free Khmer") and suspected that it had been financed by American agents. In 1963 Sihanouk abruptly cancelled U.S. loans, claiming that Cambodia's self-sufficiency was being crippled by them.

Sihanouk then moved to create a more economically independent country. The distribution of wealth through socialism, he said, would free the country from its need to borrow. He nationalized the banking, foreign trade, and insurance industries. It was Sihanouk's hope that nationalization would conserve capital. As it turned out, the policy caused Cambodia to lose much more capital than it gained. Losses developed because foreign investment declined, and domestic funds proved inadequate for the nation's needs. During this period the Cambodian economy was at a standstill, despite Sihanouk's efforts to achieve progress through a Five-Year Plan (1960–65).

Yet Sihanouk's popularity remained high throughout the country. He kept in touch with the people through the National Congress, an informal body that met with him twice a year on the grounds of the national palace. His political party, the Sangkum, gained more than two million members by 1965. But it was more of a rubber stamp for him than a source of guidance. He still behaved as though he were king.

Sihanouk's popularity did not overcome the opposition to him. Nor did it thoroughly unite the Sangkum, many of whose members did not share his political views. For this reason he was forced to reorganize the government nine times in the three years after his 1955 election victory. Shortly after the death of his father, King Suramarit, in 1960, he withdrew as prime minister. Through popular demonstrations and an election in which he received 99 percent of the vote, he was recalled to office. His mother, Queen Kossamak, occupied the royal palace while he led Cambodia's largest and most powerful party.

Yet it was evident that Sihanouk's political position was being eroded in the moment of his greatest success. Among the Cambodians who opposed him were business and military leaders who did not want a socialist country. They considered him foolhardy to try to nationalize an economy as weak as Cambodia's. The program they were willing to support included more free enterprise rather than less.

Under political attack from this group, in 1966 Sihanouk allowed competing candidates to run for Assembly offices—something not done in previous elections. To his dismay, his opponents won substantial support from the electorate. A new majority in the Assembly authorized a general named Lon Nol to organize a "national salvation" government. The Assembly noted that Sihanouk's administration had been spending $20 million more a month than it earned, and it urged Lon Nol to take whatever steps were needed to save the country from bankruptcy.

An increase in the number of northern guerrillas was another reason for Sihanouk's defeat in the election. A new rebel group called the Khmer Rouge ("Red Khmer") was organizing in the north. The Khmer Rouge differed from the Khmer Serei in that it was communist as well as nationalist. There were reports that 35,000 members of the National Liberation Front—the coalition of communist and nationalist—guerrillas in South Vietnam—had crossed the border to help the Khmer Rouge. Many Cambodian voters blamed Sihanouk for this invasion by Vietnamese guerrillas. In his effort to be neutral, he had extended diplomatic recognition both to the United States and to the National Liberation Front. According to his opponents, this merely encouraged the National Liberation Front to think that Cambodia was weak.

The members of the Front were in Cambodia for two reasons. First, they wanted to use and protect the Ho Chi Minh Trail. They used this 1,000-mile-long network of jungle roads and paths to carry supplies from North to South Vietnam and often crossed the unguarded borders of eastern Laos and Cambodia. Second, the members of the Front were in Cambodia because they regarded their war as an international one. They were applying pressure throughout the former French colonies of South Vietnam, Laos, and Cambodia.

With Cambodia's economy and neutrality both collapsing, Sihanouk confirmed Lon Nol as prime minister and went to France for medical treatment. While he was gone, demonstrations broke out in Phnom Penh. They were directed against the resident Vietnamese community, which Cambodians identified with the guerrillas. Vietnamese property was seized and burned. Sihanouk was accused of treason in the National Assembly. His opponents said

After deposing Prince Sihanouk, Cambodia chose Lon Nol to head the new government.

that he had sold arms to the enemy, allowed bribery and corruption, and ran the country as a autocrat. The legislators particularly attacked Sihanouk's cooperation with Communist China and North Vietnam. By official resolution he was dismissed and ordered not to return to the country.

But Sihanouk's popularity remained a factor in Cambodian politics. Despite his failings, his people remembered him as the hero of the independence movement and as the leader who had prevented full-scale war. Sihanouk was arrogant, but many people were willing to forgive that in a former king. Under him Cambodia made striking gains in education and in the revival of the Khmer culture. The economy was faltering, but it was difficult to estimate whether this decline was caused by Sihanouk's policies or whether it would have been worse without them.

After he was deposed as Cambodia's chief of state in 1970, Norodom Sihanouk went to Peking, China, where he was offered arms to help him resist the government that had overthrown him. He began broadcasts, beamed to Cambodian peasants, urging them to rebel against the government of Lon Nol. He accused the United States of causing his overthrow.

Sihanouk's effectiveness in arousing the peasants is shown by the growth in the number of rebels in Cambodia. There were only 3,000 Khmer Rouge when he was ousted from office. By 1973, the movement included almost 50,000 guerrillas and had set up a revolutionary government over more than one-third of the population. Sihanouk, meanwhile, became chief of state of a government-in-exile in Peking, hoping to move it to Phnom Penh if the Khmer Rouge succeeded in toppling Lon Nol. He called it the Royal Government of National Union of Cambodia, and he called its armed force the Cambodian People's Liberation Movement.

Further organizing efforts. With Sihanouk gone, Lon Nol confronted the dangerous issue of guerrilla warfare more directly than he could before. In the view of the United States and other Western powers, Sihanouk had deliberately overlooked the use of Cambodia as a sanctuary by North Vietnamese communists. They claimed that the North Vietnamese were storing supplies along the Ho Chi Minh Trail and could not be attacked because of Cambodia's "neutrality." Lon Nol accepted this view. He agreed to work more closely with the United States in order to block the guerrillas, who were beginning to join with supporters of Sihanouk.

First, Lon Nol appealed for national unity. Every city block and rural area was organized under committees to increase participation in the government. On October 9, 1970, Cambodia sought to widen its popular support by ending the 1,168-year-old monarchy. From that point it was called the Khmer Republic.

Despite his appeal for unity, Lon Nol found the country badly divided over the issues raised by the insurgents, the growing number of refugees, and the failing economy. Members of his cabinet often quarreled with each other and resigned. The communists advanced steadily and by 1970 controlled the roads over which rice was transported to Phnom Penh. Lon Nol was able to increase the size of his army from 35,000 to 200,000, yet he found that he had not enough soldiers to withstand the tide of 50,000 North Vietnamese and 20,000 Khmer Rouge guerrillas. By 1974, the guerrillas had control of 80 percent of the country, including 5.5 of its 7.4 million people.

The United States, South Vietnam, Thailand, Indonesia, and Malaysia came to the aid of the Lon Nol government during 1970–73. On the ground, American military men wore civilian clothes and were officially called advisers. They did this to avoid the implication that the United States was directly involved in the war. But in the air, thousands of American planes rained explosives, napalm, and anti-personnel bombs over suspected communist positions. From 1970–73, the U.S. Strategic Air Command carried out a total of 2,875 raids over Cambodia. They dropped more than 240,000 tons of bombs, 50 percent more than were dropped over Japan during World War II. The administration of President Nixon kept these raids secret from the American public, denying that they were taking place until Congress discovered and halted them in 1973.

The explosions, fire storms, and defoliation caused by the bombing seriously damaged the country's environment. Many of the bombs were dropped over heavily populated areas, especially in the Mekong Delta. Shortly before the raids were halted the American pilots mistakenly dropped their bombs over government-held positions. In one case they destroyed an entire village, killing 137 persons and wounding 268 others.

The suffering of the Khmer Republic in battle was compounded by the war's effects on daily life: corruption, shortages of food, and rising prices caused by military expenditures. A vocal minority arose to protest the war. Students and professionals began to demonstrate, and in 1972 impoverished families, joined by soldiers, showed their desperation by raiding the Phnom Penh market.

Current conditions. Lon Nol rejected the complaints of people who wanted to give up the war. Declaring that the country could not afford to "play the game of democracy and freedom," in 1971 he suspended constitutional law and began to rule by ordinance. Nevertheless, his suppression of criticism could not hide the fact that fewer and fewer people were confident of his ability to solve the nation's problems.

Lon Nol became increasingly desperate as the military situation deteriorated. Both students and professionals charged that the Khmer people were being manipulated by the United States. Lon Nol won reelection with 55 percent of the vote in 1972, but teachers, students, and Buddhist monks mounted more active protests against his government. He responded by tightening his political controls. His administration was dominated by fewer than one hundred men.

After an attempt on his life in 1973, Lon Nol closed all newspapers and magazines, forbade all meetings of more than five people, and arrested 55 members of the former royal family. The United States, his chief source of financial support, pressed him to broaden the responsibility for governing the Khmer Republic, but he was forced to tighten his authority as guerrilla pressures mounted. In 1973 he moved to negotiate with the guerrillas, but they rejected him. Having won almost all of the country they would fight on, they said. Their confidence was shared by 31 countries, led by Communist China, which began a campaign to replace Lon Nol's government with the Red Khmer in the United Nations.

Lon Nol promised to fight on. He tried to appease his critics by appointing a "political high council" to run the government. Although this body was not as broadly representative as the Assembly that it replaced, it was more so than the personal rule that

A small boy tried
to lead his blind grandmother
away from the horrors of
the war in Cambodia.

Lon Nol had been using. The council's concerns focused on prices, the military draft needed to bolster the army, and on mounting casualties and refugees, of whom there were at least 700,000.

Meanwhile the combined armies of the Khmer Rouge and Prince Sihanouk moved relentlessly against Phnom Penh. They surrounded the capital, depriving it of the food and munitions that the United States had been sending. In 1973 President Nixon had promised Lon Nol that "...the United States remains fully determined to provide maximum possible assistance to your heroic self-defense and will continue to stand side by side with the republic in the future as in the past." But just two years later the Americans recognized that it was impossible to support the Khmer Republic to the extent that they had before. With the main lifeline, the Mekong River, blockaded by the guerrillas, Lon Nol's military situation became increasingly desperate. In 1975 he fled the Khmer Republic, taking refuge in the U.S. "I am leaving to pave the way for a peace settlement," he said. And with his departure the collapse of the republic became certain.

Lon Nol's flight marked the end of a long war that left more than a million people dead or wounded. As many as four million—fully half of the entire population—were homeless. Yet terrifying as it was, the ordeal of the war was only a prelude to the agony that followed.

First, the victorious Khmer Rouge, joined by ordinary citizens who were furious at what they had been led to, massacred remaining supporters of Lon Nol's cause. Whoever was suspected of differing from the new leadership stood in constant danger. Tens of thousands of people were butchered.

Then, in the midst of this havoc, the Khmer Rouge ordered the almost total evacuation of the city of Phnom Penh. What may have been the largest single mass migration in history took place within a period of ninety days. More than 450,000 people, including the infants, lame, sick, and elderly, were herded onto roads into the countryside. Starving, burdened by their few possessions, thousands died on the way. Survivors were pressed into labor details on farms or in public works. Within a year, it was said, as many as a million more people perished.

The Khmer Rouge explained to furious world opinion that it needed to reduce the population of Phnom Penh to avoid epidemics and famine there. Similar policies were being followed by the new communist governments in Vietnam and Laos. The purpose seems to have been an effort to change the nature of the country's society. In all three countries shopkeepers and professionals were persecuted and driven into the countryside. The Khmer Rouge appears to have wanted a nation made up almost entirely of peasants.

To enforce its harsh demands, the Khmer Rouge government kept a large standing army long after the war. Throughout the country, soldiers carried out executions to control the population. Their chief victims were Buddhist priests and anyone who refused to labor in the ricefields or rubber plantations. During one entire year (1975-76) they prevented marriages so that people would work harder, eat less, and produce fewer children.

The principal architect of these edicts, a former schoolteacher named Pol Pot, boasted that he was creating a new kind of society. In it, he said, such institutions as marriage, families, religion, money, and cities would be swept away and replaced by socialist ones. As head of the Communist Party, Pol Pot became secretary-general of the entire government. His authority was confirmed in an election, but his critics pointed out that his was the only party qualified to present candidates. It was under Pol Pot, in 1977, that Cambodia changed its name to Kampuchea.

Pol Pot seemed invincible, but even he was subject to a much larger struggle—the struggle between the Soviet Union and China. These two giant communist neighbors had a long-standing border dispute which caused each of them to station huge armies in Central Asia. In Southeast Asia, the Soviets were attempting to block China by creating an alliance with Vietnam. Pol Pot took China's side in this dispute, and during the national emergency continuously looked to the Chinese for grain and for arms.

By 1979, the hatred of Pol Pot's repressive measures reached a boiling point in Kampuchea. A guerrilla force arose, and it won the immediate support of the Vietnamese. Suddenly this force thrust into Phnom Penh and declared that its leader, Heng Samrin, was in control of the government. As Pol Pot and his associates took flight to China and Thailand, Heng Samrin tried them *in absentia* for the death of more than a million people. They were found guilty, declared fugitives, and sentenced to death.

Three rival armies now raged across Kampuchea, compounding the anguish caused by the economic crisis. One, headed by Heng Samrin, had the support of the Vietnamese and the Soviet Union. With powerful help from the Vietnamese, it pursued remnants of Pol Pot's forces across the border with Thailand. The third army consisted in a coalition of non-communist and anti-communist guerrillas headed by Prince Norodom Sihanouk. This third army was supplied by the Chinese, who had given refuge to Sihanouk.

Each of the three sides claimed the legal right to govern Kampuchea. Heng Samrin based his claim on an election, held in 1981, in which his United Front for National Salvation was the only party allowed to offer candidates. Kampucheans are required to vote, and almost all of the 3.5 million who cast ballots favored the United Front. Pol Pot based his claim on the previous election, denying the legality of the new one. Finally, Sihanouk declared that in any free election he would be the winner.

ECONOMIC CONDITIONS AND PROBLEMS

Sources of current problems. Until the outbreak of war in 1970, Kampuchea's economy was dominated by two crops, rice and rubber. The production of rubber was almost abandoned during the war because U.S. bombing defoliated most of the rubber trees and guerrillas were overrunning plantations. Some rubber production has been revived, but this industry has far from recovered. Therefore rice is the sole important crop.

Supplemented by small amounts of corn, fruit, vegetables, sugar, textiles, and paper products, the rice crop accounts for almost 35 percent of the national product. More than 76 percent of Kampu-

The struggle for the political control of Kampuchea resulted in one of the greatest disasters in modern history, in which millions died of starvation.

chea's people are involved in its production. These two figures reveal the enormous human energy that the country invests to produce the grain. Before 1967 the Khmer people were able to increase rice production as rapidly as their population increased. Since then, wartime conditions have caused them to fall behind.

The relationship of food to population is difficult to measure during the havoc of war. During the mid-1970s, only half of the farms in Kampuchea could function. At least a million people could not work and would have starved to death without help from overseas, chiefly the United States. Rice production fell to less than 40 percent of its normal levels. Yet paradoxically as the death toll rose, more grain became available to each survivor. The population declined from about 8 million to 6 and perhaps even to 5.5 million during the height of the combat. Life expectancy at birth slipped below forty years.

Many early deaths were due to starvation. Although rice is planted in almost eight of the nine million acres in cultivation, production did not meet the country's needs. There were a number of important reasons for this. First, Kampuchea has few draft animals and almost no capital for tools. Second, over the centuries most regions have adapted certain strains of rice to their own land. Farmers have been unable or unwilling to use newer, high-yielding strains. Third, because of the war and shortages of capital, the government has been unable to build needed irrigation projects. Nor has it been able to encourage the use of chemical fertilizers and pesticides to the extent necessary. Chemical fertilizer is essential for the growth of the improved rice strains, but most Kampuchean farmers have little of it. Finally, the war has taken many acres out of production.

To date, there are no clear reports on the effects of the mass migrations and collective farms that the government has pressed upon the Kampuchean people. In the past, Kampuchean farmers clung to the relatively poor land of the Mekong Delta instead of moving to the more productive highlands. Eighty percent of the country's riceland is in this region. Less than 10 percent of the delta's land is suitable for double cropping, and all of it is subject to erosion from uncontrolled floods.

Farmers tended to stay on their land because they owned it. Their creditors usually were Chinese, members of a minority forbidden to foreclose on land or to own it in any way. Now the government has seized most, or perhaps all land. Vast numbers of people have been moved from one region to another, and farms have been organized into collectives consisting of 100 to 1,000 families each. This method of organization may solve some of the problems due to the shortage of capital. However, its usefulness in other countries, such as China, has proved limited.

Throughout the 1980s there has been widespread famine in Kampuchea. Rival armies denied each other emergency food shipments on grounds that relief was a form of military aid. Thus starvation became widespread, especially among the Kampuchean refugees living over the border in Thailand.

Trends. At the height of its economic activity during the 1960s, Kampuchea's industry and commerce never employed more than 10 percent of the population. Factory and business workers were usually drawn from the Chinese and Vietnamese minorities. Today, the numbers of Khmers in non-farming occupations is increasing, but the total number of jobs in the country is declining because of the shortage of capital and raw materials. Many factories are operating at less than half capacity.

Before the war thousands of Khmers were able to earn a large part of their income by fishing. Natural conditions in the Tonle Sap ("Great Lake") and Tonle Sab, the river below it, gave them one of the best fish supplies in the world. Shortly before the war, the supply of fish was noticeably reduced by the increasing number of fishermen. The war reduced fishing by another 40 percent, limiting a major source of protein.

In the midst of these shortages the Khmer nation must buy at least $100 million in goods overseas each year. Meanwhile it can export less than half that amount. The United States became the main supplier of goods after France left Southeast Asia, but except for emergencies, U.S. shipments were cut off in 1975. Kampuchea's economy today is increasingly linked with Vietnam, Laos, and the Soviet Union.

Foreign Relations

Under Prince Sihanouk, Cambodia tried to preserve its neutrality. Sihanouk chose to ignore increasing evidence that the North Vietnamese were using Cambodia as a base from which to attack South Vietnam. The outbreak of war in Cambodia in 1967 did not persuade him to change his policy. He warned the Cambodian rebels, but he did little to oppose them.

In 1970 Lon Nol, Sihanouk's successor, took the opposite view of how to deal with the rebels and North Vietnamese. He invited the United States and other countries to help crush them. Responding, President Nixon sent U.S. troops into Cambodia to seize guerrilla supplies. Nixon emphasized that the troops were attacking communist munitions dumps, not invading Cambodia. In the United States, however, there were massive protests against this extension of the Vietnam War. The Congress threatened to cut off military funding. Nevertheless, American pilots continued to bomb suspected enemy targets in the Khmer Republic for four years. Lon Nol's government knew of these raids, but they were kept secret from the American people and Congress.

After the United States withdrew its troops from South Vietnam in 1973, the countries of Southeast Asia became increasingly aware of Communist China's powerful new influence in its region. The Chinese gave strong support to the Khmer Rouge. Allied with the supporters of Prince Sihanouk, the Khmer Rouge had captured the entire country by 1975, and the Chinese led a movement to seat the new government in the United Nations.

For a brief time, China was the only country with which the Khmers had relations. Then in 1978 a group sponsored by Vietnam, aided by the Soviet Union, took over the government. Following this action, Kampuchea extended its relationships to Soviet bloc nations in Eastern Europe as well as to its two communist neighbors, Laos and Vietnam. Meanwhile, non-communist nations in Southeast Asia, as well as most countries elsewhere, claimed that Pol Pot's ousted government was the legal one.

The Future of Kampuchea

Only five years after it was founded, the Khmer Republic was crushed by the combined forces of the Khmer Rouge and Prince Sihanouk. The new government, led by Pol Pot, experienced an even briefer life. Pol Pot brought the country starvation and massacres before he was finally driven out.

The present government of Kampuchea is almost completely

The Khmer Republic enlisted all able hands, including women, to help fight the Khmer Rouge. Most of its productive capacity was crippled during the war.

dominated by Vietnam and the Soviet Union. It is likely to remain so. Vietnam, impoverished by years of warfare, offered to withdraw its troops from Kampuchea in 1988, but an international conference arranged to begin that process fell far short of success. That left Vietnam still immeshed in an expensive, exhausting conflict. It must continue to station 100,000 troops in Kampuchea.

In the negotiations the Vietnamese wanted to be sure that the most powerful of the three forces in the coalition they were fighting would not take over the government again. It was the 35,000-member Khmer Rouge army still led by Pol Pot, who had headed the government for four murderous years before the Vietnamese drove him out in 1979. The Khmer Rouge representatives, knowing that their strength was growing, refused to negotiate flexibly.

Peace in Kampuchea next fell to China and the Soviet Union to try to arrange. With China supporting the Khmer Rouge and the Soviets the Vietnamese, those two countries began meetings. The foreign policies of both had become less aggressive; an armistice had become possible, though it was still remote.

Whatever other countries do to or for it, Kampuchea must eventually face the same problems that it did in earlier times. Its lasting crisis arises out of poverty and its dependence on a single crop, rice. Its people, lacking raw materials or industrial capacity, have little to trade with other countries. Because of the failure of a rice crop more than a million Kampucheans were near starvation in 1987-88 alone.

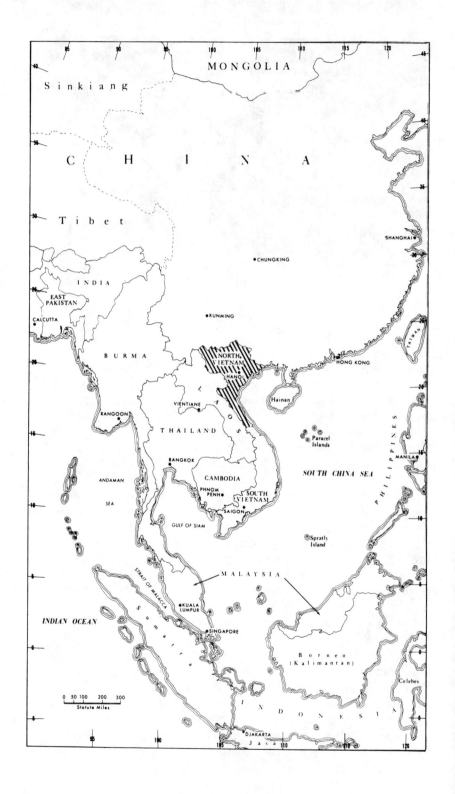

CHAPTER 5

The Independent Nations

VIETNAM: THE PATH TO UNITY

Two Countries, One People

As the French neared their collapse at Dienbienphu, Great Britain and the Soviet Union called a conference of the world's great powers and of Southeast Asian countries. The representatives met at Geneva, Switzerland, to work out a plan for stabilizing Southeast Asia. The resulting Geneva Agreement of 1954 officially divided Vietnam into two states, North and South. Among other things, it promised that the two countries would hold a joint election on the question of their reunification in 1956. The major powers pledged that they would not interfere with the two new countries, politically or militarily. The United States publicly subscribed to the Agreement but was not a party to it.

The people of North and South Vietnam had a common culture, but there were historic differences between them. While tracing the similarities, this chapter will show how and why these differences led them into the most devastating conflict of modern times. The differences were the basis of a civil war, but eventually they affected much larger populations than the Vietnamese themselves. Every other country in Southeast Asia, as well as the United States, China, and the Soviet Union, became involved in the conflict.

SOCIAL CONDITIONS AND CULTURAL LIFE

Ethnic groups. Almost 85 percent of Vietnam's 60 million people are members of a cohesive ethnic group called the Vietnamese. They are descendants of the Yueh, a tribe that apparently migrated from China in 333 B.C. A little over five feet tall, the average Vietnamese has high cheekbones, brown skin, dark eyes, and straight black hair.

In their historic movement southward, the Vietnamese absorbed the culture of an indianized people called the Chams. According to the Vietnamese, the southerners became less cohesive as they

185

encountered more Indian ideas and moved farther from the origins of their culture. Resistance to foreigners generally sprang up in the north, while the south tended to accept the powerful influence of the Khmers and French.

At both ends of the country, people are concentrated in the lowlands. In the north, the population density is greatest in the Red River Delta, and in the south it is in the Mekong Delta. Both the north and the south have large minority groups. The mountains east of the Red River, on the border with China, is home for minorities who occupy the Tay Bac Autonomous Region (south of the river) and the Viet Bac Autonomous Region (north of the river). They were settled on these lands during the Vietnam War when they expressed a desire to have their own governments.

The Meo are the largest minority in the north. About 250,000 of these short, dark people live in elevations over 3,000 feet. For this reason, other Vietnamese often refer to them as "wildcats." Smaller groups in the north, including the Tay, Tai, Nyong, Man, and Nung, are less cohesive and speak at least a dozen languages.

There are two large minorities in the south: the Montagnards

South Vietnam's rice paddies are cultivated by methods that have not changed for centuries. This is the Mekong Delta, the country's most productive area.

(French for "mountain people"), about 700,000 of whom live in the Annamite Highlands; and the ethnic Chinese. Until recent times, about a million Chinese lived in Vietnam's southern cities. This huge population originally came to Vietnam to work on plantations owned by the French, but later they entered business and rose to dominate commerce. After the Vietnam War a wave of anger against both private businesses and foreigners swept across the country. It forced the Chinese to make the cruel choice of laboring on farms or leaving the country and in either case to abandon their homes. Once scattered, many lost their lives as well.

Religion. The major Vietnamese religions are drawn from three sources: local, India, and China. Though they have different names, they are subtly mixed into a religious system which is unique to Vietnam. At least 85 percent of the Vietnamese people call themselves Buddhists. What they practice, however, is a blend of animism, Buddhism, and Confucianism. This blend is apparent even among people who have replaced religious with political concerns.

What remains of animism in Vietnam runs like an undercurrent through the life of the people. It is chiefly expressed through a popular belief in astrology or "luck," for most Vietnamese still think that their lives are governed by spirits. Individuals regularly ask astrologers to help them learn their destinies from the positions of the planets. Others conduct themselves according to the way that pebbles fall out of an overturned cup. People say that spirits make some days luckier than others, and almost every farmer calls on a "Guardian Spirit of the Village" to help him gain its favors. In precolonial times the emperor of Vietnam assigned a particular spirit to almost every village, and most of his suggestions are still remembered.

Almost every village has a sacrificial altar for its "Guardian Spirit" and for the "God of the Soil." Four ceremonies draw villagers into religious activities: "Wish for Peace," "Descent to the Fields," Ascent from the Fields," and "Appreciation at the Temple"—the latter a harvest festival. The people pay tribute to gods and saints who are thought capable of leading, protecting, and inspiring their families, communities, craft practitioners, or professions. Most village homes maintain an altar for the "God of the Hearth."

Probably their strong belief in spirits led the Vietnamese to accept the Mahayana, rather the Theravada school of Buddhism. The Mahayana school suggests that saintly teachers (*bodhisattvas*) choose to live among humans rather than remain in heaven with the Buddha, whom the school reveres as a god. The Vietnamese,

Confucianism remains
powerful in
South Vietnam.

alone among Southeast Asians, adopted this Buddhist school, which came from China.

In Vietnam as elsewhere, Buddhism encourages a sense of internal strength based upon moderation, respect for life, and compassion. It advises the Vietnamese to bear hardship and to complain as little as possible. Vietnamese children are urged to "bend as the bamboo"—to yield under pressure but not to snap. People are told to be courteous, modest, patient, and friendly in their relationships.

To these virtues, Buddhism also adds the need for selflessness, which has been sharply evident among the Vietnamese in recent times. The Buddhist faith in Vietnam is supported almost entirely by the voluntary contributions of its followers. The constant pressure to give charity, from wandering monks and in temples, steadily reminds the Vietnamese that society requires sacrifices of all individuals.

Buddhist ideals in Vietnam are complemented by those of Confucianism, which also preaches moderation, compromise, and self-discipline. Confucianism is not a religion, but an ethical system. It urges people to think that the culture of society, in the form of the ancient past and its modern traditions, is more important than the self. Heeding the call of Confucianism for ancestor worship, most Vietnamese families remained close to the burial grounds of their ancestors even when war made it difficult to do so. Most farms include a separate area for the spirits of the dead. Confucianism teaches that society is ordained by "Heaven" and survives only because people know their places in it. There are limits to each person's role in life, it suggests. The individual must accept these limits, whatever the hardship.

Almost all Vietnamese are profoundly affected by Confucianism, which exists side by side with Buddhism. They agree with its premise that society operates best when individuals follow the natural order of the universe. As a part of nature, the individual is expected to know his relationship to people, institutions, and even things. In the family, the basic unit of Confucian society, the father benevolently regulates the natural order. His counterpart in government is the emperor, who performs the same function for the whole country. In general, Confucian society grants the greatest esteem to elderly males and the least to young females, but it urges that all members of the family be protected and cherished.

About 1.5 million Vietnamese are Roman Catholics. Under French rule they kept their positions of leadership in the economy. Many of them, more highly skilled than others, kept their high positions when Vietnam was split in two. The communists of the North regarded them as agents of foreign culture, however. In 1956, feeling persecuted, more than 750,000 of them marched southward, led by their priests. Less than twenty years later they were under communist rule again.

Daoism (often spelled Taoism) was another influential, though less popular Vietnamese religion during precolonial times. It spread among the peasants while Confucianism was developing in the court. Eventually Vietnam's Daoists accepted the animist belief in magic. They claimed that spirits had the power to cure illness or deliver good fortune and should be offered sacrifices at specific times. These beliefs, like the animist ones, have not disappeared. They have been absorbed into the mainstream of Vietnamese religions.

A more isolated set of beliefs exists among more than three million people in the Mekong Delta. There, two religious sects comprise almost 40 percent of the population. One, the Cao Dai ("Third Amnesty of God"), combines Confucianism, Buddhism, and Daoism. It unites all of the world's great religious leaders in one symbol, the "Eye of God," which is represented in their cathedral northwest of Ho Chi Minh City (Saigon). The second is the Hoa Hao, a group of Buddhists whose unique interpretations of their faith includes ancient healing practices and ancestor worship. The center of activity of the Hoa Hao is southwest of Ho Chi Minh City, the former Saigon.

For all of their differences, Vietnam's religions share basic principles. Above all, they make the individual subject to a group rather than to an individual conscience. They have enabled the Vietnamese people to bear the intense suffering caused by the longest wars in recent times. Even the communist government recognizes the importance of religion in Vietnam's life. For example, it organized Catholics into the "National Catholic Liaison Committee" and the "Patriotic Catholic Church." The founder of communism in Vietnam, Ho Chi Minh, emphasized the Confucian concept that government is good conduct in practice. It was through this ideal that he was able to mobilize people in his struggle against corrupt rulers.

Ho, like China's Confucian monarchs, conceived of himself as the head of a family rather than as a detached sovereign. He had no children, but in public messages referred to himself as "Uncle Ho" and to the people as his "nephews and nieces." The Vietnamese thought of him as a leader with a "Mandate of Heaven." Ho's victories over the Japanese and French earned him popular devotion that verged on religion. Preaching the need for common action and morality, he drew on popular religions to prepare the Vietnamese for his program of national unity, communism, and social action.

Education, language, and the arts. The Vietnamese rejected the education offered them by the French, for they considered it cultur-

The richly decorated throne room in the Imperial Palace at Hué symbolizes the ancient influence of China in Vietnam. The dragon-like figures connote perfection.

ally inferior to their own. They saw it as a French device to control them. About the time of World War I, they began to question their own Confucian education, too. Their doubts arose chiefly because 100,000 of their young men were drafted by the French to help fight in the European war. When these soldiers returned home, they began dream of a modern country resembling the ones that they'd seen in Europe. Traditional training could never make this dream come true, they thought.

The mood of the soldiers quickly affected all of Vietnam. This change in the country's way of thinking stirred new interest in both the quality and quantity of education. In the past, the mandarins of Vietnam had emphasized instruction in the Chinese and Vietnamese languages, literature, and history. They taught a limited number of students. Under post-World War I reforms, new public schools emphasized science and technology as well as the humanities. So many young Vietnamese tried to enroll in them that the French were unwilling to build schools fast enough.

The Vietnamese people responded to the shortage of schools by starting their own system of education. Though the French, accusing them of teaching nationalism, arrested hundreds of teachers and students, Vietnam had 567,000 primary and secondary students by 1939. Even that was far less than the number who might have been enrolled if more buildings existed.

A few other figures demonstrate Vietnam's strong belief in education. Throughout the Vietnam War, in the midst of air raids and raging ground battles, there were 7.5 million students in both north and south. That was more than 750 percent of the 1939 number. Another 119,000 were enrolled in institutions of higher learning, despite the need to maintain large standing armies. The threat of bombing often closed urban schools, but rural ones kept teaching while fighting went on around them. By 1985, 63 percent of all Vietnamese between the ages of 5 and 19 were in schools, and literacy had reached 78 percent of the total population.

Education at all levels is identified with patriotism in Vietnam. "To study is to love the Fatherland," say officials. Every school has organizations of teachers and students attached to the government's only political party. Students carefully study communist ideas and control each other by continually repeating slogans. While studying they are told to work for the reconstruction of Vietnam. Many educational ideas have been borrowed from the Soviet Union, which financed the construction of Hanoi Polytechnical College in 1965.

Vietnamese is the language used in the schools. It contains personal pronouns that classify people according to age, education, and status and thus reflects Confucian influence among the Vietnamese people. At the same time it uses titles rather than names, even when referring to close relatives, so that animist spirits will not overhear and be aroused by the sound of a personal name. Vietnamese employs Roman letters and accent marks and so does not appear to resemble Chinese. Nevertheless, older Vietnamese people often use Chinese characters, especially during ceremonies.

Like education, the arts are used to promote support for Vietnam's government. The Vietnamese have always been drawn to literature, and the modern government uses this attraction by paying writers and poets to create patriotic works. Songs, plays, and dances are developed to call attention to the unity and accomplishments of the Vietnamese people. Ho Chi Minh himself led the way to Vietnam's use of the arts in politics. As a prisoner of the Nationalist Chinese in 1942-43, he wrote about a hundred poems. They exist today in the form of a widely admired book called *Prison Diary*. One of these poems says:

> The body is in prison
> The mind escapes outside:
> To bring about great things
> The mind must be large and well-tempered.

Throughout history, thousands of Vietnamese writers have chosen the medium of poetry to express themselves. They emphasized the ideas of order, discipline, and duty that are inherent in Confucianism. Some reflect animism and deal with the mystical. Their work became more popular after the development of Vietnam's Roman letter script during the nineteenth century.

The longest poem in the Vietnamese language is a masterpiece called *Kim Van Kieu*, by Nguyen Du (1765-1820). The three thousand lines of this tale of love and loyalty are known by most Vietnamese, who like dramas which describe their history and moral principles. So eager are the Vietnamese to read that villages often contain "Temples of Literature." In precolonial times the materials in the temples stressed Confucianism. Today they deal chiefly with communism.

Music is also an important part of life in Vietnam. People often sing while working in the fields or marching. Like workers everywhere they use music to help concentrate on monotonous jobs, but the songs also often contain moral lessons drawn from Confucianism. Operas that use the five-tone Chinese scale, rather than the West's eight-tone one, are popular. French, as well as Chinese culture, influences the Vietnamese.

Calligraphy and landscape painting are probably the most widespread visual arts in Vietnam. Some of the country's most respected rulers and scholars were also famous calligraphers. They became models for the general population, and their art is preserved in scrolls, lacquerware, and pottery.

POLITICAL DEVELOPMENTS

There were no more than five thousand communists in all of Vietnam at the beginning of World War II. Their leader, Ho Chi Minh, had become a communist after fighting in the French army in 1917-18. Ho's ultimate goal was to liberate Vietnam from France and to reform its economy, but during the war he organized resistance against the Japanese.

In 1942, as described in Chapter 4, the Nationalist Chinese arrested Ho for communist activities. They held him for two years, and when they released him it was with the understanding that he would help them by fighting the Japanese in his homeland. Ho returned to Vietnam with a substantial sum of money that he promised to use for anti-Japanese activities. His successes enabled him to take the leadership of North Vietnam by 1945.

Late in 1945, Ho issued a "Declaration of Independence of the Democratic Republic of Vietnam." It quoted from the American Declaration of Independence and the Declaration of the French Revolution, then gave these reasons for the continuing struggle of the Vietnamese people:

(The) French imperialists, abusing the standard of Liberty, Equality, and Fraternity, have violated our Fatherland and oppressed our fellow-citizens. They have acted contrary to the ideals of humanity and justice. In the field of politics, they have deprived our people of every democratic liberty.

They have enforced inhuman laws; they have set up three distinct political regimes in the North, the Center, and the South of Vietnam in order to wreck our national unity and present our people from being united.

They have built more prisons than schools. They have mercilessly slain our patriots; they have drowned our uprisings in rivers of blood. They have fettered public opinion; they have practiced obscurantism against our people To weaken our race they have forced us to use opium and alcohol. . . . In the fields of economics, they have fleeced us. . . .

Ho was able to defeat the French chiefly because the Vietnamese people accepted his view of their condition. They helped him both secretly and openly, until in May, 1954 his guerrillas forced the

The French dealt severely with insurgents in Vietnam. The ragged army of peasants, however, gained in strength and defeated France's modern army.

collapse of the French army in the siege of Dienbienphu. Professor Bernard B. Fall, a noted historian of modern Vietnam, later wrote of France's humiliation at the hands of the guerrillas who closed the siege:

> *Close to ten thousand captured (French) troops were to begin the grim death march to the Viet Minh prison camps three hundred miles to the east. Few would survive. About two thousand lay dead all over the battlefield in graves unmarked to this day.*

THE TWO GOVERNMENTS

Post-independence: the North. When the French were defeated the members of Ho's party, the Lao Dong (the "Worker's Party"), included less than 0.5 percent of North Vietnam's 20 million people, but its influence was profound. It made direct contact with the North Vietnamese people through *cadres*, party members with special skills and persuasive ability. Most cadres were young, but some were among the original two or three hundred who helped to found the Lao Dong Party in 1930. Many were women, for the party stressed the equality of the sexes. Cadres began to appear at every meeting and in all of the social institutions of North Vietnam.

The Lao Dong Party proclaimed as its goal a society in which goods and services would be more equitably distributed than in the past. It worked to develop what it called a "socialist man" instead of the traditional Confucian one. This "new man," it hoped, would be more loyal to the state than to his family, dedicating himself to the advancement of his people under a socialist system. He was expected to honor the chief of state at least as much as his own father.

The North Vietnamese communists developed their program in response to problems inherited from colonial times. Under the French, Vietnam did not control its own resources. The country's wealth was managed by an elite class made up of the few who could learn French and were willing to become Roman Catholics. The mark of membership in this class, a French education, was unavailable to most people. How the North Vietnamese overcame this elite, and what happened as a result, is a major part of recent world history.

The Lao Dong Party was determined to avoid giving control of government to an elite. But the members of the party had, in effect, become an elite themselves. They refused to allow non-party members to join the administration. To spread the party's program chapters were formed in the industries, schools, the army, and large farms of North Vietnam. Party members were organized into associations including youth, professional, and labor groups. In 1955 all of these groups were merged into one massive federation called the Vietnam Fatherland Front. By 1960 the original 5,000 members of the Lao Dong Party had grown to 300,000, and by 1965, 800,000.

The Fatherland Front easily persuaded the Vietnamese people to vote for the Lao Dong Party in every election. Ho Chi Minh never failed to win less than 98 percent of the vote in three general elections. North Vietnam used the secret ballot and permitted anyone eighteen or older to vote. Nevertheless, it offered people no alternatives to the Lao Dong Party, to which all of the 453 members of the National Assembly belonged. The Assembly was given the right to choose the country's president and other high officials.

There were elected "People's Councils" in each of North Vietnam's seventeen provinces and two autonomous regions. The councils worked closely with the national government. North Vietnam developed a judicial system called the "People's Courts." The judges, or "assessors," weighed cases against standard morality and public policy rather than against fixed law. For example, someone who failed to help develop a public project might stand accused of a major crime and suffer a jail sentence. But the same crime might be overlooked or even draw a lesser punishment at another time or place. Under these conditions it was not always possible for individuals to know when a crime had been committed or what their punishment would be after conviction. Once accused, the chances were that they would be found guilty, for the courts gave great weight to the evidence gathered by police and party investigators. Defendants represented themselves, for North Vietnam had no legal profession, nor were the assessors trained in the law.

The government used its carefully built society to help develop the new "socialist man." Writers, musicians, and artists were only given financial aid if they served the aims of the Lao Dong Party. Officials spoke daily over more than 600,000 loudspeakers in the country's schools, offices, and factories. They called on people to "Place the interests of the party and the interests of the people above one's own interest." They urged greater production, an increase in public health and sanitation, a lower birth rate, and higher moral standards including reduced gambling and drinking. They opposed wasteful celebrations, arranged marriages, and ancestor worship.

Post-independence: the South. Shortly after becoming South Vietnam's first Chief of State Bao Dai, former emperor of Annam, appointed a regional leader named Ngo Diem as prime minister. Diem promptly called on South Vietnam to decide whether or not it wanted to become a republic. A year later an election was held, and Diem became president, replacing Bao Dai. The results of the election, however, were suspiciously overwhelming. More than 98 percent of the votes were cast for Diem. Many people said the election was a fraud.

Diem's first major problem involved the capital, Saigon. There, the French and Bao Dai had given control of the police to a fraternal group called the Binh Xuyen. This organization openly collected bribes from most businesses and was licensing drugs, prostitution, and criminal syndicates. Diem ordered the army to replace the Binh Xuyen. This action won him the support of the United States, which began to send advisers and money to support his government. In 1956 alone the United States sent $270 million.

The unity of South Vietnam was soon threatened by the three million members of the Cao Dai and Hoa Hao, the two major religious sects near Saigon. The sects charged that Diem was not allowing them freedom of religion, though a new constitution guaranteed it. They formed armies totalling 35,000, but Diem's troops quickly scattered them and drove many of their leaders out of the country. His successful military action against the sects rapidly won him more support from the South Vietnamese army, whose officers represented the country's wealthiest class.

The constitution of 1956 gave the president control over the courts, army, and police. Diem exercised this enormous power by refusing to allow legal opposition. To halt what he said were conspiracies, Diem issued eight million identity cards to every adult in South Vietnam. His closest advisers were the members of his own family, for he trusted few others. His brother, Ngo Dinh Nhu, developed a spy system to keep close watch over his critics. Diem defended his suspicions by pointing out that the 900,000 refugees arriving from the North might easily include communist agents. Thus he used the desire for national security as a means of increasing his power.

Diem and his family were determined to wipe out communism in South Vietnam and proposed their own political philosophy to oppose it. This creed, called "Personalism," attracted about 20,000 followers, mostly in the army and civil service. It urged strict self-discipline which could be transferred on the social level into public morals. With the help of the Personalists, Madame Nhu, the wife of Ngo Dinh Nhu, became an influential political figure. She designed a new Family Code which restricted polygamy, concubinage, and the freedom given to men in divorce actions. She sponsored laws prohibiting birth control, boxing, cockfights, beauty contests, the sale of alcoholic beverages to minors, prostitution, and American dancing.

Because they were a leading Roman Catholic family, the Ngos soon aroused the opposition of the Buddhists. The Ngos appointed Catholics to most of the top administrative positions in government. The 750,000 Roman Catholics who came from the North in 1956 doubled the Roman Catholic population in South Vietnam. The policies of the Ngo family and the sudden increase in the number of Roman Catholics brought strong opposition from the country's Buddhists.

Unrest in the south thus had its roots in uncertainty. The South Vietnamese were not sure whether they could build a nation, though they had been given one in name. Large groups believed themselves to have been denied representation in government and within the leadership of society. It appeared to many South Vietnamese that their leaders reflected foreign principles rather than those springing from their own soil.

As this mutual distrust spread, the new government of South Vietnam refused to sign the Geneva Agreement, which ended France's efforts to keep Vietnam in 1954. It protested that instead

With increasing U.S. support, Diem developed one of the largest armies in Southeast Asia. His methods were stern, however, and he was assassinated.

of forming two countries the convention should have placed all of Vietnam under a commission of the United Nations. On these grounds, it refused to honor North Vietnam's call for national elections in 1956. Diem claimed that he was not bound by the Geneva Agreement because South Vietnam had not signed it and because North Vietnam had violated its terms. The United States supported this action.

But a coalition of reformers and communists inside of South Vietnam demanded the promised election. When they were consistently rejected, they began to organize guerrillas. Diem's agents sought to control them in 1957, beginning a round of assassinations that resulted in the death of hundreds of rural officials. The National Liberation Front (NLF), which by then had organized revolutionaries throughout the country, responded with kidnappings and murders of Diem's supporters. Hiding in the jungle, they made swift attacks and then withdrew to safety. Thus the civil war began, and soon it was to involve many other governments.

CHAPTER 6

The Independent Nations

THE VIETNAM WAR (1956-75)

CAUSES AND EFFECTS

Economic conditions. When South Vietnam gained its independence in 1955, an American economist studied its land ownership. He found that more than half of the land was owned by 2.5 percent of the population. In the crowded Mekong Delta, two-thirds of the peasants owned no land at all. The system which enabled a few people to take control of most of the land developed during the colonial period. The French did not have enough administrators to govern the large new areas they were opening in Cochin China. For this reason they helped French-speaking Vietnamese to become landlords and local rulers.

The landlords became Confucian heads of their communities and were locally powerful even when they moved to Paris or to South Vietnam's cities. They loaned money, judged disputes, and took care of the needs of peasants while collecting up to half of the annual crop for themselves. In effect these landlords were extensions of the French colonial government, which concentrated its efforts in the cities and plantations.

The peasants learned to despise the landlords and their agents. They saw young Vietnamese going to work in French-owned mines, plantations, and industries while they were left to pay high rents. They watched angrily as Vietnam's imperial and communal lands became private estates and plantations. The land was producing such export crops as rubber, coffee, and tea instead of rice for domestic consumption.

The problems of land ownership were compounded by the Indochina War. By 1955 South Vietnam's agriculture, the basis of its economy, was crippled by the destruction of 2.5 million acres of the most valuable rice farms. Canals irrigation, and farm machinery were in ruins. The average farmer owned only 2 to 5 acres or had to buy his own seeds, tools, and livestock in order to secure the 50 percent of the crop that the landlord allowed him to keep.

South Vietnam's farmlands are crowded, and there is no land to spare. Only 7.6 million of the country's 42 million acres are under intensive cultivation. Of this amount about 6.5 million acres produce wet rice. The 17,000 square miles of the central highlands have vast amounts of land that cannot be used because they lack water or arable soil. They include 350,000 acres of rubber plantations built for the French, however.

The country appeared to be recovering rapidly after the war with the French. In the Mekong Delta rice production reached its normal level between 1,000 and 1,500 pounds of rice per acre each year. The delta's farmers were able to plant only one crop a year, but they worked steadily and were making progress.

This was the situation when, in 1959, the guerrillas of the NLF began their attacks. Their chief issue was the refusal of South Vietnam to permit a national election. However, they advanced other goals to win peasant support. One was the concentration of land ownership in the hands of a few. Another was the feeling among Buddhists that they had little influence in the government. A third was widespread corruption and the breakdown of morals. All of these problems, the guerrillas said, had been brought about by foreign influences.

Political developments. The guerrillas set up a jungle headquarters and by 1960 were joined by several hundred advisers from the North. They gained control of sufficient land to set up their own government, which collected taxes, established schools, hospitals, and granaries. Diem promptly called this government the "Viet Cong" (Viet communists) to imply that his rural opposition were all agents of the North. The charge was false, but the name Viet Cong has been used to describe the rebels ever since. At the beginning of the Vietnam War the rebels consisted of a coalition of land reformers, nationalists, and communists, almost all of whom lived in the South.

The issue of land reform drew millions of peasants to the side of the guerrillas. Many landlords were executed or forced to abandon their holdings. Others were permitted to continue to own land if they limited rents to 5 to 15 percent of the annual crop.

In exchange for help against the landlords the peasants supplied food, refuge, and volunteers to the Viet Cong. The guerrillas were able to buy and store as much rice as they needed, thus depriving the government of food in the cities. By controlling the rice supply they drove prices higher each year. The government tried to block this maneuver by seizing all but one week's supply of rice from every family in the delta. In 1970 it began to store rice inventories in warehouses from which families could draw supplies once a week. Still, it bought rice at fixed prices which were lower than the guerrillas offered and so spread discontent with its economic policies.

Shortages and wartime expenditures made inflation one of the gravest problems in South Vietnam. As the rate of inflation rose from 30 percent in 1968-69 to 50 percent in 1969-70, disabled veterans, students, and the elderly became the first victims of rising prices. Rice production was increasing, yet there seemed to be too little to feed the 20 million people of South Vietnam.

The guerrillas, meanwhile, persisted because of the rugged terrain in rural South Vietnam. The jungles have no boundaries and few communications. In one early battle, fewer than 200 guerrillas were able to defeat 2,500 trained government soldiers. They triumphed, though the soldiers were supported by automatic rifles, rockets, amphibious vehicles, helicopters, and bombers. The guerrillas shot down five helicopters and killed or wounded most of the government troops. Then they faded into the canopy of the jungle, returning to villages where they were indistinguishable from other peasants.

To fight these elusive soldiers the South Vietnamese army needed five to ten times the number of men and arms possessed by the guerrillas. It was this unequal combat which soon brought outside forces into the country.

THE AMERICAN ROLE

U.S. advisers. Officially, North Vietnam disclaimed any relationship with the NLF. The United States, however, reported that about 5,000 North Vietnamese troops were stationed in the South and were supporting the guerrillas. The Americans, fearing the spread of communism in Southeast Asia, began sending advisers to South Vietnam. At this time, they had no intention of committing ground troops to a land war. They were continuing a process begun in 1950 by President Truman, who had sent thirty-five military advisers to Vietnam to help the French.

President Kennedy, who had sent 800 advisers to help the South Vietnamese, increased the number to more than 16,000 in 1961. Among them were members of the Central Intelligence Agency (CIA). Disguised as civilians, the CIA agents were given funds to sabotage guerrilla efforts in the South and to blow up at least one munitions base in the North.

The British, as well as the Americans, were advising Diem. They recalled their successes against guerrillas in Malaya. There, villagers were gathered in fortified hamlets from which the combined colonial and local forces were able to defeat the insurgents. The

At the height of his power in South Vietnam President Diem toured the front with an American adviser.

British proposed a similar policy to Diem, who used American funds to finance the plan. But in Malaya the insurgents were almost all Chinese. They could be distinguished from the general population, while the South Vietnamese guerrillas could not. The fortified hamlets therefore proved to be ineffective against the Viet Cong.

By 1962, about 80 percent of South Vietnam's rural areas were under the control of the NLF. There were more than 75,000 anti-government guerrillas in the South, and their number was growing. To resist them the Americans began to send bombers, helicopters, and artillery.

Thus while many local issues lay at the core of the struggle in South Vietnam, the region's strategic value were drawing powerful outside forces into battle. An American army, and to a much lesser extent British, French, Thai, and Korean forces, stood beside the South Vietnamese. The Vietnamese communists, meanwhile, fought alone, but were firmly supported by China and the Soviet Union.

U.S. troops. By 1962, the triumph of the guerrillas seemed inevitable. It appeared that President Diem was unable to rally South Vietnam to meet the challenge. The reasons for his failure lay in the nature of South Vietnam's society.

Much of the unwillingness of peasants to cooperate with their government stemmed from Diem's conflicts with Buddhists. Tension between the Buddhists and the government turned to violence on the anniversary of Buddha's birthday in 1963. The government refused to allow the Buddhists to raise their flag in Hue. The Buddhists organized demonstrations and were attacked by police, who killed nine persons. Then Buddhists throughout South Vietnam took to the streets, demanding the right to raise their flag and worship freely.

Soon, the Ngo family was locked in a political struggle from which it could not retreat. On the streets of Hue and Saigon, crowds of people were shocked one day to see Buddhist monks sitting in flames. The monks, using gasoline, had set fire to themselves to demonstrate moral commitment to their faith. To this desperate policy the Ngos responded forcefully, charging that the Buddhists were largely communists. Police were sent into pagodas to arrest more than 1,000 monks. Yet despite his declaration of martial law, President Diem could not prevent thousands of students from joining the Buddhist protest.

Ultimately, the government arrested almost 4,000 Buddhists. The sight of monks burning in the streets or being thrown into prisons, carried over television, turned world opinion against South Vietnam. In a further blow to his administration, Diem was revealed to have lied about the use of American funds. He had claimed to have fortified 16,000 hamlets, but an investigation showed that money had been spent on less than a tenth of that number.

Finally South Vietnam's army decided to take action. Apparently with the consent of American advisers, four generals ordered the arrest of Diem and his brother, Nhu, in 1963. Soldiers found the two men taking refuge in a Catholic church and executed them both.

After the assassination of President Kennedy in 1963, the U.S. Joint Chiefs of Staff pressed for a greater American military commitment in South Vietnam. They thought that the small guerrilla army would stand no chance against the full use of American military power. Setting up what they called "free fire zones," they ordered American pilots and South Vietnamese troops to shoot anything that moved outside the Strategic Hamlets at night. At the same time they pleaded with the new President, Lyndon B. Johnson, for the power to use American troops in South Vietnam if necessary.

The new tactics, like many others undertaken by the South Vietnamese and Americans, terrified many villagers. The free-fire zones, Strategic Hamlets, and use of napalm and defoliation aroused anger among the peasants. Nothing, it seemed, could bring them to join the fight against the guerrillas. On the contrary, most of them seemed to be giving the rebels food, shelter, and supplies. But the Americans persisted, believing that their modern weapons and overwhelming fire power could overcome the resistance.

The U.S.-South Vietnamese alliance. The South Vietnamese generals who overthrew Diem dissolved the government. In 1963, they established a Revolutionary Military Council composed of twenty-four army officers. The Council promised freedom of religious worship and a new constitution. It abolished Diem's spy system and released many of the imprisoned Buddhists, students, and other dissidents. At the same time it ordered the arrest of a number of Diem's former agents.

Diem's fall left a political vacuum that no other single leader was able to fill for almost three years. During that period, nine administrations rose and fell in South Vietnam. None could reconcile the demands of the Buddhists, Catholics, and urban intellectuals who wanted freedom of expression. Seven of these administrations came to power through violence. Buddhists and students pleaded for an end of military control, but they were met with tear gas and mass arrests. They repeatedly accused the United States of supporting a corrupt military dictatorship. The army, on the other hand, said that strong governmental controls were needed to resist communism.

In 1966, South Vietnam's military leaders formed a National Leadership Committee called the "Directorate." It was led by a former Buddhist who had become a Catholic, Major General Nguyen Van Thieu. The Directorate made Thieu chief of state. It appointed Brigadier General Nguyen Cao Ky to serve as prime minister. Thieu and Ky continued to suppress freedom of speech and of the press on grounds that the country was threatened by communist guerrillas and a severe inflation. A new constitution—the fourth since Diem's overthrow—called for civilian government, but the army continued to hold the ultimate power.

Yet Buddhist resentment against the South Vietnamese government did not end with the fall of Diem. Previously disorganized, the Buddhists formed the Popular Force Struggling for Revolution—"Struggle Force"—in 1966. When Prime Minister Ky dismissed a Buddhist general, Struggle Force staged demonstrations, strikes, and boycotts. Finally it took control of most of the northern part of South Vietnam. Ky was forced to send paratroops to overcome the Buddhists. At length he had to assure them that elections would be held.

The momentous national elections did take place in 1966. They were boycotted by Buddhists and communists, who charged that the government had prevented them from campaigning. Most of the 108 Assembly seats were won by Catholics, property owners, professionals, military men, and civil servants. In the presidential election that followed, the military displayed its continuing power by ordering Prime Minister Ky not to oppose Thieu. Ky angrily accepted the order and ran for vice president instead. Ten civilian candidates opposed the Thieu-Ky ticket, but in protest against the military control of the campaign they all refused to make public appearances. Thieu and Ky won the election, but they received less than 35 percent of the 4.8 million votes cast. Thus Thieu and Ky, although supported by little more than a third of the voters, took office for five years.

While Thieu and Ky were asserting military control over South Vietnam, Lyndon B. Johnson was preparing his 1964 Presidential campaign in the United States. He promised the American people peaceful solutions to the issues in South Vietnam. After winning the Presidency with the largest vote in American history, however, his public speeches reflected a change of opinion. Johnson kept emphasizing that the war in South Vietnam could be stopped immediately if the North Vietnamese would withdraw their support of the Viet Cong. He informed the country that two U.S. destroyers had been attacked by North Vietnamese vessels in international waters near the Gulf of Tonkin. In an atmosphere of crisis, Johnson persuaded the U.S. Congress to empower him to retaliate.

Years after these events a book of official American documents, *The Pentagon Papers*, revealed that Johnson had planned the appeal for wartime powers even while campaigning on a peace platform before the "crisis" took place. Neither he nor the U.S. Navy explained why the destroyers were in the Gulf of Tonkin. Nevertheless, the Congress was led to believe that North Vietnam had struck the first blow and authorized the President to counter-attack. Its "Gulf of Tonkin Resolution" empowered Johnson to take measures "to repel any armed attack against the forces of the United States and to prevent further aggression." Thus began the longest war in American history.

The number of U.S. troops in South Vietnam rose from 17,000 in 1965 to 542,000 in 1970. They supported a South Vietnamese army which by 1970 numbered almost one million. Meanwhile, North Vietnamese troops in the South increased from 500 in 1965 to 95,000 in 1970. The North Vietnamese troops supplemented a Viet Cong army which by 1970 numbered more than 280,000.

The army of South Vietnam proved ineffective, largely because its troops were never as dedicated as those of its adversaries. Many South Vietnamese soldiers disliked Thieu. He ruled with a strong hand, silencing his critics with long jail sentences at hard labor. His popularity declined rapidly, and there were widespread complaints about his harsh policies and corruption among government officials. Beginning in 1970, many of his candidates were defeated in elections. Thieu himself won a major victory in his campaign for reelection in 1971, drawing 94 percent of the 6.3 million votes cast. But Ky, his major opponent, said the election was "rigged beyond imagination." To protest Thieu's power, students rioted on election day in Saigon, Da Nang, and Hue, burning government and U.S. vehicles.

To compensate for their loss of power on the ground, U.S. forces, under the authority of the Gulf of Tonkin Resolution, rained bombs steadily over North Vietnam. The concentrated air attacks struck at factories, bridges, and troops. They hammered the Ho Chi Minh Trail, a network of hidden jungle roads over which more than 90,000 Vietnamese regularly carried supplies from the North to the South. The North Vietnamese learned to move mostly at night in camouflaged vehicles. The bombing placed an enormous strain on them because the planes came steadily, dropping napalm and anti-personnel weapons, as well as bombs. According to American estimates, they often suffered more than 1,000 casualties a week. Food

The Ho Chi Minh Trail crosses Laos and Cambodia, ranging between North and South Vietnam.

was in short supply, and most consumer goods were unavailable. The North Vietnamese took steps to increase their food supply and capacity for production. At the same time they moved more than a million people from the Red River Delta, one of the world's most densely populated areas, to the sparsely settled highlands. By 1965 the resettlement program was part of a general plan to reduce the number of military targets in populated areas. Almost every civilian in Hanoi was moved to the countryside.

As the war progressed, the destructive power of the bombs dropped on North Vietnam surpassed the total dropped on Europe during World War II. Yet paradoxically, the North Vietnamese continued in their determination to unite the country. They drew pride from their defiance of a larger and more powerful country. In 1966 more than two million of them volunteered to help repair bombing damage in industry. Most North Vietnamese worked more than sixty hours a week, holding jobs and afterward standing guard duty or digging trenches. They planted small vegetable gardens to supplement the dwindling food supply. In Hanoi they swept the wide, tree-lined avenues clear of bombed rubble by 5 a.m. every day. Then they went to their jobs or set out in work gangs to repair buildings, railroads, or highways.

In the ground war, the Americans and South Vietnamese learned again that neither their great numerical superiority nor their superior weapons could overcome an enemy who refused to fight for territory. The North Vietnamese and Viet Cong attacked suddenly in small groups and disappeared into the jungles. They were given refuge by villagers who either shared their convictions or were fearful of Viet Cong terrorists. The Americans defoliated trees, destroyed crops, exploded napalm, anti-personnel weapons, and electronically-controlled bombs. Still they failed to destroy the Viet Cong or its source of supplies. The Americans dominated the skies by day, but the guerrillas controlled the countryside at night. With the help of villagers, the communists were able to carry food and munitions for miles.

The guerrillas mounted three major offensives, during 1964-65, 1968, and 1972. The first of these offensives took advantage of Buddhist demonstrations in South Vietnam. It brought most of the country's rural areas and major highways under Viet Cong control. The second consisted of a coordinated attack on more than one hundred South Vietnamese towns and cities. This was the "Tet Offensive," named for the period of the lunar new year in which it took place. It was not a military victory for the communists because the Vietnamese people did not rise up against their government as the guerrillas hoped. But the offensive was startling in its boldness and destructive effects, which included an invasion of the U.S. embassy in Saigon. The Tet Offensive resulted in a massive counter attack by U.S. and South Vietnamese forces. The third major communist offensive began in the far north—the so-called "Demilitarized Zone"—in 1972. It was an effort to test the ability of the South Vietnamese army to fight independently of the Americans.

The U.S. withdrawal. In the United States, there were mounting protests against the war. President Johnson, besieged by Americans demonstrating against the slaughter in Vietnam, decided not to run again. The demonstrators next forced Richard M. Nixon, who succeeded Johnson, to proclaim a policy of "vietnamizing" the conflict. By this he meant that he would slowly build South Vietnam's ability to fight alone. Yet it became evident that the South Vietnamese were not strong enough to withstand the sustained assaults in the offensive of 1972.

The Americans then made one last desperate effort to end the war. Waves of American bombers rained destruction on North Vietnam's cities and jungles. At the same time U.S. troops, accompanied by South Vietnamese, Thais, Koreans, and Australians, invaded neutral Cambodia in 1970. Their objective was to destroy Viet Cong supplies and quickly withdraw. However, this had the effect of intensifying the guerrilla war in Cambodia. In the United States it caused mounting protests from Americans who were angry and ashamed their country's role in Southeast Asia. After the Cambodian expedition President Nixon slowly withdrew U.S. ground forces from South Vietnam. But at the same time, he continued the massive bombing and artillery attacks on the North.

By 1970, the guerrillas had set up a "Provisional Revolutionary Government" (PRG) in rural areas which they firmly controlled. Immediately afterward, negotiations were begun in Paris by the United States and South Vietnam on one hand and North Vietnam and the PRG on the other. They dragged on inconclusively while the painful war continued. When the North Vietnamese and PRG mounted its 1972 offensive, the U.S. responded vigorously. American planes sowed mines in North Vietnam's harbors and renewed raids on Hanoi and Haiphong. U.S. pilots intensified efforts to defoliate jungles and destroy food supplies. The U.S. government later revealed that it had even tried to alter North Vietnam's weather patterns by scattering ice crystals in clouds.

At last, in despair, both sides agreed to an armistice. They had been negotiating in many unproductive meetings for over four years. Then in Paris, in 1973, they announced a cease-fire and the release of prisoners. The four parties to the agreement—the two

Nguyen Van Thieu continued
the military government
in South Vietnam.

Vietnams, the guerrilla force (PRG), and the United States—
recognized the demilitarized zone between North and South as a
provisional demarcation line. The authority of the PRG extended to
about 10 percent of the South Vietnamese population and 40 percent of its land. Until South Vietnam could hold "free . . . general
elections under international supervision" its own government was
to retain control over most of its original area.

But the population in the south was growing increasingly fearful.
The government had become more repressive as U.S. forces left.
President Thieu began his second five-year term by passing legislation that discouraged most candidates from opposing members of
his "Democracy Party." By 1974 Roman Catholics, as well as Buddhists, were demonstrating against his unwillingness to grant them
freedom of speech.

Thieu responded to the demonstrators by replacing hundreds of
public officials who were charged with corruption. But the people
of South Vietnam wanted a more complete reckoning. With U.S.
forces leaving, they were both insecure and burdened by the costs of
war and inflation. They were angered by proof that the fighting
continued, though at a low but deadly level, despite the armistice.

The Paris Agreement called for the establishment of a National
Council of National Reconciliation and Concord. It was to be made
up of members of the South Vietnamese government, the PRG, and
undefined "neutralist" spokesmen. Under the Agreement, American troops and bases were to be removed within sixty days, and that
clause was fulfilled. The North Vietnamese, meanwhile, were permitted to keep, though not to expand, their existing army of
140,000 men in South Vietnam.

As U.S. soldiers were leaving Saigon in 1973, a North Vietnamese officer said, "This is an historic day. It is the first time in one hundred years that there are no foreign troops on the soil of Vietnam." But by the Fall of that year, the communists were charging that the U.S. still had 20,000 advisers in the South Vietnamese army. The U.S. government replied that it had merely followed the Paris Agreement and counter-charged that the North Vietnamese had violated the agreement by moving 70,000 new troops, 400 tanks, and 200 artillery pieces into South Vietnam.

The truce broke down throughout 1974. During that year, South Vietnam reported having killed 104,670 North Vietnamese and NLF troops. These must be added to the 859,641 North Vietnamese and NLF guerrillas who were reported killed in the Vietnam War up to the time of the truce. In addition, 165,268 South Vietnamese and 55,000 Americans were killed. About 380,000 civilians died, and more than three million others became refugees. A moral breakdown accompanied the slaughter. Seeing mass murders going unpunished, gangs began to roam the streets of South Vietnam's cities. Drug-running, black marketeering, and prostitution became rampant. The overcrowded, impoverished urban areas were unable to prevent outbreaks of cholera, scabies, smallpox, malaria, and bubonic plague. Bridges, railways, roads, schools, and communications were in ruins.

The rest of the world was not always conscious of the war's effects on South Vietnam. Yet slowly other countries became aware that the billions of dollars spent on the war were a cause of rising prices everywhere. Within two years after the American troop withdrawal from Vietnam, inflation reached 50 percent in South Vietnam and 12 percent in the United States. All of Western Europe and Japan experienced increases between those figures. This inflation caused administrations to fall and threatened whole systems of government, for countless millions of people were unprepared to pay its price.

Yet the war went on and was certain to continue. By 1975, the North Vietnamese and NLF forces were mounting a major offensive and overcame a province just 75 miles north of South Vietnam's capital at Saigon. In response to this action the United States warned that it could not stand by and watch the guerrillas conquer all of South Vietnam. American arms and supplies continued to flow to the South, but the U.S. Congress resisted the enormous expenditures that it had made there in the past. As new fronts were opened during 1975, it appeared that the government of South Vietnam would have to stand alone against the combined forces of the North Vietnamese and their allied guerrillas.

Slowly the insurgents moved into the vacuum created by the withdrawal of the Americans. During the two years of the truce they seized eleven provinces and gained control of 80 percent of South Vietnam. They advanced on Saigon, claiming they had been promised a representative government that had not been formed.

The people of the South became desperate. More than a million refugees filled their roads. Major groups, including Catholics, Buddhists, and professional people demanded President Thieu's resignation. They called for an end to the government's repression and the negotiation of an enduring cease-fire. Thieu resigned in 1975 as the Viet Cong rockets exploded just fifteen miles from Saigon. Thus relentlessly, despite an "armistice," the insurgents were finishing off their enemy in the longest, costliest war of recent times. At the same time the Americans were frantically escaping from Saigon, evacuating all personnel and records while leaving behind tens of thousands of Vietnamese to whom they had promised protection.

The havoc was clear for all to see. More than 3.3 million Americans had fought in the Vietnam War. At the final count, 58,721 were reported killed and 303,713 wounded. A decade after the end of the war 2,477 were still reported missing in action. On all sides, the total military and civilian dead numbered more than 1.3 million. There were 9 million refugees in Indochina, and more than 5.2 million acres had been defoliated by American planes spreading chemicals which were to endure for years. The Americans had given South Vietnam $24 billion and had spent $165 billion in the struggle which an American general, Bruce Palmer Jr., was later to call "the first clear failure in (American) history."

CHAPTER 7

The Independent Nations

THE PEOPLE'S REPUBLIC OF VIETNAM:
THE USES OF POWER

T HE VIETNAM WAR CAME TO AN END after the U.S. Congress refused to grant South Vietnam additional military aid. The Congress indicated that more funds would only prolong the bloodshed and make no difference in the outcome. With the resignation of President Thieu in 1975, South Vietnam's government collapsed, and the country surrendered to the Viet Cong.

The victory of the Viet Cong halted the massive military expenditures, but not all of the causes of deficits. The new government next faced the problems of refugees, reconstruction, and food shortages, among many others. It planned to solve them by inviting the communist government of the north to extend itself across the conquered land. The battle for national unity, which had lasted for twenty-two years, was over. But new battles were beginning.

RECENT POLITICAL DEVELOPMENTS

On July 2, 1976 a military parade, complete with troops, tanks, and firecrackers, roared through the streets of Saigon. It celebrated the founding of the Socialist Republic of Vietnam. The newly unified state had been founded after an election in which 99 percent of all eligible voters chose the 492 members of a National Assembly. Only members of the Communist Party were permitted to run for office.

The new government found it difficult or impossible to achieve its announced goals of ". . . peace, independence, and national concord." The country went to war again soon afterward. It also became heavily dependent on the Soviet Union and profoundly disturbed the lives of millions of its people. For ten years more, the Vietnamese people endured new hardships as their country changed its political system.

At the outset of unification, the two parts of Vietnam were equal in name only. Political power rested in the north, whose officials began a campaign of "reeducation" in the newly added land. They sent police, schoolteachers, and tax collectors southward to replace

Ho Chi Minh (1890–1969)

their former enemies in those positions. After giving Saigon its new name, Ho Chi Minh City, they made plans to reduce the city's population. Up to 700,000 people, chiefly those in business, would be moved into the countryside to become farmers, they said. Another 700,000 eventually were moved out of other cities in South Vietnam.

The goal of this policy was to attack capitalist tendencies and increase food production. The government seized shops and businesses, ordering their owners to go to work on newly organized collective farms. Vietnam's 1.1 million ethnic Chinese bore the brunt of these changes. They dominated commerce and so were the largest group affected by the reduction in businesses. After spending their lives developing businesses, they were now regarded as class enemies and told to surrender their work and savings.

To a large degree, the ethnic Chinese felt that they were being punished because they were different from the Vietnamese— different in culture, language, and appearance. Many of them, therefore, tried to escape the country. Some struggled over the mountainous north, crossing wild rivers and jungles in an effort to reach China. Others set out in small fishing boats from Vietnam's southern shores. Probably the number who fled reached 750,000. It was greatly increased by the willingness of the Vietnamese government to put refugees out to sea in exchange for personal wealth.

The Chinese were not the only people to flee Vietnam. Whoever had cooperated with the Americans or owned substantial property stood in jeopardy. So were people who persisted in believing in their individual freedoms and right to become more prosperous than others. Most of these considered escaping from the country. Within the first four years after the war, 185,000 Vietnamese refugees managed to reach the United States alone. Even after ten years had passed they kept coming, until the number soared over a half million.

The ordeal of the "boat people," as those who left by sea were called, soon became a matter of international concern. Tens of thousands of them starved. Others were attacked by pirates who took their possessions, abused their women, and murdered them. Hundreds of their vessels sank in storms or under the sheer weight of the humanity in them. The few who reached other countries—mostly Thailand, Indonesia, and Malaysia—were rarely welcome. As refugees they were costly to feed, house, and attend to medically. They threw themselves, exhausted, on the beaches of largely impoverished countries in which Chinese were often envied because of their success in business. Many, therefore, were forced to return to their deaths on the high seas.

To escape the new government—and often rounded up and banished by the government—countless Vietnamese crossed rivers and seas in small boats.

For Vietnam, the plight of the boat people had severe consequences. First, the country lost the great skills and energy of most of its business community. Second, it lost the close and valuable friendship of its giant neighbor, Communist China. Alarmed by what it saw as persecution of relatives overseas, the Chinese pleaded with Vietnam to relent in its efforts to expropriate businesses. When Vietnam refused, the Chinese sent two ships to rescue the displaced people. Vietnam turned these vessels back.

The problem of the boat people was not the only one tending to divide the communists of Vietnam and China. Of equal importance was the continuing struggle in neighboring Cambodia. In 1979, Vietnam sent 150,000 troops into Cambodia to crush a government which it considered menacing. That government, comprised of members of the Khmer Rouge (Communist Khmer), had caused havoc in Cambodia, bringing about the deaths of more than two million people. The Vietnamese set up a new government in Cambodia and began a long battle with Khmer Rouge guerrillas, whom they pursued into Thailand. Two other guerrilla armies, described in Chapter 4, also resisted the Vietnamese.

To the dismay of the Chinese, Vietnam's action in Cambodia had the powerful support of the Soviet Union. China feared that the Soviets, with whom it had a long-standing border dispute in Central Asia, now was drawing a ring around it in Southeast Asia. The Chinese protested both this alliance in Cambodia and Vietnam's treatment of its Chinese community. They suddenly brought an end to the substantial help they were giving Vietnam and began to mobilize troops on the border. In Cambodia, meanwhile, they sent arms and supplies to Vietnam's enemies.

The growing dispute between Vietnam and China caused a major shift in foreign policy that will be detailed below, and it also had an immediate political effect. Vietnam, convinced that a war with China was developing, quickly shifted back to its wartime footing. It formed a military reserve, called the National Task Force, consisting of five million potential soldiers. Funds which should have gone into reconstruction went instead into mobilization.

The reserve army was desperately needed in 1979, when 170,000 Chinese troops, supported by tanks and planes, stormed over the northern mountains. China announced that it intended only to punish Vietnam and leave, not to invade and remain. Covering a narrow area near the border, its soldiers devastated homes, farms, and equipment. The Chinese butchered more than 150,000 domesticated animals, most of them water buffaloes which were urgently needed in the production of rice. Then, confronted by a strong

Reverence for Ho Chi Minh
promoted cohesiveness
among the North Vietnamese.

Vietnamese force, they swiftly withdrew, threatening to return if policies were not changed.

Vietnam, nevertheless, was determined to pursue its efforts to establish communism in the south. In one aspect of this program they set up camps in which to batter officials of the defeated government with lectures and demands for menial labor. In another, they planned to send ten million northern communists to settle in the south, where they could teach southerners their philosophy. This huge movement of people not only would serve to affect ways of thinking, but would make better use of the country's farmlands.

ECONOMIC CONDITIONS AND PROBLEMS

Thus it seemed that the communists of Vietnam would apply their doctrine with religious zeal. It appeared that no force could prevent them from repeating in the south the program they had previously imposed upon the north.

The economy of the north had undergone a complete transformation which began when the communist government took power there. First, review boards known as "People's Courts" screened the lives and activities of every individual. They placed each person and household into one of six categories: landless agricultural workers, poor peasants, middle peasants, rich peasants, landlords, or a single category including Confucian scholars, Catholic priests, and Buddhist monks.

Next, the government took steps to seize all privately owned lands. Between one and two million acres, or from 20-40 percent of the total available for cultivation, became the basis for a rural cooperative movement. By 1956, when this program was just two years old, almost 80 percent of North Vietnam's peasants were members of agricultural teams rather than individual farmers. Cadres continuously roamed the farms to show laborers how to work together, especially during the sowing or harvesting periods. A relatively small number of peasants—about eight million—were permitted to remain as individual farmers, but they paid a special tax for the privilege.

During a transition period, there was a mixture of private and public ownership of agricultural lands. The 200 or so families who formed each collective, or "Agricultural Producer's Cooperative," paid rent directly to the private owners. The land, however, was combined with government holdings. In time, the private owners were asked to give their land to the cooperatives. Almost all did so because of social pressure and because they were told they could withdraw their contribution later if they wanted to. Few did withdraw; many, in fact, heartily supported the cooperatives because, as skilled administrators, they were given jobs on them.

In addition to land, the government took over the tools and distribution system in agriculture. At that point, private ownership on the farms was reduced to a few personal effects and houses. Storage and shipping facilities, always complex in a society which intensively produces grain, all became public property.

The relatively small number of people who did not belong to rural cooperatives worked on state farms. For the most part, these farms were developed out of the old plantations created by the French. In general the south had more plantations than the north. The managers of state farms in both regions often included former owners pressed into government service. In the north, however, plantation owners were often among the 50,000 who were executed during the course of land reform.

The government also collectivized other parts of the economy. It took over the ownership of most businesses, handicraft industries, and shops. People were encouraged to buy their raw materials and to sell their products through state-owned organizations. Advisers from Communist China and the Soviet Union encouraged the North Vietnamese to establish a system of national planning. Later, with a unified country and the Chinese gone, the Soviets continued this task. The goal, as expressed in the First Five-Year Plan, (1958-60) was "to liquidate capitalist ownership of the means of production in industry and trade."

North Vietnam was able to accomplish this goal by the 1970s, then to extend it over the more fertile, newly added lands to the south. There, even more rapid development of rural cooperatives was possible because of the northern experience. By 1985, collective farming spread over most of the 7.6 million acres under cultivation in the south. The unified state took over all enterprises, either wholly or partly. Many people in the south resisted this drastic change. To persuade them the government executed some and drove others out of the country, so that most finally accepted communist principles.

But the shift to the new economy proved to be no solution for the problems at hand. Just as in capitalist countries, prices rose in Vietnam, tripling during the first year after unification was achieved. Unemployment, too, struck Vietnam, for the government had insufficient capital to create more jobs. Typhoons and droughts, coupled with the changeover to communism, cut the food supply by 20 percent.

Thus three years after the war, Vietnam was forced to endure new hardships. Individuals received no more than 46 pounds of rice a month—and as little as 28 pounds if their work required less energy. Not only did they lack food, but clothing, housing, and medicines as well. Hungry workers were unable to produce as much as usual. The country had to spend most of its income on rice, and with almost nothing to export it experienced a soaring deficit in the balance of trade. Per capita income was less than $150 a year, one of the lowest in Asia.

It was during this difficult period that ever greater numbers of Vietnamese took flight from their country. Moving was painful for them, not only because of the perils of the journey, but because of a deep-seated belief that they should live near the graves of their ancestors. Of the more than half million Vietnamese who came to the United States from 1975-85, most settled in southern U.S. areas where jobs and climates were like those they remembered. With each passing year they adapted to their new lives, gaining menial jobs at first but making steady progress through hard work and a desire to gain educations. Like many other immigrants to America, they often suffered prejudice, but their lives had promise.

In their ancestral home, however, matters were less bright. Vietnam could not have survived without extensive help from Communist China and the Soviet Union. Both countries sent money, machinery, and advisers. But soon, because of its invasion of Kampuchea and treatment of the boat people, Vietnam lost even Chinese support.

At last the government was forced to yield some of its communist principles. A raging black market, in which people traded for prices far higher than those officially set, dominated most transac-

The tub-boat, woven of rattan, is widely used in Vietnam. Steering it takes great skill. In rapid streams it is relatively safe, however.

tions. In 1982, Vietnam acknowledged this persistence of capitalism in the marketplace. It allowed some merchants to set up their own businesses again. Yet, at the same time it taxed merchants heavily in an effort to limit their activities. The Chinese community, it said, was chiefly responsible for capitalist tendencies in Vietnam. By the mid-1980s the government had embarked on a campaign to crush the underground market which threatened its carefully planned economy.

Meanwhile, in relatively peaceful conditions, the country was making some economic progress. It began slowly to increase its cultivated acreage, irrigation, electrical output, and industry. Chemical fertilizers, new rice strains, and large irrigation projects had enhanced its ability to produce food. By the mid-1980s it had reduced its need to import rice from one million tons a year to less than 300,000 tons a year. Despite the continuing war in Kampuchea, it had almost completely rebuilt its ruined cities, plantations, and farms.

But the communist system in Vietnam had yet to match the successes of the capitalist one in neighboring Thailand. While the Thais enjoyed a rising per capita income and many more consumer goods, the Vietnamese remained one of the 25 poorest peoples in the world. Vietnamese officials explained this by reminding the world that their country was still recovering from more than 30 years of war. Thailand may be earning more money, they said, but it was dependent upon the United States, and its income was chiefly owned by a few very rich people. Vietnam continued to strive for equality of wealth. Yet there were beggars on the outskirts of Ho Chi Minh City. Throughout Vietnam people were forced to stand in line to buy items as simple as a bar of soap, which cost them as much as a day's pay.

FOREIGN RELATIONS

When Vietnam was unified, the government announced that the core of its foreign policy would be "peace and nonalignment." It promised to "establish relations with all others, irrespective of their social systems, on the basis of mutual respect for independence and sovereignty."

Ten years later, Vietnam was neither peaceful nor nonaligned. Its army, with 1.2 million men under arms the fourth largest in the world, was fighting in Kampuchea and Thailand. It dominated one neighbor, Laos, and was exchanging threats with another, China. It was clearly aligned with the Soviet Union and had relationships with most of the communist countries of Eastern Europe. Though it was also recognized by many non-communist countries, including Britain, France, Japan, and India, its trade was chiefly with the Soviet Union.

Noting that Vietnam was serving Soviet interests and had sent tens of thousands of boat people to die on the high seas, many foreign governments began to withdraw the aid they had been sending. Many regarded the battle in Kampuchea part of a wider one for all of Southeast Asia. The struggle in Kampuchea especially aroused the fears of members of the Association of Southeast Asian Nations (ASEAN)—Indonesia, the Philippines, Singapore, Malaysia, Thailand, and Brunei. They not only withdrew aid but also began to support Vietnam's enemies, the insurgents in Kampuchea.

Thailand, above all other members of ASEAN, was determined to halt Vietnamese advances. Thailand has a long history of conflict with Vietnam and rose to defend its borders when Vietnamese troops crossed them to fight the Khmer Rouge. The Thais, after rushing infantry to the Khmer Rouge camps, gave arms to the insurgents and threatened to carry the conflict into Kampuchea. For centuries Kampuchea had been a buffer between the hostile Thai and Vietnamese populations. Now this buffer had become subject to and perhaps was even being colonized by Vietnam. War between Thailand and Vietnam thus became possible.

Just as they had been during the Vietnam War, the world's largest powers were deeply involved in the struggle for the peninsula of Southeast Asia. The United States strongly supported Thailand as the only capitalist country on the peninsula. It had rejected Vietnamese efforts to reconcile and be paid for the extensive damage caused by Americans during the war. The U.S. was prepared to renew arms shipments to Thailand and perhaps to the insurgents who were resisting Vietnam in Kampuchea. China, too, seemed ready to follow this course. Meanwhile the Soviet Union relentlessly promoted Vietnamese expansion.

The new relationships between China, the Soviet Union, and the United States completely changed understandings for which tens of thousands of people had died during the war. The United States had gone to war because, in the words of President Eisenhower, "You have a row of dominoes. . . . You knock over the first one, and what will happen to the last one is the certainty that it will go over very quickly." Almost every American official thought the Chinese communists would turn over the Vietnam domino and so seize control of Laos, Cambodia, Thailand, Burma, and the Malay Peninsula. Fearing Chinese expansion, they committed American forces to Vietnam.

But the dominoes did not fall after the unification of Vietnam. The U.S. achieved through diplomacy what it could not achieve through war. Three years before withdrawing its troops from Vietnam it made contacts with Communist China and so moved closer towards the recognition of the most significant power in East Asia. Chinese policies have restrained Vietnam and its closest ally, the Soviet Union. Soviet troops and finances are being used to confront China in Central Asia. Meanwhile Vietnamese troops are spending their energies against Chinese-supported insurgents. Thus despite its inability to win the war, the United States seemed to have stemmed the tide of communism in Southeast Asia, at least for the present.

The Future of Vietnam

The revolution will proceed in leaps. The simultaneous implementation of the three revolutions in production relations, technology, and culture and ideology; the direct advance from small-scale production to large-scale socialist production; both the technical and then the scientific-technical revolutions; and the rapid crossing of the first state into the process of industrialization—all are great leaps.

Those were the confident words of *Nhan Dan* ("The People"), the official newspaper of the People's Republic of Vietnam, shortly after the victory over the United States. But in 1988, just over a decade later, the Vietnamese government announced that it was cutting its rice rations for many people to slightly more twenty-two pounds a month—the minimum for survival. Vietnam issued an international appeal for food. Nor, beyond repairing much of the widespread damage caused by wartime bombs, had Vietnam made significant technological progress. In sum, a disaster followed this small country's triumph over the greatest power on earth.

Having accomplished its victory with essentially inferior weapons, Vietnam might be forgiven for a decade of pride. Yet it was pride which brought about the disintegration of the country's master plan for its future. The production of all goods and most services declined in relation to a population growth of 2-2.5 percent a year. Except for India, no nation outside the Communist Bloc has recognized Vietnam, and few have traded with it. The Vietnamese people have seen corruption and the heavy hand of government in all that they do. They are demoralized. "Oh Government!" cries a woman in a popular Vietnamese short story after tax collectors seize the rice she was keeping for old age. "Oh party! Look at us!"

Vietnam pursued its dream of a socialist state long beyond any chance of success. In just two months of 1988 the already desperately poor population saw its currency, the dong, lose half of its value. This devaluation came at a time when inflation was soaring over 1,000 percent a year. Many people turned to the abuse of narcotics, which the government had once claimed was a plague only in capitalist lands, as a consolation for their sorrows. From 1975-88 more than 1.5 million people fled their Indochinese homeland. Taking to small boats, they chose to risk death from storms and pirates rather than face the ordeal of life in Vietnam.

At last the Communist Party of Vietnam acknowledged the need for change. Like their Chinese colleagues, the Vietnamese installed a leader whom they had previously stripped of power. Nguyen Van Linh was 77 when he assumed the Politburo's highest office, but he quickly began in the spirit of youthful reform. One of his first moves was to try to disentangle the Vietnamese army from Kampuchea, where, in 1979, it marched with the announced purpose of preventing further massacres of the Kampuchean people by their leader, Pol Pot. The Vietnamese had been fighting a coalition of three guerrilla forces ever since, and every Western country, led by the United States, had promised to isolate Vietnam until it withdrew.

Nguyen Van Linh promised that Vietnamese troops would be back home by 1992. Then he pressed reform even further. Startling the whole world, the Vietnamese turned to economic methods which, as fundamentalist communists, they had been condemning. They began to break up large collective farms into small private ones and to introduce financial incentives for individual entrepeneurs and workers. They removed some of the power of bureaucrats to strangle the economy by giving plant managers the right to run factories and bankers the power to make loans. Centralized planning disappeared, and cost accounting and quality controls suddenly spread in Vietnam. In contrast to *Nhan Dan's* revolutionary remarks a decade earlier, the Council of Ministers, in Decision 217, said Vietnam would:

> . . . *develop production and business, improve labor output, product quality and socio-economic results, create more marketable products and support services needed by society, generate an ever larger source of revenue for the state budget, and gradually improve the livelihoods of workers and civil servants.*

These changes in Vietnam's Marxist views came about a decade after Communist China introduced similar ones and about two years after the Soviet Union did so. Following the tendency of those countries, it has been trying to improve its relationships with the West. This development will be rapid if it keeps its promise to leave Kampuchea. In 1988 Vietnam also was more open to U.S. demands that it allow U.S. investigators to seek 1,758 Americans who have been missing in its jungles since the war. Such moves are certain to allow an American administration to begin a reconciliation with Vietnam.

The Vietnamese government correctly points out that the population it rules is an essentially industrious and creative one. That is shown by the largely successful adaptation of almost 900,000 Vietnamese refugees in the United States alone. But Vietnam, a country which was once committed to families, literature, music, and education has been transformed by more than fifty years of invasions. It has much work to do before it can outgrow both the physical and psychological damage of war.

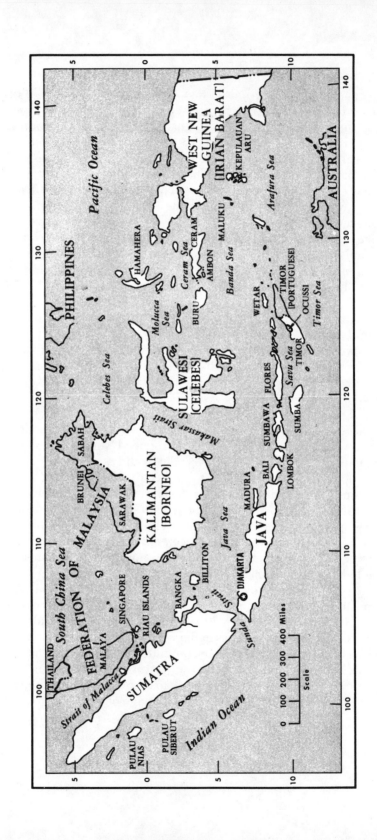

CHAPTER 8

INDONESIA

When the Japanese drove the Dutch out of Indonesia at the outset of World War II, the Indonesian people welcomed them as liberators. With Japanese help, they organized an army that warned the Dutch not to return. Soon, however, the Indonesians realized that they were no better off under the Japanese than under the Dutch. At the end of World War II they declared independence and announced they would fight either or both sides for their freedom.

British troops replaced the retreating Japanese when World War II came to an end. They tried to reconcile Indonesian nationalists with the Dutch colonial regime, but they failed. The Dutch who returned after the war were met by gunfire from the army of the newly proclaimed Republic of Indonesia. They offered to compromise by establishing a Netherlands Indonesian Union, but the nationalists refused to accept them under any conditions. Neither side was willing to trust the other. The nationalists were embittered by the memory of a harsh colonial rule. The Dutch, on the other hand, were furious with the many nationalists who cooperated with the Japanese.

SOCIAL CONDITIONS AND CULTURAL LIFE

Ethnic groups. The Javanese are the largest of Indonesia's 36 major ethnic groups. They represent about 50 percent of the total population. The second largest group, the Sundanese, comprises about 15 percent, and the Madurese are third with about 8 percent At least seven ethnic groups live on the island of Sumatra, where the dominant ethnic group is Malay.

Indonesians of Chinese ancestry represent about 3 percent of the total population but more than 90 percent of the foreign minorities. They were encouraged to move to Java by the Dutch, who used them to build forts and later gave them managerial posts in business and government. In the past, the Chinese often used the money that they earned in commerce to become "tax farmers," or revenue

225

A diverse ancestry is
seen in the face
of this Balinese girl.

collectors for the Dutch. As agents for the hated colonizers, they instantly became the enemies of the people from whom they collected money.

There are other reasons for anti-Chinese feeling in Indonesia. Disasters in China often caused thousands of refugees to crowd into the islands. The Chinese seemed to enjoy the benefits of their new society but almost never gave up their old culture. As a result, Indonesians were offended by what they thought was the Chinese sense of superiority. In 1741, Indonesians murdered many of their Chinese neighbors, and incidents of this kind have often marked the tense relations between the two people.

Attacks on the Chinese were a matter of official policy under President Sukarno. He accused them of dominating retail businesses on Java and forbade them from entering commerce outside of the cities. In 1960 he deported 100,000 of them to mainland China. Indonesia and Communist China agreed that Chinese who lived in Indonesia could become citizens of both countries at the same time if they registered to do so in the period 1960–62. Less than one-third of the Indonesian Chinese registered, however. The rest remained in the position of separatism that has so often angered their Indonesian neighbors.

In 1965 Indonesians blamed their Chinese community for a plot by communists to take over the government. They slaughtered 400,000 Chinese for what they assumed was obedience to Communist China. Nothing as violent has taken place since, but there have been a number of anti-Chinese riots. After each of them, the Chinese and Indonesians returned to their homes and their work, going separate ways as occupants of the same land. The causes of hostility have remained, and for many of Indonesia's Chinese, the national motto, "Unity from Diversity," is an empty hope. The deep anger between the two groups must be overcome if Indonesia is to achieve the equality and national pride for which it strives.

The members of Indonesia's ethnic groups are remote from each other in the country's 21 cities. Each ethnic group lives in neighborhoods called *kampongs*, which line the street and surround a community area leased to the householders by private landowners. The kampongs run along, side by side, for miles before a neighborhood changes.

Most of Indonesia's houses are small, having been built for single families. Many of them are unsanitary because of the lack of plumbing, running water, and sewage disposal. Two-thirds of the houses in Djakarta are said to be unfit for life or are substandard. Yet the cities are increasingly crowded and now contain more than 15 percent of the total population. Indonesia has three enormous metropolitan areas: Djakarta has 6 million people, Surabaja 2.1 million, and Bandung 1.5 million.

Life is much different in the countryside, where Indonesians tend to produce almost all of their own needs. The leading crops in Indonesia—rubber, rice, corn, copra, tea, and coffee—require joint efforts, and people tend to cooperate more than they can in the cities. The principle of mutual help and cooperation is a village tradition that persists throughout Southeast Asia. In Indonesia, as in most other Southeast Asian countries, it has resulted in formal codes of law based on local societies and cultures. This law, or *adat*, is administered by communities through judges who decide on conflicts regarding the individual's relationship to the community. A typical problem may involve the amount of time that a farmer gives to help till community owned lands. Besides this law, Indonesians are subject to their official laws and to their informal social pressures.

Religion. Almost 90 percent of Indonesians are Muslim, making the country one of the two largest Islamic nations in the world. Islam affects every activity in their lives, yet does not regulate them as completely as Muslims in the Middle East. Indonesians began to accept Islam in the thirteenth century, but they never completely erased the cultural influences of India. Today, most Indonesians practice their faith chiefly through ceremonies. They stress religious beliefs weddings, funerals, or the birth of children. Almost all

Indonesian men attend mosques to pray on Fridays. Thousands of Indonesians travel to Mecca every year, although the government has been discouraging the long trip on grounds that the money spent on the trip could better be given to charity. Indonesian women do not practice *purdah* (seclusion behind a veil) and in general have more social and economic independence than women in the Middle East. Indonesian Muslims also differ from those of Middle Eastern ones in the degree of their interest in commerce. Indonesians are more concerned with agriculture and fishing than with business and distant voyages. It was because of this attitude that the Dutch originally began to import the Chinese.

Indonesia has three other religious communities which, though they are small, are influential. They are the Hindus, Christians, and animists. The Hindus consist of about 3 percent of the population (less than two million people) and are concentrated on the island of Bali. There, Hindus retreated to preserve their beliefs while others were being converted to Islam on the islands of Java and Sumatra. They brought with them the caste system and belief in the multiplicity of gods that still characterize India. Their castes today are much less rigid, but the Hindu gods are still worshipped. Moreover, Hindu art forms, particularly in the dance and sculpture, are notable.

The Hindu dance and other aspects of Indian culture survive on Bali.

Almost eight million Indonesians claim to be Christians. They are scattered in the islands wherever Western missionaries came to live during the nineteenth century. What they practice, however, is often only a short step away from primitive animism. There are about five million animists in Indonesia.

Education, language, and the arts. The goal of Indonesia's educators is twofold: to train skilled workers and professional people and to strengthen national unity. Since independence, Indonesia has placed great emphasis on education and has more than doubled the number of students in schools. Children aged 6 to 12 are required to attend classes. In contrast to the 2.2 million primary grade students who were in schools when the Dutch ruled Indonesia, there are more than 11 million today. In addition, there are six million students in secondary schools. The prewar enrollment in universities was only 637. Today, there are more than 160,000 students enrolled in 39 universities and other institutions of higher learning.

The language of education is no longer Dutch, but rather Bahasa Indonesia, a variation of Malay. There are 400 distinct languages spoken in Indonesia. Almost all of these languages belong to the Malayo-Polynesian family. Children may study in their own ethnic language until the fourth grade. After that, Bahasa Indonesia is the language of instruction. This requirement is an important part of the process of nation-building among an ethnically and linguistically diverse population. If students learn a second language it is usually English, which is required in high school.

Rapid population growth is placing great strains on the school system. Many classrooms have little more than a blackboard and a few books. Disease, illness, and the lack of food force many children to quit school before they are graduated. But most students know that in an increasingly commercial society, the educational drop-out may not find a job. Unemployment in Indonesia today is almost 9 percent of the labor force. Most of these unemployed people are unskilled laborers.

Students who are disinterested in practical subjects may attend religious schools. With the exception of a few Christian institutions, all of Indonesia's religious schools are Muslim. They are financed by the government through the Departments of Education and Religion. For the most part they teach Muslim history, philosophy, and concepts of government, but supplement these courses with more technical ones. About 26 percent of all elementary school students, or almost five million children, are enrolled in the religious schools. Indonesia's religious educational system culminates in the University of Djakarta, which is administered by the Department of Religion.

Indonesia's arts, in their deepest sense, reflect the essentially cheerful and optimistic nature of its people. The most popular art form is the *wayang*, a melodrama in which puppets or actors portray ancient Arabic or Indian myths, tales, and comic scenes through music and dance. The simplest wayang is a shadow play that makes use of painted puppets. A skillful puppet master can entertain hundreds of Indonesians for hours by manipulating the two-dimensional figures behind translucent screens, in front of bright lights. The audience sees a series of moving shadows. Meanwhile, the puppet master tells the story of the play, and intermittantly a small orchestra is heard but not seen. The Hindu epic, the *Ramayana*, is a favorite play in Indonesia. It tells how a handsome young raja named Seri Rama wins a beautiful princess named Siti Dewi by shooting an arrow through forty palm trees standing in a row. But Siti Dewi is kidnapped by an ogre king who was angry because he was not invited to the contest for her hand in marriage. Rama goes through hundreds of grueling adventures until, aided by magical monkeys and a giant bird, he is reunited with his princess in the ogre's island kingdom.

Indonesian art includes some highly regarded paintings. The subject matter of many of them is the Indonesian landscape. Since the 1930s Indonesian painting had tended to be strongly realistic, showing the human despair which accompanies desperate material conditions in the country. However, modern painting also reveals the intense joy that Indonesians feel because they live in one of the world's most beautiful countries. Many of these same feelings are expressed in Indonesian textiles, jewelry, and pottery.

For the most part, Indonesian buildings are constructed of palm, bamboo, or timber. These structures may be beautifully painted or carved, but they easily decay in the moist climate. The ancient Hindu culture has left enduring monuments of stone, however. One of the most famous of these monuments is the Borobudur. This magnificent shrine, dating from the ninth century, is an enormous truncated pyramid in central Java. It is covered with intricately carved blocks of stone depicting the life of the Buddha. Seven stone terraces encircle the pyramid. Above them are three platforms from which a huge seated Buddha is visible.

The Balinese dance is another inheritance of the Hindu period. In their most elaborate performances the dancers wear stunning jewelry and costumes reminiscent of classical India, and they move in formal, stylized ways. The Balinese dance dramatizes ideas and stories from the great Indian epics, the *Ramayana* and the *Mahabharata*.

RECENT POLITICAL DEVELOPMENTS

In 1947, the Dutch attacked a nationalist force that was preparing to resist the formation of the Netherlands Indonesian Union on the island of Java. Served by a cease-fire order from the United Nations, they agreed to stop fighting after they had seized two-thirds of Java. But the Indonesian nationalists refused to quit fighting. They dissolved their army into small groups that could move quickly, attack suddenly, and withdraw into the jungles or blend with the population. There seemed no way to defeat these roving bands, which harassed the Dutch until 1950, despite their lack of money, arms, and food. Increasing Dutch severity failed to weaken the nationalist drive for independence. On the island of Makassar alone the Dutch executed 30,000 persons and still failed to destroy the spirit of rebellion. The nationalist rallying cry was *"Indonesia Merdeka"*—Indonesia, independent and free. But while the nationalists were unified in the struggle against the Dutch, they had little else in common. There was no program through which independence could be practiced. The independence movement consisted of political and religious factions and various ethnic groups. What was needed was a single unifying force—or a leader who could pull the factions together. Then suddenly one man appeared to express the most ardent nationalist hopes, and through him Indonesia was formed. He was the fiery nationalist, Achmed Sukarno.

Sukarno had been active in the independence movement since 1927. One of the few Indonesians allowed to study in Dutch schools, he had become an engineer, but his main interest was politics. Sukarno was familiar with the writings of Thomas Jefferson, especially the Declaration of Independence, and read all the works of Karl Marx. He wanted to adapt the ideas of both men to Indonesian culture.

Sukarno's intimate knowledge of Indonesia filled him with self-confidence. He recognized that his people were too diverse to create a nation, and to make them more conscious of their common destiny he coined slogans that remained uppermost in their minds. One of his first programs was called the *Pantja Sila*, or "Five Principles of the State," which included nationalism, humanism, democracy, social justice, and belief in Allah. He announced these principles during the Japanese occupation in 1945, and from that point onward they appeared in all of Indonesia's most momentous state documents, including its constitution. In rousing speeches, Sukarno also proclaimed the slogan that was to become the motto of the new nation, "Unity from Diversity."

Throughout his political career Achmed Sukarno proved himself able to communicate directly with his fellow Indonesians, who treated him as a king.

Sukarno became the chief focus of national unity, the leader who declared independence in front of his own house on August 17, 1945, just four days after the Japanese surrender. He remained the dominant political force in Indonesia for the next twenty years. His titles—"Great Leader of the Revolution" and "The Mandate of the People's Tongue"—and the ceremonies surrounding him resembled those of a king. Indonesia, however, called itself a democracy.

Post-independence. Unable to gain representation in President's Sukarno's administration, Indonesian communists began to attack the government as early as 1948. They struck from jungle refuges or from villages in which they were indistinguishable from other farmers. Sukarno's army, however, was able to defeat them. This left him freer and much stronger in the eyes of his countrymen. By 1950 the Dutch officially recognized the United States of Indonesia as part of the Netherlands Indonesian Union. They retained only West Irian (which they called West New Guinea) because, they said, the population there was not hostile to them. They offered to leave West New Guinea eventually, but gave no date. Sukarno was therefore able to claim victory over his two major enemies—the communists and the Dutch.

Nevertheless, the new government quickly fell into confusion as factions struggled to dominate the country or to become autonomous within it. It seemed impossible for Sukarno to find the "Unity from Diversity" that he sought. His task was to govern a people who were used to being ruled and who had no sense of nationhood. On Sulawesi, Christians demanded the right to keep their own army and began to fight government troops. On Java, Muslim leaders demanded independence. Another cry for an independent republic arose in the Moluccas.

In response to these challenges, Sukarno dropped the idea of a confederation of Indonesian peoples. To create a federation, it would have been necessary to maintain a parliament in which nine opposing parties were represented. Recognizing that an institution with that many political divisions would paralyze itself in debate, Sukarno imposed a "unitary government" on the country. He sought the advice of each of the major parties and ruled Indonesia much like the chairman of a corporation's board of directors. Luckily for him, the economy was expanding, and most Indonesians were willing to accept his leadership. During this period, he increased the country's social services, thus adding to his own following.

Sukarno could not ignore the growing conflicts between the non-communist West and the communist East, however. In 1951, the entry of the United States into the Korean War caused many politically conscious Indonesians to demand that he take sides. Powerful business interests fretted about the possibility that Indonesian communists were longing to seize the country, as Mao Tse-tung had recently seized China. Sukarno heeded the business interests rather than the socialists and communists who were demanding that he oppose the United States. He arrested many of the leaders of the Communist Party.

Indonesia was not used to settling political differences in parliamentary ways. To most factions it seemed that arguments could be resolved only through the use of force. Many people carried arms and threatened to use them. While political disputes grew more intense, inflation was steadily eroding the economy. It was one of the effects of the enormous expenditures made by both sides in the Korean War. Rising prices caused many Indonesians to lose faith in the government. The people of outlying islands claimed that the government was corrupt and favored the Javanese over themselves. On Java, meanwhile, there were bitter struggles among Muslims, Chinese, communists, socialists, and capitalists.

Further organizing efforts. In this atmosphere of political and economic turmoil, Indonesia was not able to hold a general election until 1955—more than five years after independence. The purpose of the election was to choose a Parliament and Constituent Assembly. At least a hundred political parties began to campaign. Many issues divided these parties. The major argument centered around the extent to which the government should be identified with the Islamic faith. Another important issue was the resentment that outer islanders felt for the Javanese, who they thought were using too much of the national budget for themselves.

The election took place after bitter campaigning. When it was clear that no single party received more than a quarter of the votes, Sukarno appeared before the Constituent Assembly. He called for the suspension of all political campaigns and voting. Indonesia was not prepared for this type of democracy, he said. Sukarno proposed a program that he called "Guided Democracy." Under it, the 283-member National Assembly was to be a forum for a coalition of parties, regional populations, and ethnic groups. Sukarno suggested that the coalition discuss the issues and then inform the new National Council, consisting of representatives of all the factions. The National Council would then decide on the course of action.

Just as Guided Democracy was being introduced, several army officers led rebellions in four provinces on Sumatra and Sulawesi. They took action to protest the larger defense budgets granted to the army on Java. When the rebel leaders demanded new governments in the outer islands, Sukarno declared a "state of war and siege." The nation was put under martial law, and Sukarno assumed all political power.

Sukarno used his new powers to press forward with his idea of Guided Democracy. He had immense popular support, and the cabinet resigned because it was unwilling to confront him. In complete control of the country, he assumed duties as head of state, head of government, and commander-in-chief of the army. Then he began to form a National Council. However, the communists, socialists, and Muslims could not all be represented on it because they refused to work together. Sukarno had to choose among these groups, and he decided to include the Communist Party of Indonesia (PKI), which had won more than 27 percent of the votes in the last election on Java.

Next, Sukarno moved against the remaining Dutch interests in Indonesia. His main purpose was to force the Dutch to surrender their base on West Irian, but a secondary goal was to bring the country's major businesses under his control. His political allies, the PKI, organized strikes and boycotts against Dutch businesses. The communist-dominated unions seized the Netherlands Trading Association, which managed two-thirds of the country's international trade. Sukarno preferred not to leave those businesses in the hands of the communists and quickly took them over in the name of the government. This policy forced thousands of Dutch citizens to leave Indonesia.

Many Indonesian politicians and businessmen objected to

Sukarno's anti-Dutch policies. They thought that it was unjust to persecute individual Dutch, but they also thought that the program would lead to economic disaster because it deprived Indonesia of its only group of skilled managers. On Sumatra, many workers contended that government ownership of business would leave them in the control of Javanese bureaucrats. They feared that corruption and incompetence would cost them their jobs. Blaming Sukarno's communist alliance for his actions, they refused to accept his leadership until he severed his connections with the PKI. In 1958, this group led a rebellion on Sumatra. Sukarno responded by sending the Indonesian Air Force to bomb the rebels. He declared a state of civil war and appealed for outside help. The United States refused to arm him, but the Soviet Union supplied him with the jet fighters that he needed to suppress the rebellion.

Sukarno's victory over the Sumatran rebels was slow to come. The fighting continued through 1961. Yet the president's show of force enabled him to rule the country as completely as any king. He closed critical newspapers, postponed elections, dissolved the Constituent Assembly and all political parties, and took sole responsibility for government. He continued his political alliance with the Communist Party. In 1960 he replaced Parliament with a House of Representatives that was half communist.

Emboldened by their political advances under Sukarno, Indonesian communists took steps to control the government more completely. They demanded the right to arm the peasants and workers as a "defense corps," to be used in the event of an internal struggle. International trade and loans from the West began to fall off

Mobs of Indonesians attacked this school and other Chinese institutions after a group of communists tried but failed to take over the country in 1965.

The attempt by communists to seize Indonesia resulted in the massacre of many Chinese. These men were held for execution.

because of the growing communist strength. Inflation, due in large part to Sukarno's military expenditures, was running at the rate of more than 600 percent a year. Thus Indonesia was being drained of its political and economic strength at a time when the Communist Party of Indonesia was able to claim a membership of about three million, with another three million in its youth division.

In 1965, a group of Indonesia's communist leaders concluded that they were in a position to undertake a *coup d'état*—the forceful and illegal seizure of the state. On September 30 of that year, they seized the national radio station and announced that a new government was being formed. That night, the communists killed six generals who refused to cooperate with them. They organized strikes and attacked public buildings the next morning. But anti-communist army officers rallied behind the leadership of General Suharto, commander of the strategic reserves. Street fighting between the two sides continued for more than three months.

It was during this period that the Chinese community was rumored to be supporting the communist uprising. Many Indonesians believed the rumors and began to attack individual Chinese in their homes and shops. In East Java, Bali, and Sumatra, the Indonesians slaughtered anyone even suspected of association with the communists. The rivers ran red with blood and were clogged with bodies. Between 3–400,000 people were killed. The Chinese lost most of their businesses and all of their schools.

Current conditions. The attack on "communists" was an indirect criticism of Sukarno because it was under his administration that they first gained a role in government. He was still too popular to dismiss immediately, but he steadily lost power and was finally removed from office in 1966. Thus ended the political career of the man who symbolized nationhood and independence for the world's fifth largest country. Through dramatic speech and behavior, he had held a diverse and widespread population together for almost twenty years. In the end his misplaced trust, inability to share authority, and Indonesia's deteriorating economy led to his downfall.

Indonesia's reaction against the Chinese caused it to seek a leader who could work more closely with the West. While Sukarno ruled, American, Dutch, and British businessmen were unwilling to make investments there. Suharto, on the other hand, accepted a mandate to attract more capital from the West, to control prices, and to manage the national budget. In 1967 the Assembly granted Suharto a full five-year term as President, and Indonesia held its first general election since 1955. Suharto was conscious of the need for stronger political opposition and encouraged Indonesia's eight minority parties to unite. Under his prodding the four parties dedicated to Islamic traditions formed the United Development Party (*Partai Persatuan Pembanguan*, or PPP), while five nationalist parties organized the Indonesian Democratic Party (PDI).

Indonesians responded favorably to Suharto at first. At the end of his fifth year in office, the country enjoyed greater prosperity and unity than ever before. Indonesia had become a leader in Southeast Asia. On the unanimous vote of the People's Consultative Congress, Suharto was reelected to a second five-year term.

It was during Suharto's second term that strains in the society began to reappear. They revealed the ever-present gulfs between Indonesia's largest racial and religious groups. In Bandung, on the island of Java in 1973, a minor traffic accident burst into a riot. Because the accident involved a Chinese, Malay students attacked and looted shops in the Chinese community. Later that year religious differences flared into riots when Muslims throughout the country demonstrated against new marriage laws. The legislation would have allowed women to initiate divorce proceedings, sharing that right with men. According to the Muslims such laws forced Christian behavior upon the country.

The most serious strains appeared as Suharto's second term drew to a close. Thousands of students organized to demand that he not run for a third term. They claimed that his closest advisers were allowing foreigners to gain control of the country. At that time, the premier of Japan, Kakuei Tanaka, was due for a state visit to Indonesia. The students shadowed him throughout the trip, protesting that Japanese companies in Indonesia were hiring more Chinese than Malays. They destroyed Japanese-made goods and businesses, and their bloody riots did not end until the army seized the University of Indonesia.

Despite the protests, Suharto won a third, then a fourth term. By the time of his fourth election campaign the voices raised against him included members of the professions and former high officials as well as students. They accused him of suppressing freedoms through the excessive use of police power. Suharto, they said, had created a government based upon bribery and favors to the rich. But in 1983, Suharto won reelection by an overwhelming majority. Thus he held Indonesia's highest office for a total of twenty years. It was a troubled time, though generally less so than when the country was ruled by Sukarno.

ECONOMIC CONDITIONS

Sources of current problems. Indonesia was near financial collapse during Sukarno's last years in power. The country had not fully recovered from the destruction of World War II, yet had been forced to shoulder additional burdens. Sukarno budgeted half of the Indonesia's income for the military. By 1963 the government was spending more than it earned. Sukarno paid for deficits by increasing the supply of money, and this added to the financial pressures. His military expenditures, among others, caused prices to soar. Rising population was another cause of shortages and fiscal strain. Between 1960 and 1966, the cost of living in the city of Djakarta increased by 635 percent. The

A roadside market in rural Indonesia may consist of little more than a few wives of farmers, sitting beneath a tree with plates of food to sell.

national rate of inflation rose to 650 percent in 1966.

As he took more and more power, Sukarno ignored these problems. He spent his efforts building the army and a huge bureaucracy. His administration employed approximately 50,000 people in the 1940s. By the time he left office, government employees numbered almost 1.5 million. Meanwhile, the country was forced to buy rice abroad to feed its starving millions, and industry was hampered by a lack of capital and skilled managers. Today, only 23 percent of the workforce is involved in industrial and commercial enterprises. Indonesia must buy such items as tires, paper, and clothing abroad. It cannot make all that it needs, though it has the raw materials to do so.

The decade ending 1985 brought substantial economic gains to Indonesia. These gains were in large part based on rising oil prices, which were artificially set by the Organization of Petroleum Exporting Countries (OPEC), including Indonesia. At the outset of this ten-year period, the income from oil sales accounted for half or more of the country's total revenues. While inflation declined, Indonesia's rate of growth soared to 7 and 8 percent a year. The annual per capita income, which was only $55 in the 1950s, was twice that by 1975. It rose to $575 by the mid-1980s.

Then suddenly an economic crisis struck Indonesia, along with all other oil-producing countries. In the wake of a worldwide recession, the use of oil declined, and so did oil prices. Indonesia fell victim to an oil glut and was forced to devalue its currency, the rupiah, by 27.5 percent. The country, which until that point was able to sell enough raw materials and products abroad to pay for its substantial imports, faced the need to borrow heavily in order to keep its economy going.

In the effort to fulfill the goals of four five-year plans, Indonesian farmers have been able to produce increasing amounts of food. For the most part foods are grown on small farms, and the methods used on them are still primitive. Most field workers use their hands, ancient tools, and bullocks, instead of machines. More than 66 percent of Indonesia's workforce labors in agriculture, yet the country must regularly import food. By contrast, less than 3.5 percent of the U.S. population, using modern equipment, is able to produce more food than Americans can consume.

In Indonesia, small farmers grow rice, corn, cassava roots, sweet potatoes, and copra, while the plantations produce rubber, coffee, tea, and sugar. Most farms range between one and five acres, barely large enough to support their own laborers. Many

The people of Java, who occupy the most densely populated land in the world, compete for relatively few jobs. There, even the youngest children must work.

farmers are sharecroppers on land owned by others. They pay rents ranging from 50-70 percent of their crop.

Trends. Upon taking office in 1966 General Suharto moved quickly to remedy Indonesia's economic problems. He devised a program called "Repelita," a word formed from Indonesian words meaning "Five-Year Development Plan." The plan was designed to increase food supplies, improve transportation, increase manufacturing output, and encourage family planning. Suharto concentrated on increasing education, skills, and public health facilities. This coordinated economic program succeeded in reducing inflation and increasing foreign investment. The new capital thus gained helped Indonesia to develop more of its oil, tin, copper, and nickel deposits. Indonesia held its position as the

With a population of more than 4.5 million, Djakarta is one of the largest cities in the world. It is critically short of housing, sanitation, and food.

world's second largest producer of natural rubber and the eighth largest producer of oil. It also developed its tin mines, and its production of that vital mineral reached 10 percent of the world's total.

The first Five-Year Plan established a pattern for the three plans that followed it. Agricultural output was to be increased, with the hope of making Indonesia independent of rice imports. The plans have also aimed at raising industrial production, much of which, such as rice milling, is based on agricultural output. If farmers have no surplus beyond their own needs, factories have little to process. On the other hand, farmers desperately need such industrial products as fertilizers, farm machinery, and pesticides. Indonesia's factories, concentrated in one area between Djakarta and Surabaja on Java, are still too small to produce sufficient goods for farmers. Most factories in Indonesia make household goods and operate at far less than full capacity. Food production has been increasing, but not enough to make the country self-sufficient.

Five-year plans have greatly increased Indonesia's economic stability. Though the purchase of rice overseas still takes a large part of the foreign trade budget, the country has often managed to earn as much as it spent abroad. The recent decline in oil prices will deprive it of much of its income, however, and the balance of trade is likely to become less favorable in the future.

FOREIGN RELATIONS

The harshness of Dutch colonial rule caused most Indonesians to fear and suspect any foreign influence. After gaining independence, Indonesia became the leader of Southeast Asia's anti-West faction. In 1955 it invited 29 Asian and African countries to a conference at Bandung. There, they discussed a "United Front" against colonialism, and Sukarno described his foreign policy as "nonaligned but not neutral." That is, he claimed that he would not consistently side with either the communist or noncommunist blocs in the world community. Still, he steadily cut Indonesia's ties with the West and seemed to favor Soviet policies.

Indonesia's fears of Western influence in its region were reflected in its relations with its nearest neighbor, Malaysia. When Malaysia was formed in 1963, it incorporated the former British territories on the island of Kalimantan (Borneo): Sarawak, Sabah, and the sultanate of Brunei, as well as Singapore and Malaya. Sukarno considered Malaysia's extension to Kalimantan, where Indonesia also owns territory, as a hostile act. He sent guerrillas into Malaysia, but the British repulsed them. Sukarno then declared that the invasion was only the beginning of what he called the "Confrontation" with Malaysia, which he called a British puppet. Indonesia's guerrilla warfare in Malaysia continued until Sukarno left the presidency in 1966.

Another expression of Indonesia's anti-Western attitudes came in 1965 when it resigned from the United Nations. Sukarno claimed that the UN was dominated by the world's "Old Established Forces," which he identified as the leading Western powers. With the help of Communist China, he offered to found an organization to rival the UN, called "New Emerging Forces." The members of the new organization, he said, would come almost entirely from Asia and Africa. Like the "Confrontation," this policy of Sukarno was revised when Suharto came to power in 1966.

Under Suharto, Indonesia settled its differences with Malaysia. He said the purpose of Indonesia's foreign policy was "to serve the national interest, particularly our urgent economic interest at present." He dropped most other aspects of the aggressive anti-Western posture that Sukarno had presented. Indonesian diplomacy began to improve international trade and relations with the British, Dutch, and Americans. Indonesia repaid the Dutch for some of the destruction of their businesses during the 1960s. In return, it received a loan from them. A small guerrilla movement on Kalimantan (Borneo) is said to be financed by Dutch business-men, but thus far Indonesia has not officially held the Dutch responsible for the fighting. Indonesia has completely replaced the Dutch on West Irian. The island, inhabited by 700,000 Papu-ans, is shared with Australia. Indonesia's relationship with both Australia and New Zealand has been friendly and unmarked by conflict.

This change in attitude affects the United States, too. Sukarno had often charged that Americans were seeking to impose a new imperialism on Indonesia. He seized a number of large American businesses. Committees of Indonesians began to supervise the enormous holdings of the Standard Oil Company of New Jersey and the Royal Dutch Oil Company on Java and Sumatra. Sukarno used the same tactic with respect to the large facilities of the United States Rubber Company. But these policies have also been reversed under President Suharto. Acknowledging the need for Western capital and managerial skills, Suharto has encouraged Americans to help increase Indonesia's rubber and oil production.

The growing willingness of Indonesia's government to cooper-ate with foreign countries has helped it during times of stress. Since Suharto came to power thirteen countries, including the United States, Great Britain, France, Japan, and Australia, granted aid to Indonesia when its food supplies declined to the danger point.

This new spirit of cooperation has come under severe tests. Many other countries began to question it during an incident involving the Portuguese half of the island of Timor, part of the Indonesian archipelago which lies closest to Australia. The peo-ple of that colony, which the Portuguese had seized from the Dutch in the seventeenth century, declared in 1975 that they would seek independence. Indonesia feared this possibility because an independent government on the island might have harbored guerrilla movements. After a long struggle in which it sent "volunteers" to fight a communist movement in East Timor, Indonesia claimed the whole island, with its 1.5 million people, as its own. In the U.S. Congress, Indonesia was accused of starv-ing and torturing prisoners in East Timor. However, the Indone-sian government was not shaken. It continues to hold the former Portuguese colony.

Indonesia has attempted to become a leading country in its region. In 1962 the Philippines encouraged the formation of the Association of Southeast Asia (ASA). This organization was seri-ously weakened because of conflicts between the Philippines and

Malaysia, as well as Sukarno's hostility. Reversing Sukarno's policy with respect to regional cooperation, Suharto in 1967 helped to found the Association of Southeast Asian Nations (ASEAN), which includes all of the nations of Southeast Asia except Burma and Vietnam. ASEAN provides a basis for effective economic and political cooperation on a regional basis.

THE FUTURE OF INDONESIA

Indonesia's future will be closely related to the world market for petroleum, its most profitable export. When the price paid for oil was relatively low, during the 1960s, the nation found it increasingly difficult to provide adequate food, clothing, and shelter for its people. Conditions improved sharply during the 1970s because oil prices were soaring. By the mid-1980s a worldwide recession had reduced the consumption and, therefore, the price of oil. Indonesia's income fell, and hard times returned.

The price of oil may rebound again some day. Yet whether or not it does, Indonesia must eventually face its problem of population increases. It is adding between 3 and 4 million people every year to a population which has reached 167 million. Indonesia is presently the fifth most populous country in the world, after Communist China, India, the Soviet Union, and the United States. Its growth rate, between 2 and 2.5 percent a year, compares with the world average of 1.76 percent a year.

This increase is chiefly concentrated on the islands of Java and Sumatra. The staggering burden is shown by a few figures. There were only five million people on Java and Madura in 1815. By 1985, though they could not be properly counted, there were an estimated 90 million. This means that in 170 years the population has multiplied eighteen times. One Javanese county has a population density of almost 2,500 people per square mile—thirty-nine times greater than the United States. By the mid-1980s the Java-Madura area had between 65 and 70 percent of Indonesia's population but only 7 percent of its land. The average density on Java was well over 1,500. The island of Sumatra contains between 15-20 per cent of the total population, but the island of Kalimantan (Borneo), which is as large as France, contains less than 5 per cent of the total.

The problems caused by rising population contribute to political unrest. With 153 million people, Indonesia is presently the world's fifth most populous country, and it continues to grow at the rate of about 2 percent a year. The slaughter of Chinese in 1965 and the ethnic riots of the following decades were one expression of the fear that outsiders were taking advantage of the national weakness.

Today, social and economic pressures are increasing in Indonesia. They may foreshadow future conflicts. Only the wealthiest are able to buy meat, fish, and fresh vegetables. The masses of people live chiefly on a diet of rice and sweet potatoes supplemented by coconuts and a little fruit. The country is short of housing; two or three families are often forced to live together in single-family homes. In the growing cities of Djakarta (6 million), Surabaja (2.1 million), and Bandung (1.5 million) thousands of people sleep in shacks made of discarded wood and tin, in the streets, or under bridges. The annual per capita income is just $580.

During the recent past, substantial revenues from the sale of oil have brought stability and progress to Indonesia. In human terms, for example, improved economic conditions enabled the country to increase life expectancy at birth from 44 to 49 years during the decade ending 1985. This gain in life span, however, means that resources must be divided among more people and that more services must be developed. Only a small fraction of Djakarta receives city water and electricity. Inadequate sewage is a breeding ground for disease and early death. Most drinking water in Indonesia is still drawn from streams that are polluted by sewage, bathing, washing, or poor drainage.

Many groups have been angered by rising costs, unemployment, and the increasing military control over their lives. As soon as General Suharto was made president he brought hundreds of his fellow officers into the government and began to curtail freedom of speech. The army, one of the best organized political forces in Indonesia, moved promptly to imprison his critics. He appointed almost 60 percent of the Parliament, and in return in 1988 Parliament re-elected the 66-year-old former general to a fifth five-year term.

Though under its military government Indonesia has become self-sufficient in the production of rice, it has also fallen deeply into debt, corruption, and even outright thievery among officials. Inefficient, it has become increasingly dependent on Japanese loans to survive. Yet its natural resources are of enormous importance to the whole world. The tin, oil, rubber, natural gas, copper, copper, nickel, tin, timber in this single country are vital to many others. If Indonesia can correct its troubled political system, control its population growth, and acquire needed capital and technology, it could become one of the most prosperous nations in Asia. It is, however, far from doing so.

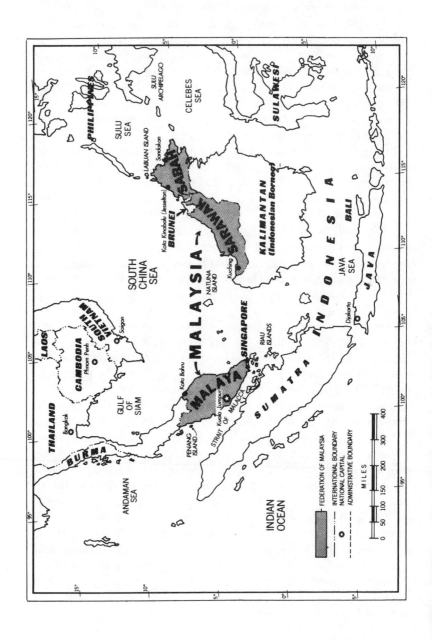

CHAPTER 9

The Independent Nations

MALAYSIA

---

*The Japanese moved quickly into the Malay Peninsula at the begin-
ning of the Pacific phase of World War II. They were able to take
the area without destroying its economy. Later, the Allies were
forced to damage much of Malaya's productive capacity during
their counterattack, however. As part of their war effort the Allies
armed Chinese refugees whom the Japanese had persecuted in the
cities and villages. Using British weapons, many of the Chinese
became guerrillas behind Japanese lines.*

*After the war, the British tried to centralize the governments of
the peninsula and the Straits Settlements but were blocked by the
sultans of the peninsula. The sultans would agree to join a
federation only if they could keep most of their political authority.
Even limited plans for a Malay Federation were opposed by
Malayan communists, who began to fight for the complete withdrawal of the British. But the British refused to leave until they
could be sure that the country would not explode into a racial war.
In 1952 the Malay, Chinese, and Indian communities seemed ready
to work together, and the British planned to create the Federation
of Malaya. The new nation began its history in 1957, at a time when
its racial and political tensions were reduced but far from removed.
The Federation began its first years struggling to reconcile large
groups that were essentially suspicious of each other, and many
people wondered whether it could survive.*

SOCIAL CONDITIONS AND CULTURAL LIFE

Ethnic groups. The Malays are an agricultural people who call
themselves "sons of the soil" (*bumiputera*). They have been involved
in rice growing, coconut harvesting, and fishing for centuries. A
1969 survey showed that of the four million Malays in the country

247

during the 1960s, only 20,000 owned businesses. Most Malays live in villages, forming large, extended families whose members reckon descent from both the mother and the father.

The Malays are the country's largest ethnic group, representing 45 percent of the population. People of Chinese ancestry, the next largest ethnic group, make up about 35 percent of the population. The British brought many of the Chinese to Malaysia to build roads, mines, and plantations when it became apparent that the Malays were unable or unwilling to take these jobs. The Chinese drifted to the cities when they finished their projects, and they began to open stores. Largely poor and illiterate when they arrived, the Chinese prospered and soon were earning up to 50 percent more than the Malays. The success of the Chinese was due to their cultural cohesiveness and the fact that the Malays refused to compete with them in business.

As the Chinese gained surplus capital, they sent for their families in South China. This numerical growth helped them to move their ancestral culture to Malaya. The Chinese brought Confucianism, Buddhism, and Taoism to their adopted country. They established Chinese schools and organized more than 1,000 voluntary associations, guilds, and secret societies to act as unofficial governments for their communities. Today, Malaysia's Chinese dominate the country's businesses and professions and supply most of the labor in manufacturing and mining. But their wealth, influence, and sense of cultural superiority have caused deep resentment among the Malays.

About 10 percent of Malaysia's population originated in India, Pakistan, and Bangladesh. The British brought these minorities to work in the mines and plantations that the Chinese had built. The

This Malay dancer
is celebrating
the harvest festival.

Many of the tribesmen on Kalimantan (North Borneo) use blowpipes and poisoned darts to catch their prey. The members of some tribes are headhunters.

families of most Malaysian Indians migrated from Tamil Land, in South India. In Malaysia they maintain Indian culture without its caste system. About 20 percent of them are Muslims about 5 percent are Christians. Most Malaysian Indians are farmers, but in recent years some of them have opened businesses in Kuala Lumpur. They make up about 20 percent of the city's population, which in 1975 was 453,000.

Finally, about 10 percent of Malaysia's population consists of tribal people and immigrants from Thailand, Burma, the Philippines, and Arab countries. West Malaysia's tribal people are descendants of the earliest inhabitants of the peninsula. About 50,000 of them live in the interior jungles. The largest tribe there is the Senoi, which occupies the foothills and mountains. About 20,000 members of the Jakun tribe live in East Malaysia, where they are farmers. Neither the Senoi nor the Jakun have accepted Islam. The most widely known tribe in Malaysia is the Iban, or Sea Dayak, headhunters whom the first Europeans to arrived called the "wild men of Borneo." Other tribes of "Borneo" (now called Kalimantan) are the Land Dayak, Melanau, Kayan, and Kenayah.

Thus Malaysia's ethnic groups represent various stages of development ranging from Stone Age culture to a modern commercial society. Malays have occupied the land for centuries, but today comprise less than half of the total population. The Malays share the land with newcomers from China and the Indian subcontinent, as well as with their predecessors, the people of the jungle.

Religion. Almost all Malays are Muslims. This faith binds them together more powerfully than any other social force. A Malay who denies his faith is likely to be cast out of his community. About 44 percent of the population are followers of Islam.

The influence of Islam on Malaysia is far greater than the percentage of its followers indicates. Islam is the state religion, and nine of the thirteen district rulers are sultans ("defenders of the faith"). The sultans control the operation of the mosques, which are the center of social activity in every Malay community. Moreover, the national government levies a religious tax on Muslims to finance their institutions. It also grants Muslims the privilege of enforcing their religious laws through special courts. The judges in the courts are responsible to the sultans. Thus the nine sultans are political as well as religious leaders.

The sultans all belong to a Conference of Rulers in Malaysia. Every five years this Conference selects the Supreme Head of Malaysia. Penang, Malacca, Sarawak, and Sabah, all have small Muslim populations and are not represented in the Conference. Their chiefs are appointed by the Supreme Head, but the members of Malaysia's Parliament are elected by the entire population.

Because of its large ethnic minorities, Malaysia provided for constitutional guarantees of religious freedom. However, the constitution states that religious freedom is "subject to public order, health, and morality." In the predominately Malay states, "public health, order, and morality" are determined according to Islamic standards.

Muslim mosques
are at the center of
most Malaysian communities.

Laws concerning marriage, divorce, and property-owning are basically Muslim in intent. Muslims may be punished for failing to pay their religious taxes, for drinking liquor, or for disobeying the holy laws. Muslims are required to observe their dietary regulations and may not eat food prepared by non-Muslims. Muslim wives who refuse to obey their husbands may be punished, too. Non-Muslims are judged under the constitutional law which is administered in secular courts.

Another law, which has vital significance and force in the villages, is the customary law (*adat*). It predates the acceptance of Islam by the Malay people and may often conflict with Islamic law. According to *adat*, for example, brothers and sisters must share equally in the possessions of the family. By contrast, Muslim law favors men over women and awards brothers twice as much as it does sisters when an estate must be distributed. The secular courts are expected to resolve these conflicts of law.

Most of the important events in Malay lives revolve around the practice of the Muslim religion. Until a boy is ten he is given intensive training in Islamic law. Then he is introduced into manhood through a circumcision ceremony. He is prevented from making close relationships with girls until he is old enough to marry. When a young man wants to marry, his parents will find a mate for him and usually plan a Muslim ceremony that lasts up to seven days. Malay parents keep close bonds with their children throughout their lives and are particularly attached to their daughters, who they hope will care for them in their old age.

Education, language, and the arts. In its development of a national education system, the government has often had to yield to pressures from its largest ethnic groups. The Chinese refused to give up private education and kept their own schools open after public school hours. Indians had fewer private schools but taught their languages in families. Nevertheless, the government succeeded in making six years of education free and compulsory for all students within walking distance of schools. It began to print uniform textbooks for the first time during the 1950s. These books used the official language, Bahasa Malaysia. Sarawak and Sabah, however, preferred their own textbooks, printed in English. Both regions were allowed to continue to use English for the indefinite future. The tribal people constituted another exception to the national education system, for they were barely taught at all.

Nonetheless, Malaysia has made impressive strides in nation-building through its improvements in the educational system. When its national education policy was conceived in 1952, there were few public schools in the country. The urban centers offered mostly

Chinese and missionary training, and in the rural areas mosques were the main source of education. About 35 percent of West Malaysians and less than 20 percent of East Malaysians were enrolled in schools. Within fifteen years school enrollment soared to almost half of the school-age population in both East and West Malaysia. Today, there are more than two million students in Malaysia's secondary schools and about 15,000 in the institutions of higher learning. The government's budget for education increased from 2.7 percent of the national income in 1957 to 4.6 percent in 1967. The figure is still rising.

Malaysian schools tend to favor the Malay community more than the Chinese, Indian, or Pakistani ones. The government offers financial support to Malay students and promises jobs to Malays who stay in school long enough to graduate. Whenever there are fifteen or more Muslim students in a class the teacher is required to give some instruction in Islamic history and traditions, whether or not there are non-Muslims in the class, too.

The development of schools has rapidly increased literacy in Malaysia. In 1947, only 38.7 percent of the population of West Malaysia and 17 percent in East Malaysia could read and write. Today, 51 percent of the West and 25 percent of the East are literate. The government has claimed even greater recent gains, but statistics are lacking.

Literacy is measured in terms of a knowledge of Bahasa Malaysia, the national version of Malay speech. The national language has been used throughout the school system since the 1960s, although Chinese, Indians, Pakistanis, and tribespeople even now insist upon using their own languages. As we have seen, the schools of Sarawak and Sabah continue to use English.

Malaysian arts reflect the country's ethnic diversity, for each ethnic group preserves its culture in them. Malay literature borrows from the Hindu classics and adds Arabic names to the plots. The Chinese and Indian Malaysians have their own classics, written centuries ago in their ancestral homelands. Each of these three major groups has its own forms of music.

Malay literature originally was communicated verbally. After the fourteenth century some of it was recorded in Arabic, but mostly it was rendered in the form of plays or proverbs. Today it takes the form of the Malay Shadow Play, or *Wayang Kulit*. This art form integrates Malaysian music and narratives from the Hindu epic, the *Ramayana*. Seated behind a transluscent screen near a bright light, a narrator operates hand puppets made of painted leather, the shadows of which are thrown onto the screen. He chooses from among more than a hundred puppets, each a character in the story.

The puppeteer in the Malaysian shadow play sits behind a translucent screen on which the shadows of his puppets are magnified for the audience on the other side.

Meanwhile he tells the tale of how Raja Seri Rama's wife, Laksamana, is kidnapped and taken to a southern island by the evil king, Maharaja Rawana. Malaysians watch this play for hours, until after many adventures Laksamana is recovered by her heroic husband. The whole performance may take weeks. Between narrations a small orchestra of flutes, flageolets, or bamboo harmoniums, drums, and clappers plays in the background.

Malay music is rarely separated from the other arts or from religion. At religious ceremonies two choirs often chant alternating verses from the Qu'ran. Malay dancing is designed to describe personal or historical experiences and often is accompanied by dialogues between performers and the audience. Malays enjoy dancing, but their Muslim faith forbids men and women from dancing with one another. The women who dance usually have abandoned religion and even then are often forced by Muslim law to dance alone or with other women.

Malaysia's most famous literary work is the *Malay Annals*. Written in the fifteenth century, it describes the historical development of the Malay people in and around Malacca. Other Malay tales often personify an animal, such as a mouse, in the fashion of Aesop's fables in ancient Greece.

From the fifteenth century onward many more Malay works were written in Arabic. Later, the schools established by the British became more influential and caused the Malays to translate Western political ideas into their own language. There was no Malay fiction in the Western sense until 1929, and few novels dealt with social or political themes until after World War II. The Malays continued to enjoy their own classic form of romantic poetry, which is illustrated in this sensitive English rendering of a *pantun*, or brief poem:

> *The fate of a dove is to fly—*
> *It flies to its nest on the knoll;*
> *The gate of true love is the eye,*
> *The prize of its quest is the soul.*

Malaysia has been less productive in the visual arts than in the literary ones. Islamic law forbids the representation of living things and so limits painting and sculpture in Muslim countries. Malays produce fine metalcraft containing elaborate decorations, which are not restricted by their religion.

The country has not produced much notable architecture, chiefly because it has lacked the labor and materials for monumental works. Its architectural styles are not unique and tend to be borrowed from India, China, Arabia, and the West.

RECENT POLITICAL DEVELOPMENTS

Post-independence. When World War II ended, Chinese guerrillas roamed the jungles of the Malay Peninsula. We have seen how the Japanese drove the Chinese out of the cities and villages and how the British armed them to help fight the Japanese. Using the weapons supplied by the Allies, the Chinese later became determined to create a Malayan revolution that would duplicate the one that Mao Tse-tung was carrying forward in China. This period of guerrilla warfare was called the "Emergency."

The British and Malayans fought the guerrillas through a unique program called the "New Village Policy." Through it the British built new villages for 450,000 Chinese who were living as squatters near the mines and prewar plantations. The British fortified these villages to reduce the number of contacts between Chinese guerrillas and the rest of the Chinese population. Thus the guerrillas were cut off from their source of supplies and support.

This program became increasingly effective in Malaya because the guerrillas were easily distinguished from the ethnic Malays. In the chapter on South Vietnam we will see how a similar policy, called the "Strategic Hamlet Program," failed because the guerrillas there were members of the ethnic majority which often joined the rebellion. In Malaya, the British ultimately extended their New Village Policy to include 130,000 members of non-Chinese minorities. They built 500 new villages, each containing from 50 to 13,000 people.

During the "Emergency" the British suspended constitutional guarantees and populated the new villages by force when necessary. But in most cases the peasants moved into the villages voluntarily.

They usually gained more food, better sanitary conditions, and more security behind the barricades than outside of them. Twelve years after the fighting began, most of the guerrillas were defeated. Some fought on and still do today, but the "Emergency" was declared over in 1960. While it lasted, thousands of lives were lost and millions of dollars spent on warfare. But the decline in fighting meant that at last Malaya was able to look forward to a period of relative internal peace, in which the new nation could be economically, politically, and socially strengthened.

Further organizing efforts. The Federation of Malaya was not a nation in the same sense that Burma, Thailand, Indonesia and the Philippines were nations. It was a collection of ethnic groups whose principal reason for union was a common colonial experience. The Muslim religion and Malayan culture provided the base upon which the nation grew. Behind the Federation, offering military protection and membership in the Commonwealth, stood Great Britain.

During the 1960s the British recognized that their days in Southeast Asia were ending. They were willing to continue their military alliance with Malaya but were unable to justify expenditures in their nearby possessions of Singapore and North Borneo. Accordingly, the British proposed to include Singapore and their North Borneo colonies—Sabah (British North Borneo), Sarawak, and Brunei—into a new federation, called Malaysia.

Singapore and Malaya were initially reluctant to give wholehearted support to the formation of Malaysia. We will see in a later chapter how Singapore's population had reservations about the plan because their economy and school system were stronger than those on the peninsula. The Malays, on the other hand, resisted merger with Singapore because they did not want to increase their already large Chinese population. The people of North Borneo were even less enthusiastic about joining the new country. One of their reasons was a fear of arousing the hostility of Indonesia. Sabah, Sarawak, and Brunei share the vast island of Borneo (known to Malays as Kalimantan) with Indonesia. The Indonesians, having recently fought the Dutch for freedom, strongly opposed Western interests anywhere in Southeast Asia. Finally, the sultanate of Brunei resisted the plan for Malaysia because it did not want to share the wealth from its large oil reserves. In 1963, violent demonstrations took place against the British in Brunei. Operating from the safety of Indonesian territory, guerrillas took advantage of the discontent by striking across the border at Brunei. They were defeated, but later Brunei's sultan announced that it would remain outside of Malaysia.

Besides Indonesia, the Philippines opposed the formation of

Malaysia. The Filipinos asserted a right to Sabah as part of the Sulu Archipelago, their southernmost chain of islands. Both Indonesia and the Philippines feared economic competition from Malaysia. To resolve these differences the heads of the three countries met in 1963. Indonesia and the Philippines agreed to accept Malaysia only if a United Nations survey in Sarawak and Sabah showed that the populations there were in favor of it.

The United Nations conducted its survey and announced that the people of Sarawak and Sabah were overwhelmingly in favor of joining Malaysia. Therefore, the Federation of Malaysia was proclaimed at Kuala Lumpur on September 16, 1963. Simultaneous ceremonies took place in Singapore, Sarawak, and Sabah. During the Kuala Lumpur celebrations a flock of doves was released, symbolizing Malaysia's desire to live in peace with its neighbors. But there was no peace. Indonesia's chief of state, Achmed Sukarno, tried to overturn Malaysia through an undeclared war called the "Confrontation" (1963–66). Sukarno failed, however, and Malaysia brought together more than nine million people, living in an area 1,600 miles wide, under a common government. Great Britain was committed to defend the new country, and Australia and New Zealand joined in its support.

Current conditions. Malaysia's most difficult problem was the resentment stirred among Malays by the growing influence and wealth of the resident Chinese. In the 1960s the government tried to equalize differences between the two communities through its social and economic policies. But change did not come rapidly enough. In 1969 the fury of Malays exploded into a violent ethnic disturbance. The incident caused the government to intensify its efforts to help the Malay community catch up with the Chinese population.

The Chinese and Indians were not permitted to enter businesses or become citizens as easily as Malays. At the same time, Malays were encouraged to take more responsibility in society. The government established quotas from Malays in schools, professions, and the civil service. It gave tax incentives to businesses willing to hire Malays.

Some non-Muslims criticized the government for aiding the Malays at the expense of other ethnic groups. But the government responded by saying that the nation could not survive if the Chinese continued to gain strength while the Malays lost it. The new Malaysian constitution assured the minorities that their basic liberties would be protected and that they would receive equal protection under the law. It empowered the Supreme Head to "safeguard the special position of the Malays and the legitimate interests of the other communities."

Tungku Sir Abdul Rahman of Negri Sembilan State became Malaysia's Supreme Head in a traditional Muslim ceremony. He is shown here with his wife.

We will see in the next chapter how and why Singapore became an independent city-state in 1965. The separation of Singapore allowed Malaysia to enjoy much greater political stability by reducing the number of Chinese in the Federation. The ruling Alliance Party was the most important political force in Malaysia. Organized in 1952, this party had been the first to unite the leaders of Malay, Chinese, and Indian associations when the country was still in the hands of the British. Its initial success had been the deciding factor in persuading the British to withdraw. By 1965, with Singapore detached from the country, the Alliance Party was able to renew its claim to national leadership.

The party advanced its program of giving the Malay population special assistance. This policy was carried out by Tungku Abdul Rahman, the head of the party and the prime minister of Malaysia. "The Tungku," as he was called, was one of the most durable leaders in the history of Malaysia. The son of a Siamese princess and a sultan of Kedah, he studied law in England before returning home to enter politics.

The Tungku managed to keep the government functioning by enabling each of the major ethnic groups to influence the policies of the Alliance Party. The party formed a joint committee of representatives from the Malay, Chinese, and Indian associations which formed the "popular front." After meeting to discuss policies, these representatives returned to their members to advise them of what had been negotiated. This system gave Malaysia political stability until 1969. In that year the Alliance Party unexpectedly lost an election. The parties that gained at the polls mainly appealed to ethnic interests rather than to national ones.

The 1969 election reflected growing division among Malaysia's ethnic and economic groups. After the election, Chinese and Indian voters marched through the streets of Kuala Lumpur to celebrate the defeat of the Alliance Party. Suddenly fighting broke out between the marchers and the Malay observers. The death of two hundred people made this one of the worst ethnic riots in Malaysia's history. The government declared a state of emergency. The Supreme Head vested political power in a newly formed National Operations Council that included the Prime Minister, his deputy, and military and business leaders. There were six Malays, one Chinese, and one Indian on the Council.

The Council ruled for twenty-one months. Parliamentary government was suspended. At last the Council returned authority to Parliament and to a National Unity Council whose task was to encourage ethnic unity. Then, in 1970, the Tungku resigned as Prime Minister, ending a career of fifteen years in that office. He was replaced by his deputy, Tun Abdul Razak bin Hussein, who had, like him, studied law in England. At the same time the sultan of Kedah, Tungku Abdul Halim Mu'azzam, became Malaysia's Supreme Head.

Following these changes, the Malays continued to dominate the government of Malaysia for the next decade. A coalition headed by leaders of the United Malay National Organization (UMNO) gained overwhelming majorities in the Parliament. After the death of Tun Abdul Razak in 1976 another member of this party, Hussein bin Onn, succeeded him, and in 1981 Datuk Seri Mahathir bin Mohamad, deputy president of the UMNO, became Prime Minister. Both leaders continued the stable, prosperous course upon which Malaysia had embarked.

But the problem of racial conflict in Malaysia did not end. It took a different form—friction with Chinese from nearby Vietnam. The newcomers, in flight from Vietnam's hostile government, set out in small boats and at last reached Malaysia after escaping storms, pirates, and starvation at sea. Tens of thousands of them, driven by winds and tides, managed to land in Malaysia, but were greeted there by a government that threatened to shoot them on sight. At least fifty thousand finally were settled on islands near the Malay Peninsula. Malaysia's unwillingness to shelter these homeless people by itself at last led to an international conference which sought to help the "boat people" of Vietnam.

ECONOMIC CONDITIONS AND PROBLEMS

The British built the foundations of Malaysia's modern economy. Their objective was to develop sources of cash income, rather than to shape a balanced economic system. Therefore, they concentrated their investments in tin mines and rubber plantations, neglecting the country's basic need to produce more food and diverisfy its industries. The British also failed to develop forest products, though 70 percent of the country is covered by forests. Tin and rubber became the mainstays of the economy. Nonetheless, under the British the per capita income rose rapidly and reached the level in Japan, despite Japan's much larger population.

By 1985, this was no longer true. Japan's per capita income had soared to more than $8,500, while Malaysia's was $714. Yet the per capita income in Malaysia was 50 percent greater than it had been a decade before, and the country was among the most economically healthy in Southeast Asia. Its income from international trade exceeded expenditures by more than 50 percent. This one country was producing 35 percent of all the world's tin and rubber, as well as increasing amounts of oil and hardwood. By the 1980s the development of offshore wells had enabled Malaysia to begin exporting oil to the nearby nations which were clamoring for it, such as Singapore and Japan.

But Malaysia's dependence on tin and rubber continues. These two products are the main source of support for a much larger

Malaysia's Chinese maintain their own culture and have become the wealthiest ethnic group in the country, with an income far exceeding the Malays.

population than existed during colonial times. Rubber alone gener-
ates up to a half of all the revenues from abroad and employs up to
a half of the labor force. This one industry is so profitable that
immediately after World War II it alone was credited with preventing the bankruptcy of the United Kingdom.

Today, synthetic rubber has captured a large share of the world
rubber market. To compete with the synthetics, Malaysia must
plant thousands of new, higher-yielding rubber trees. This expensive process is not easily financed. Only large plantation owners,
many of whom are Europeans, can afford to make the investment.
The less prosperous owners, meanwhile, must struggle against the
economic tides and often are threatened with bankruptcy. Malaysia
also faces severe problems in its tin industry. Someday, certainly, its
supply of ore will give out. Thus the economic dependence on tin
and rubber has placed Malaysia in a dangerous position.

For the present, international markets consume all of the tin and
rubber that Malaysia can produce. The country puts most of its
energies into the development of mines and plantations, which
mostly lie on the west coast between Kedah and Singapore. Too
little money is available for the development of new sources of food.
Malaysia's rate of population growth has declined in recent years
from 3 to 2.5 percent, but even at the lower rate will double in less
than twenty-nine years. New farms are not easily created, and
more than 40 percent of the work force labors on the present ones.
Thus it is difficult to see how Malaysia will be able to feed all of its
future population.

Malaysia has produced a series of five-year plans aimed at reducing poverty, social stress, and unemployment. In its second plan the
country established a goal of "restructuring Malaysian society to
reduce and eventually eliminate the identification of race with
economic function," but it changed little. Essentially the Malays,

The National Mosque at Kuala Lumpur symbolizes Malaysia's determination
to maintain its religious traditions while creating a modern community.

who by the mid-1980s represented half of the population, remained agricultural, and the Chinese, with 36 percent, commercial. Many of the laborers were Indians, who comprised about 10 percent of the population.

Under the five-year plans the economy has continued to grow and diversify, producing amazing growth rates ranging from 6 to 11.3 percent in 1976. By 1985 inflation had settled into the 3 percent range, making Malaysia's one of the most stable economies in Asia. There were many other healthy signs. Before World War II the country was forced to import two-thirds of its rice. In recent years its rice yields per acre have been increasing, despite a climate that is not the best for rice-growing. More intensive rice cultivation, double-cropping, the use of new strains, and terracing have enabled Malaysia to reduce its rice imports to one-third of its consumption.

Malaysia has little industry. Most of its factories are based on tin and rubber products or on handicrafts. The nation has developed one of the largest shipyards in Southeast Asia. It is also rapidly building a highway transport system to replace the old railways and river traffic that the British developed to bring tin and rubber down from the highlands. Lacking coal, Malaysia has not been able to refine all of its own ores, but has some small mills. It also has a large fishing industry.

FOREIGN RELATIONS

In recent years Malaysia's central foreign policy goal has been to lead its troubled region towards neutrality between the world's great powers. The departure of American forces from Vietnam in 1975 opened the way for a new struggle, between China and the Soviet Union, for control of this vital region. Malaysia opposes communism, but to help avoid collisions it has improved its relations with all three Communist countries. At the same time it has maintained friendships with Japan and the United States, its two largest trading partners.

Malaysia has also sought to maintain friendly contacts with its nearest neighbors, Indonesia, the Philippines, and Singapore. The Malaysian government and Indonesia agreed to allow each other to pursue guerrillas over the unmarked borders on Kalimantan. Trade between the two countries has been increasing. Improved relations with the Philippines has opened the way to more regional cooperation. In the 1960s Malaysia, Indonesia, and the Philippines took steps to form "Maphilindo," an association designed to increase regional social and economic cooperation. The new era of friendship with its neighbors permitted Malaysia to help found a broader organization, the Association of Southeast Asia (ASA) in 1967.

ASA was not broad enough to succeed. Therefore Malaysia, the Philippines, Thailand, and Singapore organized its successor, the Association of Southeast Asia Nations (ASEAN). The new agency was more promising than either of its predecessors. It quickly set about organizing economic cooperation in the region. ASEAN has helped Malaysia to make neutralism the cornerstone of its foreign policy. Fearful of arousing Communist China, its giant neighbor, it refused to join the Southeast Asia Treaty Organization (SEATO), which was organized by the United States to resist the spread of communism in the region.

Malaysia's large Chinese-speaking population is an important factor in its relationship with Communist China. The Malaysian government does not want to provoke any part of its largest minority. The People's Republic of China has renounced any claim that overseas Chinese are its citizens, but almost certainly would resent their mistreatment. Trade between China and Malaysia has been increasing rapidly.

In addition to its defense agreements with Great Britain, Malaysia has many reasons to continue friendly relations with the British Commonwealth. It has strong commercial and cultural ties with the English. Malaysian students and merchants often travel to Australia and New Zealand, and many of them speak English.

THE FUTURE OF MALAYSIA

Malaysia's stability depends upon the willingness of its ethnic groups to cooperate with one another. Each of them is vital to the country's economic progress. The Malays contribute the food, the Chinese the professional and commercial skills, and the Indians much of the labor to run the plantations that are a main source of revenue. Conflicts among the ethnic groups echo immediately in the economy. They jeopardize Malaysia's position as one of the most prosperous countries in Southeast Asia and represent a continuing source of internal tension.

But the Malaysian government is determined to risk upsetting ethnic stability in order to gain ethnic equality. The government realizes that the Malays have bound themselves to agricultural jobs that will always be less profitable than the commercial ones held by the Chinese. Therefore, the government's basic policies are designed to stimulate the participation of Malays in businesses and the professions. At the same time, it has been holding back the Chinese and Indians in those fields. The civil service is required by the constitution to hire four Malays for every Chinese or Indian.

There are dangers in these policies. If pressed too hard, the minorities may react against government restrictions. Malaysia's ethnic tensions are most clearly revealed in the schools. The use of Bahasa Malaysia as the language of education offends the Chinese, who prefer to study in their own language. People of Indian ancestry are equally irritated by the need to learn a second language. Both Chinese and Indian students continue to learn their own languages after school hours. Their sense of cultural pride often causes them to clash with Malay students in schools. This source of friction is accepted by the Malaysian government as unavoidable. It believes, no doubt correctly, that nationhood can only be fostered through the use of a national language and the development of a national culture.

Despite problems in the school system, there has been substantial progress in the field of education. During the 1980s the government reported that 94 percent of all qualified students, including Malay, Chinese, and Indian, were attending primary schools. More than 48 percent were attending secondary schools. As a result, literacy was said to have soared in 75 percent of the population. Even life expectancy at birth, which hovers about fifty years in many countries of the region, was said to be an astonishing sixty-four years.

But Malaysians have paid a substantial price for these gains: their civil liberties. Politicians, claiming that national security would be threatened by dissent, have suppressed almost all criticism on grounds that it might lead to ethnic clashes. In 1988 Prime Minister Mahathir Mohamad ordered the arrest of ninety-one newspaper reporters, consumer advocates, human rights campaigners, and leaders of social and religious minorities. He also seized and tried six Supreme Court justices, as well as his leading political opponent in Parliament. Mahathir next banned all public meetings and closed four newspapers. To protest the dumping of radioactive waste or to represent a radical Muslim group was to risk jail. Four women were imprisoned on grounds that they had visited the Philippines; they were accused of seeking to repeat in Malaysia the popular uprising which overthrew Ferdinand Marcos in the neighboring islands.

Throughout the world, champions of democratic freedoms protested these actions on the part of the Malaysian government. Mahathir did not change his course, however. He drew legitimacy from Malaysia's Internal Security Act , which permits the government to arrest anyone on relatively vague charges for any length of time. Some of Mahathir's critics, such as Prince Abdul Rahman, said that the Internal Security Act had led to a dictatorship. But the prince, who was in his mid-eighties and was the most widely venerated person in Malaysia, was one of the few who were above arrest for

The Malaysian landscape is one of the most beautiful in the world, with lush vegetation and many forest animals, of which the argus pheasant is one.

criticism.

Thus Malaysia may be said to have solved some of its material problems while suppressing its political ones. And the government is certain to pursue more of them, often successfully, while claiming that a unified population is needed to do so. Malaysia's population, for example, is poorly distributed. This problem is more important in Malaysia than overpopulation, though the country's 15.2 million people are increasing at the high rate of 2.5 percent a year. To open new lands the government will have to use firm measures which will further endanger civil liberties.

The government is committed to the development of the 70 percent of Malaysia which is covered by forests. Large areas are being prepared for planting; many more will become available in the near future. More double-cropping, irrigation, and effective fertilizing must be developed. The economy must be diversified through the better use of Malaysia's valuable antimony, bauxite, copper, and gold reserves, as well as its tin, rubber, and oil. But even if its prosperity reaches new heights Malaysia's gains may prove to be ashen if they are made at the expense of liberty. There will be a day, as history has shown, when even the most restrictive of governments must yield to the demands of its people for political as well as economic freedom.

CHAPTER 10

The Independent Nations

SINGAPORE

Before World War II, Singapore was the heart of the British Empire in Southeast Asia. It was regarded as an invincible island fortress, shielded from attack by the mighty British Navy. The Japanese demolished that illusion at the beginning of the Pacific phase of the war. Isolating Singapore from its source of supplies, they forced the fleet there to surrender and overran the British military base.

The British regained Singapore after the war, but with diminished prestige on the island. They turned the city into a semi-independent Crown Colony. Singapore governed its own internal affairs but relied upon the British for the management of its foreign policy. Later, the British proposed to include Singapore in a new Malay Federation by combining it and other Straits Settlements with the Malay States. But the Malay rulers rejected the idea of merger with Singapore, whose large Chinese population might have controlled them politically. Singapore remained an independent Crown Colony when the Federation of Malaya was organized in 1957. Outsiders were deeply concerned about Singapore's ability to survive in its isolated position. The people of the island, however, were determined to overcome their handicaps, and how they have managed to do so is one of Southeast Asia's great success stories.

SOCIAL CONDITIONS AND CULTURAL LIFE

Ethnic groups. Of Singapore's 2.2 million people, about 1.7 million are Chinese. Like Chinese everywhere in Southeast Asia they migrated to escape poverty, natural disasters, warfare, or tyranny in their homeland. The Chinese were also drawn by economic opportunities on the island. Between 1850 and 1930, tens of thousands of them immigrated in the hope that they could earn enough money to return home to support their families. But these strong, resilient people usually decided that they would remain in Singapore or Malaya instead of returning home.

Frightened by the massive influx of an ethnic minority, the Malays began to restrict Chinese immigration to the peninsula in 1933. But the Chinese population kept growing, particularly in Singapore. Most of the immigrants were young and hard-working. By taking over commercial jobs that the Malays did not seem to want, they gained control of Singapore's commerce and industry. A few came as impoverished farmers and became industrial million-aires. The great majority, however, owned small shops and worked long hours to make a bare living.

The British encouraged the growth of the Chinese community in Singapore. There were only 150 Chinese on the island when Thomas Stamford Raffles (later Sir Thomas) claimed it for the British Empire in 1819. Raffles admired the energy and initiative of the Chinese and invited more of them to settle under British protection.

Other ethnic groups began to arrive as the British developed the port. The city's population was about 35,000 in 1840. Most of these people were Chinese, but Malays began to immigrate after Great Britain extended its control over nearby islands. The Malays and Indian merchants came to share in the new prosperity created by tin mining and shipping. As the British progressed toward a federation of Malay states, Singapore became the only metropolis in Malaya. Its population rose to three times that of Kuala Lumpur, the largest city on the Malay Peninsula, and reached about 400,000 by the turn of the century.

The proportion of Chinese among Singapore's total population continued to hover about 75 percent. By the end of World War II there were more than 725,000 Chinese on the island. Thus Singapore contained about 25 percent of all the Chinese in Malaya. Today, 76 percent of its population is Chinese, 14 percent Malay, and 8 percent Indian and Pakistani. People often call Singapore the "Third China"—after mainland China and Taiwan.

Religion. More than 70 percent of the Chinese in Singapore are Buddhists, Confucianists, or Taoists. Like Chinese throughout Southeast Asia, they respect the past, honor their own ancestors, and tend to follow the social structure that their religions teach. Both Buddhists and Confucianists accept the idea of a paternalistic ruler in a well ordered society. Buddhism, Confucianism, and Taoism may exist in varying degrees in the same individual.

The young people of Singapore are less concerned with religion than their parents. In many ways they are also less mindful of tradition than their countrymen elsewhere in Southeast Asia. The flood

Singapore is the world's most densely populated country, with 9,761 persons per square mile. This street is not far from a modern financial center.

of ideas from Communist China and their own brisk commercial society have deeply influenced Singapore's young Chinese. China's Cultural Revolution, which renounced Confucianism, ancestor worship, and the reverence for history, had parallel effects in Singapore. Religions which are faithfully accepted in agricultural societies seem less important in the thoroughly urban atmosphere that Singapore provides.

In addition to the Chinese religions, those of the Malay Peninsula and subcontinent of India are represented in Singapore. The city's Malays and Pakistanis are almost all Muslims, and most of the Indian practice Hinduism. Singapore also has a large European and Eurasian community which is either Christian or agnostic.

Education, language, and the arts. The children of Singapore are required to attend free primary schools for six years. Students are offered a combination of academic, commercial, and technical subjects in well-equipped secondary schools, but are not compelled to attend them. The elementary schools enroll more than 375,000 students, and the secondary and vocational schools enroll more than 150,000. All told, the island maintains more than 500 primary and secondary school. It also supports two universities with almost

13,000 students, as well as three technical institutes with a total enrollment of more than 4,000.

Singapore's schools teach in any one or combination of four languages: English, Chinese, Malay, and Tamil. Children are required to learn at least two of these languages. Since English is used in government and business, 60 percent of all students study it, while about 33 percent study in Chinese. Singapore's Chinese population uses three different dialects, for it originated in three separate provinces of South China. For this reason Singapore's Chinese may not always understand each other's speech. Many speak Mandarin, the official Chinese language, as well as their own dialect, however.

Malay is another frequently used language in Singapore. All Malays and some Chinese use it when they are dealing with people from Malaysia, their second largest trading partner. The majority of Indians in Singapore speak Tamil, the language used in the part of South India from which they or their families came. Some also speak Pakistani and Sinhalese.

The arts of Singapore blend those of China, India, Malaysia, and Indonesia, and all are influenced by Western styles. The population supports music, painting, literature, and the theater to a degree not found in many other countries. Movies, imported from the United States, Taiwan, and India, are among the most popular cultural

Singapore's Tao Payoh Housing Estate maintains its own market, shopping centers, and schools. This couple is watering the estate's vegetable gardens.

events on the island. Singapore's architecture reflects the country's special combination of Asian and Western ideas. Buildings resembling those in New York and London rise above rows of narrow shops in which Chinese families both live and work. Western-style houses and apartment buildings spread into the suburbs. Not far from them are huts made of wood or corrugated iron, topped by thatched roofs.

Singapore's population is more than 70 percent literate. It consumes vast quantities of books, newspapers, and magazines. The socialist government operates radio and television stations and broadcasts daily in all four official languages.

RECENT POLITICAL DEVELOPMENTS

Post-independence. When it was a semi-independent Crown Colony after World War II, Singapore governed its own domestic affairs but recognized the power of Britain to control its foreign relations. Its tendency was to press for complete independence. Like others in Southeast Asia, the people of Singapore had lost much of their respect for Western governments during the war. About 30,000 Japanese had forced the surrender of more than 100,000 Britons by cutting them off from their source of supplies. The British were further humiliated when the Japanese forced them to perform hard labor in public.

After the war, the people of Singapore saw themselves as the equals of the British rather than their inferiors. In 1948, Singapore overwhelmingly rejected the British by granting 43 of the 51 seats in the new Legislative Council to the People's Action Party (PAP). The PAP strongly supported complete independence for Singapore. It wanted a socialist economy but was anti-communist. In its foreign policy it proposed that Singapore remain a member of the Commonwealth and continue its military relationship with Britain. However, it stood for total self-rule, and it quickly set about this task.

Further organizing efforts. Recognizing that it would have to leave Singapore soon, Great Britain negotiated to include the city in the new Federation of Malaysia which was being formed out of its Straits Settlements, Malay States and North Borneo colonies. The PAP supported this move, for few people thought it would be possible for Singapore to stand alone. Political changes in China were provoking strikes and terrorist activity in Singapore's industries. The PAP offered to make Malay its first official language, despite Singapore's overwhelming Chinese population, if it could join the new federation. But the Malays opposed Singapore's socialist tendencies as well as its ethnic composition. At that time, Malaya was suffering from a guerrilla war in which the rebels were almost all Chinese. Therefore it resisted the inclusion of more Chinese into its population.

Singapore also had reservations about the proposed merger. It feared that because of its greater wealth it would be paying a disproportionate amount of taxes as part of Malaysia. It was also concerned about the possible deterioration of its economy and school system if it were subject to the political influence of Malays. Members of the PAP thought that the Malays might prevent them from carrying out their socialist program, which proposed that government plan the economy and participate with private investors in the development of industry.

These political divisions blocked the development of the Federation of Malaysia until 1963. At last, there was a compromise. Singapore was added to Malaysia on terms that differed from those allowed the rest of the country. It was granted a lower tax rate and the right to control its own economic and educational systems. For its part, Singapore agreed to reduce its political influence within the Federation, It accepted only fifteen seats in the Malaysian Parliament, although it was entitled to more. Its citizens were allowed to become citizens of Malaysia, but the tests by which people became citizens were more difficult for the Chinese than for the Malays.

Singapore's mayor, Lee Kuan Yew, put an unexpected interpretation on the compromise agreement after the Federation was created. He had agreed not to involve Singapore directly in Malaysian politics, yet sponsored nine candidates for Parliament in the 1964 elections. Lee had gained a reputation as a brilliant politician and economist who wanted to extend his influence into Malaysia. His socialist policies had been successful in Singapore without the help of the city's large communist faction.

Lee's candidates were badly defeated in the election. Only one gained a seat in the Parliament, while Malaysia's ruling Alliance Party won 89 seats. With its power confirmed, the Alliance Party dealt severely with the Chinese socialist leader. Lee met with Alliance Party leaders, and in 1964 the two sides agreed that Singapore would no longer be part of the Federation of Malaysia. On August 9, 1965, Singapore became the world's only true independent city-state.

Current conditions. Many observers believed that Singapore would be unable to survive outside of Malaysia. Its people had no sense of national identity and borrowed their culture from other countries. Racial tensions between Chinese, Malays, Indians, and Pakistanis often exploded into violence.

Lee, who was chosen prime minister of the new country, regarded these problems as inescapable in what he called Singapore's "rugged society." But the scope of the problems could be

Lee Kuan Yew, President of Singapore, is given much of the credit for the country's successful government.

reduced, he said. To cope with them he gathered increasing power in his office. His People's Action Party had controlled the government since 1959; it was unopposed since Singapore's separation from Malaysia in 1965. In the face of increasing crime and threats posed by sympathizers of Communist China, Lee appealed for a stronger government. His administration abolished trial by jury for capital offenses in 1970, replacing it with trial by two judges from whose decisions the defendants could appeal. He closed two newspapers in 1971, charging that their editors were bribed by agents of Communist China.

By the early 1970s there were fifteen political parties in Singapore, but few of them had the strength to challenge Lee's political power successfully. The People's Action Party controlled all of the seats in the legislature. In 1972 Lee called for a new election, though his five-year term had eight months to go. Once again Lee was confirmed as Prime Minister. His party won 70 percent of the vote. It promptly used its mandate to declare that Singapore would remain independent unless two-thirds of the population decided to invite annexation by another country.

Lee's new success at the polls quickly led to a one-party government in Singapore. Managing with a firm hand, he claimed the power to license the owners of newspapers and threatened to close papers which he said were printing "purient and permissive" stories. To limit congestion downtown he taxed all drivers with cars there. He tried to affect education by insisting that students learn English as well as the languages of their own ethnic groups. In 1983 he even offered the services of government in helping educated women find equally educated mates. Only such marriages, he said, would gain for Singapore the new talent that it needed to survive. To bring more skilled people to the country Lee advertised in overseas newspapers, offering inducements to professionals to immigrate.

Such complete powers of government were certain to lead to abuses in time. By the 1980s, they began to appear. According to Amnesty International, an organization which monitors the violation of human rights throughout the world, Singapore had begun to seize and torture its critics over a period of years. While denying that it had used torture, Lee's government appeared to be admitting this policy when, in 1981, it released two political prisoners who had been held without charge for seventeen years. The government announced later that it had arrested members of the one group which opposed Lee, the Workers' Party, for distributing pamphlets.

Thus Lee seemed willing to sacrifice political rights in exchange for material progress. While he had resolute opposition in the political arena, few people in Singapore denied that he had enabled the tiny city-state to achieve an astonishing prosperity.

ECONOMIC CONDITIONS AND PROBLEMS

"You may take my word for it," Thomas Stamford Raffles said, "Singapore is by far the most important station in the East; and as far as naval superiority and commercial interests are concerned, of much higher value than whole continents of territory."

Raffles made this statement soon after he founded a British base on the island in 1819. Few people shared his vision. The land was nothing more than a swamp, and the 150 people who lived on it occupied a few run-down houseboats. But under Raffles Singapore's trade grew steadily. It rose to $3 million within one year and to $13 million within five years after it was founded. The island's commercial success was assured after 1832, when it became the capital of the British Straits Settlements. (The Straits Settlements included Penang and Malacca, as well as Singapore.) The British made Singapore a separate colony in 1867 to prepare it for the surge of East-West trade that they expected to result from the opening of the Suez Canal.

Singapore's greatest assets were its deep water port, its position between Malacca and the South China Sea, and a population that was determined to achieve commercial success. During the nineteenth century, Chinese laborers swarmed into Malayan tin mines and during the early twentieth were drawn to work in the peninsula's rubber plantations. Most of the Chinese passed through Singapore. Many stayed or returned. These tough, hard-working laborers quickly established themselves as part of the foreign trade industry that sprang up around Raffles' duty-free port. Singapore became East Asia's major wholesaler and transshipper.

Today, Singapore is the fourth largest port in the world and has developed a substantial air transport industry. The entire country contains 239 square miles—less than New York City. Lacking food and mineral resources, it serves as processor, manufacturer, and broker for larger producers of raw materials. Singapore processes and sells more than half of its imports abroad. Much of its manufacturing is accomplished in the famous Jurong Industrial Estate, where about 255 modern factories occupy 7,000 acres of former swampland. Singapore is developing another 6,000 acres for this industrial area. It ships steel, tin, rubber, and cement from its own plants and transships ores, latex, and rice for its neighbors. It is a leading shipbuilder and repairer. As an agent for others it has become one of Asia's great financial centers. By 1985, at the end of its second decade, it was generating an annual per capita income of $4,100—286 percent greater than just ten years before.

Sources of current problems. As it has in other countries, prosperity has acted as a brake on the growth of population in Singapore. In 1957 the growth rate was 4.4 percent, the highest of any country in the history of the world. Then Lee began to enforce a British policy, begun in 1953, of halting the immigration of Chinese and Indians. In 1972 he placed economic penalties on couples who had more than two children. His program drove the rate of population growth down to 2.7 percent by 1975 and to 1.2 percent, or about the rate in Japan, the United States, and Western Europe, by the mid-1980s.

Even this reduced rate of growth leaves the country with the greatest density of any other in the world. The average square mile in Singapore contains 10,700 people, making a total of more than 2.5 million. The same effect would be achieved if slightly more than 80 percent of the population of the entire world were to pack itself into the United States.

Trends. Singapore's economy has continued to grow in recent years, and its future remains promising. In 1984 the gross national product increased by 8.2 percent, in contrast to 6.3 percent two years earlier. The country's progress may be subject to abrupt changes, however. Singapore is a commercial agent rather than a producer, and so it is vulnerable to worldwide conditions. A slump in the economies of its major trading partners, especially Japan, Great Britain, and the United States, spell disaster for Singapore.

Yet if disaster comes, it is likely to be temporary. Singapore, like Hong Kong, is in the best possible position to benefit from the vastly increased trade which will result from an awakening China. Multinational companies have established headquarters there, waiting for the inevitable time when Asia's vast population achieves something more like equality in world markets.

According to Lee Kuan Yew, Singapore has been drifting away from the traditional Chinese values which he favors. He opposes many practices which are widespread in the West, including the use of birth control pills, frequent lawsuits, and heated political discussions. He preferred a strong central government to the kind of diversity found in the United States. Despite his views, Singapore was moving steadily towards greater freedom, especially in its treatment of women. Many of the country's women, it seemed, were at last able to enter professions and make appointments without the permission of men.

FOREIGN RELATIONS

Singapore is a socialist state, but its economy is firmly linked to capitalist countries. Therefore it has aligned itself more with Western policies than with those of Communist China or the Soviet Union. In its own region, this has meant opposing communist expansion. Singapore has denounced Vietnamese moves into Laos and Kampuchea, and it has given the strongest possible support to Thailand in its effort to remain capitalist and independent.

Singapore's defenses are linked to Great Britain, Australia, New Zealand, and Malaysia. Through a treaty in which each state is an equal partner, these countries established a military force on Singapore to replace the one which the British withdrew in 1970. The present defense force is only a token, however. Authorities acknowledge that it has more diplomatic than military importance.

Singapore's relationship with Japan and China has, in recent years, become a pivotal element in the nation's foreign policy. Both countries are important to Singapore, not only from an economic, but from a military point of view.

THE FUTURE OF SINGAPORE

Singapore's government has persuaded some of the world's largest companies to invest in its enterprises. It did so by offering to risk capital with them in the development of industries. In recent years, the Japanese especially have become active on the island. The Sumitomo Chemical Company built a one-billion dollar petrochemical complex there in 1973. Other large companies were built with the help of loans from the United Nations. These striking economic gains gave Singapore a better chance to survive than almost any other country in Southeast Asia

The demand for goods and services in Singapore has been in-creasing steadily with the growing population. Until now, the economy has been able to supply them. Almost everyone in Singapore has water and electricity, unlike many of the people of Djakarta and other Southeast Asian cities. Computers are used everywhere; almost everyone in the country uses them, either to collect wages, pay bills, or transact banking.

Singapore's housing program has been called miraculous. The nation's first development plan called for the production for 51,000 apartments in five years. By 1966, this goal was exceeded by at least 3,000 units. More than a third of the nation's budget has been poured into social programs, principally housing, education, and medical care.

All of these gains are unique in Southeast Asia and possibly in the rest of the world, too. They have been achieved by effective planning and by the enormous energy expended by a dedicated population. Certainly the skills of Lee Kuan Yew have been a factor. But after guiding the city-state to unprecedented prosperity for twenty-nine years, Lee Kuan Yew thought not only of retirement, but of immortality. He said that his son, Brigadier-General Lee Hsien Loong, would succeed him. He pursued longstanding efforts to create a superior population by encouraging young people of proven intelligence to marry—a form of eugenic monument to his own achievements.

Facing his critics, Lee Kuan Yew banned some local and international newspapers. In 1988 he ordered the arrest of twenty-two young men and women, many of them active Roman Catholics, on grounds that they probably were Marxists seeking to overthrow him. In Singapore, under the British International Security Act which the government inherited, it is legal and even common for police to surveil and detain suspects. Some were tortured.

Though it will soon lose its immensely leader, the young nation of Singapore appears to have a brighter future than ever before. Barring war or a collapse of the world economy, it is likely to reach historic levels of financial success. It must, however, find a political system which is based upon more than a single chief of state. At the same time, it must reconsider its human and political goals as well as its political ones.

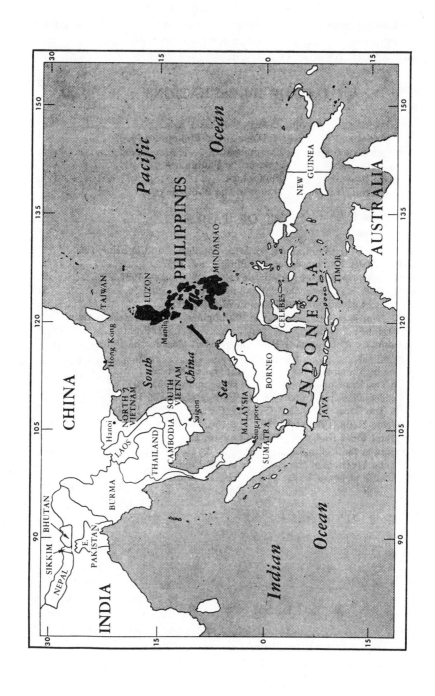

Chapter 11

THE PHILIPPINES

*The Philippines achieved independence at a time when its economy
and morale were at the lowest points in history. The country was
devastated during World War II, and the losses were a source of
bitterness and quarreling. Filipinos were especially divided over the
issue of how to treat former collaborators of, the, Japanese. They
were unable to decide how to share in the reparations promised to
them by Japan and the United States.*

*Communist guerrillas in central Luzon had been among the most
effective fighters against the Japanese. They presented the government with its most urgent political problem after the war. A debate
arose over whether to let them participate in the new government,
share in the reparation, and receive back military pay for their wartime services. The communists demanded the right to hold office in
the Philippines at a time when the new country was struggling
against the threat of starvation, bankruptcy, and chaos in the cities.*

Social Conditions and Cultural Life

Ethnic groups. The dominant ethnic group in the Philippines is
Malay. The Malays originated in Mongolia and migrated to the
Malay Peninsula, from which they moved to Indonesia and the
Philippines. Other Malays may have come by way of China. The
Malays took over coastal lands, driving older inhabitants into the
jungles. The older inhabitants were chiefly Negritos whose
descendants persist, though in diminishing numbers, in the interior
lands of the modern country. The Malays have brown skin, black
hair, flat noses, and high cheek bones. They are small and slender,
while the Negritos are slightly smaller and darker.

The only other large ethnic group in the Philippines is Chinese.
This community makes up less than 1 percent of the total
population. The Chinese create anxieties among Filipinos, as they
do in the other countries of Southeast Asia. The Chinese population

has risen from about 40,000 in 1900 to more than 500,000 today. It has increased largely because of growing numbers of refugees coming from mainland China, many of them young women of childbearing age.

Filipinos are concerned lest the Chinese community grow too large to control. Certainly the influence of the Chinese in the Philippines is greater than their numbers suggest. They are particularly influential in the areas of banking, merchandising, food processing industries, and transportation. Some of the country's most important leaders have been of mixed Filipino-Chinese ancestry. Yet people defined as "Chinese" are not permitted to become citizens in the islands.

Religion. Before the Spanish arrived in the sixteenth century Filipinos worshipped spirits, and today there are still signs of their ancient religion in their practice of Christianity. Farmers may bless seedlings effusively, pleading with the spirits of the grain before planting takes place. They may build a bamboo cross in a field in the hope that it will drive off the evil spirit that brings pests. Filipinos practice their Christian faith enthusiastically, giving dramatic pageants that draw people from remote islands. Many of them also believe that talismen and charms are useful for curing diseases.

About 80 percent of all Filipinos are Roman Catholics. Under the

Filipinos are among the most devout Roman Catholics in the world. Throngs celebrate the Day of the Black Nazarene, seeking miracles.

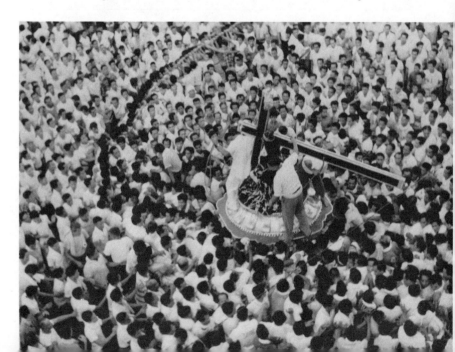

Spanish the Roman Catholic Church was the principal agent for introducing Western culture to the Philippines, and priests began to exert a greater social and cultural influence on Filipinos than any other group. There is a church in almost every town and signs of Christianity in almost every home. About 7 percent of Filipino Christians belong to the Independent, or Aglipayan Church of the Philippines. This church was begun early in the twentieth century by a priest named Gregory Aglipay, who resented the way that Spanish priests were treating Filipinos on their lands.

About 10 percent of the population is Muslim. More than two million members of the Muslim faith in the Philippines are centered on the southern part of Mindanao, the nation's second largest island. They represent a quarter of the total population on Mindanao. As neighbors of Indonesia they have long felt a greater affinity for the nearby Muslim government in Djakarta than for the more remote Christian one in Manila. They fought Spanish and American efforts to bring them under the authority of the Philippines. Today, armed by Muslim countries, they continue to demand the right to secede.

Education, language, and the arts. Filipinos have a high regard for education and respect learned, creative people. Many of their heroes, such as José Rizal, were writers and political thinkers. In Spanish times almost all of the education in the Philippines was administered by priests. Today, although there are still many religious schools in the islands, there is a large public school system with more than 7.1 million students in primary and secondary schools and between 350,000 and 400,000 in institutions of higher learning. As a result, the literacy rate stands at 88 percent, one of the highest in Southeast Asia.

Poverty significantly affects the number of children who can afford to attend schools in the Philippines. About a third of school-age children are not enrolled. Only about half of the children who enter kindergarten finish the first four years. There are not enough supplies or textbooks, and often a whole class has to share a few of them.

Students are taught their own languages for the first two years of their schooling. Philippine languages are based on the Malayo-Polynesian linguistic group and so are close to Indonesian speech. There are 75 main language groups in the islands, but only eight of them are in wide use.

The lack of a common language has been one of the major obstacles to the development of national consciousness in the Philippines. Tagalog, the language used on the heavily populated island of Luzon, is understood by about 50 percent of the population, but the people who speak it are chiefly concentrated in one area. The schools teach in a modified form of Tagalog called Pilipino, which combines major regional languages with the one of Luzon.

English is the second official language in the Philippines. It is understood by about 40 percent of the population and is taught in elementary and secondary schools for at least 40 minutes a day. Most government officials and other professionals use English, but the popular media find it necessary to use Filipino to reach the majority of people. Spanish became the third official language in the Philippines in 1952 and probably is more widely understood than either Tagalog or English. Thus someone who moves to an area where his own language is not spoken may have to learn Tagalog, English, and Spanish to be understood by everyone. The problem is especially severe because many children either fail to go to school or drop out of it and so never learn a second or third language.

In the arts, Filipinos have developed a vigorous literary tradition and are among the world's most skillful woodcarvers, designers, and craftspeople. Before the nationalist period their literature was chiefly oral, consisting in tales and legends, but after the work of José Rizal the islands produced an increasing amount of political writing. Filipinos are also a musical people and preserved their own forms of song and the dance through the long years of occupation by the Spanish and Americans.

RECENT POLITICAL DEVELOPMENTS

On July 4, 1946, the new Philippine Republic inaugurated its first president, Manuel Roxas, before a crowd of 200,000. Visitors came from around the world to witness the event. This bright beginning of the republic was clouded by problems. People who had been compensated for wartime losses received less than half the value of their properties. People who had suffered most were bitter because a few Filipinos profited during the Japanese occupation. Moreover, profiteers roamed the country, making fortunes by taking and selling the billion dollars worth of food, clothing, and equipment that had been abandoned by Japanese and American troops.

In his first State of the Nation message Roxas announced that the Philippines had only a fifth of the income needed to operate the government. The country was almost bankrupt, he said. He went on to describe its condition: the Philippines had suffered the destruction of most of its farms, transportation, mines, mills, and public health facilities. Guerrillas, epidemics, and widespread violence were threatening the very life of the new nation.

But more important than the material destruction and shortages

Manuel Roxas (1892–1948)

was the morale and attitude of the Philippine people. War and its brutality, the changing governments and loyalties, and the massive destruction and loss of lives had broken down traditions. People were forced to struggle for survival. During the Japanese occupation Filipino leaders had told the people that it was patriotic to steal from the government. It was difficult for starving people to suddenly stop the habit when the legitimate government of the Philippines returned to power.

The new government also faced a serious problem with regard to Filipinos who had collaborated with their Japanese conquerors. It was not possible for the government to identify and punish collaborators. The role of Filipinos during the war had been to minimize Japan's benefits from the occupation of their country. Almost everyone had been forced to collaborate to some extent. A few people, however, cooperated more willingly than others. Because most of these few escaped punishment after the war, others were tempted to put their own interests ahead of their country's. Loyalty to the nation was a recent and fragile concept. A more powerful and overriding one was loyalty to kinship groups.

Kinship is the strongest emotional bond in the Philippines. People enjoy a kind of closeness that is unequalled in most other countries. There may be one bed for all of a family's children, even when there is money and room for more. Uncles, aunts, and in-laws share the same roof and give each other emotional and financial support. The Philippines New Civil Code of 1953 acknowledges the power of the family structure by declaring that "every intendment of law or fact leans toward the validity of marriage ... the authority of parents over their children, and the validity of defense for any member of the family in case of aggression." The Code also reminds Filipinos that "grandparents should be consulted by all members of the family on important family questions."

After the republic was formed the power of family life in the Philippines tended to block effective government. Politicians who were elected to office saw no reason why they should not help their relatives to gain government jobs, benefits, or contracts. Anyone in authority usually was a godfather (*compadre*) or godmother (*comadre*) to dozens or even hundreds of people and felt obliged to help them. If the help was not personally deserved outsiders tended to call it "corruption," but Filipinos regarded it as a "debt of the inside." Thus family loyalty often interferes with good government. standards.

Post-independence. After World War II political events in the Philippines were powerfully affected by the existence of a guerrilla army in the mountains of Luzon. This army had its origin in the communist movement that had become active during the 1930s. The Communist Party of the Philippines was outlawed in 1931, but the mistreatment of peasants by landowners created an issue that could not be suppressed. Membership in the party increased during the decade.

There were enormous differences between rich and poor. While most people faced malnutrition in the streets or fields, a few had fortunes to waste. The communists refused to accept the idea that the

Slums and modern buildings exist side by side in Manila.

government and economy could be reformed. They insisted upon leading strikes and sabotaging industry to bring down the government, which responded by arresting many of them. By 1938, however, the threat abated and some of the communist leaders were set free.

On central Luzon the communists championed the idea of land reform. This region historically supplied most Filipino rebels, and during the 1930s it produced a group of communists who organized assaults against landowners. When the Japanese came in search of rice during World War II they met some of the bitterest resistance mounted in the islands there. One of the most effective leaders of the resistance movement was Luis Taruc. His forces were called the "Anti-Japanese People's Liberation Army," or Hukbalahaps—the "Huks" for short.

Taruc was a jungle fighter who was able to lead a striking force suddenly and effectively, then to withdraw into the marshes or jungles. He differed politically with the U.S. and Filipino governments as well as with the Japanese. Therefore Filipino landlords (*caciques*) took him to be their enemy, though they were allied with him against the Japanese. Peasants who had grievances against the landlords and the United States; to seat them in Congress might trolled central Luzon with 10,000 active soldiers and at least 100,000 irregulars. To defend themselves against his seizures of their land many landlords set up their own private armies.

Taruc kept substantial peasant support after World War II. Voters on central Luzon sent him and six other former "Huks" to the Philippine Congress. President Roxas refused to allow them to claim their seats. The Huks, he said, were in armed revolt against the landlords and the United States. To seat them in Congress might jeopardize the rights of the Americans whom the Philippine government was pledged to protect. Roxas took this position out of his own sense of antagonism for Taruc's political views. Before he became president Roxas was a lawyer who represented large sugar companies, many of which were financed by Americans.

Denied the right to participate in government and the right to claim back military pay from the United States, the communists returned to the jungle. They charged that many collaborators had been able to gain damage claims and back pay that was rightfully theirs. But the Filipino and American governments knew that if all collaborators were punished only the communists would benefit because they had never been governed by the Japanese.

Thus the jungle war was resumed. Taruc said that the new fight would be against corruption in government and the exploitation of the peasants. His organizing efforts were made easier by the rising cost of food. During the immediate postwar period rice and many other necessary products were 500 times more expensive than before the war.

Like Mao Zedong, who was winning peasant support in China by the same methods, Taruc created simple slogans telling the people that he was their sole champion. He set up a government and held trials of landlords who had collaborated with the Japanese. In time the Huks came to govern more than 500,000 people. Weakened by the Japanese destruction of its army, the shortage of food and materials, and inflation, the government could do little about the Huk threat. The Huks were able to supply themselves by seizing arms left by the Japanese and Americans, but they were also able to call on thousands of villagers for support.

Roxas sent troops to central Luzon to fight the rebels. Many battles were fought in the jungles and rice paddies. The Huks persevered, slowly draining the government of its funds and energy. In 1948, President Roxas died, and his successor, Elpidio Quirino, offered to negotiate with Taruc. Quirino offered to give the Huks complete amnesty and the right to gain representation in the Congress if they gave up the fight. But by this time it appeared to Taruc that he could gain more by continuing the struggle. He was encouraged by Mao Zedong's triumph in China in 1949.

By 1950 the Filipino government ran out of money to pay its army, and it borrowed from the United States. This loan would not last long. The country needed a more permanent solution. At the request of the Filipinos, American military advisers were sent to Manila to determine what it would take to defeat the Huks. The United States, too, was being pressed militarily by the outbreak of war in Korea. To fight there the U.S. needed the free use of its 158,000-acre facility in central Luzon, the Clark Air Base-Fort Stotsenburg Reservation. But Taruc was increasingly active in that vicinity. It became necessary for the Americans to send armored trucks with the supplies that they shipped to the base.

Partly because of the Americans, the Filipinos changed their strategy in the war with the Huks. They were advised to turn the control of their army over to Ramon Magsaysay, the new Secretary of Defense. Magsaysay had been a jungle fighter in the war against the Japanese and knew the tactics of the Huks. He personally led combat teams into the battle. Slowly the peasants came to trust the government troops when they realized that they had Magsaysay's complete protection. To counter Taruc's claim that only communists would help them against landlords, Magsaysay appointed lawyers to help peasants in court cases. These efforts brought increasing numbers of peasants to the government. By the end of

1950 the Huk threat noticeably declined. Taruc surrendered in 1954. Not all of his followers quit fighting, however. Some of them are still undefeated in the deepest jungles of Luzon.

Further organizing efforts. In 1949 Elpido Quirino won the presidency in a bitter election contested by José Laurel. The following year, Quirino was forced to admit that the Philippines could not survive without American help. But the Americans were no longer willing to help unless the Philippines could learn to help itself. The U.S. loaned the Philippines $50 million to meet a payroll and at the same time insisted that action be taken to gain fiscal stability.

The Americans regarded the Philippines as more important than ever because of the new communist government in China. The Americans were seeking to bolster their military defenses throughout Southeast Asia. President Truman announced U.S. support for the French in Indochina, the Nationalist Chinese on Taiwan (Formosa), and for the South Korean government. Substantial American supplies were sent to Japan for transshipment to U.S. troops in Korea. The Philippines had become one of the keystones of U.S. military strategy in the Pacific.

A former undersecretary of the U.S. Treasury, Daniel W. Bell, was sent to the islands to determine what could be done about the problems of Filipino unemployment, low wages, inflation, shortages of funds, and the lack of industry. He decided that most of these problems were caused by rising population, corruption in government, inadequate development of industry, and the willingness of officials to do the bidding of the powerful landlord class. Bell pointed out that if Filipinos wanted the benefits of industrialization they would have to accept the loosening of family ties that industrialization usually causes. His report did not spare the United States in its criticism of the administration of the Philippines. It said that the Filipino people were no longer willing to hear their country called the "showplace of democracy in Asia" when it was near disaster.

At first the Bell Mission caused the Filipinos to enact social reforms in the areas of land ownership, minimum wages, and working conditions. Then the promised U.S. funds were delivered. Within two years, however, it was evident that the landowning class had prevented the government from pursuing the reforms and was as powerful as ever. The average diet and wage were not substantially increased. Corruption in government did not abate. The national economy remained weak.

The success of Ramon Magsaysay against the Huks caused many Filipino politicians to think of him as a potential president. He was regarded as President Quirino's best cabinet member. In 1952 the

45-year-old Magsaysay switched political parties in order to run against Quirino. He had the backing of the large sugar and financial interests and swept into office. His national popularity was so great that he was able to win by appealing directly to the people instead of by making promises to the politicians who normally controlled elections. His majority was two to one out of five million votes cast.

For the first time in Filipino politics an incumbent lost and permitted the orderly transition of power. As Quirino stepped aside Magsaysay was inaugurated on December 30, 1953, beginning an immensely popular administration. He reduced official corruption and gave people a greater voice in their government. But to the dismay of all Filipinos, he was killed in a plane crash in 1957. He was succeeded by his vice president, Carlos P. Garcia, who in 1961 was defeated by Diosdado Macapagal in the presidential elections. Macapagal proved to be a lackluster president and in 1965 was replaced by a hero of World War II, Ferdinand E. Marcos.

Current conditions. Marcos, sixth president of the Philippine Republic, became the first chief executive to win a second term. He frankly disapproved of the American concept of "democracy" for the Philippines. It is a political system that does not fit Filipino society, he said. Marcos contended that American-style elections simply would not work in a country whose people were hungry, often unpaid, and usually uninformed. At the height of his popularity in 1970 he summoned a convention whose purpose was to revise the constitution. This convention was held at a time when the annual per capita income had fallen to about $231 from a high of about $300. People were dissatisfied with the state of the economy. They had heard rumors of huge bribes that were being passed to officials, including talk of high jobs that were being bought and sold. Therefore they appeared ready to accept a change in their form of government.

The desire to form a new kind of government represented a startling departure from American concepts. In the American view, freely elected representatives could develop welfare programs and adjust the striking injustices caused by differences between the rich and poor. In reality, the legislators almost always represented the upper class. When Manuel Quezon became the first president of the Philippines in 1946 he looked back to assess this period of stewardship. American-style democracy, he said, had done nothing more than awaken the Filipino people to expectations that were not fulfilled. Quezon, himself, often ignored the Filipino Bill of Rights "in order to get things done."

The Filipino constitution gave extraordinary powers to the president. He was allowed to suspend elected officials, including mayors

Ferdinand E. Marcos declared that the Philippines could not survive unless the government were given complete power to manage the country.

and governors. He was empowered to choose judges, treasurers, and chief legal officers in the provinces. He needed the consent of a committee of the Congress, but it was subject to his political influence. He also commanded the National Constabulary through the Department of Defense. Thus while the Philippines adopted many American ideas in government, it modified them for its own purposes.

Twenty-six years after the Philippines declared independence, President Marcos negotiated to eliminate still more American ideas from government. Shortly before he was legally bound to step down from the presidency he announced support of a parliamentary system that would have enabled him to have an unlimited term of office. This idea met resistance at the constitutional convention, but Marcos was able to overcome it because emergencies were threatening the country. About 25,000 Muslims had taken up arms against the government on Mindanao Island and the Sulu Archipelago. Marcos attacked them with planes and troops, but they fought on, creating hundreds of thousands of refugees. Another rebellion flared in central Luzon. There, successors of the Huks fought under the name "New People's Army." Marcos was able to point to these and other disheartening incidents. He called attention to bribery, election frauds, inflation that continued at the rate of 18 percent a year, and a series of volcanic eruptions and earthquakes during the period 1968–70.

Events moved more swiftly after a demonstration by young communists and students in front of the presidential palace in 1970. Police and the students clashed, and twenty demonstrators died. In protest of this incident, bombs and hand grenades were thrown at political speakers in many parts of the country. Then on September 20, 1072, a cabinet minister was ambushed in his car. The communists said that this incident was a hoax by which Marcos planned to seize power. Marcos replied that a revolution was threatened. He disbanded Congress and proclaimed martial law.

Early the next morning, police began to arrest the first of 10,000 politicians, journalists, and educators whom Marcos counted among his opposition. He proclaimed a "New Society" which he said would use strong central control to end corruption and inflation and break up concentrations of wealth. His opponents charged that, far from representing the poor, Marcos spoke for landlords and U.S. business interests. Filipino critics of the United States charged that the Americans were supporting Marcos to protect their investments in the islands. Some of them resisted Marcos but were quickly suppressed.

The evidence presented by the critics of the U.S. was circumstantial but strong. American investments in the Philippines increased from $149 million to almost one billion dollars between 1950–70. Twenty-four of the largest Filipino businesses were owned by Americans. American interests in the Philippines were protected by the terms of the Laurel-Langley Agreement, which was due to expire in 1974. The Agreement guaranteed that Americans would be treated equally with Filipino businessmen. It permitted them to own up to 40 percent of jointly held Filipino companies, and many American individuals or corporations bought land in the islands. Marcos' opponents were quick to point out that after declaring martial law he reversed a decision of the Filipino Supreme Court which had ruled that Americans could not hold private agricultural lands. Finally, opponents charged that the United States was training Marcos' police force, supplying them with helicopters, transport aircraft, machine guns, recoiless rifles, and other weapons.

Marcos' opponents included a wide spectrum of political opinions not ordinarily associated with one another. Some were professional people angered by the loss of their civil liberties. Others were officials of the Roman Catholic or Protestant churches who regarded Marcos' actions as dictatorial. Still others were communists. An underground was formed. Some of its members went to join the New People's Army in central Luzon. Others tried to organize resistance in the cities. Throughout the reaction to his declaration of martial law he tenaciously held power. He won the support of some people who previously seemed committed to democratic government. One, a famous war hero, diplomat, and newspaper owner named Carlos P. Romulo said that "...among people who never know where the next meal is coming from and are prone to disease and poverty, free speech is a remote ideal and certainly less important than finding the means for bare survival."

To prove that he had popular support, Marcos formed "citizens' assemblies" which he used instead of an election on the new constitution. He called on the new assemblies, which included everyone over the age of fifteen, to approve both the constitution and his own increasing powers. More than 90 percent of the assemblies did approve, enabling him to declare, "Martial law is an exercise of the sovereign power by virtue of the people's will. . . ." He gained a similar election victory in 1975. But his opponents charged that he failed to allow a secret ballot and charged that he had threatened to punish anyone voting against him.

The support that he claimed from "citizen's assemblies" enabled Marcos to declare himself chief of state for another seven years, beginning in 1973. Then he moved quickly to show positive results. He assured the population of its security by hiring more police and imposing a curfew. He also persuaded Filipinos voluntarily to turn in more than a half million guns. Afterward he claimed to have reduced crime and set about planning land reforms. In 1975 he took steps to organize a "volunteer citizens army" that was intended to support his tenure in office.

All of this was at the expense of democracy. Strikes were outlawed. Leading members of the opposition were imprisoned or exiled. Critical newspapers were suppressed. Marcos worked to improve the economy and was helped by the worldwide increases in the price of commodities and gold, both of which the islands export. But while his strong central controls brought some material benefits, they also cost the Philippine people their political freedoms.

By the 1980s, threats to national security were greater than ever before. They had gone far beyond the level in 1972, when Marcos gave them as reasons to declare martial law. On the southern islands of Mindinao, Sulu, and Jolo, Muslim guerrillas had driven 1.5 million people from their homes, forcing the government to triple the size of its army. Financed by Muslims in the Middle East, they demanded their own state, one based upon Muslim principles.

Mindinao was also the source of a menace which, because it was spreading to other islands, was more dangerous than the Muslims. This threat consisted in the New People's Army (NPA), which had grown from just five members in 1972 to something between 10-20,000. The leader of the NPA, Jose Maria Sison, was a lawyer who had attended the University of Manila with Ferdinand Marcos. He was a communist and so went underground when martial law was

During the 1960s the Philippines helped to originate the "Green Revolution" by introducing new rice strains. Fertilizer shortages now curtail this progress.

declared. Sison followed the examples of the revolutions in China and Vietnam, where communist guerrillas had won the support of the populations by offering social justice when the government did not. Members of the NPA hid in the jungles and entered cities at night. They seized government property, murdered public officials, held secret meetings, and vanished during the day.

Corruption was one reason for the growing success of communists on Mindinao. It had become deeply rooted in the society. On the local level it was characterized by public officials who often took bribes or worked with criminals. Nationally it was characterized by Marcos himself, who seemed strongly to favor his friends and family when making appointments. His wife, Imelda, was head of the National Youth Movement, Minister for Human Development, and Governor of Greater Manila. He enabled his son, Ferdinand Jr., to become Vice-Governor of his home province at the age of twenty-two. General Fabian C. Ver, Chief of the Armed Forces, was his third cousin.

Such actions were common. Throughout the Philippines, leaders in business and government generally promoted their friends and relatives before even considering people of merit. It was by this means, chiefly, that between 5 and 10 percent of the population gained control of more than half of the national wealth.

The followers of Sison declared themselves enemies of corruption. They held trials of officials and often executed those who, they said, had enriched themselves at the public's expense. Since the law often failed, they sought to replace it, punishing petty thieves and men who beat their wives or children as well as criminal mayors. In this way, as the communists of China and Vietnam had done before them, they began to win popular support.

The appeal of communism waned in most of Southeast Asia, but not in the Philippines. By 1985, there were communist guerrillas in all of the country's seventy-three provinces. They claimed control of more than one-fifth of the rural areas. In secret negotiations with Marcos they demanded the right to become a legal party and to eliminate U.S. military bases from the Philippines.

Most of the country's political action, meanwhile, focused on Marcos. He had sought to win legitimacy by holding a series of referendums beginning in 1976. Although he permitted the election of a 200-member National Assembly in 1978, he did not allow it to overrule him without a two-thirds majority. Marcos thus was secure in his position. Reelected President in 1981, he lifted martial law but continued tight controls over his critics.

Between Marcos and communist insurgents stood a growing number of people who demanded that democracy be restored. Priests, who have a powerful influence in a country which is 83 percent Catholic, remained in the leadership of this movement, which gained tens of thousands of workers, students, and professionals. After every election, and often when other causes gave rise, the critics of Marcos appeared in the streets with placards to demonstrate their grievances. They were almost always met by club-swinging police and soldiers. The violence became more intense as opponents of Marcos began to place bombs in public places.

The problems of crime, inflation, unemployment, public corruption, and the invasion of private rights by police and the military united the demonstrators. However, no other issue brought so many of them forward as the murder of a single man, Benigno S. Aquino.

He was a senator who protested when martial law was declared in 1972. As he attracted followers, he moved into a direct conflict with President Marcos. He was among thousands of Filipinos imprisoned for his attacks upon the government, but he drew national attention to himself by fasting in prison for forty days. In 1977, the government charged Aquino with treason, possession of an illegal handgun, and the murder of a colleague. He was found guilty, but Marcos heeded public protests and ordered a new trial.

Aquino was still awaiting his new trial when, in 1980, he suffered a heart attack in prison. Marcos then allowed him to travel to the United States for treatment, but only on the condition that he not discuss politics there. Aquino promptly offended many supporters of the government by denouncing Marcos as soon as he reached the United States. Then, three years later, he returned to the Philippines to continue his resistance to Marcos. Three soldiers met his plane. They offered to protect him and forbade all others to accompany them as they escorted him to the airport. Suddenly shots rang out, and two men lay dead. One was Aquino, with a bullet in the back of his brain. The other was a known killer.

The mysterious death of Senator Aquino inflamed the Philippines. More than two million people were said to have marched through the rain to witness his burial. They included people never before allied—students, businessmen, housewives, and members of the clergy. In thousands of churches Aquino was hailed as a martyr, a symbol of resistance to repression. After a long investigation, General Ver, the Chief of Staff of the Armed Forces—Marcos' third cousin and old friend—and twenty-five others were named as co-conspirators. They included two other generals, six lesser officers, sixteen soldiers and one civilian. But important witnesses began to disappear. The soldiers were not held in jails but in comfortable residences. Often the Marcos administration granted them ceremonial honors while they were defendants.

It took more than 18 months for the investigation and trial to end, and when it was over in 1985 the Supreme Court of the Philippines declared all of the defendants innocent. The three members of the court, all of whom had been appointed by Marcos, declared that the known killer found dead near Aquino's plane was the probable killer. Over protests from millions of Filipinos, the United States, and other governments, Marcos reinstated General Ver as Commander-in-Chief of the Army. The President next, however, surprised his adversaries by offering to prove that he was still the most popular figure in the country.

Marcos was almost 70 years old and often had been ill. He had promised to retire at the end of his term in 1987, but he chose to seek five more years in office. Many people feared that he was setting up a dynasty through his wife and son and so rallied behind a single opposing candidate, Corazon C. Aquino, widow of the late senator. She had been a housewife all of her life, but she pledged herself to learn the ways of government and began campaigning vigorously. Tens of thousands of Filipinos swarmed to hear her speeches and those of her vice-presidential candidate, Salvador H. Laurel, a former legislator who brought a substantial number of followers to her support in exchange for promises of shared power. Meanwhile Marcos campaigned on his record, pledging to continue economic advances and the struggle against the communists.

In the final days of the campaign, Marcos displayed the supreme confidence that persuaded him to call the election. He could have continued to rule as an almost absolute monarch. Instead he submitted himself to the will of the people. He and his wife appealed to sentiment, reminding Filipinos that he had been a wartime hero and was an experienced national leader. They dressed in floraled shirts and floppy sunhats, strummed ukuleles, and sang romantic duets instead of giving speeches.

Marcos was sure of himself, apparently, because he regarded his opponent as inadequate for the rigors of campaigning. He and his wife remarked that Mrs. Aquino "should learn how to appear as a woman, do her hair better, and stay out of politics." In firm control of the media, he was able to deny her access to television interviews. Newspaper editors, seeing some of their colleagues murdered for supporting her, refused to report her speeches.

Yet Mrs. Aquino seemed to be gaining, judging by the hundreds of thousands of people who appeared to hear her speak. She hammered at Marcos's record, calling him her "number one suspect" in the murder of her husband. She charged him with corruption and the theft of public funds, and she pointed out that the starvation, unemployment, and anger which racked the Philippines all had risen during the Marcos regime.

These accusations gave rise to an atmosphere of breathless tension when the election took place. Marcos, angry and frightened, put the armed forces on alert. Troops and tanks roamed the streets, but people streamed to the polls for the first election since martial law had been declared. According to members of the U.S. Congress who went to witness it, the election was "one of the most corrupt in history." Gunmen invaded polling places to steal ballot boxes. They dumped tens of thousands of ballots cast for Mrs. Aquino into gutters. They manipulated computers and gave the names of countless dead voters to registrars in order to gain ballots for Marcos.

Despite this substantial corruption, Marcos seemed to have gained no clear victory. After long delays he announced, therefore, that he was turning the issue over to the Parliament, which he controlled and which, in time, declared him the winner. Then the thirteen members of the Supreme Court, all of whom he had appointed, ratified this judgment.

Furious with the denial of their rights, the people of the Philippines took their case into the streets.

The housewife and the dictator. "What on earth do I know about being President?" asked Corozon Aquino during an interview shortly before the election in the Philippines. A housewife, widow of the assassinated leader of the opposition party, she had neither experience nor training in matters of government. Her only staff consisted of two houseservants. She had been born into a wealthy family and attended private schools in Manila, Philadelphia, and New York. Her majors were in mathematics, French, and law.

Marcos, on the other hand, was considered the most skillful politician in the Philippines, having controlled the government for more than twenty years. Under his firm declaration of martial law and a Constitution which he had written, freedoms vanished and the country plunged deeper into poverty and rebellion. American investigators reported that Marcos, though working for $5,600 a year, had become one of the richest men in the world, with a hidden fortune of more than $3 billion. In contrast to Mrs. Aquino's two houseservants he commanded the entire army, almost all elected officials, and every appointed official. To win votes he lowered taxes and utilities rates with a wave of his hand.

Yet, according to the U.S. observers, Corozon Aquino had won the presidency, and they marveled at the forces she had rallied against overwhelming odds. Chiefly she offered her husband's name and her own innocence, but she also had the powerful support of thousands of members of the Catholic clergy. The Pope disapproved of political action by priests and nuns, but they, more than any other social leaders, won votes for Mrs. Aquino out of a fear that their country's moral standards were declining. Despite their desire for political neutrality, the clergy could not tolerate the sight of children selling themselves in the streets to get food. The masses of poor heeded the clergy, voting though they despaired of ever gaining decent lives. Even wealthy Filipinos supported Mrs. Aquino because they knew that the vast differences between them and the poor could not be sustained without rebellion. The entire country was sickened by life in a corrupt society—of cheating, bribing, and starving.

Marcos denied that he had lost, however, and claimed another six years in office. The dispute could have cost tens of thousands of lives, but it was resolved in relative calm because of the determination of most of the people in the Philippines. The struggle began when both Marcos and Aquino announced that separate inaugurations would take place, one in the Malacanang Palace, the other in a social club in suburban Manila. Marcos, declared Mrs. Aquino, would be overthrown by nonviolent action. But as demonstrations for her began, Marcos called on troops to break them up.

Filipinos of all ages and classes stood before the armed forces, with nuns and priests, usually bearing huge crosses and statues of the Virgin Mary, in the lead. Merchants, housewives, executives, and the poor joined together to face tanks and personnel carriers

Led by nuns and clergymen, millions of Filipinos confronted armed troops and tanks which Ferdinand Marcos sent to enforce martial law in Manila.

lumbering through the capital, often persuading soldiers to join them rather than fight for Marcos.

As demonstrations proceeded, two of Marcos's highest officials went over to the side of the people. They were Defense Minister Juan Ponce Enrile and Lt.-General Fidel V. Ramos, Deputy Chief of the Army Staff. Along with a few men and provisions, they occupied the headquarters of the Defense Ministry. Throngs of Aquino supporters heard of this defection and poured out of their homes to protect the small force from the tanks which were launched against them.

The American government, which had long supported Marcos, then suddenly reversed itself. It had been giving Marcos $54 million a year to overcome hunger and communism in the Philippines, but now it saw that even its bases in the islands were in jeopardy. When Marcos lost control of the central television station during his inauguration, and when grenades exploded in the courtyard of the presidential palace, the Americans were shaken. A U.S. Senator, Paul Laxalt, who was both a friend of Marcos and of President Reagan, called him to urge, "I think you should cut and cut cleanly."

Shaken, Marcos begged Aquino to let him share the presidency or at least remain in the islands, but she refused. Marcos, no longer confident either of the army or of popular support, accepted a U.S. offer of refuge in Hawaii and began to pack, secretly ordering that stacks of freshly printed money be put into his luggage, along with priceless jewels and art works. Then he, the closest members of his family, and eighty staff members left in an American plane.

Democracy—what Filipinos came to call "People Power"—triumphed, ridding a country of its dictator. With Marcos gone, more than a million Filipinos burst into the Malacanang Palace to see what their taxes had bought for the family that had ruled them. In a country where the per capita income was $822 a year, starving people in Manila saw a 25-foot dining table on which there was still some caviar. They wandered through rooms filled with Persian carpets, authentic Chinese antiques, gold fixtures, diamond-studded statues, private chapels, pools, and spas. The closets were filled with exquisite clothes and thousands of pairs of shoes which Mrs. Marcos had bought with millions spent in New York, London, and Paris. On her bed, people used to eating the food normally given to animals read her motto on a pillow: "I love champagne, caviar, and cash."

The Aquino Administration. Once in office, President Aquino faced problems more challenging than the overthrow of Ferdinand Marcos. The entire government had been shaped in Marcos's image. He had selected almost all of the country's judges and administrators. His supporters had created or condoned the suppression of all liberties and the arrest, torture, and often murder of political adversaries. Starving, diseased people filled the slums, and many of the wealthy paid no taxes. A communist rebellion was raging in the mountains.

During the first three months in office, President Aquino moved swiftly to reverse Marcos's assault on human rights. She restored fundamental liberties. Then she began to reshape the structure of government by appointing a select commission charged with the task of rewriting the Constitution. To deal with the communists she released Jose Maria Sison, founder and first president of the Communist Party in the islands, as well as many other leading political prisoners. They had been captured and often tortured when Marcos ruled. Aquino's action won the trust of many of the rebels, some 1,200 of whom emerged from the jungles to surrender. Later, the Communist Party of the Philippines announced that it was willing to negotiate a truce with the new government.

Despite her efforts to reconcile diverse groups, Aquino had critics. Many intellectuals in the Philippines doubted her ability to govern, and some questioned her appointments. She had named Senator Salvador H. Laurel, who had become Vice-President, as her chief administrator. Laurel was the son of the puppet whom the Japanese had set up in the Philippines during World War II and was widely regarded as a wealthy seeker after political power. Aquino also appointed Juan Ponce Enrile as her Minister of Defense, rewarding him for helping to overthrow Marcos, under whom he held the same job. Enrile and his supporters in the army, it was said, might well attempt to take power if Aquino's efforts to reconcile with the communists fail. A more popular appointment than Enrile was that of Lt.-General Fidel V. Ramos, widely considered a hero of the rebellion. He was made Chief of Staff.

Most Filipinos, ignoring criticism, seemed willing to give their new President time to correct wrongs that had been accumulating. They welcomed her inaugural remarks:

> *The Filipino people have established a new government bound to the ideals of genuine liberty and freedom for all. . . . I say to you, holders of People Power, if anyone in government does not listen to what you have to say, bring it to my attention through structures that will be set up for that purpose. . . . I urge the people to watch over the government. . . . I will be uncompromising about corruption, graft, nepotism, usurpation and abuse of power and authority, against extravagance, incompetence, and abuse of human rights; and we will guarantee the basic freedoms of speech, assembly, thought, and nonviolent action.*

Corozon Aquino stunned the world by leading the rebellion against Marcos.

ECONOMIC CONDITIONS AND PROBLEMS

Sources of current problems. When the United States granted independence to the Philippines in 1046, the two countries agreed that trade between them would be tariff-free for eight years. The makers of American cars and machinery found large markets for their products in the islands during the free trade period. On the other hand Filipino manufacturers had little expensive equipment to sell in the United States. American investments in the islands increased rapidly, especially in the sugar, fruit, timber, and food processing and export industries. The new republic was no longer a political ward of the United States. Instead, it was economically dependent.

In 1955 the Laurel-Langley Agreement allowed the Filipinos to increase some tariffs on imported goods so that their own industry could be developed. At the same time the U.S. was allowed to impose tariffs on Filipino imports, though at a slower rate. The Laurel-Langley Agreement covered the period through 1974. For its entire duration both countries were committed to giving equal treatment to each other's businessmen. Like free trade, this agreement helped the Americans much more than the Filipinos. They were more much more influential in the islands than Filipino businessmen were in the U.S. Legal equality served them well.

During the 1960s the Filipinos became acutely aware that their industry was not growing as fast as they had expected. They had to buy most of their manufactured goods, as well as much of their food, from abroad. The high cost of these purchases deprived them of money for the expansion of domestic industries, although they were raising tariff barriers to protect them. According to the Filipino government, too much money was being retained by the landlords. A very few Filipinos were in control of most of the country's income. Eighty percent of the population was earning less than the average.

The land ownership system in the Philippines was developed during the Spanish period. The landlords, or *caciques*, gained title through rights given by the Spanish crown. Wealthy Filipinos, priests, and Spanish nobles built huge holdings and hired peasants for the hard physical labor. The owners often moved to the cities, meanwhile charging peasants up to 55 percent of their crop as rent. Under American rule, the government passed laws designed to control the amounts paid to landlords. The landlords usually evaded these laws by means of bribes or in the confusion about who owned land. Less than 20 percent of all estates were officially surveyed.

In recent years Filipino peasants have been forced to work for as little as 25 cents an hour. These workers pay most the costs of production, thus taking all of the risk if the crop fails. When they fall into debt, the landlords charge them high interest rates. Their loans and contracts often bind them to servitude for years. Analysts agree that the land-tenure system has blocked all efforts for the improvement of agriculture. Yet it seemed impossible to force the landowners to change the system. Because of it the peasants suf- fered high rents, evictions, poor credit, and mistreatment. The enormous size of large plantations is a related problem. Some Fili- pino and American corporations have such huge holdings that they can control the prices paid for agricultural products by contracting for all of the crops which small farmers produce in their region.

The land-tenure system and shortage of capital has so weakened agriculture in the Philippines that it is dangerously inefficient. Though some 70 percent of the population is involved in agricul- ture, it supplies only 40 to 50 percent of the national income. Rice, which Filipinos call *palay*, is the main crop. As recently as the 1970s the average yield was only 25 bushels per acre. Luckily rice is not as popular in the Philippines as it is in most other Southeast Asian countries. Filipinos have been supplementing their diets with maize since colonial times. For that reason they grow rice on less than half of the planted land, a relatively low figure for their region. Maize covers about 20 percent, and sugar coconuts, abaca (Manila hemp), vegetables, and fruits are other leading crops. The sale of foods alone bring in almost three-fourths of the annual income from abroad.

There are three major kinds of farming: slash-and-burn, planta- tion, and small holding. Slash-and-burn is practiced mainly by tradesmen who occupy the mountainous areas in the interior of Luzon. They cut vegetation over a large area, burn it, and use the ashes to fertilize the soil for their crops. After several years the soil is depleted, and the farmers move their village to another part of the jungle, where they repeat the process. Plantation farming is practiced by the large landowners, including hereditary owners and corporations. Some of the largest companies in the islands are American-owned producers of sugar, hemp, and coconuts for export.

The holders of small plots are by far the most numerous farmers. They are divided into the upland and lowland cultivators. In the uplands they grow dry rice, covering about 15 percent of the total acreage with it. Dry rice is not a highly productive crop, but Filipinos have been raising it for 3,000 years. At Baname, in the Mountain Province of Luzon, there are more than 14,000 miles of rice terraces. In the lowland areas farmers depend on rains to flood their fields, which they plow with bullocks as they have for centuries. Only about a third of the total acreage used by rice farmers is irrigated.

Trends. Today, much of the land is being put to better use than it was just fifteen or twenty years ago. New strains of rice are being adapted to the land and climate of the Philippines, resulting in higher yields per acre. The International Rice Research Institute, founded on Luzon to improve agriculture, has contributed to the use of new higher-yielding strains of rice. These strains now are used in approximately half of the total crop. The use of more fertilizer and irrigation have enabled farmers to gain up to 5,000 pounds of rice per acre. That's up to twice the amount yielded by the old strains.

The economic position of the Philippines also is improving because of worldwide demand for some of the country's other products. The Philippines is a major producer of fish and lumber. World population increases have brought about large new markets for its timber, mahogany, and bamboo, which its workers turn into furniture and rattan mats. Some highlands formerly inhabited only by tribal people now are being invaded by woodsmen and their machines.

Minerals supply more than 10 percent of the income in the Philippines. The country is a leading producer of copper, which provides about 70 percent of the total mineral wealth. It is also one of the world's ten largest producers of gold. Under joint ventures with foreign investors it has discovered large offshore oil reserves. The prices of gold and oil have fluctuated widely in recent years. Though presently low, any income they bring will be of great service.

All of this economic progress would be of greater value to the nation if it reached more people. Under present conditions those who benefit are mainly the *caciques* (landlords) and *illustrados* (educated class), rather than the peasants *(taos)*. These wealthier classes have the capital and ability to profit from economic advances, while the peasants struggle along at subsistence wages. The annual per capita income in the Philippines was only $231 in 1970. Within fifteen years it had risen sharply to more than $770. This increase, due to changing prices in world commodity markets, may be deceiving, however. First, it was accompanied by an inflation in prices. Second, it was not well distributed. Because so few people control so much of the wealth in the Philippines, the per capita figure cannot reveal the extent of poverty. Most cities include festering areas in which the poor are little more than squatters.

People by the tens of thousands cluster on land owned by the state or private individuals. Their main connection with government is through police who come to suppress rampant crime. Their contact with outside society is mostly through eviction agents who come to claim the land for other purposes.

Such social conditions can only produce a highly conservative population. Most Filipinos must struggle to maintain their own lives, their families, and cultures. They have little energy left over to help create a more vital nation.

In addition to these fundamental economic problems, President Aquino must seek to correct trends that became well established during the twenty years of rule by Ferdinand Marcos. After he left, investigators disclosed that corruption in government had become an institution. They reported, for example, that he or his relatives had received up to $80 million from a single American company which wanted to build a nuclear plant in the Philippines. In his final reelection campaign alone Marcos spent more than $500 million of public funds to grant bonuses, special privileges, or bribes in exchange for votes. The chief victims of this kind of corruption were the unemployed, who in some districts comprised more than 40 percent of the population. The chief beneficiaries were the few who had become enormously wealthy, often chiefly because they knew or were related to powerful members of government.

Marcos had further damaged the economy by allowing large corporations to do his planning. In many cases they proved inefficient or greedy, leaving the country poorer for it. When Aquino took office in 1986, the gross national product had been declining at the rate of 5 percent a year for three years. Marcos had granted state monopolies in some of the few commodities which were bringing in revenues from abroad, such as cocoa, coconuts, and sugar. Inefficiency in these industries became rampant at a time when prices for their products were falling. Moreover, inflation had reached 60 percent a year, doubling the cost of living every twenty months or so. Seeing these setbacks, foreign investors had been withdrawing their vital capital from the islands.

Thus Corozon Aquino faces a long battle in her efforts to shape a new economy in the Philippines.

FOREIGN RELATIONS

Its relationship with the United States dominates the foreign policies of the Philippines. There are strong bonds between the two countries. These bonds grew out of mutual respect for democracy and Christianity. They are also based upon shared experiences.

Side-by-side, they fought to roll back the Japanese assault during World War II. Later, Filipino soldiers fought beside Americans in the Korean and Vietnam wars.

People of the Philippines know that many of their finest institutions, such as universities and medical facilities, were built with American help. They have been inspired by U.S. freedoms and acknowledge that Americans have been generous with financial aid after earthquakes, volcanic explosions, and other disasters. Most Filipinos realize that their country might not have survived the attacks of the Huks without U.S. aid. They regard the U.S. as their most important ally.

The presence of as many as 30,000 American troops on Philippine soil also serves to link the two countries. The Philippine Military Assistance Act of 1946 guaranteed that the United States would defend the islands against attack. Under this treaty, the U.S. maintains its only major bases between the Indian Ocean and Japan. The large bases at Clark and Subic Bay are only two of twenty-three in the islands. The Philippine people own these bases and rent them to the Americans under a lease which is due to expire in 1991. Under regular reappraisals of the lease, the Philippines gains substantial American aid. The last reappraisal, a five-year agreement, took place in 1983 and brought $180 million in economic and military assistance to the islands. While protecting the Philippines against attack, it also gave the United States a position from which it could defend itself far from its own shores.

But the relationship between the Philippines and the United States is not always smooth. Many Filipinos think that American investors take far more than they give to the islands. In their view the U.S. is still using the Philippines as a colony, but in the economic and military sense rather than the political one. They point out that major American companies have always gained substantial advantages from Philippine presidents and say that bribery may be one reason.

There are differences among Filipinos over whether the U.S. bases should be permitted to remain in the islands. Some, both within communist and liberal elements, would like to end all American influence in the Philippines. They were angered by the U.S. State Department's willingness to support Marcos for almost twenty years. Only a rising tide of sentiment in the U.S. Congress and population brought official American policy to the support of Corozon Aquino.

Against this opposition, there are many Filipinos who insist that the Americans not only protect the islands but also help to buttress the economy. They point out that the Americans pay more than

$900 million a year to rent the land on which the bases had been built. In addition, Americans spend at least $300 million a year in the Philippines because of the bases, and in 1986 the U.S. government gave over $250 million in aid. President Aquino, pleased when the United States became the first foreign country to recognize her administration, has said that she would support the agreement for the bases at least through its expiration in 1991. She pointed out, however, that her weakened country will need substantially more aid if it is to prevent further starvation and civil war.

The relationship between the new Philippine government and the United States was further cemented by actions of the Soviet Union during the rise of "People Power." The Soviets, hoping to confuse and disrupt the Filipinos during their struggle for democracy, supported Marcos to the end. They also declined to recognize the Aquino administration during its first days. Asked whether she was willing to work with the Soviets, Aquino, immediately after taking office, said, "I haven't even thought about it." Perhaps she, like many leading Westerners, understood the dangers inherent in the growing Soviet fleet in the Pacific.

In its own region, the Philippine government has paid a price for its support of the United States. Filipinos, who differ from their neighbors in that they are both Christian and capitalist, are often rebuked because of their alliance with the United States. Theirs is the only Southeast Asian country willing to allow American businessmen the free right to invest. These factors, plus the military alliance with the U.S., have raised suspicions among other Asian countries.

Most Filipinos have accepted at least some Western culture through their religion, commerce, and social institutions. Yet they continue to regard themselves as part of the culture of Malay people and want to participate in regional activities. In 1962 the Philippines initiated the Association of Southeast Asia (ASA) to promote mutual assistance among Asian countries. When ASA failed to attract many members it lapsed and was replaced by the Association of Southeast Asian Nations (ASEAN). ASEAN has been trying to solve mutual development and economic problems in Southeast Asia. In 1966 the Philippines also helped to found the Asian Development Bank during an international conference held in Manila.

When Malaysia was founded in 1963 the Philippines disputed its claim to Sabah, a British colony on Kalimantan (Borneo). For this reason the relationship between Malaysia and the Philippines has not always been friendly. Muslim guerrillas in the Sulu Archipelago and Mindanao apparently have been supplied by unofficial Muslim sources in Malaysia. During this dispute Indonesia has sided with the Philippines. Relations between the Philippines and Indonesia have not always been cordial, but Filipinos regard Indonesia as the source of their culture and are generally well disposed to it. Since World War II they have also looked more favorably on the Japanese, especially since Japan paid them $800 million in reparations. They have generally followed the position of the United States with respect to Communist China. The growing power of Japan and China are essential considerations in its development of foreign policy.

THE FUTURE OF THE PHILIPPINES

In its report on the assassination of Senator Aquino, the committee of distinguished jurists investigating the case described current conditions in the Philippines. The report said that the assassination "brought into sharper focus the ills pervading Philippine society . . . including the breakdown of peace and order, economic instability, subversion, graft and corruption, and an increasing number of abusive elements in what are otherwise noble institutions in our country—the military and law-enforcement agencies."

This candid appraisal of the problems in the Philippines is clearly supported by a few facts. The tendency of Philippine society has been to divide limited resources among more and more people. The production of food has risen rapidly, but not nearly as fast as the population. It stands at more than 52 million and is rising at the rate of 2.4 percent a year.

These problems are of relatively recent origin, but they are increasing. In 1902 the population of the Philippines was only 7.5 million and life expectancy at birth was about 13 years. Even in the 1970s population was slightly less than 40 million. Today it 55 million. Life expectancy at birth, now 57 years, is one of the highest in Asia. This means that Filipinos must find ways to support growing numbers of older people at a time when most families earn less than $75 a month. Probably the majority of people suffer from malnutrition, starvation, or disease.

All of this makes social change inevitable. Though thick jungles and volcanic mountains cover much of its land, the Philippines must pack in 415 people per square mile. By contrast, there are 64 people per square U.S. mile. By the end of this century, at the present growth rate, the Philippines will be approaching a population which is 45 percent of the present American one. They will be forced to live in an area three-fourths the size of California.

This trend was caused by a number of factors. The most important of them may have been the control of death by disease and violence during the American colonial period. American public health efforts enabled Filipinos to reduce smallpox, cholera, bubonic plague, rinder-pest, beri-beri, and malaria. They made the country safer for large families, which multiplied rapidly. People were encouraged by their religious leaders to produce more children. Finally, agricultural societies traditionally believe that large families help to accomplish their tasks.

All of this means that the Philippine people, despite their heroic victory over tyranny, now must consider basic changes in their social as well as in their political life. Two years after their revolution they conceded that President Aquino had brought a new standard of morality to government, but they began to speak of a "culture of corruption" in which money could buy anything.

In 1988, assassinations were as common as they had been under Marcos. Communists still accumulated weapons in the slums and jungles, while right-wing terrorists, often with the support of high-ranking soldiers, made sporadic efforts to seize the government. But Filipinos have not accepted central controls in the past and are not likely to now, whether from the left or the right. Their present major concern is not how to begin another revolution but how to reform age-old habits. The success of their new government depends on answers to these questions:

1) Can President Aquino command the loyalty of the diverse groups which enabled her to replace Ferdinand Marcos, or will the military, supported by business leaders who fear economic collapse, set up a new dictatorship?

2) Can the Aquino administration, by improving the economy, reducing the huge foreign debt, and encouraging land reform, correct the vastly uneven distribution of wealth?

3) Will the Philippines be able to placate its more violent critics, such as the communists, in time to increase its total wealth, or will it be drained by continuing insurrection and the greed of its landowners?

4) Can ways be found, acceptable to both religious and social groups, through which population may be limited, or will it be limited by poverty, disease, and possibly rebellion?

The Philippines has one of the greatest assets that any country can possess: an educated, alert, and highly intelligent people. Now that it has reasserted its political democracy, it must turn its economic potential into a reality for all of its people, rather than for merely a few. To do so it will need much help from abroad, but ultimately success or failure will depend upon it alone.

APPENDIX A

STATISTICAL PROFILE OF ASIAN NATIONS

All figures were assembled in 1986, reflecting data obtained earlier. They are given for relative purposes only and should not be considered currently precise.

1. Population in millions.
2. Area of country in 000's sq.mi.
3. Population density per sq. mi.
4. Percentage population increases.*

5. Years for population to double.
6. Average life expectancy at birth.
7. Per capita income in dollars.†
8. GNP in billions of dollars.

	1.	2.	3.	4.	5.	6.	7.	8.
Bangladesh	98.7	55	1,775	2.7	27	48	130	105
Burma	37.6	261	144	2.5	28	55	180	5.6
China	1,043	3,696	282	1.2	60	67	296	301
India	768	1,183	605	2.2	32	52	260	190
Indonesia	167	741	226	1.7	42	52	560	87
Japan	121	147	827	0.6	120	76	10,100	1,204
Kampuchea	7.2	69	104	2.5	27	45	159	1.1
Laos	4.1	91	45	1.7	42	50	152	.6
Malaysia	15	127	122	2.4	30	70	1,870	27
Pakistan	100	307	326	2.7	27	50	370	35
Philippines	54	116	472	2.5	28	64	760	39
Singapore	2.5	239	10,704	1.1	65	73	7,100	16
Taiwan	19.1	14	1,376	1.4	51	72	3,040	46
Thailand	51	198	258	1.8	40	63	812	40
Vietnam	60	128	462	2.5	27	52	170	1

*World average, 1.8; U.S, .7
†U.S., $16,270

APPENDIX B

GLOSSARY

---

adat (ah-DAT)—The traditional law; enforced by village councils, it often parallels national and regional legislation.

Allah (AHL-lah)—The Islamic name for God.

Anawratha (ah-nau-Raw-tah)—The Burman king who became a Buddhist in 1056. Through his conquests Anawratha spread Buddhism throughout the western coast of the Southeast Asian Peninsula.

Angkor (ANG-core)—Capital of the Angkor Dynasty, and site of sacred buildings whose construction was begun during the reign of Jayavarman II in the ninth century A.D.

animism—The belief, older than contemporary organized religions, that spirits dwell in all things, governing the universe for good or for ill.

Annam (an-NAHM)—"Pacified South," the name given by Chinese conquerors of Vietnam to that country's central, largely mountainous district. The independent Vietnamese discarded the name, but the French restored it.

Anti-Fascist People's Freedom League (AFPFL)—Nationalists, largely led by Aung San and other members of the "Thirty Comrades," who gained independence for Burma and controlled most of its political life through 1958.

Association of Southeast Asian Nations (ASEAN)—An association of Thailand, Malaysia, the Philippines, Indonesia, and Singapore, formed in 1967 to promote cultural and economic development in Southeast Asia.

barangay (bah-RAHN-gay)—The small boats in which Malays apparently spread through the islands of the Pacific; the name was later given to small administrative districts in the Philippines.

barrio (bahr-REE-oh)—A village administrative district under the Spanish in the Philippines. The name has persisted and is often applied to Filipino settlements in cities.

batik (bah-TEEK)—"Resist," a form of patternmaking in cloth, so named because wax is used to repel dyes from specific areas. It is most widely practiced in Malay countries.

bodhisattva (bod-his-AHT-vah)—In the belief of Theravada Buddhists, a previous incarnation of Buddha; in Mahayana belief, a Buddhist who has achieved Nirvana but delays his entry to Heaven in order to help humanity.

Buddha (BOO-dah)—"The Enlightened One" of India, Prince Siddhartha Gautama or his images.

bumiputera (boo-me-POOT-era)—A Sanskrit word meaning "son of the soil," it is applied to themselves by the Malays of Malaysia and by the Malaysian government to Malays, Dayaks, and tribespeople.

brahman (BRAH-man)—A member of the highest caste in Hinduism, a teacher or priest. (May be rendered "brahmin").

Brahman (BRAH-man)—The Supreme Reality, with whom all Hindus seek union. (May be rendered "Brahma.")

Burman—A member of the largest ethnic group in Burma.

Burma Socialist Program Party (BSPP)—The ruling party in Burma since 1962, one presently headed by General Ne Win.

Burmese—A citizen of Burma, whether a member of the Burman or of smaller ethnic groups.

caciques (kah-SEEKS)—The relatively small group of landlords in the Philippines. Their power as a class is often derived from precolonial chiefs who were granted land by the Spanish, or from the Spanish themselves.

cadre (CAH-dre)—A highly trained spokesman for communist governments or organizations in North Vietnam, Laos, and Cambodia, one who communicates the policies of the ruling group in many areas of life.

Central Intelligence Agency (CIA)—The official American organization which is designed to fulfill the aims of U.S. foreign policy under cover, and which has been active in Southeast Asia.

chao (KAH-oh)—Among animists, the Thai word for the guardian spirits of the home or farm.

Chettyar (CHET-yar)—Member of an Indian subcaste which is comprised chiefly of traders and moneylenders. Many of them moved to Southeast Asia and became prominent landowners in Lower Burma.

Cochin China (COACH-in CHI-na)—The southernmost of the three administrative districts when the French governed Vietnam.

Confucius (con FEW-shas)—The Latin form of the name Kung Fu-tse (joong-foo-dzah) (551–479 B.C.), whose philosophy of social order has pervaded Chinese culture until recent times.

cooperative—In North Vietnam, an economic unit such as a farm or factory in which almost all private property is pooled and income is distributed according to the contribution of the members.

datu (dah-TOO)—A chief in a precolonial Malay population; the word is still used in Muslim parts of the Philippines.

Daw—The term of highest respect for Burmese women.

devarajah (devah-RAH-jah)—In indianized cultures, the faith in which the king is identified with a god.

encomienda (en-com-IYEN-dah)—"To trust," a system of land tenure under which Spanish colonial authorities placed much of the best acreage in the Philippines under the administration of Spanish nobles and priests.

extended family—A family in which the parents, their mothers and fathers, children and daughters-in-law and grandchildren live together.

Five Pillars of the Faith—The basic practices of the Islamic faith, including commitment to Allah, regular prayer, charity fasting in a holy month, and a journey to Mecca.

French Indochina—The regions of Tonkin, Annam, Cochin China, Laos, and Cambodia, all of which the French were forced to surrender to nationalist forces by 1954.

Gautama, Siddhartha (GAU-tamah, Sid-HARTH-ah)—The Indian prince (ca. 503–483 B.C.) who became known as Buddha (the "Enlightened One"), founder of the great philosophical religion, Buddhism.

Gujaratis (guj-ahr-AHT-ees)—Members of the merchant class who live on India's northwest, or Coromandal Coast. Many of them became successful traders in Southeast Asia.

Hadith (HAD-dith)—A collection of statements and stories about Muhammad which comprises the Islamic code.

hadj (hahj)—The visit to Mecca which every devout Muslim is expected to make at least one.

Hinayana Buddhism (hin-ah-YAN-ah boo-dhism)—The "Lesser Way" of Buddhism, a name drawn from the disdainful description of traditional Buddhism by a newer school, called Mahayana, in the first century A.D. *See also* Theravada Buddhism, Mahayana Buddhism.

Ho Chi Minh Trail—A network of jungle roads and paths more than 1,000 miles long, ranging between North and South Vietnam and crossing eastern Laos and the Khmer Republic.

Hukbalahap (HOOK-bahl-ah-HAP)—"Anti-Japanese People's Liberation Army," or "Huks" for short; the guerrilla force organized by Luis Taruc on central Luzon during World War II. Dominated by communist, the Huks attacked the landowning system government after the war.

ilustrados (ill-us-TRAD-os)—The educated class in the Philippines.

indios (in-DEE-ohs)—The name, less respectful than *"taos,"* sometimes given to peasants in the Philippines.

Indochina War—The struggle between the National Liberation Army and the French for the control of Vietnam, beginning 1946 and ending in 1954.

Islam (IS-lam)—"Submission to Allah."

kampong (KAHM-pong)—A district or neighborhood, usually comprised of people of common backgrounds in Indonesia.

Karenni (care-EN-ee)—The "Red Karen," the former name for people of Burma's Kayah State, whose people changed their name to distinguish themselves from the rebellious Karens.

karma (Kar-mah)—The shell around the soul which according to Hindu and Buddhist doctrine is a consequence of action and so affects future rebirths.

Khmer Issarak (kh-MER ISS-arak)—A nationalist movement founded in Cambodia to fight the French in 1946.

Khmer Rouge—A group of communist guerrillas who opposed the rule of Prince Sihanouk until he was deposed in 1970.

Khmer Serei (kh-MER Ser-EYE)—The "Free Khmer" who were part of the Khmer Issarak in Cambodia but retained their independence when most of the rest of their nationalist organization joined Prince Norodom Sihanouk's government in Cambodia in 1949.

Lan Xang (lan ZANG)—"Million Elephants," the Buddhist kingdom founded with the help of Khmer rulers in 1353 A.D. Forerunner of modern Laos, Lan Xang was conquered by Siam (Thailand) in the eighteenth century and did not regain its independence until the defeat of the French.

Lao (LAH-oh)—The ethnic group, related to the Thais, who live along the Mekong River in Laos and comprise the largest of the 60 ethnic groups in that country.

Lao Issara (LAH-oh ISS-ara)—"Free Lao." The coalition of Laotian nationalists organized to fight the French in 1945.

Lao-tzu (lah-OH-tze)—China's first great Taoist (born ca. 604 B.C.)

longhouse—A series of connected houses, raised on stilts, often built above or near water in East Malaysia and among some tribes in West Malaysia.

Lower Burma—The delta of the Irrawaddy River and the mouths of the Pegu and Sittang rivers, forming the part of Burma annexed by the British in 1853; the British drained Lower Burma's swamps and so enabled the Burmese to make it one of the world's most productive rice regions.

Luang Prabang (loo-AHNG pra-BAHNG)—The royal capital of Laos.

Mahabharata (mah-HAB HARAH-tha)—The philosophical epic poem of India which means literally, "Great Bharat," the early name for India.

Mahayana Buddhism (MAH-ha YARN-ah BOO-dhism)—The "Greater Vehicle," a name given in the first century B.C. to a major school of Indian Buddhism which altered the religion, permitting the rise of new saints (bodhisattvas) in order to increase its appeal. It is practiced in Vietnam.

Majapahit (mah-jah-PAH-eet)—The Javanese kingdom founded in 1293 A.D. after the destruction of Sri Vijaya by the Mongols. Monopolizing the spice trade, it extended from the Malay Peninsula to most of contemporary Indonesia and lasted three centuries.

Malayan Union—The British proposal to join the Straits Settlements and the states of the Malay Peninsula after World War II; it was rejected because the Malays feared any increase of their Chinese population.

Marx, Karl (1818–83)—The political philosopher whose concept of government motivated revolutionary movements throughout Southeast Asia, as well as other regions.

Mon (mon)—The early settlers of Lower Burma, through whom Indian culture was spread to the Burmans and Thais.

Muhammad (ma-HAM-mad)—An Arabic merchant (570–632 A.D.) who founded the Islamic faith.

Muslim (MUS-lim)—A believer in Islam; a follower of Muhammad. (Also Moslem.)

National Front for the Liberation of South Vietnam (NFL)—A coalition of South Vietnamese insurgents founded in 1960 and ultimately dominated by its communist members.

National Liberation Army (NLA)—The armed force organized by the Viet Minh to prevent the return of France to Vietnam after World War II.

Neo Lao Hak Sat (NLHS)—The "Lao Patriotic Front," the organization of guerrillas which formed the military arm of the Provisional Revolutionary Government (PRG) in Laos.

New Village Program—The plan by which the British organized rural Chinese in Malaya into new communities after World War II. Through it they defeated a guerrilla movement which was largely comprised of ethnic Chinese.

Nirvana (nirv-AHN-ah)—Literally, a "blowing out" of the soul after death, the aim of all Hindus and Buddhists who believe that in the absence of Nirvana, the soul painfully wanders from life to life.

nuclear family—The basic family, comprised of parents and their children.

Panchatantra (PAHN-cha-TAHN-tra)—A collection of children's tales about animals in ancient India, resembling Aesop's *Fables.*

Pantja Sila (PAHNT-gha SEE-ah)—The "Five Principles" of Indonesia proclaimed by Achmed Sukarno and recounted ever since in many official documents: faith in Allah, international or humanitarian, democracy, social justice, and national identity.

Pathet Lao (PAth-et Lah-o)—"Lao State," the largely communist movement who fought under Prince Souphanouvong and won recognition as part of the government of Laos.

phi (fie)—Spirits which in the belief of animists inhabit all things and serve humanity for good or evil, according to whether they are pleased by human behavior.

Pilipino (pill-ip-EEN-oh)—A variation of Tagalog which is designed to increase understanding of the tongue throughout the Philippines.

Provisional Revolutionary Government (PRG)—The political division of the coalition of insurgents who organized in South Vietnam in 1959 under the name, National Front for the Liberation of South Vietnam.

purdah (PUR-dah)—The practice of seclusion of women in Muslim societies, characterized by the wearing of veils in the presence of all men excepting those among the closest relatives.

Pyidawtha (pie-ie-DAHW-tha)—"Happy Land," a Burmese plan for socialism, first announced in 1952.

rajah (RAH-jah)—A district ruler who governed for a sultan in the nineteenth century. The term has been retained for local princes and governors in Malaysia.

Rama (RAHM-ah)—The hero of the epic, *Ramayana*, symbol of light and goodness, said to be an incarnation of the god Vishnu.

Ramayana (RAHM-ah-YAHN-ah)—The greatest Sanskrit epic of India, probably composed in the third century B.C.; second in importance only the the *Mahabharata* in Indian culture, it is referred to and staged frequently in all modern indianized societies.

sangha (SANG-ha)—The Theravada Buddhist monkhood.

Shan (shahn)—A Thai-speaking people who live in Burma's mountainous Shan State.

sitio (seet-EEH-oh)—A lesser village or hamlet, usually part of a *barrio*.

Southeast Asian Treaty Organization (SEATO)—A military pact for the defense of Southeast Asia, including the United States, Great Britain, France, Australia, New Zealand, the Philippines, and Thailand.

Sri Vijaya (sree-vij-AY-ah)—The seafaring empire centered on Sumatra from the seventh to the twelfth centuries A.D. It was destroyed by the Mongols and replaced by Majapahit.

stupa (STOO-pah)—A burial mound or domed temple supposed to contain some relics or remains of Buddha.

sultan—"Defender of the Faith," a title given to a Muslim ruler who is both the religious and civil head of his region. Malaysia has eight sultans who, as part of the Conference of Rulers select the Supreme Head of State.

Tagalog (tah-GAH-log)—The people who live in lower Luzon and their language. Their language is the first official one in the Philippines.

Taoism (DAH-o-ism)—A faith developed by the Chinese philosopher Lao-tze (born ca. 604 B.C.), whose verses in the *Tao teh ching* ("The Book of the Way of Life") urged people to recognize themselves as part of the natural order rather than as manipulators of it.

taos (TAH-os)—The name often given to the peasants of the Philippines.

Thai (tie)—A people who were driven out of South China by Mongols in the thirteenth century and settled in many parts of Southeast Asia, concentrating in Thailand and Laos.

Thakin (THAY-kin)—"Master," the salutation taken by Burmese students in Rangoon University when the British occupied Burma and were reserving that title for themselves. The "Thakins" became leaders of the Burmese nationalist movement.

Theravada Buddhism (THERE-ah-VAHDA BOO-dhism)—"Teachings of the Elders," the traditional name given to Buddhist scriptures before the rise of Mahayana Buddhism in the first century A.D. from Ceylon, where it was driven by the Mahayanist, Theravada Buddhism spread throughout peninsular Southeast Asia.

Tonkin (TONG-kin)—The northernmost, industrialized third of Vietnam when it was governed by the French, covering the delta of the Red River.

U—The term of highest respect for Burmese men.

Upper Burma—The British designation for the region they annexed in 1886, covering the northern half of modern Burma.

utang na look (oot-ahng-nah-loob)—A "debt inside oneself," signifying the responsibilities of the individual within the kinship system that pervades society in the Philippines.

Vientiane (vee-eht-YAHN)—The administrative capital of Laos.

Viet Cong (Viet CONG)—A contraction of the name Viet Nam Cong San ("Vietnamese communists") which was given by President Ngo Dinh Diem of South Vietnam to his adversaries, the insurgents who in 1959 formed the National Front for the Liberation of South Vietnam.

Viet Minh (Viet MINH)—The "League for the Independence of Vietnam," a coalition of nationalists organized in North Vietnam in the 1920s.

Vietnam Fatherland Front—A coalition of social and political organizations which serves to communicate between the North Vietnamese people and the ruling party, the Lao Dong.

Vishnu (VEESH-nu)—The benevolent god of the Hindu Triad (Vishnu, Siva, Brahma); he appears often in the oral and written literature of Southeast Asia and in Indonesia is often shown riding the mythical bird, Garuda.

wat (waht)—A group of buddhist structures surrounded by a wall, usually the center of social and religious activity in the countries of Southeast Asia.

APPENDIX C

THE SEARCH OF ASIAN PEOPLES*

Carlos P. Romulo

This declaration by former Ambassador Romulo in 1954 proved to be one of the most prophetic in recent history.

1. The Asian peoples will no longer tolerate the shackles of colonialism. What they want is a status of equal partnership and voluntary cooperation with other peoples.
2. The Asian peoples are fired with an aspiration to human dignity and economic well-being which can no longer be held in abeyance.
3. The Asian peoples will not fight for the vague concept of a free world; they will fight on the side of the free world only if they have a stake in freedom themselves.
4. The West must work with and through the responsible nationalist movements in Asia rather than through puppet regimes that have no popular support. By denouncing and opposing genuine freedom movements in Asia as Communist-inspired, the West, in fact, exposes such movements to Communist infiltration and control. The objective must be to isolate Communist agitation from the legitimate nationalist aspirations of the Asian peoples.
5. Military measures are at best a short-term device for staving off an immediate threat of Communist aggression. The long-term struggle against communism, however, requires economic and financial assistance that will enable the Asian peoples to raise their standards of living.
6. Assistance should be offered on a basis of equality and mutual respect, and not as a special favor with political strings or as a disguised survival of colonialism.
7. As there can be no world peace without Asia, so there can be no economic stability in the world without Asia. You cannot neglect Asia and, by continuing to pour dollars into Europe, expect to stabilize the world economy, including the European economy itself.
8. Asian political, economic and social organization is predominantly on an authoritarian pattern. Therefore, it should not be assumed that the Asian peoples will automatically adopt democracy of the Western type; rather, they will adopt it with necessary modifications and only as it demonstrates its superiority in the actual experience of daily life.

---

*Carlos P. Romulo, Filipino diplomat and newspaper publisher, *Congressional Record*, v. 100, pt. 6, June 9, 1954, pp. 7972–7973 (83rd Cong., 2d sess.).

9. Asian neutralism must be recognized partly as the result of a genuine desire for peace, partly as dictated by the serious internal problems of many countries in the region, and partly as inspired by a lingering distrust of the motives of the colonial powers.
10. The Asian peoples will not give their support to any program, policy or course of action affecting Asia that is taken without consulting them.

APPENDIX D

DECLARATION OF INDEPENDENCE OF THE DEMOCRATIC REPUBLIC OF VIETNAM*

"We hold truths that all men are created equal, that they are endowed by their Creator with certain unalienable Rights, among these are Life, Liberty and the pursuit of Happiness."

This immortal statement is extracted from the Declaration of Independence of the United States of America in 1776. Understood in the broader sense, this means: "All peoples on the earth are born equal; every person has the right to live to be happy and free."

The Declaration of Human and Civic Rights proclaimed by the French Revolution in 1791 likewise propounds: "Every man is born equal and enjoys free and equal rights."

These are undeniable truths.

Yet, during and throughout the last eighty years, the French imperialists, abusing the principles of "Freedom, equality and fraternity," have violated the integrity of our ancestral land and oppressed our countrymen. Their deeds run counter to the ideals of humanity and justice.

In the political field, they have denied us every freedom. They have enforced upon us inhuman laws. They have set up three different political regimes in Northern, Central and Southern Vietnam (Tonkin, Annam and Cochin China) in an attempt to disrupt our national, historical and ethnical unity.

They have built more prisons than schools. They have callously ill-treated our fellow-compatriots. They have drowned our revolutions in blood.

They have sought to stifle public opinion and pursued a policy of obscurantism on the largest scale; they have forced upon us alcohol and opium in order to weaken our race.

In the economic field, they have shamelessly exploited our people, driven them into the worst misery and mercilessly plundered our country.

They have ruthlessly appropriated our rice fields, mines, forests and raw materials. They have arrogated to themselves the privilege of issuing banknotes, and monopolized all our external commerce. They have imposed

---

*Information Service, Vietnam Delegation in France, *The Democratic Republic of Vietnam* (Paris: Imprimerie Centrale Commercials, 1948), pp. 3-5. Proclaimed Sept. 2, 1945.

hundreds of unjustifiable taxes, and reduced our countrymen, especially the peasants and petty tradesmen, to extreme poverty.

They have prevented the development of native capital enterprises; they have exploited our workers in the most barbarous manner.

In the autumn of 1940, when the Japanese fascists, in order to fight the Allies, invaded Indochina and set up new bases of war, the French imperialists surrendered on bended knees and handed over our country to the invaders.

Subsequently, under the joint French and Japanese yoke, our people were literally bled white. The consequences were dire in the extreme. From Quang Tri up to the North, two millions of our countrymen died from starvation during the first months of this year.

On March 9th, 1945, the Japanese disarmed the French troops. Again the French either fled or surrendered unconditionally. Thus, in no way have they proved capable of "protecting" us; on the contrary, within five years they have twice sold our country to the Japanese.

Before March 9th, many a time did the Viet Minh League invite the French to join in the fight against the Japanese. Instead of accepting this offer, the French, on the contrary, let loose a wild reign of terror with rigor worse than ever before against Viet Minh's partisans. They even slaughtered a great number of our *"condamnés politiques"* imprisoned at Yet Bay and Cao Bang.

Despite all that, our countrymen went on maintaining, *vis-à-vis* the French, a humane and even indulgent attitude. After the events of March 9th, the Viet Minh League helped many French to cross the borders, rescued others from Japanese prisons and, in general, protected the lives and properties of all the French in their territory.

In fact, since the autumn of 1940, our country ceased to be a French colony and became a Japanese possession.

After the Japanese surrender, our people, as a whole, rose up and proclaimed their sovereignty and founded the Democratic Republic of Vietnam.

The truth is that we have wrung back our independence from Japanese hands and not from the French.

The French fled, the Japanese surrendered. Emperor Bao Dai abdicated, our people smashed the "yoke" which pressed hard upon us for nearly one hundred years, and finally made our Vietnam an independent country. Our people at the same time overthrew the monarchical regime established tens of centuries ago, and founded the Republic.

For these reasons, we, the members of the Provisional Government representing the entire people of Vietnam, declare that we shall from now on have no more connections with imperialist France; we consider null and void all the treaties France has signed concerning Vietnam, and we hereby cancel all the privileges that the French arrogated to themselves on our territory.

The Vietnamese people, animated by the same common resolve, are determined to fight to the death against all attempts at aggression by the French imperialists.

We are convinced that the Allies who have recognised the principles of equality of peoples at the Conferences of Teheran and San Francisco cannot but recognize the Independence of Vietnam.

A people which has so stubbornly opposed the French domination for more than 80 years, a people who, during these last years, so doggedly ranged itself and fought on the Allied side against Fascism, such a people has the right to be free, such a people must be independent.

For these reasons, we, the members of the Provisional Government of the Democratic Republic of Vietnam, solemnly declare to the world:

"Vietnam has the right to be free and independent and, in fact, has become free and independent. The people of Vietnam decide to mobilize all their spiritual and material forces and to sacrifice their lives and property in order to safeguard their right of Liberty and Independence."

Hanoi, September 2nd, 1945
Signed: Ho Chi Minh, *President*

APPENDIX E

LETTER TO LYNDON B. JOHNSON*

Ho Chi Minh

On February 10, 1967, I received your message. This is my reply.

Vietnam is thousands of miles away from the United States. The Vietnamese people have never done any harm to the United States. But contrary to the pledges made by its representatives at the 1954 Geneva Conference, the United States Government has ceaselessly intervened in Vietnam, it has unleashed and intensified the war of aggression in South Vietnam with a view to prolonging the partition of Vietnam and turning South Vietnam into a neocolony and military base of the United States. For over two years now, the U.S. Government has with its air and naval forces carried the war to the Democratic Republic of Vietnam, an independent and sovereign country.

The U.S. Government has committed war crimes, crimes against peace and against mankind. In South Vietnam, half a million U.S. and satellite troops have resorted to the most inhuman weapons and the most barbarous methods of warfare, such as napalm, toxic chemicals and gases, to massacre our compatriots, destroy crops and raze villages to the ground.

In North Vietnam, thousands of U.S. aircraft have dropped hundreds of thousands of bombs, destroying towns, villages, factories, roads, bridges, dikes, dams and even churches, pagodas, hospitals, schools. In your message, you apparently deplored the sufferings and destructions in Vietnam. May I ask you: Who has perpetrated these monstrous crimes? It is the U.S. and satellite troops. The U.S. Government is entirely responsible for the extremely serious situation in Vietnam.

The U.S. war of aggression against the Vietnamese people constitutes a challenge to the countries of the Socialist camp, a threat to the national-independence movement and a serious danger to peace in Asia and the world.

New York Times, March 22, 1967.

The Vietnamese people deeply love independence, freedom and peace, but in the face of the U.S. aggression, they have risen up, united as one man. Fearless of sacrifices and hardships, they are determined to carry on their resistance until they have won genuine independence and freedom and true peace. Our just cause enjoys strong sympathy and support from the peoples of the whole world, including broad sections of the American people.

The U.S. Government has unleashed the war of aggression in Vietnam. It must ease this aggression. That is the only way to the restoration of peace. The U.S. Government must stop definitively and unconditionally its bombing raids and all other acts of war against the Democratic Republic of Vietnam; withdraw from South Vietnam all U.S. satellite troops; recognize the South Vietnam National Liberation Front; and let the Vietnamese people settle themselves their own affairs. Such is the basic content of the four-point stand of the Government of the D.R.V., which embodies the essential principles and provisions of the 1954 Geneva Agreements on Vietnam. It is the basis of a correct political solution to the Vietnam problem.

In your message, you suggested direct talks between the D.R.V. and the United States. If the U.S. Government really wants these talks, it must first of all stop unconditionally its bombing raids and all other acts of war against the Democratic Republic of Vietnam. It is only after the unconditional cessation of the U.S. bombing raids and all other acts of war against the D.R.V. that the D.R.V. and the United States would enter into talks and discuss questions concerning the two sides.

The Vietnamese people will never submit to force; they will never accept talks under the threat of bombs.

Our cause is absolutely just. It is hoped that the U.S. Government will act in accordance with reason.

APPENDIX F

EXERPTS FROM THE CONSTITUTION OF THE DEMOCRATIC REPUBLIC OF VIETNAM*

Chapter II. Economic and Social System

. . . Art. 11. In the Democratic Republic of Vietnam, during the present period of transition to socialism, the main forms of ownership of means of production are: state ownership, that is, ownership by the whole people; co-operative ownership, that is, collective ownership by the working masses; ownership by individual working people; and ownership by the national capitalists.

Art. 12. The State sector of the economy, which is a form of ownership by the whole people, plays the leading role in the national economy. The State ensures priority for its development.

Constitution of the Democratic Republic of Vietnam (Hanoi: Foreign Languages Publishing House, 1960).

All mineral resources and waters, and all forests, undeveloped land, and other resources defined by law as belonging to the State, are the property of the whole people.

Art. 13. The co-operative sector of the economy is a form of collective ownership by the working masses.

The State especially encourages, guides and helps the development of the co-operative sector of the economy.

Art. 14. The State by law protects the right of peasants to own land and other means of production.

The State actively guides and helps the peasants to improve farming methods and increase production, and encourages them to organize producers, supply and marketing, and credit co-operatives, in accordance with the principle of voluntariness.

Art. 15. The State by law protects the right of handicraftsmen and other individual working people to own means of production.

The State actively guides and helps handicraftsmen and other individual working people to improve their enterprises, and encourages them to organize producers, and supply and marketing co-operatives in accordance with the principle of voluntariness.

Art. 16. The State by law protects the right of national capitalists to own the means of production and other capital.

The State actively guides the national capitalists in carrying out activities beneficial to national welfare and the people's livelihood, contributing to the development of the national economy, in accordance with the economic plan of the State. The State encourages and guides the national capitalists in following the path of socialist transformation through the forms of joint State-private enterprise, and other forms of transformation.

Art. 17. The State strictly prohibits the use of private property to disrupt the economic life of society, or to undermine the economic plan of the State.

Art. 18. The State protects the right of citizens to possess lawfully-earned incomes, savings, houses, and other private means of life.

Art. 19. The State by law protects the right of citizens to inherit private property.

Art. 20. Only when such action is necessary in the public interest, does the State repurchase, requisition or nationalize the appropriate compensation means of production in city or countryside, within the limits and in the conditions defined by law.

Art. 21. Labor is the basis on which the people develop the national economy and raise their material and cultural standards.

Labor is a duty and a matter of honor for every citizen.

The State encourages the creativeness and the enthusiasm in labor of workers by hand and brain. . . .

APPENDIX G

MANIFESTO OF THE NATIONAL FRONT FOR THE LIBERATION OF SOUTH VIETNAM*

... The NFLSV undertakes to unite all sections of the people, all social classes, nationalities, political parties, organizations, religious communities, and patriotic personalities, without distinction of their political tendencies, in order to struggle and overthrow the rule of the U.S. imperialists, and their stooge, the Ngo Dinh Diem clique, realize independence, democracy, peace and neutrality, and advance toward peaceful reunification of the fatherland. The program of the NFLSV includes the following 10 points:

1. To overthrow the disguised colonial regime of the U.S. imperialists and the dictatorial Ngo Dinh Diem administration, lackey of the United States, and to form a national democratic coalition administration. . . .
2. To bring into being a broad and progressive democracy, promulgate freedom of expression, of the press, of belief, of assembly, association and movement, and other democratic freedoms; to grant an amnesty to all political detainees, dissolve all concentration camps dubbed "prosperity zones" and all "resettlement centers," abolish . . . anti-democratic laws.
3. To abolish the economic monopoly of the United States and its henchmen, protect homemade products, encourage home industry; . . . to help NorthVietnamese people who had been forced or enticed to go south . . . to return to their native places if they so desire; and to provide jobs for those among them who want to remain in the South. . . .
4. To carry out land rent reduction, guarantee the peasants' rights to till their present plots of land, and redistribute communal lands in preparation for land reform. . . .
5. To eliminate the enslaving and depraved U.S.-style culture; to build a national and progressive culture and education, eliminate illiteracy, open more schools. . . .
6. To abolish the system of American military advisors, eliminate foreign military bases in Vietnam and build a national army defending the fatherland and the people. . . .
7. To guarantee the right of equality between men and women and among different nationalities, and the right to autonomy of the national minorities; to protect the legitimate interests of foreign residents in Vietnam; to protect and take care of the interests of overseas Vietnamese.
8. To carry out a foreign policy of peace and neutrality; to establish diplomatic relations with all countries which respect the independence and sovereignty of Vietnam.

---

*Vietnamese News Agency (Hanoi), in English, February 4, 1961.

319

9. To reestablish normal relations between the two zones as a first ste toward peaceful reunification of the country. . . .

10. To oppose aggressive wars and actively defend peace. . . .

APPENDIX H

THE LAST WILL AND TESTAMENT OF HO CHI MINH*

Even though our people's struggle against U.S. aggression, for national salvation, may have to go through more hardships and sacrifices, we are bound to win total victory.

. . . the war of resistance against U.S. aggression may drag on. Our people may have to face new sacrifices of life and property. Whatever happens, we must keep firm our resolve to fight the U.S. aggressors to total victory.

Our mountains will always be,
Our rivers will always be,
Our people will always be,
The American invaders defeated,
We will rebuild our land ten times more beautiful.

No matter what difficulties and hardships be ahead, our people are sure of total victory. The U.S. imperialists will certainly have to quit. Our fatherland will certainly be reunified. Our fellow countrymen in the South and in the North will certainly be reunited under the same roof. We, a small nation, will have earned the signal honor of defeating, through heroic struggle, two of the big imperialisms—the French and the Americans—and of making a worthy contribution to the world national liberation movement.

*Witnessed and published September 3, 1969 by Le Duan, first secretary of the Workers' Party; Truong Chinh, President of the National Assembly; Vo Nguan Giap, Defense Minister; Pham Van Dong, Prime Minister; Duy Trinh, Deputy Prime Minister and Foreign Minister; and Le Duc Tho, Politburo member.

APPENDIX I

THE RETURN OF PEACE TO VIETNAM*

Le Duc Tho

Dear friends, the struggle of the Vietnamese people for independence and liberty has lasted nearly 30 years. In particular, the resistance in the last 13 years with its many trials was the most difficult in the history of our people's struggle against foreign invasion over several centuries.

It is also the most murderous war in the history of the movement of national liberation of the oppressed peoples throughout the world.

Finally, this war has deeply stirred the conscience of mankind.

The negotiations between our Government and the Government of the United States of America for a peaceful settlement of the Vietnamese problem has lasted nearly five years and have gone through many particularly difficult and tense moments.

But we have overcome all obstacles and we have at last reached the agreement on ending the war and restoring peace in Vietnam.

This agreement will be officially signed in Paris in a few days.

The just cause triumphs over the evil cause. The will to live in freedom triumphs over cruelty.

The conclusion of such an agreement represents a very big victory for the Vietnamese people. It is the crowning of a valiant struggle waged in unity by the army and the people of Vietnam on all fronts, at the price of countless sacrifices and privations.

It is a very big victory for the fighting solidarity of the peoples of the three countries of Indochina who have always fought side by side against the common enemy for independence and liberty.

It is a very great victory for the Socialist countries, the oppressed peoples and all the peace-loving and justice-loving peoples throughout the world, including the American people, who have demonstrated their solidarity and given devoted assistance to the just struggle of our people.

The return of peace in Vietnam will be greeted with immense joy by our people. At the same time, it will answer the hope which has so long been harbored by the American people and the peace-loving peoples in the world.

With the return of peace, the struggle of the Vietnamese people enters a new period. Our people, lifting high the banner of peace and of national concord, is decided to strictly apply the clauses of the agreement maintaining peace, independence and democracy and heading toward the peaceful reunification of its country.

---

*Statement made at a press conference in Paris, January 24, 1975; full text of the press conference printed in the *New York Times*, January 25, 1973.

It will also have to rebuild its war-devastated country and consolidate and develop its friendly relations with all the peoples of the world, including the American people.

Heavy tasks still await us in this new period. But the Vietnamese in the North as in the South, at home as abroad, rich in their traditions of unity and perseverance in struggle, following a just policy, strengthened by the close solidarity of the peoples of Laos and Cambodia and benefiting from strong aid from the Socialist countries and all the peace-loving countries of the world, will be able to smooth out all difficulties and victoriously accomplish their tasks.

At a time when peace is dawning on our country, in the name of the Government and people of Vietnam we wish to address our warm thanks to the Socialist countries, to the governments of many countries and to the peoples of the entire world for the sympathy they have shown toward the just struggle of the Vietnamese people and for the active help given in all fields.

In the past years, how many fighters for peace in many countries have known repression and prison, and certainly even sacrificed their lives in the fight they carried out to support the resistance of the Vietnamese people. These noble internationalist feelings and these sublime sacrifices occupy forever a place in our hearts.

The signature of the "Agreement for the Cessation of War and the Reestablishment of Peace in Vietnam" is only a first victory, because the task of strictly applying the agreement is important.

Anxious to maintain peace, independence and democracy and heading toward reunification of the country, the Vietnamese people will act in a unified manner to insure the correct and serious application of the clauses of the agreement which will be signed in a few days, and at the same time it will show vigilance towards reactionaries who try to sabotage the agreement.

But we must say that the situation in our country and in the world is developing in an extremely favorable way for the cause of the Vietnamese people.

We have the conviction that the dark designs of the reactionary forces in the country and abroad to obstruct the application of the agreement, or to sabotage it, can only fail.

The Vietnamese people have, therefore, every reason to believe in the victorious accomplishment of its tasks in the new period. No reactionary force will be able to slow down the march forward of the Vietnamese people.

APPENDIX J

VICTORY STATEMENT OF THE PROVISIONAL REVOLUTIONARY GOVERNMENT OF SOUTH VIETNAM*

The long war of resistance of the Vietnamese people against the American aggression for its independence and its freedom has just ended victoriously. The population of the People's Liberation Armed Forces of South Vietnam, supported and staunchly helped by their brothers in the North, have brought the uprising and attacks against the war repressive machine set up by the U.S. in South Vietnam to a successful end.

The capital of South Vietnam, Saigon, was liberated. The U.S. aggressors were compelled to pull out. The puppet administration in Saigon as a whole, which is a tool of the U.S. neocolonialist policy, has fully collapsed. This is a complete bankruptcy of the strategy of neocolonialist aggression carried out by the U.S. for more than a decade.

Henceforth, South Vietnam is free and independent. The sacred testament of our beloved President Ho Chi Minh is realized. This is a victory of historic significance for the South Vietnamese population and for the Vietnamese nation as a whole. It is at the same time a just victory of the cause of peace, national independence and justice of the peoples over the world.

In this eventful day, I want to reaffirm that the policy of the P.R.G. has always been and will be a policy of great union and national concord. Yesterday, the P.R.G. rallied with this policy all strata of the population with a view to achieving the struggle of the population for its legitimate aspirations for peace, independence, democracy and national concord.

Today and tomorrow, it will mobilize with this policy all forces in order to build, in recovered peace, a peaceful, independent, democratic, neutral and prosperous South Vietnam and to progress toward peaceful reunification of Vietnam.

This policy of great union and national concord of the P.R.G. specially aims at erasing hatred and divisions and offering a place and a role to all inhabitants irrespective of their past in the tremendous task of reconstruction and building.

With regard to foreigners present in South Vietnam, according to the 10-point policy of the P.R.G., their lives and property are protected but they are asked to respect the independence and sovereignty of Vietnam and to observe the policies of the revolutionary power.

In international affairs, South Vietnam will carry out a foreign policy of peace and nonalignment. It will be prepared to establish relations with all countries irrespective of their political and social systems on the basis of

---

*The New York Times, April 30, 1975.

323

mutual respect for independence and sovereignty and accept economic and technical aid from any country with no political conditions attached.

Allow me, in the name of the P.R.G. and the people of South Vietnam, to express our warm thanks to all socialist countries of national independence and all peace and justice-loving peoples, including the American people who have supported and helped our people in its just struggle.

The victory gained today is also theirs. We are convinced that they will continue to support and help our people in the building and reconstruction of our country.

APPENDIX K

THE WHEEL OF THE LAW

Ho Chi Minh

The wheel of the law turns
without pause.

After the rain, good weather
In the wink of an eye.

The universe throws off
its muddy clothes.

For ten thousand miles
the landscape

Spreads out like a beautiful brocade.
Light breeze. Smiling flowers.

High in the trees, amongst
the sparkling leaves

All the birds sing at once.
Men and animals rise up reborn.

What could be more natural?
After sorrow comes joy.

APPENDIX L

EXCERPTS FROM THE AGREEMENT ON THE RESTORATION OF PEACE AND RECONCILIATION IN LAOS*

Art. 1. A. The desires of the Lao people to safeguard and exercise their cherished fundamental national rights—the independence, sovereignty, unity, and territorial integrity of Laos—are inviolable.

B. The 9 July 1962 communique on the neutrality of Laos and the 1962 Geneva agreement on Laos are the correct basis of the policy for peace, independence, and neutrality of the Kingdom of Laos. The parties concerned in Laos, the United States, Thailand, and other foreign countries must strictly respect and implement this agreement. The internal affairs of Laos must be conducted by the Lao people only, without external interference.

C. To achieve the supreme objective of restoring peace, enhancing independence, implementing national concord, and restoring national unification, and due to the present reality in Laos, which has two zones under the control of the two sides, the internal problems of Laos must be solved on the spirit of national concord and on the basis of equality and mutual respect, with neither side trying to swallow or oppress the other side.

D. To safeguard national independence and sovereignty, implement national concord, and restore national unification, the people's various rights and freedoms must be absolutely respected—for example, privacy, ideology, speech, press, writing, assembly, establishing political organizations and associations, candidacy and elections, traveling, living where one wants, and establishing business enterprises and ownership. All acts, regulations, and organizations that violate these rights and freedoms must be abolished.

Art. 2. Beginning at 1200 on 22 February 1973, a cease-fire in place will be observed simultaneously throughout the territory of Laos. . . .

Art. 6. General free and democratic elections are to be carried out to establish the national assembly and permanent national coalition government, which are to be the genuine representatives of the people of all nationalities in Laos. The principles and procedures of the general elections will be discussed and agreed upon by the two sides. Pending the general elections, the two sides must set up a National Provisional Coalition Government and a National Political Coalition Council within 30 days at the latest after the signing of this agreement, to implement all the agreements signed and to administer national tasks.

Art. 7. The new National Provisional Coalition Government is to be composed of representatives of the Vientiane Government side and the Patriotic Forces side, in equal proportions, and two intellectuals who advocate

*New York Times, Feb. 22, 1973.

peace, independence, neutrality, and democracy, who will be agreed upon by both sides. The Prime Minister must be a person who is not a member of the representatives in the Government. The National Provisional Coalition Government is to be set up in accordance with special procedures by royal decree of His Majesty the King. It will perform its duties in accordance with principles unanimously agreed upon by both sides. It will have the responsibility to implement all agreements reached and the political program agreed upon by the two sides—for example, in implementing and maintaining the cease-fire, permanently safeguarding peace, completely implementing popular rights and freedoms, implementing the policy for peaceful foreign relations and for independence and neutrality, for coordinating all economic development plans, expanding culture, and accepting and distributing all aid materials from all countries aiding Laos. . . .

APPENDIX M

POLITICAL PROGRAM OF THE NATIONAL UNITED FRONT OF CAMBODIA*

. . . The Cambodian society . . . will be rid of all defects impeding its rapid and full bloom . . . . The National United Front declares that "power is, and will always be, in the hands of the progressive, industrious and genuine working people who will ensure our motherland a bright future on the basis of social justice, equality and fraternity among all Khmers." The people are the source of all power.

The democratization of Cambodian society is being carried out in the liberated zone at present and will be carried out in the whole country in the following ways:

—Guarantee to all Cambodians, except traitors, . . . the freedom of vote, . . . of standing for election, . . . of speech, the press, opinion, association, demonstration, residence, travel at home and going abroad, etc. Safeguard the inviolability of the person, property, wealth and privacy of correspondence.

—Guarantee effective equality to both sexes. . . . Encourage by all means the cultural and professional development of women to enable them fully to participate in the common struggle . . . .

—Buddhism is and will remain the state religion. Bu the National United Front recognizes and guarantees the freedom of all other religions and beliefs . . . .

—Look after with the greatest solicitude the needs of our disabled servicemen and the families of our fighters who gave their lives for the country, and reserve a privileged treatment for them.

---

*Programme Politique du Front Uni National du Kampuchea (FUNK) (Peking?), May 1970?

. . . —See to it that the legitimate rights and interests of minority (groups) . . . are respected.

The National United Front is dedicated to building and developing an independent national economy by relying principally on the resources and productive forces of Cambodia. This economic policy finds concrete expression in:

—Freeing the national economy from persons who engage in profiteering, smuggling, blackmarketeering and inhuman exploitation of people.

—Protecting and guaranteeing the rights of ownership of land and property in accordance with the laws of the state.

—Confiscating the land and property of traitors who are active accomplices in the pay of the American imperialists and who have committed crimes against the people. The land and property seized will be distributed among the needy peasants.

—Guaranteeing to the peasants the right of ownership of the land they cultivate. Establishing a fair system of land rent and interest rates on loans.

—Helping the peasants resolve the agrarian problem through a fair solution of unreasonable debts.

—Helping the peasants increase production . . . . Protecting and developing cooperation and the good customs of mutual aid in the countryside.

—Ensuring conditions for secure and rational farm management and the economical marketing and transportation of products.

—Encouraging the formation of trade unions. Guaranteeing security of employment and reasonable remuneration to the working classes. Improving working conditions. Ensuring a system of social insurance.

—Developing the industrialization of the country and carrying out a rational industrial policy so that production will meet the principal needs of the people . . . .

—Encouraging the national bourgeoisie to set up and manage well enterprises beneficial to the people . . . .

—Helping artisans raise and diversify their production and ensure the sale of their products on the best terms.

—Developing means of transportation and communications.

—Safeguarding the interests of students, intellectuals and civil servants; providing employment for those "without occupation" and the unemployed in accordance with their ability and helping them develop further their ability to serve the country.

—Maintaining the nationalization of the banks and foreign trade.

. . . —Encouraging and developing exports, limiting imports to products necessary to the national economy. Protecting national products from foreign competition.

—Safeguarding the purchasing power of the *riel* and improving the public finance.

. . . The policy of the National United Front concerning education and culture is based on the following points:

—Develop the good traditions of the Angkorian civilization.

. . . Build a national culture based on patriotism and love for work well done and love of art. Protect historical relics and monuments.

—Khmerize gradually the curricula for education, including higher education.

—Adopt the national language as the sole official language in the public services.

—Adapt the programs and methods of education to the needs of the country.

—Encourage and assist scientific research and experimentation. . . .

—Promote research in our national history, which is often distorted by foreign authors, and include it in educational programs.

—Ensure continuous education through regular school terms or vocational training.

—Develop pre-school education. . . .

Ensure free education and provide scholarships for needy children and youth.

—Ensure and support an extensive political, civic and cultural education among the people and the youth. Help every citizen realize his duties to himself, to society and to the people. Instill actively the ideas of public interest and service to the community. . . . This political, civic and cultural education should be carried out at all levels (of government), in factories, shops, cooperatives, in the capital, provinces, districts, villages and families. Develop the ideas of morality, honor, national dignity, patriotism, mutual aid, usefulness of collective labor, the sense and nobleness of rendering sacrifices for the people's cause, the spirit of working conscientiously and practicing economy, and respect for public property.

The foreign policy of the National United Front is one of national independence, peace, neutrality, non-alignment, solidarity and friendship with all peace-loving and justice-loving peoples and governments. The National United Front maintains relations of friendship and cooperation with all countries according to the five principles of peaceful coexistence and the spirit of the United Nations Charter regardless of their political system and ideology. It will not participate in any military alliance, nor does it allow any foreign country to set up military bases or station troops and military personnel on Cambodian territory for the purpose of aggression against other countries. The National United Front does not accept the protection of any country or of any military alliance. In the common struggle against American imperialism, the National United Front pursues a policy of friendship, militant solidarity and cooperation with Laos and Vietnam according to the principle that the liberation and the defense of each country are the affair of her own people and that the three peoples pledge to do their best to support one another according to the desire of the interested country on the basis of mutual respect. In addition, Cambodia is ready to make concerted efforts with Laos and Vietnam to make Indo-China genuinely a zone of independence, peace and progress, where each nation preserves its integral sovereignty with the sympathy and support of the peoples and governments of the socialist countries, non-aligned countries and peace-loving and justice-loving countries in the world, including the American people. . . .

DEMOCRATIC RIGHTS MAY NOT BE USED AS MASKS*

President Suharto

. . . Everything has to be done in a constitutional way! The purpose of the New Order is precisely to uphold the constitution and democracy. If unconstitutional tendencies arise I will go back to the attitude I took on October 1st, 1965, when I served the people by confronting the P.K.I. who wanted to trample on the constitution and the Pantja Sila.

At that time nobody came to encourage me. Did the leaders of the political parties offer me support? No. No one of the youth came to me either. No. Nor any of the students. But I didn't care who was behind me. In fact there was only one person, my wife. She said to me simply: "Be strong in your faith." That was my wife's message to me on October 1st. That was my encouragement and it gave me enough strength to urge the people to overcome the P.K.I.

Later, after this had succeeded, the Pantja Sila Front and the Generation of '66 were formed and then the movement to hasten the process of overcoming the deviation. And I was urged to act unconstitutionally to speed up the process of correction.

This I firmly rejected. I already knew my mind. Acting according to the constitution was a matter of principle for me. Because all corrections had to be made by constitutional means, the special and general sessions of the Interim People's Consultative Congress were convened, and so on. Everything was done constitutionally, so the people were the ones who took the decisions. My responsibility was to ensure that the changes were not effected by unconstitutional means. And, thank God, I was successful.

After that there was more pressure on me to take steps outside the constitution. But, as I say, thank God, I was successful. If I had acted unconstitutionally in the situation at that time when divisions were so sharp I can just imagine what the picture would have been. There would have been civil war and our situation would probably be very different today.

Thank God, we were able to overcome those difficulties. I have been criticized for doing things too cautiously. I have been abused as a "slow but sure" Javanese, as a Javanese who is like a walking snail, like a snail whose shell is too big and heavy for its body. Never mind. The main thing was to safeguard the state and the nation.

---

*Address of the president at the Opening of the Pertaminia Hospital, January 6, 1972 (Pidato Presiden pada Pembukaan Rumah Sakit Pertamina, Tanggal 6 Djanuari 1972) (Djakarta: State Secretariat, 1972).

329

For that reason, if there are now people trying to act in defiance of the constitution, I will go back to the attitude I took on October 1st, 1965. Quite frankly, I will smash them, whoever they are! And I will certainly have the full support of the Armed Forces in that.

And that goes, too, for those who make use of their democratic rights and use those as their masks, who use their rights to excess in any way that suits them. Those rights are like spices: Used excessively, they spoil everything. And if the spoiling of democracy is going to result in the disturbance of order and the general security situation, the disturbance of national stability and the disturbance of development, that is something I will not stand for. Lest you don't understand what I mean by "I will not stand for it" let me say frankly that I will take action. If those people take no notice of warnings and continue to act as they have been I will take action. And if there are legal experts who hold that it is no longer possible for the President to do that, that it would be against the law for me to act against those responsible for these violations—if they want to be stubborn about it—all right, that is simple. In the interest of the state and the nation, I can invoke the Order of March 11, 1966, to declare a State of Emergency. If necessary I can do that even without the existence of an emergency. If those people are going to continue to create chaos I will take it upon myself to act, in my responsibility to the people and to God.

As I said before, it is unexceptionable for there to be differences of opinion in a democratic state, in a democratic environment. But there are limits to differences of opinion. The limits are set by the need for democracy to be in harmony with the calling of our struggle. The calling of our present struggle is to develop, to give content to independence. For development, political and economic stability are essential. And political stability requires order and security.

APPENDIX O

THE RADICALIZATION OF SOCIETY*

Ferdinand E. Marcos
President of the Philippines

Long before the British came, India had an ideology rooted in the long and continuing search for the origin and the meaning of life, a tradition that exalted meditation above action, the primacy of spiritual over material concerns. She had the Hinduist and Buddhist religions. She had a long tradition of village politics, the basis of the *samiti*, or general assembly, of the Vedic period, and of republicanism, the institutions of which developed around the eighth century. Gandhi's non-violent revolution is an original form of protest, but it had its roots in indigenous ideology.

China, on the other hand, has a rich political tradition. The concept of the

---

*Excerpted from *"Today's Revolution: Democracy,"* Manila, 1971.

"Mandate of Heaven" anticipates the people's democratic right to revolt when the ruler has become unjust or ineffective. The *pao chia* system is a device for collective responsibility, and it is, quite possibly, the ancient crutch that holds the Communist concept of democratic centralism, as the "Mandate of Heaven" provided the indigenous power of the Communist revolution.

We understand, of course, that India and China had their size and ancient civilizations going for them before the period of colonialism. But these civilizations exerted an influence all over Asia that barely touched the Philippines. The influence of Islam, on the other hand, was arrested in Sulu—Islam with its socially conscious tenet that its devotee should not sleep when there is a hungry man within a hundred miles.

It is, however, the inaccessibility of the Philippines that gave her the Christian religion and the panoply of Western democratic thought, the nineteenth century enlightenment ideology of Rizal and the individualist ideology of our contemporaries. What would have been our political culture, one wonders, if we could have had for an ancient base for freedom a modified or even a corrupted form of the Chinese *pao chia* system? Could we have readily acquired the political habit of reconciling our private inclinations with the public good, our individual wishes with collective purposes? Or would ancestor worship have been transformed into a sense of historic responsibility?

While it is undeniably true that four centuries of colonization have left their mark on us, our very awareness, our own decision to be free, can only mean that we are prepared to account for ourselves. We cannot be forever holding other peoples responsible for our present condition. The foreign overlords have gone and Filipinos have taken their places: a native oligarchy has displaced the foreign one. That we have been colonized can no longer excuse us.

This society that we live in is of our own making. The fault is not in our stars but in ourselves.

Ours tends to be an oligarchic society. This simply means that the economic gap between the rich and the poor provides the wealthy few the opportunity of exercising undue influence on the political authority. But it does not mean that all the rich and all the privileged constitute an oligarchic class, for many of them—in government, business and even the clergy—are socially conscious enough to acknowledge the necessity of revolutionizing the social order. When I speak, therefore, of oligarchy, I refer to the few who would promote their selfish interests through the indirect or irresponsible exercise of public and private power.

What, to begin with, do we mean by "oligarchy?" . . .

The concentration of a community's wealth in the hands of small minority must result in an oligarchic society. When this society exists side by side with a democratic political authority, as in the case of the Philippines, the consequence is an oligarchic order, or an "oligarchic democracy"—a term employed on Athenian democracy because only a very small percentage of its population—to the exclusion of women and slaves—enjoyed political rights. In our case, every citizen enjoys political rights, which, however, are not *effectively* exercised because of social and economic inequalities.

How is this so? In the first place, the intervention of wealth in the political sphere produces corruption. And when this practice permeates the whole of society itself, the result is social corruption and moral degeneration [and] the failure of a glorious revolution. Now we realize that this condition can also promote a political culture which equates freedom with self-aggrandizement, and the politics of participation, so essential in a democracy, with the pursuit of privilege.

A society based on privilege is the inevitable result, to the extent that the masses themselves, following the example of those above them, seek their own middling and often illusory "privileges." Corruption at the top is matched by social corruption below. The oligarchic elite manipulate the political authority and intimidate political leaders; the masses, in turn, perpetuate a populist, personalist and individualist kind of politics.

The permeation of oligarchic "values" is also managed through the control of the means of mass communication. It is no longer a secret that the displeasure of the oligarchs is communicated through radio and television commentaries and newspaper columns. The media have become the weapon of a special class rather than serve as a public forum. The so-called "editorial prerogative" has been used to justify what is best described as "selective journalism."

The control of media has perpetuated the simplistic politics that have been obstructive of meaningful change, the "radical change," more honored in the pretension than in the performance. It has been remarked how media owners soon reverse their social—progressive—ideas when it comes to their own labor problems. One must note that the popular prejudice against any increase in taxes, even when these are earmarked for development projects, has primarily been the work of media.

The freedom of the press is sanctimoniously invoked whenever the work of media is criticized. But is its hospitality to the most spurious statements and the most outrageous allegations a fair step in, say, improving the quality of political debate, or keeping the people well-informed? Do media not promote the decadence of the masses by reducing the discussion of national issues to the level of entertainment? The usual excuse is the "low taste" of the masses, but pandering to, exploiting it, assuming the judgment to be true, cannot deserve the abused name of "public service."

It is quite revealing that the very radicals whom the media pretend to sympathize with allude to it as the "reactionary press." The sweeping accusation is that the press will lengthily and noisily commit itself to the peripheral issues of our society but not to the fundamental ones: for example, private property. . . . We have yet to hear a voice from the media concurring with the proposition that the existing property laws, derived largely from our Spanish past, perpetuate the oligarchic society and ensure, in turn, the continuing corruption of the political authority. But what does radical change, the revolutionization of society, mean but striking at the roots of the present social system? . . .

The search for "better men in politics," a "higher political morality," is the oligarch's ready answer to the problem of change. Not institutional change, not the restructuring of society, but "getting rid of politicans," the accursed of society, but without whose interventions in an oligarchic-influenced government the needs of the masses could not have been satisfied, even if haphazardly. In this sense, the maligned politician, serving his own desire for power, is the stabilizing element of the oligarchic society, promoting the special interests of the privileged, on the one hand, and lulling the masses with patronage, on the other. But why is the oligarchic master contemptuous of his political servitor, his stabilizing factor? Simply because there are more of him elsewhere—and because he is a servitor. But the politician accepts his status out of his own design: in time, should he stay in the oligarchical conspiracy, he too can become his own oligarch.

Under this system, the search for "better men in politics" is largely a pious sham. And when that sham is discovered, when it can no longer sustain itself by pandering to the few and humoring the rest, the masses will just have to take power into their hands.

All this will depend, however, on the capacity of the political authority to re-assert its will, which is the will of the sovereign people. It is the political leadership that is called upon to revive the atrophied will of the political authority. A re-orientation must proceed; society must be revolutionized.

. . . At the outset, we note three goals that we have in common with the new nations of Asia, Africa, and Latin America. These are nationalism, modernization, and democracy. Let us see how these goals fit into the ideological framework.

The nationalism of the Third World is new in that it departs radically from Western, or the old, nationalism. The impact of Western nationalism on Asia, Africa and Latin America was imperialism; the impact of the new nationalism on the West is decolonization. The old nationalism colonized and exploited other people in order to develop its own societies. That is why Marxist hopes for a world proletarian revolution were grossly disappointed: the condition of the working classes of the metropolitan cities vastly improved because of the benefits of imperialism. It has been observed that all of the demands of the *Communist Manifesto*, except the abolition of private property, have been realized in the capitalist countries of the West, thus weakening the appeal of communism. But we can go even further: the welfare and socialist states of the West have been established not by social revolution but by imperialism: colonialism built Western socialism. But the new nationalism, even with socialism or communism as a goal, cannot pursue the development of its own societies by imperialist means; it can only, if it chooses, "colonize" *its own*.

Salvador de Madariaga once asserted that there is such a thing as government colonizing its own people. This is a valid criticism of the totalitarian state, which strengthens and develops the society out of the exploitation of its own people. The mobilization of Cubans for the great sugar harvest and the Chinese people for the Great Leap Forward and the Great Proletarian Cultural Revolution, collectivization and the rest, are instances of "colonization." But the moral issue is not exactly the same, for the exploitative government justifies itself with the socialization of wealth.

This, in fact, is the problem of the new nationalism: that it has to develop its own societies in far less time and more rapidly than the old nationalism developed theirs with the exploitative machinery of imperialism. The leaderships of the new nationalism are, on the other hand, faced with the problem that no Western leader has had to face in two or three hundred years: the problem of a Moses, Solon, Lycurgus, and Hammurabi. From out of this difficult and complex condition have arisen the various ideologies of the developing nations.

There is common among these ideologies a commitment to democracy, on the one hand, and socialism (with the exception of the Philippines, Liberia, and Malaysia), on the other. But is is a democracy that no Western democrat would regard as such, and a socialism that will not satisfy the consummate socialist. There are, to begin with, collective, guided or basic, and elitist democracies, or to cover a wider range, Mao Tse-Tung's New Democracy. Ayub Khan sums up the more or less general concept of democracy in his four prerequisites:

1. It should be simple to understand, easy to work, and cheap to sustain.
2. It should put to the voter only such questions as he can answer in the light of his own personal knowledge and understanding, without external prompting.
3. It should insure the effective participation of all citizens in the affairs of the country up to the level of their mental horizon and intellectual caliber.
4. It should be able to produce reasonably strong and stable governments.

The Western witness to the operation of these prerequisites in the developing societies is liable to dismiss the word "democracy" as either a fraud or a convenient label for an actually repressive ideology. For he will see one-party political systems, authoritarian rule, weak assemblies, press censorship, and militarism. But let him go back to the experience of his country at a similar period (for there cannot be an exact period for the problems of the new nations), and he will understand that the militarism of some new nations is as much the instrument of national unification as it was for then developing Western countries; moreover, the new militarism looks inward, not outward, for imperialist purposes. As for the other restrictions on freedom long customary among Western democracies, they follow from the principle of a strong government needing strong leaders, and that, moreover, the Western democracies were not less "despotic" at a similar period of national development. . . .

It is quite certain that the new nations, if allowed to develop without the threat of subversion or domination and the Trojanism of some classes of economic aid, will eventually create societies which may well be the monuments to the creative intelligence of mankind. But they must at present develop themselves under severe and often discouraging conditions, largely relying on their political wits.

When it comes to modernization, the whole issue turns on the question of "models"—Indian or Chinese? It would seem that insofar as the economic principle is concerned, there is a strong family resemblance: like China, India is committed towards a "real socialist basis of society." The difference, as Nehru saw it, was in the existence of parliamentary institutions in India. But India is a "collective democracy" and China is a "people's democracy." Necessarily, Nehru thought that the establishment of a socialist society in India would be gradual, although he did not think that the Chinese mode of development was much faster.

The only Asian countries which make no concession, however rhetorical, to socialism, are Taiwan, South Korea, South Vietnam (which are best described as "militant" democracies), Malaysia, and Japan. It is interesting to note that the ruling Alliance Party of Malaysia, which postulates "property-owning democracy," considers ideology "dogmatic" and prejudicial to "pragmatism."

But as any serious scholar knows, there is a bit of ideology in every theory and a bit of theory in every ideology. It is not often easy to draw the line. The common observation is that while a theory is abandoned the moment it is shown to be false, an ideology is not; moreover, it is often impervious to refutation, since ideology presupposes "a conditioned mind," which cannot see things in any other way.

Be that as it may, the prevailing ideology in the Third World is a limited socialist or "collective" democracy.

Considering that we share the same goals of nationalism, modernization, and democracy, how is it that the Philippines never formulated a limited socialist-democratic ideology? One reason is the nature of our "apprenticeship" in democracy. From the earliest days of the American Occupation, it was generally assumed that Philippine independence would be restored at a definite date. In barely a century, personal freedom, individualism, and private initiative became deeply ingrained in the society as enduring values.

The "free enterprise" economic system, on the other hand, found favor with the advanced classes in Philippine society, and for many years, this system, along with the democratic political order, offered a high social mobility.

Another reason is that the leaders of the Philippine struggle for independence, owing to the autonomy of Commonwealth politics, did not have to go in exile to pursue their objectives. In the case of the other new nations, their leaders were exiled, and most of them drawn to the socialist groups in Europe, which, of course, were firmly opposed to imperialism and colonialism. It was from these socialist groups that the exiled leaders learned the technique of mass political organizations.

Thus the dominant principle in Philippine political society is, by contrast, "unlimited" democracy and a "free enterprise" economic system. However, there is a socialist and communist minority whose organizational aim is to politicalize the masses—that is, force them into a mass revolutionary party. This minority provides the friction in society, the antagonism between the classes, insofar as their objective is the armed overthrow of the existing political and social order. Their appeal, now as before, rests on the glaring economic gap between the rich and the poor.

It is the social and economic setting of Philippine democracy that calls for radical change, but because the political culture abets the status quo, that too has to be radically changed. The question is whether these objectives necessitate the formulation of an ideology. Now an ideology should reflect the historical experience, hopes, fears and expectations of a people. No two nations are exactly alike, no two revolutions. And living as we do in a revolutionary age, the ideology towards the remaking of society or the making of a new society must necessarily reflect the tendencies of the times.

In this sense, an ideology need not be a rationalization or a distorted explanation, let alone the justification of special or class interest; it must fill a general and vital need of human beings in a given community. The purpose was to offer an understanding of the times and a practical national guide. The theory, therefore, of Democratic Revolution is the Ideology that seeks to transform society. Democracy, in sum, *is* the Revolution.

On this basis do we look forward to a new society. . . .

Until the super-industrial nations of the world can miraculously agree on an effective plan to infuse the Third World with their affluence, the new nations will have to design their societies according to the indubitable fact of their poverty. And in the present world order, these nations cannot develop themselves fast enough to catch up with their problems. Poverty is the principle of life in Asia, Africa, and Latin America. Their peoples will not wait for economic development and political and social change to follow one another in a grand, stately sequence. This was possible in the era of imperialism; it is possible now.

. . . the democratization of wealth and property must proceed, if the alternative of socialization, or abolition, is to be avoided. Democratization simply means the "sharing" of private wealth with the entire society, and this calls for the regulation of property for collective *human* ends. Thus, private wealth and property are not abolished, for this will stultify private initiative and turn man into a pure collective being. (As Winston Churchill wisely observed, "no man is wholly an individualist or wholly a collectivist.") But the unbridled use of wealth and property mocks the ends of human society, for it accomplishes "the elevation of the few and the degradation of the many."

In this profoundly social century, the wealth of the few, like the power of the few, is a violence on the poor; it becomes, when exercised irresponsibly, a New Barbarism. Just as power can be democratized by popular representation, free speech, and other free institutions, private wealth should be democratized by regulation for the worthy ends of human society. The communist answer to the violence of wealth is its abolition, but it also strikes the very heart of human initiative, and, above all, in the pursuit of collectivist ends, tends to restrict the precious area of personal freedom. It should be emphasized at this point that our concern with private wealth and property is based on democratic principle, for while communism destroys personal freedom, the unrestricted control of wealth and property by a few private individuals similarly restricts the personal freedom of the rest. As Alexander Hamilton observed some two hundred and fifty years ago, the man who has control over another man's subsistence also exercises control over his will.

We envision, therefore, a new society in which equality of opportunity is not a fraud but a fact. An oligarchic society may sincerely believe in equality of opportunity but so long as there is a wide economic gap, the opportunity does not in fact exist. True equality of opportunity begins at the *starting line*, when a human being is born. This simply means that a few should not be born "with everything" while the many have nothing.

When we proceed from this premise, everything else follows: the radicalization of society begins.

DECLARATION OF MARTIAL LAW IN THE PHILIPPINES*

Ferdinand E. Marcos

My Countrymen:

As of the 21st of September, I signed Proclamation No. 1081 placing the entire Philippines under martial law. This Proclamation was to be implemented upon my clearance, and clearance was granted at 9:00 in the evening of the 22nd of September. I have proclaimed martial law in accordance with powers vested in the President by the Constitution of the Philippines.

The proclamation of martial law is not a military takeover. I, as your duly elected President of the Republic, use this power implemented by the military authorities to protect the Republic of the Philippines and our democracy. A republican and democratic form of government is not a helpless government. When it is imperiled by the danger of a violent overthrow, insurrection, and rebellion, it has inherent and built-in powers wisely provided for under the Constitution. Such a danger confronts the Republic.

Thus, Article VII, Section 10, paragraph (2) of the Constitution, provides:

"The President shall be Commander-in-Chief of all the Armed Forces of the Philippines and, whenever it becomes necessary he may call out such armed forces to prevent or suppress lawless violence, invasion, insurrection, or rebellion. In case of invasion, insurrection, or rebellion or imminent danger thereof, when the public safety requires it, he may suspend the privilege of the writ of habeas corpus, or place the Philippines or any part thereof under martial law."

I repeat, this is not a military takeover of civil government functions. The Government of the Republic of the Philippines which was established by our people in 1946 continues. The officials and employees of our national and local governments continue in office and must discharge their duties as before within the limits of the situation. This will be clarified by my subsequent orders which shall be given wide publicity. . . .

We will explain the requirements and standards or details as soon as possible. But any form of corruption, culpable negligence, or arrogance will be dealt with immediately.

The Armed Forces is already cleaning up its own ranks. I am directing the organization of a military commission to investigate, try, and punish all military offenders immediately. For more than any other man, the soldier must set the standard of nobility. We must be courageous but we must be humble and above all we must be fair. As this is true of the soldier, it must be true of the civilian public officer. . . .

---

*Radio address by President Ferdinand Marcos, Manila, September 12, 1972.

Persons who have nothing whatsoever to do with such conspiracy and operations to overthrow the Republic of the Philippines by violence have nothing to fear. They can move about and perform their daily activities without any fear from the Government after the period of counter-action is over.

The persons who will be adversely affected are those who have actively participated in the conspiracy and operations to overthrow the duly constituted government of the Republic of the Philippines by violence.

But all public officials and employees whether of the national or local governments must conduct themselves in the manner of a new and reformed society.

In addition to this, I issued General Orders for the government in the meantime to control media and other means of dissemination of information as well as all public utilities. All schools will be closed for one week beginning this coming Monday. The carrying of firearms outside residences without the permission of the Armed Forces of the Philippines is punishable with death; curfew is established from twelve o'clock midnight to four o'clock in the morning; the departure of Filipinos abroad is temporarily suspended; exceptions are those of official missions that are necessary. Clearances will be given by the Secretary of National Defense. In the meantime, rallies, demonstrations are prohibited. So too are strikes in critical public utilities.

I have ordered the arrest of those directly involved in the conspiracy to overthrow our duly constituted government by violence and subversion.

It is my intention beginning tomorrow to issue all the orders which would attain reforms in our society.

This would include the proclamation of land reform all over the Philippines, the reorganization of the government, new rules and conduct for the civil service, the removal of corrupt and inefficient public officials and their replacement and the breaking up of criminal syndicates.

Again I repeat—this is the same government that you—the people—established in 1946 under the Constitution of the Philippines.

There is no doubt in everybody's mind that a state of rebellion exists in the Philippines.

The ordinary man in the streets, in our cities, the peasants and the laborers know it. Industrialists know it. So do the government functionaries. They have all been affected by it. This danger to the Republic of the Philippines and the existence of a rebellion has been recognized even by our Supreme Court in its decision in the case of *Lansang vs. Garcia*, dated December 11, 1971.

Since the Supreme Court promulgated this decision, the danger has become graver and rebellion has worsened or escalated. It has paralyzed the functions of the national and local governments. The productive sectors of the economy have ground to a halt. Many schools have closed down. The judiciary is unable to administer justice. Many of our businessmen, traders, industrialists, producers, and manufacturers stopped their operations. In the Greater Manila area alone, tension and anxiety have reached a point where the citizens are compelled to stay at home. Lawlessness and criminality like kidnapping, smuggling, extortion, blackmail, armed robbery, illegal traffic in drugs, gunrunning, hoarding and manipulation of prices, corruption in government, tax evasion perpetuated by syndicated criminals, have increasingly escalated beyond the capability of the local police and civilian authorities.

The usually busy centers of the area such as cinema houses, supermarkets, restaurants, transportation terminals and even public markets are practically deserted. Battles are going on between elements of the Armed Forces of the Philippines and the subversives in the Island of Luzon at Isabela, Zambales, Tarlac, Camarines Sur, Quezon; and in the Island of Mindanao at Lanao del Sur, Lanao del Norte, Zamboanga del Sur, and Cotabato.

If this continues even at the present rate, the economy of the country will collapse in a short time.

In one province alone—Isabela—where the Communist Party and the New People's Army have sought to establish a rural sanctuary, they are now in control of 33 municipalities out of 37. Other towns are infiltrated severely by these armed elements. In this province alone, the supposed invisible government of the Communist Party has been organized through the Barrio Organizing Committees (BOCs), totaling 207 in twenty-five towns, compared to 161 in twelve towns in early 1971. . . .

The armed elements of the New People's Army under the Communist Party of the Philippines (Maoist faction) have increased to about 10,000, which includes regulars as well as farmers in the daytime and soldiers at night. This is an increase of 100 per cent in a short period of six months. It has increased its mass base to 100,000. Their front organizations' operations have increased tremendously. Example of such a front organization is the Kabataang Makabayan (KM), the most militant organization of the Communist Party, which has increased its chapters from 200 in 1970 to 317 up to the end of July 1972, and its membership from 10,000 in 1970 to 15,000 up to the end of July this year. The Samahang Demokratiko ng Kabataan (SDK), an outspoken front organization, had also increased its chapters from almost none in 1970 to 159 at the end of July this year and has now 1,495 highly indoctrinated and fanatical members. . . .

The subversives have organized urban partisans in the Greater Manila area. They have been and still are active. They have succeeded in some of their objectives.

The violent disorder in Mindanao and Sulu has to date resulted in the killing of over 1,000 civilians and about 2,000 armed Muslims and Christians, not to mention the more than five-hundred thousands of injured, displaced, and homeless persons as well as the great number of casualties among our government troops, and the paralyzation of the economy of Mindanao and Sulu.

I assure you that I am utilizing this power vested in me by the Constitution to save the Republic and reform our society. I wish to emphasize these two objectives. We will eliminate the threat of a violent overthrow of our Republic. But at the same time we must now reform the social, economic, and political institutions in our country. The plans and orders for reform to remove the inequities of that society, the clean-up of government of its corrupt and sterile elements, the liquidation of the criminal syndicates, the systematic development of our economy—the general program for a new and better Philippines—will be explained to you. But we must start out with the removal of anarchy and the maintenance of peace and order.

I have had to use this constitutional power in order that we may not completely lose the civil rights and freedom which we cherish. I assure you that this is not a precipitate decision—that I have weighed all the factors. If there were any other solution at our disposal and within our capability which we could utilize to solve the present problem, I would choose it. But there is none.

I have used the other two alternatives of calling out the troops to quell the rebellion and suspending the privilege of the writ of habeas corpus. But the rebellion has not been stopped. I repeat, it has worsened. . . .

All other recourses have been unavailing. You are all witnesses to these. So we have fallen on our last line of defense.

You are witnesses to the patience that we have shown in the face of provocation. In the face of abuse and license we have used persuasion. Now the limit has been reached. We are against the wall. We must now defend the Republic with the stronger powers of the Constitution.

To those guilty of treason, insurrection, rebellion, it may pose a grave danger. But to the citizenry, whose primary concern is to be left alone to pursue their lawful activities, this is the guaranty of that freedom.

All that we do is for the Republic and for you. Rest assured we will continue to do so.

I have prayed to God for guidance. Let us all continue to do so. I am confident that with God's help we will attain our dream of a reformed society, a new and brighter world.

APPENDIX Q

THE BURMESE WAY TO SOCIALISM*

THE REVOLUTIONARY COUNCIL OF THE UNION OF BURMA does not believe that man will be set free from social evils as long as pernicious economic systems exist in which man exploits man and lives on the fat of such appropriation. The Council believes it to be possible only when exploitation of man by man is brought to an end and a socialist economy based on justice is established; only then can all people irrespective of race or religion, be emancipated from all social evils and set free from anxieties over food, clothing and shelter, and from inability to resist evil, for an empty stomach is not conducive to wholesome morality, as the Burmese saying goes; only then can an affluent stage of social development be reached and all people be happy and healthy in mind and body.

Thus affirmed in this belief the Revolutionary Council is resolved to march unswervingly and arm-in-arm with the people of the Union of Burma towards the goal of socialism.

In setting forth their program as well as in their execution the Revolutionary Council will study and appraise the concrete realities and also the natural conditions peculiar to Burma objectively. On the basis of the actual findings derived from such study and appraisal it will develop its own ways and means to progress.

The Burmese Way to Socialism (Rangoon: Director of Information, 1962).

In its activities the Revolutionary Council will strive for self-improvement by way of self-criticism. Having learned from contemporary history the evils of deviation towards right or left the Council will with vigilance avoid any such deviation.

In whatever situations and difficulties the Revolutionary Council may find itself it will strive for advancement in accordance with the times, conditions, environment and the ever changing circumstances, keeping at heart the basic interests of the nation.

The Revolutionary Council will diligently seek all ways and means whereby it can formulate and carry out such programs as are of real and practical value for the well-being of the nation. In doing so it will critically observe, study and avail itself of the opportunities provided by progressive ideas, theories and experiences at home, or abroad without discrimination between one country of origin and another.

The fundamental concept of socialist economy is the participation of all for the general well-being in works of common ownership, and planning towards sufficiency and contentment of all, sharing the benefits derived therefrom. Socialist economy aims at the establishment of a new society for all, economically secure and morally better, to live in peace and prosperity.

Socialist economy therefore opposes any pernicious economic system in which man exploits man, and self-interest and self-seeking are the motivating forces.

Socialist economy does not serve the narrow self-interest of a group, an organization, a class, or a party, but plans its economy with the sole aim of giving maximum satisfaction to material, spiritual and cultural needs of the whole nation.

Socialist economy is the planned, proportional development of all the national productive forces.

"Productive forces" is the collective term for natural resources, raw materials, instruments of production, accumulated capital, peasants, workers, intelligentsia, technicians, know-hows and experiences, skills, etc.

Socialist economy proportionally plans, on the basis of the population and productive forces, for sufficiency and abundance of consumer goods. While improving the standard of living and increasing the purchasing power of the nation it also expands production. Socialist economy thus solves the problem of unemployment and ensures security of a means of livelihood for every individual.

In order to carry out socialist plans such vital means of production as agricultural and industrial production, distribution, transportation, communications, external trade, etc., will have to be nationalized. All such national means of production will have to be owned by the State or cooperative societies or collective unions. Amongst such ownerships State ownership forms the main basis of socialist economy. State ownership means ownership by the whole nation itself, whereas ownership by cooperatives or collectives means group-ownership by respective concerns. But as all forms of ownership will have to operate within the framework of socialist national planning they are interdependent.

In building up an economy according to socialist plans every able individual will have to work according to his ability. The material and cultural values that accrue will be distributed in accordance with the quantity and quality of labor expended by each individual in social production.

In our Burmese socialist society equalitarianism is impossible. Men are not equal physically and intellectually in the respective quantity and quality of service they render to society, and differences are therefore bound to exist. But at the same time social justice demands that the gaps between incomes are reasonable, and correct measures will be taken to narrow these gaps as much as possible.

A socialist democratic state will be constituted to build up a successful socialist economy. A socialist democratic state is based on and safeguards its own socialist economy. The vanguard and custodian of a socialist democratic state are primarily peasants and workers, but the middle strata and those who will work with integrity and loyalty for the general weal will also participate.

Parliamentary democracy called "The People's Rule" came into existence in history with the British, American and French Revolutions against feudalism. It happens to be the best in comparison with all its preceding systems.

But in some countries the parliament has been so abused as to have become only the means by which the opportunists and properties people deceive the simple masses.

In the Union of Burma also, parliamentary democracy has been tried and tested in furtherance of the aims of socialist development. But Burma's "parliamentary democracy" has not only failed to serve our socialist development but also, due to its very defects, weaknesses and loopholes, its abuses and the absence of a mature public opinion, lost sight of and deviated from the socialist aims, until at last indications of its heading imperceptibly towards just the reverse have become apparent.

The nation's socialist aims cannot be achieved with any assurance by means of the form of parliamentary democracy that we have so far experienced.

The Revolutionary Council therefore firmly believes that it must develop, in conformity with existing conditions and environment and ever changing circumstances, only such a form of democracy as will promote and safeguard the socialist development.

These then are the fundamentals of socialist economy.

In marching towards socialist economy it is imperative that we first reorientate all erroneous views of our people.

Fraudulent practices, profit motive, easy living, parasitism, shirking and selfishness must be eradicated.

We must so educate the people that to earn one's living by one's own labor and to see dignity in one's own work comes into vogue. We must educate, lead by example and guide the people away from the base notion that it is beneath one's dignity to work by the sweat of one's brow.

Attempts must be made by various correct methods to do away with bogus acts of charity and social work for vainglorious show, bogus piety and hypocritical religiosity, etc., as well as to foster and applaud bona fide belief and practice of personal morals as taught by ethics and traditions of every religion and culture. We will resort to education, literature, fine arts, theatre and cinema, etc., to bring into vogue the concept that to serve others' interests is to serve one's own.

In our road to socialism the existing bureaucratic administration is a big stumbling block. To achieve our socialist aims with this effete machinery is impossible. Steps will have to be taken to remove this bureaucratic machinery and lay firm foundations for a socialist democratic one.

The existing Defense Services will also be developed to become national armed forces which will defend our socialist economy.

The Union of Burma is an economically backward agricultural country. The national productive forces need to be continually developed to build up socialist economy. That is why various productions that would be compatible with existing conditions and time will have to be planned and developed. While modernizing the agricultural production which forms the main basis of the national economy such industries as would be commensurate with the natural resources and capabilities of the country will also be developed. In doing so national private enterprises which contribute to national productive forces will be allowed with fair and reasonable restrictions.

On the full realization of socialist economy the socialist government, far from neglecting the owners of national private enterprises which have been steadfastly contributing to the general well-being of the people, will even enable them to occupy a worthy place in the new society in the course of further national development.

As the Union of Burma is a country where many indigenous racial groups reside, it is only when the solidarity of all the indigenous racial groups has been established that socialist economy which can guarantee the welfare of every racial group can be achieved. In striving towards fraternity and unity of all the races of the Union we will be guided by what General Aung San, our national leader, said at the A.F.P.F.L. conference held at the middle terrace of the Shwedagon Pagoda on January 20, 1946:

> "A nation is a collective term applied to a people, irrespective of their ethnic origin, living in close contact with one another and having common interests and sharing joys and sorrows together for such historic periods as to have acquired a sense of oneness. Though race, religion and language are important factors it is only their traditional desire and will to live in unity through weal and woe that binds a people together and makes them a nation and their spirit a patriotism."

We, the peoples of the Union of Burma, shall nurture and hug a new patriotism as inspired by the words of General Aung San.

The Revolutionary Council believes that the existing educational system unequated with livelihood will have to be transformed. An educational system equated with livelihood and based on socialistic moral values will be brought about. Science will be given precedence in education.

Our educational target is to bring basic education within the reach of all. As regards higher education only those who have promise and enough potentialities and industriousness to benefit from it will be specially encouraged.

The Revolutionary Council believes that other social services such as Health, Culture, etc., shall flourish in direct proportion to the tides of socialist success like the lotus and the water's height, and will accordingly work towards this end.

The Revolutionary Council recognizes the right of everyone freely to profess and practice his religion.

In marching towards the goal of socialism the Revolutionary Council will base its organization primarily on the strength of peasants and other working masses who form the great majority of the nation. It will march also hand-in-hand with those who will work with integrity and loyalty for national interest and well-being of the people.

The Revolutionary Council will therefore carry out such mass and class organizations as are suitable for the transitional period, and also build up a suitable form of political organization.

When political organizational work is carried out socialist democratic education and democratic training will be given to the people so as to ensure their conscious participation. (The Revolutionary Council believes and hopes that there will come about democratic competitions which will promote socialist development within the framework of socialism.)

The aforesaid are in outline the belief and policy of the Revolutionary Council of the Union of Burma.

The Revolutionary Council has faith in the people, and in their creative force.

The Revolutionary Council believes that the people will, with an active awareness of their duties and responsibilities, play their part in full in this national revolutionary progressive movement and program under the leadership of the Revolutionary Council.

The Revolutionary Council reaffirms and declares again that it will go forward hand-in-hand with the people to reach the goal of socialism.

Let us march towards socialism in our own Burmese way!

APPENDIX R

BIBLIOGRAPHY

The mark (*) indicates a book especially useful for young readers, as well as for adults.

Journals & Periodicals (to 1986)

Asia, American Asian Review, Asian Survey, Far Eastern Quarterly, the United Nations Population, Vital Statistics Reports, and The New York *Times*

Encyclopedia Brittanica Yearbook, Keesing's, Facts on File, Contemporary Southeast Asia, Encyclopedia Americana Yearbook, World Almanac. *See also* articles on individual countries in the encyclopedias *Brittanica* and *Americana, The Associated Press Almanac* and the Far Eastern Economic Review Yearbook.

Books

AUNG-THWIN. *Pagan: The Origins of Modern Burma*. Honolulu: University of Hawaii, 1985.
Discloses how Burma's earliest past presaged its present and probably its future.

BAIN, CHESTER A. *Vietnam: The Roots of Conflict*. Englewood Cliffs: Prentice-Hall, 1967.
An excellent survey of Vietnam's history from the end of the Nguyen Dynasty to 1967.

BASHAM, ARTHUR L. *The Wonder that Was India*. New York: Taplinger, 1968; Grove Press, 1959; Sidgwick & Jackson, 1983.
The best available survey of India's pre-Muslim culture, illustrated, is useful in the study of Southeast Asia.

BLOODSWORTH, DENNIS. *An Eye for the Dragon: Southeast Asia Observed, 1954-1970*. New York: Farrar, Strass, and Giroux, 1970.
A British journalist's account of the origins of war.

BUNGE, FREDERICA M., *et al. The Country Study Series*. Washington, D.C.: U.S. Government.
The American University's superb volumes, offering comprehensive data on Malaysia (1985), North Vietnam (1981), Laos (Donald Whitaker, 1979), Khmer Republic (Donald Whitaker, 1973), and Indonesia (1983).

BURKI, SHAHID JAVED. *Pakistan: A Nation in the Making*. Boulder: Westview, 1985.
Through an examination of historical and cultural factors, shows the roots of the ongoing struggle for stability.

BUTTINGER, JOSEPH. *The Smaller Dragon*. New York: Praeger, 1958.
Easily read, written by an Austrian statesman and scholar who wrote one of the first substantial works on Vietnam from prehistory to the conquest by the French.

_____. *Vietnam: A Political History*. New York: Praeger, 1968.
A condensation of the 2,000 page, *The Smaller Dragon*.

_____. *Vietnam: A Dragon Embattled*. 2 vols. New York: Praeger, 1968.
Carries the history of Vietnam into the 1960s.

CADY, JOHN F. *The History of Post-War Southeast Asia: Independence Problems*. Athens: University of Ohio Press, 1975.
An incisive political-economic study by a noted scholar in this field.

_____. *Southeast Asia: Its Historical Development*. New York: McGraw-Hill, 1964.
Becoming obsolete, but one of the better broad perspectives on the entire region.

_____. *A History of Modern Burma*. Ithaca: Cornell University Press, 1958.
A dated but useful work of scholarship.

*CAMPBELL, JOSEPH. *The Masks of God: Oriental Mythology*. New York: Viking, 1962.
Brilliant discussions of Asian mythology, with contrasts to the West.

*CARMICHAEL, JOEL. *The Shaping of the Arabs*. New York: The Macmillan Co., 1967.
A thorough and valuable study which should be related to Southeast Asia.

CHAFFEE, FREDERIC H. *et al. Area Handbook for the Philippines*. Washington, D.C.: U.S. Government Printing Office, 1969.
A guidebook, including statistics and maps, to all aspects of the Philippines.

*CHAMPION, S.G. and SHORT, D. (eds.). *Readings from World Religions*. New York: Fawcett World, 1968 (paperback).

Succinct essays about, and readings from, the texts of the world's eleven most influential religions.

CHANDLER, DAVID P. *A History of Cambodia.* Boulder. Westview., 1983.
An especially comprehensive survey of a rapidly changing history.

CHANG, PAO-MIN. *Kampuchea Between China and Vietnam.* Singapore: Singapore University Press, 1985.
Analyzes the causes and effects of the power struggle of which Kampuchea has been the victim.

CREEL, H.G. *Chinese Thought from Confucius to Mao Tse-tung.* Chicago: University of Chicago Press, 1953. A popular, well-written survey of Chinese intellectual activity to post-revolutionary times.

COEDES, GEORGES. *The Indianized States of Southeast Asia.* Honolulu: University of Hawaii, East-West Center Press, 1968.
A perceptive study, translated.

COMMITTEE OF CONCERNED ASIAN SCHOLARS. *The Indochina Story.* New York: Bantam Books, 1970 (Paperback).
A documented study of the causes of the Vietnam War.

CORPUZ, ONOFRE D. *The Philippines.* Englewood Cliffs: Prentice-Hall, 1965.
A rare overview of a complex nation.

CRESSEY, GEORGE B. *Asia's Lands and Peoples.* New York: McGraw-Hill, 1963.
A widely accepted geography, useful though obsolete in places.

*DEBARY, W.T. (ed.). *Sources of Indian Tradition.* New York: Columbia University Press, 1958.
The best available compilation of original material and commentary on India.

_____. (ed.). *The Buddhist Tradition in India, China, and Japan.* New York Random House, 1972 (Paperback).
The best available short collection of original material and commentary.

DOMMEN, ARTHUR J. *Laos: Keystone of Indochina.* Boulder: Westview, 1985.
An agricultural economist, writing from a historical perspective, discusses Laos's present role and its probable future.

DEDIOS, EMMANUEL S. (ed.). *An Analysis of the Philippine Economic Crisis.* Honolulu: University of Hawaii Press, 1985.
Reveals the menacing depths of the problem and its implications.

DONNISON, CRAIG. *The Rise & Demise of Democratic Kampuchea.* Boulder: Westview, 1984.
Unravels one of the most complex and anguishing stories in modern political science.

DUIKER, WILLIAM J. *Vietnam Since the Fall of Saigon.* Athens: Ohio University Press, 1986.
The motives and methods of the government which triumphed in the Vietnam War.

DUTT, ASHOK K. (ed.). *Southeast Asia: Realm of Contrasts.* Boulder: Westview, 1985.
A symposium—essential because of the subject's complexity—dealing with the geography, economy, culture, and development of the entire region.

FAIRBANK, J.K. *et al. A History of East Asia.* Boston: Houghton Mifflin, 1973.
A standard in its field.

FALL, BERNARD. *Anatomy of a Crisis.* New York: Doubleday, 1969.
A narrative about the Vietnam War, written by a professor who later was killed there.

*FENOLLOSA, E. *Epochs of Chinese & Japanese Art.* 2 vols. Baltimore: Dover Publications, 1963.
A good introduction to the history and aesthetics of Chinese and Japanese art, useful in the study of Southeast Asia.

FISHER, C.A. *South-east Asia: A Social, Economic, and Political Geography.* London: Methuen, 1964.
A major accomplishment in its field, though now dated in many respects.

*FITZGERALD, FRANCES. *Fire in the Lake: The Vietnamese and the Americans in Vietnam.* Boston: Little Brown, 1972.
A prize-winning account of the origins of the Vietnam War.

GOLAY, FRANK H. (ed.). *The United States and the Philippines.* Englewood Cliffs: Prentice-Hall, 1966.
Various perspectives on a unique relationship.

GORDON, FRANK H. (ed.). *The United States and the Philippines.* Englewood Cliffs: Prentice-Hall, 1966.
Analyzes the scope and depth of political tensions.

GULLICK, J.M. *Malaysia*. New York: Praeger, 1969.
A scholarly account from the earliest times to post-World War II.

HERZ, MARTIN F. *A Short History of Cambodia*. New York: Praeger, 1958.
Though limited and aging, this brief exposition touches the high points to the period following World War II.

HO CHI MINH. *On Revolution: Selected Writings. 1920-60*. New York: International Publishers, 1970.
Basic thought of the Vietnamese leader.

_____. *Prison Diary*. New York: Bantam Books, 1971.
Widely admired, highly-compressed poems reflecting Vietnam's culture and determination.

HUNTER, GUY. *South-east Asia*. London: Oxford University Press, 1966.
Examines the region from the perspective of race, culture, economics, and nationalism.

JONES, HOWARD PALFREY. *Indonesia: The Possible Dream*. New York: Harcourt Brace Jovanovich, 1971.
A hopeful account by a former U.S. ambassador.

KAHIN, G.M. (ed.). *Governments and Politics of Southeast Asia*. Ithaca: Cornell University Press, 1965.
An excellent compendium by a group of specialists.

KENNEDY, JOSEPH. *Malaya*. New York: St. Martin's Press, 1962.
A reliable work by a British scholar, recounting history to independence.

KING, JOHN KERRY. *Southeast Asia in Perspective*. New York: Macmillan, 1956.
Includes brief histories of Southeast Asian countries at the end of World War II, showing the rise of communism and nationalism

*KRAMER, SAMUEL NOAH (ed.). *Mythologies of the Ancient World*. New York: Doubleday & Co., 1961 (Anchor Paperback).
Good sections on the mythologies of China, India, and Japan are included.

*LANDON, MARGARET. *Anna and the King of Siam*. New York: John Day, 1944.
After reading Anna Leonowens' 1870 book, *The English Governess at the Siamese Court*, the author conducted interviews and created her own account, a romantic fiction which is nevertheless influential and reached other media.

*LARKIN, JOHN A. and BENDA, HARRY JR. *The World of Southeast Asia: Selected Historical Readings*. New York: Harper & Row, 1967.
A good source of annotated materials.

*MAO TSE-TUNG. *Selected Works*. New York: International Publishers, 1954-56.
Official publication of Mao's most important writings.

McCOY, ALFRED W. & DE JESUS, EDILBERTO. *Philippine Social History*. Honolulu: University of Hawaii Press, 1982.
Brings together the countless strands, from precolonial to modern times.

MILLER, HARRY. *A Short History of Malaysia*. New York: Praeger, 1965.
An early general history, written as the country began.

MILLS, LENNOX, A. *Malaya: A Political and Economic Appraisal*. Minneapolis: University of Minnesota Press, 1958.
An excellent study of the diverse groups and economic problems during the post-World War II period.

_____. *Southeast Asia*. Minneapolis: University of Minnesota Press, 1964.
Contains economic and political data, showing the relationship of financial position and foreign policy.

MILNE, R.S. & MAUZY, DIANE K. *Malaysia: Tradition, Modernity, and Islam*. Boulder: Westview, 1985.
In less than 200 pages this volume touches upon all aspects of progress and conflict in a rapidly developing country.

NAKAMURA, HAJIME. *Ways of Thinking of Eastern Peoples*. Honolulu: East-West Center Press, 1964.
One of the most insightful books of its kind, covering India, China, Tibet, and Japan, reflects on Southeast Asia.

PAXTON, JOHN (ed.). *Statesman's Yearbook*. New York: St. Martin's Press, 1974-75.
A good source of statistics on land, population, and government to 1975.

PENDLETON, ROBERT L. *Thailand*. New York: Duell, Sloan & Pearce, 1962.

*Raskin, Marcus G. and Fall, Bernard B. *The Viet-Nam Reader*. New York: Random House, 1965.

An excellent collection of original materials, compiled by two who criticized the U.S. role in the Vietnam War.

*Ravenholt, Albert. *The Philippines: A Young Republic on the Move*. Princeton: Van Nostrand, 1962.

Uncritical and journalistic, but with some useful information.

Reichauer, E. and Fairbank, J.K. *A History of East Asian Civilizations*. 2 vols. Boston: Houghton Mifflin Co., 1961-64.

A brilliant study of China and Japan by two noted scholars.

_____. *East Asia: The Great Tradition*. Boston: Houghton Mifflin, 1960.

One of the most widely noted surveys of Asian thought and action.

Scalapino, Robert A. (ed.). *The Communist Revolution in Asia*. Englewood Cliffs: Prentice-Hall, 1965.

Perceptive essays, edited by a political scientist who has advised the U.S. State Department.

Shinn, Rinn-Sup. et al. *Area Handbook for Handbook for India*. Washington, D.C.: U.S. Government Printing Office, 1969.

A guidebook, including statistics and maps, to all aspects of India.

*Sihanouk, Norodom. *My War with the CIA*. New York: Random House, 1972.

Prince Sihanouk's description of the U.S. role in Cambodia.

Steinberg, David Joel et al. *In Search of Southeast Asia*. Honolulu: University of Hawaii Press, 1985.

A massive effort by six prominent historians to reveal Southeast Asia in its many complex facets.

Tarling, Nicholas. *A Concise History of Southeast Asia*. New York: Praeger, 1966.

Analyzes the origins of nationalism.

Tate, D.J. *the Making of South-East Asia* (vol 2). *The Western Impact: Economic & Social Change*. Oxford: Oxford University Press, 1979.

An impressive contribution to the ongoing study of the effects of colonialism.

Taylor, George R. *The Philippines and the United States: Problems of Partnership*. New York: Praeger, 1964.

A candid exposition, written by Americans.

United Nations. *Economic Survey of Asia and the Far East*. New York: United Nations Publishing Service, 1981.

The most complete data available to publication.

*U.S. Department of Defense. *the Pentagon papers*. New York: Bantam Books, 1971.

Essential for an understanding of the U.S. role in Southeast Asia.

Weber, Max. *The Religions of China*. Glencoe: Free Press, 1957.

A pioneering sociologist analyzes China's major faiths.

Whitaker, Donald P. et al. *Area Handbook for Laos*. Washington, D.C.: U.S. Government Printing Office, 1972.

Wint, Guy (ed.). *Asia Handbook*. Harmondsworth: Penguin, 1969.

A compilation of statistical data gathered as nations developed.

Woodcock, George. *The British in the Far East*. New York: Athenaeum, 1969.

A vivid account of British colonialism.

*Wu, Nelson, I. *Chinese and Indian Architecture*. New York: Braziller, 1963.

A splendidly illustrated and annotated short survey.

*Yohannan, John D. (ed.). *A Treasury of Asian Literature*. New York: John Day, 1956 (Also Mentor Paperback).

Well-chosen excerpts from works which helped to shape Asian history.

APPENDIX S

INDEX

Acapulco, 43
adat, 229, 251
AFPFL. *See* Anti-Fascist People's Freedom League.
Aglipay, Gregory, 281
Agrarian Law, 51
Aguinaldo, 47, 61-62
Air America, 155
Alaungpaya, 34
Albuquerque, Alfonso, de, 41, 43
Allah, 7, 39. *See also* Muslims.
Alliance Party, 99, 257-58
Allies, 94, 247
Amboyna, 42, 48
Americans. *See* United States.
Ananda Pagoda, 32
Anawratha, 31, 32
Ang Chan, 28
Angkor, 27, 169
Angkor Thom, 28
Angkor Wat, 27, 168-70
animism, 2-3, 109-10, 128-29, 149-50, 230, 280
Annam, 27, 36, 37, 58, 59, 79, 86, 93-97
Annamite Mountains, 23
Anti-Fascist People's Freedom League, 88, 105, 113
anyeint pwe, 111
Aquino, Benigno S., 293-4
Aquino, Corozon, 294-99
Arakan Mountains, 54, 112
Arakanese (Arakans), 33, 107-08, 112
archipelagoes, 16-17
architecture. *See* "arts" under country.
Armee Clandestine, 155.
"Asia for the Asiatics" slogan, 85
"Asian Co-Prosperity Sphere," 83, 86
Asian Development Bank, 120, 123
Assam, 54
Associated States of Indochina, 96
Association of Southeast Asia (ASA), 261-62, 305
Association of Southeast Asian Nations (ASEAN), 144, 246, 262, 305
astrology, 3, 11, 128-29

Attlee, Clement, 88
Aung San, 82, 86, 87, 88-89, 105
Australoids, 22
Ava, 33, 34, 54
Ayuthia, 30, 31, 130

Bahasa Indonesia, 100, 231
Bahasa Malaysia, 251, 252
Bali, 7, 228, 230, 232
Ba Maw, Dr., 76, 232
Banda Islands, 35
Bandung, 229
Bangkok, 30, 126, 129, 130, 131, 135
Bangladesh, 107, 112, 248
Bantam, 42
Bao Dai, 79, 93-94, 96
barrios, 44
Bataan, 101
Batavia, 48, 49, 50, 53
Batdamban, 65 84
Bell, Daniel W., 287
Bhumibol Aduljadej, King, 90, 133
"boat people", 214-153, 258
bodhisattva, 4
Bodhisattva Avalokitesvara, 5
Bonifacio, Andreas, 47
Borneo, 35, 54, 57, 99. *See also* Kalimantan.
Borobudur, 35, 232
Bowring Treaty, 138
Brahmans, 3, 25, 26, 128, 129
British, 34, 50, 52-57, 64, 65, 73-77, 84, 87-88, 89, 98, 100, 105, 107, 108, 126, 161, 227, 248, 253, 267-68, 271
British East India Company, 53, 54
British Malaya, 68, 73-75, 97-99, 103, 268. *See also* Federated Malay States, Malaysia.
Brooke, James, 54
Buddhism, 2, 3-6, 25, 28, 29, 31, 32, 37, 55, 56, 108-09, 114, 148-49, 151, 166-67, 187-89. *See also* Mahayana Buddhism, Theravada Buddhism, "religion" under country.

Budi Utomo, 72
Burma, 11, 12, 19, 20, 31, 33, 34, 37, 54-57, 65, 75-77, 82, 85, 87-89, 103, 105-23
  agriculture, 117-20, 122
  children, 106-07,
China, relations with, 120-22, 123
Chinese in, 117
  civil war, 112; constitution, 115; corruption, 116; economy, 116-20; employment, 115; education, 110; elections, 113, 115; ethnic groups, 105-08; families, 106; food supplies, 116; foreign relations, 120-22; future, 122-23; foreign relations, 120-22 future, 122-23
  guerrillas, 115; houses, 106; Indians in, 117, 121 land, 117-18, 122; land ownership, 118; language, 110; literacy, 110; minerals, 119
  minorities, 115, 117; military, 114; nationalization, 117, 121; People's Congress, 115; per capita income, 120 political groups, 113-115; population, 122; raw materials, 119-20; religion, 108-10; population growth, 122
  "respect" names, 107; universities, 116; villages, 106
  socialism in, 116ff.
Burma Independence Army, 76, 87
Burma Road, 77, 84-85
Burma Socialist Program Party (BSPP), 114-15
Burmans, 24, 27, 31, 32, 33, 34, 75-76, 105-07, 114-115
Burmese, 34, 54, 75-75, 105-06 See also Burmans (identical).

caciques, 45, 63
Cambodia. See Kampuchea, Khmer Republic.
Canton, China, 78
Cape of Good Hope, 41, 48
Catholics, 58, 59, 166, 189, 190, 197, 280-81
Cavite, 46
Celebes, 35. See also Sulawese.
Central Intelligence Agency (CIA), 153, 155,
Ceylon, 5, 28, 42, 151. See also Sri Lanka.
Chams, 27, 28, 37

Champa, 25, 37
Champassak, 90, 147, 153
Chao Phraya River, 17, 30, 126, 132, 141
Chenla, 26
Chettyars, 56, 108
Chiengmai, 29, 31, 127, 151
China, 1, 31, 33, 34, 36-38, 44, 58, 67, 77, 78, 84-85, 93, 94-95, 98, 106, 120-21, 125, 161, 179, 182, 279, 287. See also Chinese; Chinese influence; Chinese, massacres of; People's Republic of China.
Chinese, 14, 24, 34, 48-49, 51, 56, 61, 66, 72, 74, 75, 76, 77, 89, 97-99, 108, 110, 115, 117, 133, 134, 213, 267-71, 279-80
Chinese, massacres of, 45, 49, 86, 228, 258. See also "boat people".
Chins, 88, 108
Christianity, 42, 108-09, 128, 231, 269, 280-81
Christians, 114, 127, 231, 280-81
Chulalongkorn, King, 65
Chungking, 77
cities, 14-16, 20-21, 48, 52, 72, 75, 131, 267-77
Clark Air Base, 286
Cochin China, 58, 59, 79, 86, 93-97
Coen, Jan Pieterzoon, 48
coffee, 19, 48-49, 52, 59
Communist China. See People's Republic of China.
communist movements, 73, 68-79, 94-95, 100, 112, 152, 156, 236-38, 247, 254-55, 284-85
Confrontation, the, 256
Confucianism, 8-9, 11, 36, 37, 60, 78, 248, 268-69
Cultural Revolution, effects of, 117, 121

Dayak tribe, 249
Dekker, Eduard, 51
Democratic Republic of Vietnam, 95. See also Vietnam.
devaraja, 4, 25-26, 169
Dewey, Admiral George, 62
Diem, President Ngo Dinh, 9, 172
Dienbienphu, 97
Diponegoro, Prince, 51
Diu, 41
Djakarta, 48, 100, 229.

Dutch, 47-52, 71-73, 84. *See also* Indonesia.
Dutch East Indies, 71-73, 84. *See also* Indonesia.

Eightfold Path, 4
Eisenhower, President Dwight, D., 161
elections, 66, 79, 113, 152, 170, 173, 176, 235-36, 272, 288
Emergency, the, 254
encomienda system, 44
Enrile, Gen. Juan, 297
Ethical Policy, 52, 72

families, 10-12, 20-21, 60. *See also* under country.
Federated Malay States, 54, 57
Filipinos, 11-12, 279-82. *See also* Philippines.
Five Pillars of the Faith, 7
Flying Tigers, 77
food supply, 56, 282
Four Noble Truths, 4
France, 50, 57-61, 77-79, 86, 90-99, 147, 148, 151, 153, 161, 168, 170
French Indochina, 77-79, 84, 86-87, 90-97, 153, 165
Funan, 26

galleons, Spanish, 43, 44
Gandhi, M.K., 67-68
Garcia, President Carlos, P., 288
Geneva Conference of 1962, 154, 162, 197-98
Germany, 165
Giap, Vo Nguyen, 96-97
Goa, 42
gold, 1, 19, 33
Great Britain, 50, 52-57, 73, 77, 87-89, 91, 98-99, 103, 161, 254-56, 267-68, 271
Great Depression,52, 66, 69-70, 80
"Green Revolution", 159
guerrillas, 62, 91-92, 95, 95, 97, 98, 101, 102, 112, 133, 153-57, 165, 166, 173, 175-77, 233, 254-55, 271, 282, 284
Guided Democracy, 236
Gujaratis, 24, 38
Gulf of Tonkin Incident, 205, 206

Haiphong, 95, 96,

Hanoi, 58, 78, 91
Harding, President Warren G., 80
Hare-Hawes-Cutting Bill, 81
Hatta, Muhammad, 73, 100
headhunters, 1, 2, 249
Heng Samrin, 179
Himalayas, 1
Hinayana Buddhism, 5, 6. *See also* Theravada Buddhism.
Hinduism, 3, 4, 25, 28, 230
Ho Chi Minh, 190, 192-4, 213
Ho Chi Minh Trail, 206
Ho Chi Minh City, 213
Hue, 58, 79,
Hukbalahaps, 285-87, 289

illustrados, 63
Independent Church of the Philippines, 281
India, 1, 33, 34, 74, 75, 76, 77, 87, 89, 99, 108, 110, 121, 125-26, 248-49, 252, 257, 268
Indians, 56, 74, 75, 76, 77, 87, 89, 99, 108, 110, 115, 117, 125-26, 248-49, 252, 257, 268
Indianization, 14, 25, 26, 28, 29, 31, 32, 34, 39, 229-30
Indonesia, 11, 19, 51-52, 69, 71-73, 85, 99-100, 166, 227ff., 255, 281
    anti-Chinese feeling, 228-229; arts, 232; attacks on Chinese, 238, 239; cities, 229; Communist Party, 236; communist uprising, 238; crops, 229; economy, 240-42; education, 231; ethnic groups, 227-29; foreign relations, 244-46; future, 246-47 language, 231; law, 229; political developments, 233-39; religion, 229-31; student rebels, 239-40
Indonesia Merdeka, 233
Industrial Revolution in Europe, 50
Irrawaddy River, 17, 23, 105, 122
Islam, 6-8. *See also* "religion" under country.
islands, 1, 16

Japan, 37, 67, 70, 73, 76, 77, 78, 81, 83-103, 105, 122, 125, 133, 135, 147, 227, 239, 247, 262, 282-83, 285
Java, 13, 19, 26, 34-35, 47, 48, 50-52, 53, 227, 230, 233, 235
Jayavarman II, 26-27

Jayavarman VII, 28
Johnson, President Lyndon B., 205
Jones Act, 80

Kachins, 87, 108, 114, 115
Kalimantan (Borneo), 2, 14, 245, 249, 305
kampongs, 229
Kampuchea, 11, 19, 27, 28, 58, 59-60, 64, 84, 86, 89, 92-93, 103; capital, 180 crops, 179-80; economy, 179-81; foreign relations, 182; future, 182-3; government, 142, 178-79; land use, 181; life expectancy, 180; massacres, 178; population, 178, 180; urban depopulation, 178 *See also* Khmer Republic.
Kampuchean refugees, 138
Karenni State, 112, 114
Karens, 55, 76, 88, 89, 107, 112, 115, 126
Kaundinya, 25-26
Kawthule State, 107, 112
Kedah, 34, 53, 65, 74,
Kelatan, 74
Kennedy, President John F., 201
kha, 148
Khmer Islam, 166
Khmer issarak, 92
Khmer Republic (Cambodia), 23, 26, 165-83 economy, 172; education, 167-68; ethnic groups 165-66; literacy, 168; political developments, 170-77; population, 178 *See also* Cambodia, Kampuchea.
Khmer Rouge, 173-77
Khmers, 23, 25, 26, 27, 28, 29, 30, 31, 37, 206
King and I, The, 65, 129
Kipling, Rudyard, 56
Kong Le, 154
Koran. *See* Qu'ran.
Korat Plateau, 18
Korea, 37
Korean War, 113, 161, 235
Kuala Lumpur, 54, 99, 249, 256, 268
Kublai Khan, 28
Kyansittha, 32, 33

Lan Xang, 29

Lao, 28-29, 148
Lao Issara, 90
Lao Lum, 148
Laos, 11, 12, 23, 59-61, 84, 86, 90-92, 103, 147ff.; agriculture, 147-160; arts, 151-52; communist movement, 156, 163; economic conditions, 157-59; economic trends, 159-61; education, 150-51; ethnic groups, 148; foreign policy, 161-62; forests, 162-63; future, 162-63; government, 157; land use, 157-59; languages, 151; literacy, 160; medical facilities, 156; Pathet Lao, 153; political developments, 152-57; population, 158-59; raw materials, 159; refugees, 154, 162; religion, 148-50; Royal Laotian Government, 153; ruling families, 153; U.S. bombing, 154-55
Lao Sung, 148
Lao Tai, 151
Lao Thai, 126, 148
Lao Theung, 148, 150
Lao-tze, 9-10
Laurel, Jose P., 101
Laurel, Salvador H., 294, 299
Laurel-Langley Agreement, 290, 291-92, 299
League for the Independence of Vietnam, 79 *See also* Viet Minh.
Lee Kuan Yew, 272-73
Lenin, V.I., 71, 79
Leonowens, Anna, 65, 129
Leyte, Battle of, 101-02
Liberal System, 51-52, 71
Light, Francis, 53
literacy. *See* "literacy" under country.
longhouses, 14
Lon Nol, 173, 175-77, 182
Luang Prabang, 59, 90, 147, 148, 153, 156, 157, 158
Luzon, 39, 102, 285, 289, 290

MacArthur, General Douglas, 101
Madurese, 227
Magellan, Ferdinand, 43
Magsaysay, Ramon, 286-88
Mahabharata, 7, 151, 152, 232
Mahayana Buddhism, 5-6
Majapahit, 35, 38-39
Malacca, 31, 35, 39-40, 42, 43, 47-48,

53, 54, 98, 99, 250
Malaya. *See* British Malaya.
Malaya, Federation of, 99, 102, 213-14, 247, 267
Malayan Union, 98
Malays, 22, 31, 34-35, 36, 53, 89, 227, 247-49, 255, 256, 257, 268, 279, 305
Malay Shadow Play. *See* Wayang Kulit.
Malaysia, 11, 97-99, 166, 255-56; arts, 252-53; "Confrontation," the, 256; economy, 259-61; development of 255-56; education, 251, 263; Emergency, the, 255; ethnic groups, 247-49; foreign relations, 261-62; future, 262-63; government, 254-63; language, 251-52, 263; literacy, 252, 263; mines, 248; political developments, 254-58; population growth, 260; raw materials, 261; religion, 249-51; tribes, 249
Manchu Dynasty, 67
Manchuria, 77
Mandalay, 84, 112
Mandate of Heaven, 8-9
Manila, 44, 45-46, 62, 80, 101
Mao Zedong (Tse-tung), 161, 235, 254, 286
Marcos, President Ferdinand. *See* "politics" under Philippines.
Marx, Karl, 68, 70, 79, 102
Marxism, 70-71, 73, 82, 88, 102-03, 115. *See also* "Politics" under Burma, Laos, Kampuchea, Malaysia, Vietnam.
Max Havelaar, 51
McKinley, President William, 62
Mecca, 7, 230
Mekong Delta, 59, 158, 166, 176, 181, 207, 222
Mekong River, 17, 25, 29, 84, 148, 158, 159
Meo, 126, 155
Mexico, 43
Mindanao, 44, 281, 289
Moluccas, 35, 41, 42
Mongkut, King, 65, 129
Mongols, 24, 28, 33, 35, 37-38, 41, 125, 148
Mongoloids, 22, 23, 24
Mons, 23, 29, 30, 31, 32, 33, 34, 108, 126, 130

monsoons, 17
mosques, 40, 250, 252
Music. *See* "arts" under country.
Muslims, 2, 24, 38-40, 44, 51, 72, 75, 77, 98, 112, 114, 127, 166, 229, 230, 235, 249-51, 281, 289

Nacionalista Party, 79
Naga tribes, 115, 121
Napoleon Bonaparte, 50
National Council of National Reconciliation and Concord, 197
National Front for Indochina, 92
National Indonesian Party, 73
Nationalist China. *See* Republic of China.
National Liberation Army (NLA), 94
Negri Sembilan, 57
Negritos, 12
Neo Lao Hak Sat (NLHS), 92, 155-56
Netherlands Indonesian Union, 233
New People's Army, 289, 290
New Society, 290
New Village Policy, 254, 255
Ne Win, 113-15, 117ff.
Ngo family, 9
Nirvana, 4
Nixon, President Richard M., 154, 177
NLHS. *See* Neo Lao Hak Sat. North Borneo Company, 54
North Vietnam. *See* Vietnam.
Nu, U, 109, 113-14

oil, 1, 55, 81, 242
"Old Established Forces," 242
opium, 74
Osmena, Sergio, 101

"pacification," 96
paddies, 12-13,
Pagan, 32
Pakistan, 112, 268
Pakistanis, 115
Panchatantra, 151
Paris Agreement, 208-09
Pathet Lao, 153, 154
Pearl Harbor, 85
Pehang, 57
Penang, 53, 98, 99, 250
Pentagon Papers, the 217
People's Action Party (PAP), 271
People's Councils, Burma, 114, 115

"People Power", 298
People's Republic of China, 133, 174
Perak, 57
Perlist, 65, 74
Phahol, Phya, 00
Phaulkon, Constantine, 64
Phetsarath, Prince, 90, 147
phi, 128
Phibul Songgram, 66, 133-34
Philippines, the, 11, 19, 36, 39, 43-47, 79-82, 85, 255, 279ff.
  arts, 282; civil service, 68; clergy, role of, 296-7; Commonwealth State, 81; communists in, 284-86; corruption under Marcos, 296, 298; density, 306; disease in, 306; early history, 43-47; education, 281; ethnic groups, 279-80; government, 298, 292; foreign policy, 303-306; kinship system, 283-84; land reform, 63; land under Spanish, 44-45; language, 281-82; life expectancy, 306; Marcos, President, 288-69, 291, 302; Marcos, Imelda, 292; martial law, 291-93; Marxism in, 103, 284-86, 291; minerals, 302; Muslim rebellion, 291ff.; per capita income, 302; political developments, 282-84; population, 306-07; poverty, 284; religion, 200-81, 293; rice, 302; and Soviet Union, 305; and U.S., 61-64, 101, 290ff., 300, 303-05; World War II, 86-87, 101, 279
Phnom Penh, 28, 166, 168, 173, 175, 176
Phoumi Nosavan, 153-54
Pilipino, 282
pirates, 38, 45
Plain of Jars, 18, 154, 158
plantations, growth of, 49, 51, 59, 60
Polo, Marco, 41
populations. *See* under country.
Portuguese, 33, 41-43
Potsdam Conference, 94
Prabang, 29
Pri Banomyong, 66, 89-90, 102-03, 125, 132-33
Prince Wellesley, 53
Provisional Revolutionary Government (PRG), 155-56
purdah, 11, 230
Putera, 100
Pyidawaha (Burma), 116
Pyus, 31

Quezon, President Manuel, 79-80, 101, 288
Quirino, President Elpidio, 286, 287
Qu'ran, 7, 8, 253

rain, 1, 18
Raffles, Sir Thomas Stamford, 50, 53, 268
Rama the Great, 29, 30
Ramayana, 7, 132, 11, 152, 232, 252
Ramos, Lt.-General, 297
Rangoon, 34, 54, 55
Rangoon University, 76
Ramkambaeng University, 135
raw materials, 19, 83, 84, 86, 100, 121ff.
Razak, Tun Abdul, 258
Red Guards, 112
Red River, 17
Red River Delta, 36
religions, 2-10; *See also* animism, Buddhism, Christianity, Confucianism, Islam, Daoism (Taoism).
Republic of China, 287
Revolutionary Council, Burma, 114
rice, x, 12-13, 36, 59, 76, 107, 108, 135, 157
Rizal, Jose, 47, 282
Romulo, Carlos P., 290
Roosevelt, President Theodore, 62
Roxas, President Manuel, 282-83, 285-86
Royal Laotian Army (RLA), 154-55
rubber, 1, 19, 54, 59, 74, 76, 126
Russia, 67. *See also* Soviet Union.
Russian Revolution, 70

Sabah, 54, 57, 99, 250, 255, 256, 298
Saigon, 58, 84, 189. *See also* Ho Chi Minh City.
Sailendra, 34
Salween River, 17
Sangkum, 170
Sanya Thammosak, 136-37
Santa Thomas, College of, 45
Sarawak, 57, 99, 250, 255, 256
Sarekat Islam, 72
Sarit Thanarat, 134
Saw, U, 76, 89
schools. *See* "education" under country.
SEATO. *See* Southeast Asia Treaty Organization.
Sison, Jose Maria, 291-92, 298

South Vietnam. *See* Vietnam.
Selangor, 57
Seni Pramoj, 137
settlers, early, 22-24
shahada, 7
Shan Plateau, 112
Shans, 33, 89, 107, 114, 126
Shwe Dagon Pagoda, 108
Siam, 29, 30, 31, 57, 58, 59, 64-66
Siemreab, 26, 30, 31, 57, 58, 59, 64-66
Siemreab, 26, 65, 84, 93, 165, 170-75, 181
Sihanouk, Norodom, 3, 92-93, 165, 170-75, 179, 181, 182
Singapore, 18, 20, 53, 54, 98, 99, 255, 256, 267-77
    area, 275; arts, 270-71; economy, 274-75; education, 269-70; ethnic groups, 267-68; foreign relations, 276; future, 276-77
    language, 270-71; literacy, 271; merger with Malaysia, 271-72; political developments, 271-74; population, 268; religion, 268-69; trends, 275-76
Sisavong Vong, King, 90
Sittang River, 17
slash-and-burn agriculture, 12, 14, 36, 108
Son Noc Thanh, 92
Souphanouvong, Prince, 91-92, 147, 152, 153, 154
Southeast Asia Treaty Organization (SEATO), 161
Souvanna Phouma, Prince, 91, 147, 152
Soviet Union, 71, 79, 89, 103, 191, 212, 223
Spain *See* Philippines, Spanish.
Spanish, 43-47, 281. *See also* Philippines.
Spanish-American War, 61-62
Spice Islands, 41, 47
Sri Vijaya, 34-35, 36
Straits of Malacca, 34, 42
Straits Settlements, 54, 74, 98, 247, 267, 271, 274
Strategic Hamlets, 254
stupa, 131
Suez Canal, 50, 72
Suharto, General, 238
Sukarno, Achmed, 73, 100, 102, 228, 233-39, 256
Sukothal, 29, 31

Sulu Archipelago, 36, 39, 44, 256, 305
Sumatra, 34, 35, 38, 51, 227, 230, 236, 237
Sundanese, 227
Sun Yat-sen, 67-68
Surbaja, 229
Suramant, King Norodom, 171, 172
Survayarman II, 28, 27
System of Correlation of Man and the Environment, The, 114

Taft, William Howard, 63
Tagalog, 281
Tagalog Rebellion, 62
Tamil Land, 249
Taoism (Daoism), 9-10, 189, 248
Tao teh ching, 9
Taruc, Luis, 285-87
tax farmers, 227
Tay Bac Autonomous Region, 186
teakwood, 19, 54, 118
temperatures, 18
Tenasserim, 54, 107, 108
Tet Offensive, 207-08
Thailand, 11, 12, 15, 19, 31, 34, 97, 125-45, 154, 162, 181
    arts, 111, 130-32; Communist Party, 89; constitution, 89, 133; economy, 139-41, 143; education, 129-30; ethnic groups, 125-27; foreign policy, 142-44; future, 144-45; government, 132-38; hill tribes, 126; indebtedness; king, 90; languages, 130; literacy, 130; population, 125, 130, 139; religion, 127-29; reparations, 89; student activists, 136; World War II and after, 76, 84, 89-90, 91
Thakins, 76, 87, 89, 105
Thais, 28, 29, 30, 31, 32, 33, 34, 38, 59, 148, 166, 170
Thanom Kittikachorn, 134-37
Theravada Buddhism, 28 108-09, 148-49, 151, 166-67, 187
Thieu, General Nguyen Van, 204ff.
Thirty Comrades, the, 76, 87, 112
Tibet, 105
Timor, 42, 48
tin, 1, 54, 55, 59, 59, 74, 76, 126
Tonkin, 58, 59, 79, 84, 93-97
Tonle Sap, 26
Trailok, King, 31
Tran Hung Dao, 37

transmigration, 3-4
Trengganu, 74
Tribute System, 49, 50
Tripartism, 154
Tripitaka, 151
Tungku, the, 257-58
Tydings, McDuffie Bill, 81

Unfederated States of Malaya, 74
Union of Indochina, 59, 91
United Malays National Organization (UMNO), 98
United Nations, 91, 198, 256
United States, 50, 61-64, 77, 85, 91, 121, 133, 134-35, 143, 152, 153-54, 172, 175, 176, 196, 201-11, 237, 285-97
U.S. bombing, 154-55, 159, 162, 175
Unity from Diversity slogan, 233

Vajiravudh, king, 65-66
Vasco da Gama, 41
Ver, General Fabian, 292, 294
Vientiane, 90, 147, 148, 153, 156
Vietnam
   "boat people", 213-14; economy, 199-201, 216-20; education, language & arts, 190-93; ethnic groups, 185-87; foreign relations, 220-21; future, 221-34; government, 194-98; politics, 193-93, 200-01, 212-16; religion, 187-90; social conditions, 185-93; South Vietnam, 196-98; People's Republic of, 212-23; population, 185-86; U.S. in, 201-11
Vietnam War, 143, 199-211
"vietnamization" of war, 218
Vishnu, 25
Voksraad, 72
volcanoes, 1, 19

wat, 108, 149-50, 167
wayang, 232
Wayang Kulit, 252
West Irian, 234
Wilson, President Woodrow, 79, 80
Wood, General Leonard, 80
World War I, 66, 76, 78, 80
World War II, 1, 82, 83-103, 105, 108, 125, 147, 153, 165, 190, 227, 247, 267, 271, 279, 282, 285

Xieng Khouang, 90, 147, 153

Yangtze River, 24
Yen Bay, 78
Young Men's Buddhist Association, 75
Yueh, 24, 36, 186